Atomic Age Cinema

The Offbeat, The Classic and The Obscure

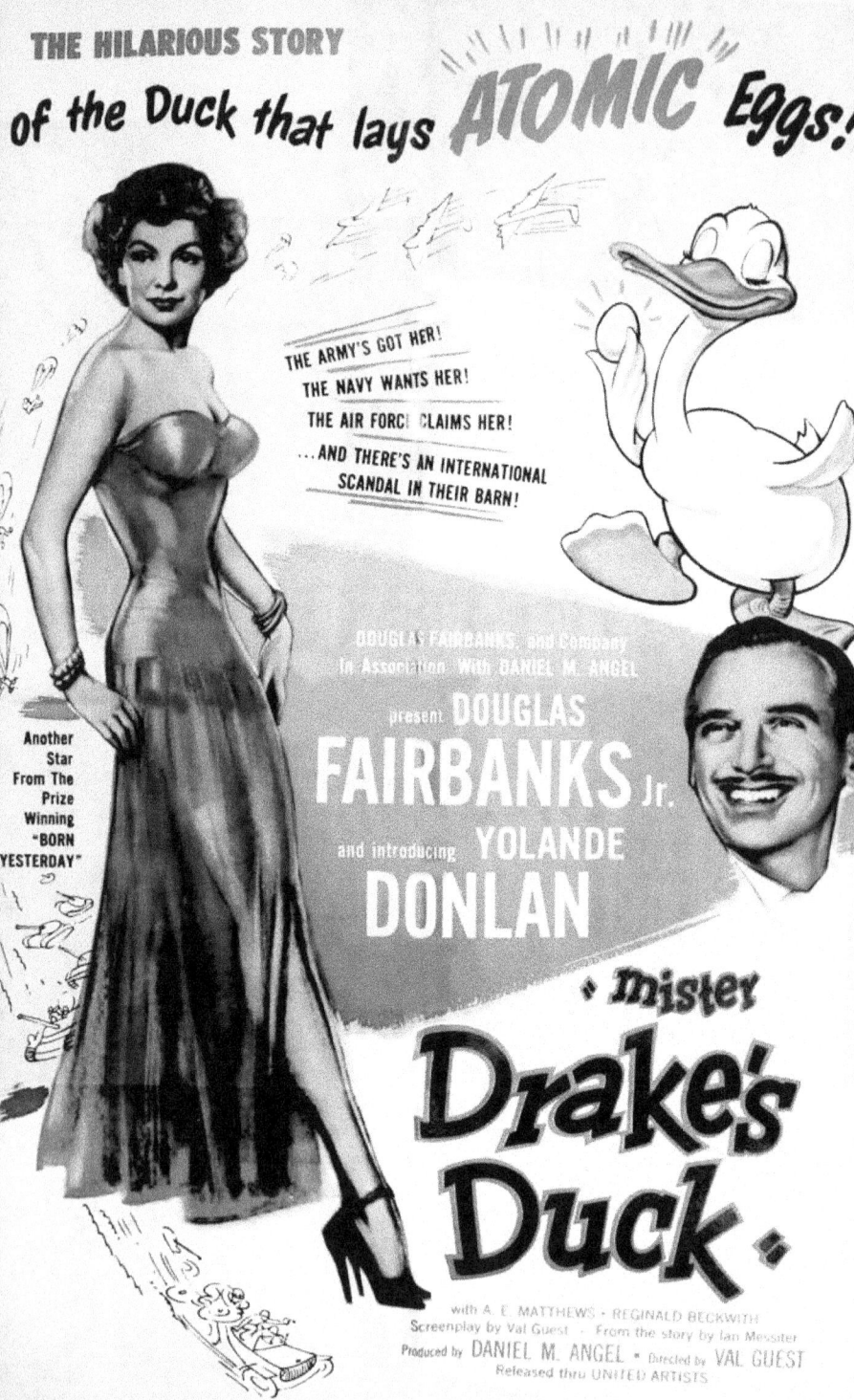

Atomic Age Cinema

The Offbeat, The Classic and The Obscure

by Barry Atkinson

Midnight Marquee Press, Inc.
Baltimore, Maryland, USA; London, UK

Copyright © 2014 by Barry Atkinson
Interior Layout by Gary J. Svehla
Cover Design by A. Susan Svehla
Copy Editor: A. Susan Svehla

Midnight Marquee Press, Inc., Gary J. Svehla and A. Susan Svehla do not assume any responsibility for the accuracy, completeness, topicality or quality of the information in this book. All views expressed or material contained within are the sole responsibility of the author.

Without limiting the rights under copyright reserved above, no part of this publication may be reproduced, stored in or introduced into a retrieval system, or transmitted, in any form, or by any means (electronic, mechanical, photocopying, recording or otherwise), without the prior written permission of the copyright owner or the publishers of the book.

ISBN 978-1-936168-44-6
Library of Congress Catalog Card Number 2014938440
Manufactured in the United States of America

First Printing by Midnight Marquee Press, Inc., May 2014

Dedication

To my wife Janet, whose countless hours of research and investigation have enabled me to include, in this book, many rare and hard-to-come-by films that otherwise would have been overlooked.

And to Gary and Sue Svehla for their continued support.

Table of Contents

9	Foreword
10	Chapter 1 – The '50s Reign Supreme
13	Chapter 2 – An A-Z of the 1950s
17	Chapter 3 – The Studios, Actors and Directors
25	Chapter 4 – Soundtracks: The Composers
34	Chapter 5 – Let's Take Another Look: Part One
49	Chapter 6 – Godzilla and Rodan: Japan vs. America
54	Chapter 7 – Fifty Fabulous Lines of Dialogue from the 1950s
61	Chapter 8 – Atomic Age Underdogs
96	Chapter 9 – Chaney, Karloff and Lugosi in the 1950s
112	Chapter 10 – Gill-Man Number One!
116	Chapter 11 – Cahn's Sci-Fi B-Movie Par Excellence
121	Chapter 12 – Bring on the Girls!
130	Chapter 13 – Let's Take Another Look: Part Two
145	Chapter 14 – To Colorize or Not to Colorize
152	Chapter 15 – Gigantis and Varan: Toho's Forgotten Monsters
157	Chapter 16 – Regal by Name – Not Quite by Nature!
163	Chapter 17 – Monster Number One: Life Before CGI

168	Chapter 18—A Monster of Foreign Delight— and a Nod to Verne
173	Chapter 19—British Sci-Fi: From a Duck to a Dinosaur
192	Chapter 20—Two Schlock Classics!
199	Chapter 21—Let's Take Another Look: Part Three
213	Chapter 22—The Abominable Snowman in the 1950s
219	Chapter 23—Let's Get Serious
224	Chapter 24—Under the Knife: Franju's Surgical Masterpiece
228	Chapter 25—Tales of Mystery, Imagination, Noir, Horror and Suspense—British Style
253	Chapter 26—From Around the World
277	Chapter 27—A Classic Short
279	Chapter 28—A Monster Double Bill: Mexican Dinosaur Meets Outer Space Turkey
283	Chapter 29—Fifty Fabulous '50sScenes
289	Chapter 30—Spawn of Dr. Jekyll
293	Chapter 31—The Adventures of Jungle Jim in the Atomic Fifties
310	Chapter 32—Science vs. Folklore
314	Chapter 33—Closing Credits: A Hammer Favorite

Phyllis Kirk as Sue Allen encounters a 3-D skeleton from *House of Wax* (1953).

Foreword

"From the point of view of the cinema, there wasn't that much around in the 1950s." Written by a 20-something film critic in an English newspaper in August 2012, this young upstart couldn't have been more wrong if he'd tried. That particular decade was a fabulously fertile spell for the cinema buff and baby-boomer generation as the industry reached a creative high. Classic motion pictures were issued fast and furious, becoming a cornucopia fit for a king. Westerns? *Shane, High Noon, The Searchers, Rio Bravo.* Musicals? *Oklahoma, Carousel, Singin' in the Rain, South Pacific.* War? *The Bridge on the River Kwai, Paths of Glory, From Here to Eternity, The Dam Busters.* Crime? *The Big Heat, Riot in Cell Block 11, The Detective Story, Al Capone.* Drama? *On the Waterfront, Giant, Rebel Without a Cause, Ace in the Hole.* Hitchcock? *North by Northwest, Strangers on a Train, Vertigo, Rear Window.* Comedy? *Some Like it Hot, The Ladykillers, Road to Bali, Genevieve.* Romance? *Three Coins in the Fountain, Roman Holiday, Gentlemen Prefer Blondes, Raintree County.* Epics? *Quo Vadis, The Ten Commandments, Ben-Hur, The Robe.* Foreign? *Seven Samurai, The 400 Blows, Rififi, The Wages of Fear.* Disney? *Cinderella, Lady and the Tramp, Peter Pan, Alice in Wonderland ...*

And then, from cinema's exciting Atomic Age ... Horror: *House of Wax, The Curse of Frankenstein, The Fly, Dracula.* Science Fiction: *The Day the Earth Stood Still, The War of the Worlds, Invasion of the Body Snatchers, The Thing from Another World.* Monsters: *The Beast from 20,000 Fathoms, Godzilla, Tarantula, 20 Million Miles to Earth.* Fantasy: *The 7th Voyage of Sinbad, Journey to the Center of the Earth, The Land Unknown, Journey to a Primeval Age.*

For those enraptured by *cinema fantastique* from its earliest beginnings, the 1950s was an unequivocally the decade that quite literally had it all—in spades. No other 10-year fantasy time span can hold a candle to it. Every type of genre was offered to satiate the appetite and stir the imagination, allowing us, within the confines of a darkened auditorium, to journey into a 70-to-80-minute mainly black-and-white world populated by giant rear-projected insects and humans, mad doctors, huge scorpions, colossal spiders, murderous aliens, flying saucers, vampires, walking trees, Frankenstein Monsters, mummies, dinosaurs, spaceships, zombies, ghouls, blobs, werewolves and garishly rendered planets. Men were clean-cut heroes, women sassy, sexy and intelligent, nothing dragged in the pace department, scripts were literate, pre-CGI effects mind-boggling, direction straight to the point, everything backed by memorable soundtracks—and, in stark contrast to today's politically correct climate, both sexes chain-smoked like crazy! It was a golden age that has never been repeated or surpassed, a diverse fantasy tapestry woven by a wealth of motion picture studios ranging from the major (Universal-International) to the minor (Howco International). This book presents a potpourri of all things related to the fabulous '50s, a validation of that decade if you like, incorporating throughout its 33 chapters personal opinions and deliberations. And if any fledgling horror enthusiast wonders if there *is* fantasy cinematic life before the year 2000, the following pages will set out to prove conclusively that there was. Accept no substitute!

Chapter 1
The '50s Reign Supreme

1945: The H-bomb is dropped on Hiroshima and Nagasaki, Japan signaling the dawn of the Atomic Age. 1947: A UFO crash is sighted at Roswell, New Mexico, with guarded reports of alien life forms. 1950: Horror, science fiction and fantasy cinema undergoes a renaissance linked to the atom bomb, Cold War paranoia and the uncertain knowledge that "out there," other intelligences may be monitoring us. 1951: Britain's infamous "X" certificate is born, the innocence of '30s and '40s horror fantasy swept aside as the old legends are given a radical makeover, rational science replacing the folklore of yesteryear. A full-scale fusion of horror and science fiction is underway, accommodating a younger, more fashionable audience; monsters, aberrations of nature caused by radiation, take centerstage and television usurps radio as the new medium of mass entertainment. 1957: Hammer's *The Curse of Frankenstein* in one fell swoop creates the modern-day horror movie, elevating the genre to a higher level and influencing countless filmmakers around the world.

It's a fact—the explosion of fantasy films that sprung forth unchecked from the 1950s bore little resemblance to the product of the previous two decades. It was more in keeping with the times and leaves an immense body of work of such complexity that it continues, to this day, to be analyzed, discussed, eulogized, criticized, written about or simply enjoyed.

In compiling this book, I have had to refer to, on occasions, my earlier publication *You're Not Old Enough Son* (Midnight Marquee Press, 2006). That's not to say I'm going to rake over old ground, but in reflecting on cinema in the 1950s, be it horror, science fiction, fantasy, war, Western, social drama or any other genre, I am going to briefly reiterate some inescapable points to those readers born outside of the United Kingdom, in case certain facts confuse. Being English, consideration of the systems in place that governed the screening of motion pictures in British cinemas needs to be addressed; other countries didn't necessarily adopt those same procedures. If you are writing about cinema as it was presented in the United Kingdom, you *have* to mention both film classification and film censorship—the two go hand-in-hand and are inseparable; inexorably linked, dictating who can see what, and when.

James Arness, without makeup, but wearing the alien suit, backstage during the production of *The Thing from Another World.*

In January 1951, the British Board of Film Censors introduced the "X" certificate, effectively banning any

Christopher Lee poses in front of a photo of himself as the Creature from *The Curse of Frankenstein* (1957), during a publicity campaign.

persons under the age of 16 from entering a cinema when an X-rated movie was showing. RKO's *The Thing from Another World* and James Cagney's gangster thriller *White Heat* were early recipients of what is now commonly regarded as cinema's most notorious classification. Next to the "X" was the "A," almost as bad because you had to be 14 and over to see an A-rated picture, although, if under 14, you could get in to a theater if accompanied by an adult. The "U" certificate was suitable for all. As the lights were extinguished and heavy brown/red curtains rolled back from the screen on squeaking rollers urgently in need of lubrication. The first thing postwar English families would be confronted with in those capacious, pitch-black auditoriums was the film's certification details, as shown on page 16. This image is truly iconic, from a distant age, as much a part of the '50s cinema scene as the movie about to watched, indelibly etched into the minds of a past generation of British movie lovers.

So in Britain, the feast of '50s fantasy goodies let loose during the late 1950s/early 1960s, the majority of which emanated from America, remained out-of-bounds to those kids itching to see them. Why? Because the censor's office, fueled by self-righteousness and perceived by some as guardians of the nation's morals, slapped "X" and "A" certificates on most of these sought-after pictures. Even fairly innocuous efforts such as *Invasion of the Hell Creatures* (aka *Invasion of the Saucer Men*), *Bride of the Monster* and *The Incredible Petrified World* were deemed suitable for one's mothers and fathers only, falling victim to the dreaded "X" rating. This unbridled censorship precipitated an immense feeling of frustration among England's cinema-mad youth, leading to the kind of escapades I wrote about in *You're Not Old Enough Son.*

Then there were the program presentations themselves. Unless the picture was a major horror, fantasy or sci-fi release (*House of Wax*, *The Fly*, *Forbidden Planet*, *The 7th Voyage of Sinbad*, Hammer's colorful output), most fantasy fodder, even brand-new releases, were relegated to the fondly remembered Sunday one-day slot, being regarded as not prestigious enough for a week's run and lacking appeal for a mass audience. On this particular day of the week, and for that day only, the American fantasy movie had its chance to rule the roost, one tremendous double bill after another drawing in the crowds. In the United Kingdom, films such as *This Island Earth*, *The Deadly Mantis*, *Earth vs. the Flying Saucers*, *The Black Scorpion* and scores of others were denied a major release date at the time they were issued. Viewed with a certain amount of disdain

Teenagers from Outer Space was re-titled *The Gargon Terror* in the United Kingdom.

by the major chains, they would eventually appear with various fantastic movies a few years later on the Sunday circuit or late-night shows. From 1961 to 1969, young British horror addicts, who had spent years straining at the leash, finally got the chance to catch up on all those wonders ogled at in the pages of *Famous Monsters of Filmland*, and it goes without saying that British television **never** broadcast the type of horror fodder that was shown regularly on American TV in the 1950s. The censor, whose powers extended to the small screen, would not allow it.

As regards film titles, I have stuck to the British name, mentioning the U.S. alternative where appropriate. Example: *Blood is My Heritage* in England became *Blood of Dracula* in the States; Hammer's *Dracula* (1958) became *Horror of Dracula* in America; *Grip of the Strangler* became *The Haunted Strangler*; *Behemoth The Sea Monster* became *The Giant Behemoth*; *The Trollenberg Terror* became *The Crawling Eye*; *Timeslip* became *The Atomic Man*; *The Gargon Terror* was known as *Teenagers from Outer Space*; *Night of the Demon* was slightly retitled *Curse of the Demon*; *The Fantastic Disappearing Man* morphed into *Return of Dracula*; *Teenage Frankenstein* became *I Was a Teenage Frankenstein* and *The Devil's Commandment* (*I Vampiri* in Italy) turned up as *Lust of the Vampire*.

Horror, science fiction and fantasy reached an artistic peak from 1950 to 1959, which is all the more amazing when we stop to consider the low budgets and somewhat primitive resources filmmakers had at their disposal compared to the seemingly unlimited funds and technical innovations the moviemakers of today have at their disposal. You don't believe me? Then read on! (Note: Throughout this book, I refer to a vast number of movies as being "Not available on DVD." That means not *officially* available. They can, with perseverance, be purchased from various outlets, but don't expect state-of-the-art picture quality. If you want something bad enough, picture quality has to be sacrificed in the name of acquisition.)

Chapter 2
An A-Z of the 1950s

A is for John Agar. A critic once wrote of Bing Crosby: "Crosby was always a pleasure to watch, even if he simply walked out on set." So was John Agar. Whether a seafaring man of action (*The Golden Mistress*), a suave, sexy doctor (*Tarantula*), an anthropologist (*The Mole People*) or a smooth salesman (*Attack of the Puppet People*), the easy-going, charismatic performer breezed effortlessly through his films without making one false move. In many a fan's eyes, Agar was the decade's topmost B horror movie actor—his is the one name, above all others, guaranteed to bring back fond memories of underage British kids sneaking into X-rated features like *Revenge of the Creature*.

B is for B movies, in all shapes, sizes and (occasionally) colors. Fans gained far more pleasure from watching something like *The Hideous Sun Demon* than sitting through a big-budget color production. "X" certificate B movies meant grainy, scratched celluloid experienced in dingy, musty dives wreathed in cigarette smoke; viewed 50 years later, they still do!

C is for censorship, in particular British censorship. Thank you, Mister Censor, for giving young English film buffs such a hard time throughout the '50s and '60s. We were dying to see all those golden delights from the pages of *Famous Monsters of Filmland*—but you wouldn't let us!

D is for *Dracula*. Hammer proved that the old legend wasn't dead and buried—it was just waiting to be resurrected in a bloodier format. Terence Fisher's masterful revamping (no pun intended!) of Bram Stoker's classic novel of the undead remains one of the decade's finest horror movies and probably, in terms of worldwide influence, England's most important '50s feature film.

E is for *Eyes Without a Face*. Continental horror pictures started to make their presence felt with the 1956 release of Riccardo Freda's groundbreaking *I Vampiri*. However, it is Georges Franju's 1959 masterpiece that's the outright winner in the surgical horror stakes, still revered today as a seminal slice of continental medical madness, a little too realistic for some tastes.

F is for Frankenstein. Still alive and well after all these years in such diverse produc-

Boris Karloff opens the grave of the Haymarket Strangler, from *Grip of the Strangler*.

tions as *The Curse of Frankenstein*, *The Revenge of Frankenstein*, *Frankenstein 1970* and *Frankenstein's Daughter*. You can't keep a good monster down!

G is for Gordon—Bert I. Gordon. *Beginning of the End*; *The Amazing Colossal Man*; *Earth vs. the Spider*; *War of the Colossal Beast*, among his roster. Never in the history of fantasy cinema has a back-projection screen been used so much, and to such questionable effect!

H is for Harryhausen. The stop-motion supremo was responsible for a trio of indispensable '50s monster classics: *The Beast from 20,000 Fathoms*, *20 Million Miles to Earth* and *The 7th Voyage of Sinbad*. His other work wasn't all that bad, either.

I is for *I Was a Teenage Werewolf*. Gene Fowler, Jr.'s wolf man opus kick-started the trend in teenage horror movies, ranging from the good (this one), the bad (*Teenage Caveman*) to the ugly (*Teenage Monster*).

J is for Jungle Jim. Don't all laugh—Columbia's 14 *Jungle Jim* potboilers made in the '50s (the initial two date from the late '40s) define the oft-used phrase "guilty pleasure." Hilarious hokum like this only appears once in a lifetime, so ignore the critics' put-down comments, sit back and enjoy the very ultimate in daftness! You will not be disappointed!

K is for Karloff. The one-time King of Horror put in some decent performances in the 1950s, still following the same furrow he plowed so successfully in the previous two decades. *Grip of the Strangler* and *Frankenstein 1970* showed that the old master hadn't lost his magic touch and wasn't going to be so easily upstaged by any pretender to the horror throne.

L is for Lugosi. Boris' old sidekick didn't fare as well, since most of his movies seem a last-gasp effort to relive former glories. *Mother Riley Meets the Vampire* and *Plan 9 from Outer Space* failed to showcase his hammy talents and are *not* the swansongs he would have wished to bow out on.

M is for monsters. From rampaging prehistoric animals to oversized insects, the '50s practically invented the phrase "monster movie." No other decade since has matched this decade for sheer variety, or the ingenuity it took to bring them to the big screen.

N is for Lori Nelson. Heroines in '50s horror movies acted with conviction and looked swell. Lori Nelson is a typical example: Blonde, pretty, intelligent and feminine. No wonder John Agar wasted little time in getting to grips with her in *Revenge of the Creature*!

O is for octopus, namely the six-tentacled giant cephalopod that rises from the depths in *It Came from Beneath the Sea*. Not one of Ray Harryhausen's better features, even though the octopus is a corker.

P is for petrified. That's how I saw some of my pals become when faced with the mutant in *Day the World Ended*, Leo G. Carroll's melted features in *Tarantula*, William Castle's trickery in *House on Haunted Hill* and Steven Ritch turning into *The Werewolf*.

Serves them right for sneaking into X-rated flicks when only 14 years old (as was I at the time!)

Q is for Quatermass, a name plucked at random out of a London telephone directory by writer Nigel Kneale. It became a name forever linked with alien terror; the two '50s *Quatermass* movies and three BBC television serials became classics of their type, scared a nation half to death and made newspaper headlines. What a shame that *Quatermass and the Pit*, the most thought provoking of the three, never made it onto the big screen in the '50s.

R is for *Return of* and *Revenge of*. Add the rest and you'll probably, without too much trouble, come up with a '50s horror title.

S is for *The 7th Voyage of Sinbad*, a colossus among fantasy pictures and one of the biggest financial successes of the decade. "How was it all done?" must have crossed the minds of a generation of youngsters as Harryhausen's Cyclops strode out of a cave in all its awesome glory.

Producer Richard Gordon and Bela Lugosi pose on the set of (*Old*) *Mother Riley Meets the Vampire* (1952).

T is for *The Thing from Another World*. The Holy Grail of film debate is this: Which title qualifies as the '50s best-ever sci-fi movie. There are classics galore to choose from, but my personal choice, taking into consideration plot, direction, acting, script, score, atmosphere and dynamics, is Howard Hawks' trailblazer. But then, what about *Invasion of the Body Snatchers*, or *The Quatermass Experiment*, or…

U is for Universal-International. No doubt about it, Universal's monster movies were a cut above the rest, although in retrospect, Columbia and United Artists weren't all that far behind in quality product. *Creature from the Black Lagoon, Tarantula, This Island Earth, The Incredible Shrinking Man, The Deadly Mantis* and *The Monolith Monsters* were among the company's undisputed gems that put bums on seats by the thousands, in the early '60s English cinemas.

V is for *The Vampire*. The bloodsucker meets *film noir* in United Artists' 1957 spine-tingler, a little gem that remains unnoticed by the majority, but the film deserves wider recognition.

W is for *The War of the Worlds*. The originals are always the best and George Pal's 1953 alien-invasion flick proves it. Fifty-two years later, Steven Spielberg and Tom Cruise, armed with $130 million, failed to trounce director Byron Haskin's colorful actioner. The earlier version packs an almighty wallop; Spielberg's effort is a damp

squib by comparison.

X is for "X" certificate. No other film classification has the association with adult movies that Britain's notorious rating possesses. Although phased out in 1984, "X" still stands for "Keep Away—You Are Too Young to Watch!"

Y is for Yeti. Strangely enough, the monster-laden '50s failed to do justice to this legendary creature. Only Toho's uncut *Half Human* comes close to capturing the myth surrounding the Himalaya's little-seen beastie.

Z is for the grade Z productions. Edward D. Wood, Jr. (*Night of the Ghouls*), Jerry Warren (*Teenage Zombies*), Phil Tucker (*Robot Monster*), Tom Graeff (*The Gargon Terror*), W. Lee Wilder (*Killers from Space*), Ray Kellogg (*The Killer Shrews*), Ronnie Ashcroft (*The Astounding She-Monster*) and Herbert Tevos and Ron Ormond (*Mesa of Lost Women*); all should hang their heads in shame. But, on the other hand, the '50s wouldn't be *quite* the same without them!

Chapter 3
The Studios, Actors and Directors

At the beginning of the 1950s, the chiefs of Hollywood's seven major players—Universal-International, 20th Century Fox, Paramount, Warner Bros., MGM, United Artists and Columbia—had to decide whether or not to take a financial risk and jump with both feet onto the snowballing fantasy bandwagon following the unexpected successes of *Destination Moon, The Day the Earth Stood Still, When Worlds Collide* and *The Thing from Another World.* Universal's fortunes were in the doldrums following a spectacular run of classic horror pictures in the '30s and '40s; Fox tended to concentrate on big-budget productions with A-list stars, as did glamour studio MGM; Warner Bros. (along with Universal) put most of their efforts into that reliable old crowd-puller, the Western; United Artists showed a preference for drama; Columbia was the serial specialist and Paramount dealt with all genres, right across the board, including expensive epics. As the new wave of horror, fantasy and science fiction took hold of audiences' imaginations and gained impetus, how did the big seven react to this fresh, atomic-themed genre? What did they come up with to appease cinema crowds, and what is their lasting legacy to fans of the fantastic?

To any underage English horror film buff sneaking into cinemas during the late '50s/early '60s, fervently hoping to catch the latest A-rated or X-rated presentation, Universal appeared to hold a monopoly on horror films. It certainly gave a damn good impression of doing so. Everywhere you looked in those days, a Universal double bill was showing on a Sunday: *The Creature Walks Among Us* c/w (coupled with) *Tarantula*; *Monster on the Campus* c/w *The Land Unknown*; *The Mole People* c/w *Curucu, Beast of the Amazon*; *The Thing that Couldn't Die* c/w *Curse of the Undead*; *The Monolith Monsters* c/w *The Incredible Shrinking Man.* That large black-and-white spinning globe was as familiar to us as Paramount's mountain, Fox's searchlights, Warner Bros.' shield, Columbia's statue and MGM's roaring lion. Also fast becoming familiar were Universal's roster of players: John Agar, Nestor Paiva, Jeff Morrow, Rex Reason, Ross Elliott, Gregg Palmer, Grant Williams and Richard Carlson, plus all those sassy female leading ladies. From a very early age, I quickly latched onto the fact that a certain Jack Arnold was the genius behind a lot of these stylish monster-feature films. Arnold, like Edward L. Cahn, Roger Corman and many other fantasy directors, originated from the Budd Boetticher school of filmmaking. Boetticher's spare Westerns are classics of their

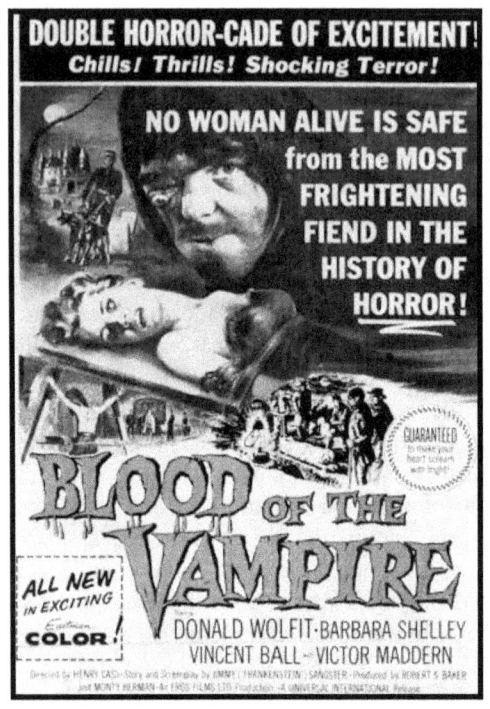

kind; stripped to the bone, not an ounce of fat, almost minimalist in conception and brief. They are masterpieces in filmic simplicity, lean and mean. That's how Arnold's exciting movies came across to us youngsters in the dark confines of an auditorium; no flab, no flapping around, nothing superfluous to requirements, just fast-paced storytelling embodying tremendous, horrifying shocks that jolted us out of our seats.

Yes, a cursory glance at the "What's on next week" section in the local papers of that time showed that Universal appeared to rule the roost in the 1950s, but on closer inspection, this isn't quite the case. From the perspective of the movies that constitute the theme of this book (horror, sci-fi, fantasy, *noir*, thriller, serials), Universal's total amounts to 27, including productions given a Universal worldwide distribution (*Blood of the Vampire*, *The Man in the White Suit*). Columbia, on the other hand, triumphs over the others with 41; United Artists is next with 35 (they also distributed quite a few minor features); Fox with 13; Warner Bros. 13; Paramount 10; and super-rich MGM, not overly interested in adding horror pictures to their glossy stable, a lowly six. From Japan, Toho scored eight. In the wings were secondary outfits Allied Artists with 23 and American International Pictures not far behind with 22. Britain's Hammer clocked up 22. That's a grand total of 220. But if you take into account the considerable output from the minor studios on both sides of the Atlantic, plus foreign features, the true figure of every fantasy genre motion picture released between 1950 and 1959 may never be accurately known. A conservative figure would be in the region of 400. On average, that's 40 a year, the peak years being 1956-1958. Today, most horror/fantasy films are made by independent, straight-to-DVD companies and screened only at frightfests. Mainstream fare is few and far between, perhaps a couple per month, if we're lucky. And very few possess the staying power that is the hallmark of the fantasy movie from that glorious postwar decade.

Did one American film company's work differ greatly from another's? Were Universal's highly professional pictures more elaborate than those made by United Artists? How about Columbia's extensive repertoire, or Allied Artists' and American International's imaginative, low-budget offerings. The answer has to be "no, not all that much," although there are subtle variations in plot and execution. Universal had their gill-man, tarantula, shrinking man, one-eyed alien, monolithic crystals and mole people, all in black-and-white. But United Artists' output was just as prolific: *The Monster That Challenged the World*, *The Black Sleep*, *The Vampire*, *The Four Skulls of Jonathan Drake*, *I Bury the Living* and *It! The Terror from Beyond Space* are the equal to anything that Universal conjured up. So are Columbia's *The Werewolf, 20 Million Miles to Earth, The Mad Magician* and *Night of the Demon*. And lesser mortals Allied Artists' contribution in this decade was a staggering mix of the incredible and the improbable: *The Cyclops, The Maze, Indestructible Man, The Disembodied, Attack of the 50 Foot Woman, World Without End, Invasion of the Body Snatchers, The Wasp Woman, Not of this Earth, Frankenstein 1970, Daughter of Dr. Jekyll, House on Haunted Hill, From Hell It Came*—what a wonderful list to sink your teeth into!

American International's films were similar in style to Allied Artists' and just as popular with punters, producing low-budget flicks that packed a punch: *Teenage Frankenstein, Blood is My Heritage, It Conquered the World, Day the World Ended, The Brain that Wouldn't Die, Attack of the Puppet People, The Amazing Colossal Man*. AIP, led by James Nicholson and Samuel Z. Arkoff, was responsible for kick-starting the '50s craze in drive-in teen horror pictures, producing films focusing on hot-rodders and rock 'n' roll; *I Was a Teenage Werewolf* is the definitive example of the '50s teenage horror film, and it's a memorable one at that.

It was really left to the major studios to come up with, on the odd occasion, a costly blockbuster in color. Paramount scored a big critical and commercial hit with *The War of the Worlds*, as did Warner Bros. with *House of Wax* and Disney with *20,000 Leagues Under the Sea*. Fox achieved huge box-office takings with *The Fly*

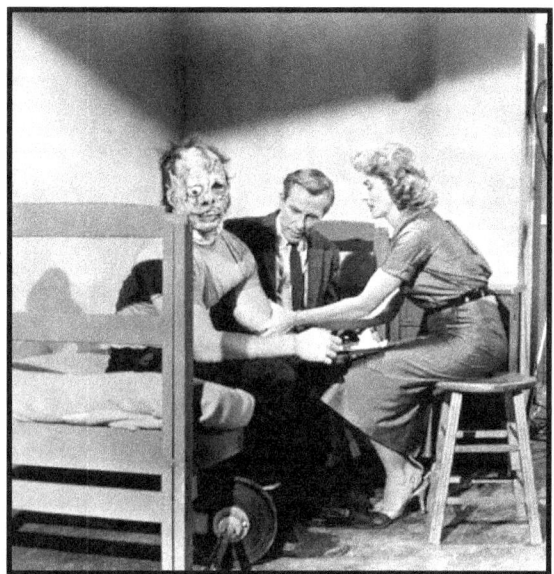

Gary Conway's Monster, scientist Whit Bissell and assistant Phyllis Coates from *Teenage Frankenstein* (aka *I Was A Teenage Frankenstein* in the U.S.A.)

and *Journey to the Center of the Earth*, both in color and CinemaScope. Even mighty MGM managed to produce a '50s undisputed masterwork, the influential *Forbidden Planet*. But to most '50s fantasy diehards, going to the movies was associated with black-and-white gritty images caught in countless stuffy flea-pits, squeezed into cramped, scuffed seats and watched through a blue haze of tobacco smoke, happily a cinematic experience long since gone.

You could rely on the independents to inflict pain and suffering on an audience, making these quick-buck producers wish they had never parted with their hard-earned cash: Astor (*Robot Monster*); Planet Filmways (*Killers from Space*); Howco International (*Teenage Monster*); Topor (*The Gargon Terror*); Topaz/Eros (*Fire Maidens from Outer Space*); GBM/Governor (*Teenage Zombies*); Hollywood International (*The Astounding She-Monster*); and, of course, Edward D. Wood, Jr.'s tawdry handiworks. These artistically bankrupt undertakings, conceived by hack moviemakers, the infamous "Kings of the Awful," were a poor substitute for the real article, the cinematic equivalent of

bootlegs, but every decade has its fair share of clunkers, so why not the 1950s? No one grade Z director was any better/worse than the other; there's very little to choose from between Jerry Warren, Ed Wood, Phil Tucker, Tom Graeff and Ronnie Ashcroft. Richard Cunha was marginally more proficient than most, directing four camp classics for Astor in 1958: *Frankenstein's Daughter*, *Giant from the Unknown*, *Missile to the Moon* and *She Demons*. Each cost around $65,000, each took a week to film and all have left their dubious mark. After completing his glorious schlock quartet, Cunha seemed to have vanished off the face of the earth.

Hammer Films reigned supreme in the United Kingdom following the unprecedented successes of *The Quatermass Experiment* and *The Curse of Frankenstein*. No other British film company could hope to compete with their financial acumen, brought about by making a series of smash-hit horror pictures which rank with the finest coming from America and the best the '50s had to offer. Hammer offered deep, rich Technicolor; artistic direction; a meticulous attention to period set design; an exceptional ensemble of classically trained stage actors; intelligent, finely written scripts; and an air of Englishness unique to the company's painstaking production values—that was the Hammer way. Pushing the boundaries as far as violence and blood and guts went, Hammer engaged in a long-running battle with the censor's office; Hammer, much to the fans' delight, epitomized the British "X" certificate picture to a tee. How many motion pictures could make front-page headlines nowadays? Hammer, who flew the flag for Britain's film industry during the '50s, accomplished it twice with *The Curse of Frankenstein* and *Dracula*. That's how high their profile was in the British public.

Apart from Lee, Cushing, Price, Lugosi (he was still around—just), Chaney and Karloff, a roll-call of actors/actresses found inhabiting one horror feature after another, year in, year out, would read like this: Marshall Thompson, John Agar, Dabbs Greer, Richard Denning, William Hopper, Kenneth Tobey, Richard Carlson, Rex Reason, Jeff Morrow, Hugh Marlowe, John Carradine, Morris Ankrum, Gregg Palmer, Nestor Paiva, Robert Shayne, Whit Bissell, Paul Birch, Ross Elliott, Robert Clarke, William Hudson, Michael Gough, Grant Williams, Harry Lauter, Peter Graves, André Morell, Francis Lederer, Tor Johnson, Gregory Gay, Ray "Crash" Corrigan, Don Megowan, Brett Halsey, Arthur Franz, Lyle Talbot, Forrest Tucker, Allison Hayes, Barbara Wilson, Charlotte Austin, Joan Taylor, Sally Todd, Susan Cabot, Mara Corday, Mala Powers, Yvette Vickers, Beverly Garland, Hazel Court, Barbara Shelley, Lori Nelson, Gloria Talbott, Peggie Castle, Sally Fraser and Faith Domergue.

From the "playing a role" point of view, each and every one of the above turned in believable performances, whatever task was ordained for them. Agar stands out as the all-American regular guy, a likeable actor with whom audiences felt comfortable. Good-looker Denning could be waspish at times, Thompson authoritative, Tobey bullish, Morrow also bullish and Carradine, slumming it somewhat all the way out of the 1940s, slightly arrogant. The women were all bright and attractive, resulting in some memorable pairings: Agar and Corday in *Tarantula*; Agar and Nelson in *Revenge of the Creature*; Hopper and Taylor in *20 Million Miles to Earth*; Tobey and Margaret Sheridan in *The Thing from Another World*; Denning and Corday in *The Black Scorpion*; Tobey and Domergue in *It Came from Beneath the Sea*; Kevin McCarthy and Dana Wynter in *Invasion of the Body Snatchers*; James Mason and Arlene Dahl in *Journey to the Center of the Earth*; Thompson and Shawn Smith in *It! The Terror from Beyond Space*; Jock Mahoney and Smith (again) in *The Land Unknown*; Cushing and Yvonne Furneaux in *The Mummy*; Gene Barry and Ann Robinson in *The War of the Worlds*; Carlson and Julia Adams in *Creature from the Black Lagoon*; Tim Holt and Audrey Dalton in *The Monster that Challenged the World* and Reason and Leigh Snowden in *The Creature Walks Among Us*. All made up the romantic element of the film they were starring in and none outstayed his or her welcome. Besides, teenage girls could ogle the males while their boyfriends fantasized about the females, all gorgeous to a fault.

Chief among fantasy/horror directors (with the number of their '50s fantasy titles listed after the dates, excluding serials) were Roger Corman (1926-present; 11), Terence Fisher (1904-1980; 10), Edward L. Cahn (1899-1963; 9), Jack Arnold (1916-1992; 7), Bert I. Gordon (1922-present; 7), Nathan Juran (1907-2002; 6), Val Guest (1911-2006; 5), Lee Sholem (1913-2000; 4), W. Lee Wilder (1904-1982; 4), Edward Bernds (1905-2000; 4) and Herbert L. Strock (1918-2005; 4). Other names saluted by aficionados include Edgar G. Ulmer (1904-1972), Fred F. Sears (1913-1957), Spencer G. Bennet (1893-1987), Edward Ludwig (1899-1982), Byron Haskin (1899-1984), Robert Day (1922-present), Howard W. Koch (1916-2001), Eugene Lourie (1903-1991), William Castle (1914-1977), Jerry Warren (1925-1988), Edward D. Wood, Jr. (1924-1978), and from Japan, Inoshiro Honda (1911-1993; 7 titles).

Many of the above names made numerous Westerns, serials and TV programs in addition to horror: Lee "Roll 'em" Sholem (known for bringing all his films in on time and budget), in particular, directed scores of television Westerns (*Cheyenne*, *Bronco* and *Sugarfoot*) as well as *Whirlybirds*, nearly 1,300 in total. Spencer G. Bennet was in the chair for four of Columbia's *Jungle Jim* series of potboilers (Sholem directed a couple himself) and the Sam Katzman-produced cliffhangers *Atom Man vs. Superman* (1950), *Mysterious Island* (1951) and *The Lost Planet* (1953). Jack Arnold's interest in the genre waned rapidly: After switching from Universal to Paramount for *The Space Children* in 1958, he returned to Universal, directing the riveting Audie Murphy Western *No Name on the Bullet* (1959) before quitting the horror scene altogether. Many other directors followed suit, entering the world of the TV series, having left their indelible print on '50s fantasy.

Claimants for the decade's most consistently creative director are Arnold, Cahn, Fisher and Honda. Jack Arnold used unfamiliar locations for his projects, allowing space for his characters to react accordingly. Arnold utilized these disquieting settings to great effect, a requisite backdrop in six of his seven horror/sci-fi pictures, as crucial to the overall ambience as the protagonists themselves: Richard Carlson menaced by aliens in the desert (*It Came from Outer Space*); children befriending an alien blob among the desolate seascapes in *The Space Children*; Carlson and Denning in the Black Lagoon, up against the gill-man; John Agar battling *Tarantula*, again in the director's favorite locale, the desert; and tiny Grant Williams fighting for survival in the inhospitable habitat of the family cellar. Even the Miami environment in *Revenge of the Creature* took on an air of foreboding, but not to John Agar and company—this time 'round, the director turned the tables by creating an urban locality hostile to the gill-man. Arnold produced five classic horror yarns for Universal, all virtually templates for the likes of Spielberg who, as a youngster, no doubt sat through *Creature from the Black Lagoon* and *Tarantula* and thought "One day…"

The prolific Edward L. Cahn roamed far and wide in his career, freelancing from one studio to another. From Italy came *Curse of the Faceless Man*; teenage horror received the Cahn treatment in *Invasion of the Hell Creatures*; the supernatural cropped up in *The She-Creature*; atomic science produced the *Creature with the Atom Brain*; The

Four Skulls of Jonathan Drake dealt with zombies and voodoo and the director took off for Mars in *It! The Terror from Beyond Space*. Cahn and Arnold were alike in that they lulled an audience into a false sense of security before hitting them over the head with a thunderbolt or two. They also expertly utilized strident musical arrangements to give their pictures maximum impact to genre fans. The body of work left by these two horror maestros is priceless.

From shaky beginnings (*Spaceways*, *Four Sided Triangle*), Terence Fisher grew into one of the '50s most revered directors. With a deliberate attention to detail almost unheard of, he breathed new life into the dusty old classics of yore; his careful, almost relaxed, camerawork took in the Gothic splendors of *The Curse of Frankenstein* and *Dracula* before closing in for the kill on Christopher Lee's frightful visage in both films, provoking the wrath of the censor's office and causing an avalanche of faintings in British cinemas. With these two productions plus *The Revenge of Frankenstein* and *The Mummy*, Fisher came up with possibly four of the greatest horror features of the 1950s.

Inoshiro (Ishiro) Honda's monster movies aren't exactly refined; he was quite content to let his titanic rubber-suited creatures do the talking. But he was a revolutionary filmmaker, treading virgin territory by constructing intricate model cities and then allowing the likes of *Godzilla* and *Rodan* to trample them underfoot. The original edit of *Half Human* shows an atypical personal approach in his work, more character-based than usual, while the full-length version of *Varan the Unbelievable* is a Japanese masterpiece waiting to be discovered. People don't really matter in Honda's films; in a way, they're victims, food for the monster. He does, though, manage to concentrate on human emotions in small doses; favorite leading man Kenji Sahara was allowed a few moments of screen smooching Japanese-style (all very polite) in *Rodan*, for instance, before Honda probably yelled, "Katto!" and went back to organizing the destruction caused by his gigantic flying reptiles. Massively influential, Honda and his team's '50s monster productions, especially *Godzilla*, still resonate through fantasy cinema to this day.

However, even these luminaries had their off days: Arnold's *Monster on the Cam-*

pus lacks the *joie de vivre* of his previous five pictures, a competent but bog-standard man-into-monster outing; Cahn's dull *Voodoo Woman* isn't in the same league as his magnificent *It! The Terror from Beyond Space*; Fisher's *Spaceways* is, for want of a better word, boring and *The Mysterians*, although colorful, doesn't match up to Honda's powerful, X-rated *Godzilla* and *Rodan*.

What about Roger Corman, I hear you ask? Corman, admittedly, is there with the best of the rest with 11 titles under his belt, but in this writer's opinion, he falls a smidgen short of greatness. *Not of this Earth*, *The Wasp Woman* and *Day the World Ended* represent the best of Corman's work from this period, tightly knit and resourceful; *Attack of the Crab Monsters*, *The Undead* and *A Bucket of Blood* are okay in patches. The less said about the director's two major blips, *Viking Women and the Sea Serpent* and *She Gods of Shark Reef*, the better! Corman found his milieu in the 1960s with his splendid Poe adaptations. His '50s output is ever so slightly erratic in content, ranging from the good (*It Conquered the World*) to the corny (*Teenage Caveman*). However, it's a grave error to underestimate Corman's pictures because "corny" was the name of the game in '50s fantasy!

The rest of the pack produced agile, workmanlike efforts containing flashes of brilliance, the pictures sometimes static, other times fluid; their combined ventures were tremendously entertaining, guaranteeing, by the lurid name of the film alone, a near-to-full house in the days when celluloid was the main source of entertainment for millions of families throughout the land. A fantastic tableau formed by film companies, from giants to small fry; directors varying from the innovative to the amateurish; and actors either professional or wooden. These are the names and faces that were behind those scores of fantasy flicks that enthralled us so much half-a-century ago. One of the main purposes of this book is to ensure that these names never fade from memory;

cinema as a whole owes so much to their hard-won endeavors.

Chapter 4
Soundtracks: The Composers

Once upon a time in movieland, a one-to-four minute piece of music known as the title score was the prelude, or curtain raiser, to what was to follow. Then, the film composer was deemed as important as the director, the producer and the stars, a key figure within the production organization. That opening score, over a short space of time, had to convey to an expectant audience a musical summary of what they were about to experience. It had to seize them by the scruff of the neck and make them sit up and take notice, to involve them from the outset. The title score was, in a way, a movie's major selling point, as much as the promotional poster, the billboards and the stills. And it didn't end there. From films lasting an hour to epics approaching the four-hour mark, a composer, or musical arranger, had to carry out the following key tasks: Complement the visuals throughout and create an appropriate aural backdrop; decide which scenes required music, and which scenes didn't; underscore nuances; cue a short passage of notes to prelude a scene of importance; keep the tempo going by the shrewd insertion of time signatures; play with an audience's emotions; raise and lower the audio level where necessary by the use of cadences; and to produce themes and codas that would stay in the public's minds long after they exited a cinema. These were the hard-and-fast rules governing film composing and they resulted in a decade ringing with momentous music. Alfred Hitchcock went on record to say that Bernard Herrmann's legendary soundtrack to *Psycho* (yes, it's a 1960 film but illustrates a point) was as important to the film's success as his expertise behind the camera. Likewise, Elmer Bernstein's magnificent music in *The Ten Commandments* is a symphony in its own right, commanding the attention for close-on four hours; Cecil B. DeMille's Old Testament epic just wouldn't be the same without Bernstein's magisterial melodies bringing it to life.

Like many other aspects of film-making in the 21st Century, the once mighty soundtrack is a thing of the past. Many films nowadays dispense with a title score altogether (step forward Mel Gibson's *Apocalypto*) and what passes as soundtrack music is often no more than a background burble, an out-of-context pop song tagged onto the *closing* credits—yes, even the all-important opening credits are being phased out. What you get for your money in many cases is a choral cacophony that can hardly be termed "music" at all. A bombardment of very loud, unrelated

Alfred Hitchcock poses in a publicity shot with music composer Bernard Herrmann.

Music composer Dimitri Tiomkin

chords with no discernible melody, leitmotif or musical pattern—nothing more. To hammer home the message, I often listen to a compilation CD embracing 40 theme titles taken from mainly 1950s fantastic films (a couple from the '40s and '60s are included); to put together such a list from today's fare would be a futile exercise.

Horror, science fiction and fantasy film productions of the '50s, on all levels, were blessed with a raft of imaginative composers. These artists ensured that the paying customer's ears would be bathed by a half-decent score, even if the events didn't quite live up to the musical expectations blasted out over the opening 60-second credit list. In fact, customers expected it! It's a testament to the abilities of a composer like Frank Worth that he could conjure up a mood of "I'm really enjoying this" in an audience that had paid good money to watch Ed Wood's tatty *Bride of the Monster*. His over-enthusiastic arrangements helped paper over the cracks in both plot and special effects, raising the film by at least one notch. He wasn't alone—awful efforts such as *Robot Monster*, *Killers from Space* and *Beginning of the End* relied heavily on composers to at least garnish their cheapskate fare with a dash of relish, to give the impression that perhaps their works of art weren't quite as bad as some critics thought.

Once in a while, a noted Hollywood composer, a colossus in his chosen field, would lend his talents to the fantasy scene on a one-off basis and then, having left his mark, depart for greener pastures. Russian-born Dimitri Tiomkin (1894-1979; 133 scores; four Oscars) achieved precisely that with *The Thing from Another World*, one of the top five fantasy soundtracks of the decade. Tiomkin's incidental music drips with otherworldly menace, a blueprint of how to enhance scenes to give them maximum impact. Maurice Jarre (1924-2009; 166 scores; three Oscars) had also dipped his toes in the genre with *Eyes Without a Face*, his discordant, out-of-kilter arrangements frayed the nerve-endings. With *Ben-Hur* looming on the horizon, Hungarian Miklos Rozsa (1907-1995; 98 scores; three Oscars) still found time to create an almost religious-type backdrop to *The World, the Flesh and the Devil*. Bernard Herrmann (1911-1975; 82 scores; one Oscar) contributed immensely to *Journey to the Center of the Earth*, *The 3 Worlds of Gulliver*, *The 7th Voyage of Sinbad* and *The Day the Earth Stood Still* while managing to liven up a few Hitchcock masterpieces along the way, his brooding, woodwind-based music becoming firm favorites with soundtrack enthusiasts.

But these were the giants; a whole host of other composers ensured that fantasy fodder from Universal-International, United Artists, Allied Artists, Columbia and American International, among others, received some form of musical recognition,

Music composer Herman Stein

whether it was a B movie or had A movie status. Many of these gifted men of music emigrated from Europe, the land of the great composers, and had come from a classical music background. Their combined output in the sphere of TV and film composing in all genres is nothing short of phenomenal. For instance, Polish-born Paul Sawtell (1906-1971) racked up 443 titles in his long career; Austrian Hans J. Salter (1896-1994) 412; Russian Mischa Bakaleinikoff (1890-1960) 459; Albert Glasser (1916-1998) 435; Paul Dunlap (1919-2010) 133; Herman Stein (1915-2007) 101; Frank Skinner (1897-1968) 380; Gerald Fried (1928-present) 120; Henry Mancini (1924-1994) 274; Ronald Stein (1930-1988) 79; Darrell Calker (1905-1964) 165; and Heinz Roemheld (1901-1985) 462. Add to these the names of James Bernard (1925-2001), Gerard Schurmann (1924-present), Henry Vars (1902-1977), Les Baxter (1922-1996), Von Dexter (1912-1996), Frank Worth (1903-1990), Bert Shefter (1902-1999), David Buttolph (1902-1983), Ernest Gold (1921-1999); Buxton Orr (1924-1997), Edwin Astley (1922-1998), Leith Stevens (1909-1970), Irving Gertz (1915-2008), Raoul Kraushaar (1908-2001), John Seely (1923-2004) and Josef Zimanich (1892-1973). That list gives some idea of the wealth of talent that helped, in their own individual ways, elevate '50s horror, science fiction and fantasy soundtracks to an artistic level not experienced before or since. The influence of the old classical masters can be heard throughout these composers' works; many scores sound more like extracts from overtures than simply film music, such is their richness and depth.

Horror/monster movie soundtracks may have been credited to one composer, but in a lot of cases this wasn't entirely true: In the big budget A productions, yes; but in monster movies, mostly thought of as Bs by studio execs, no. A low-budget picture's score was quite often composed of a patchwork of themes plundered from the company's music library, stitched together with professionalism by a soundtrack arranger; as many as 18 to 20 composers could unknowingly contribute to a movie such as *20 Million Miles to Earth*, using between 25 to 95 separate cues taken from all manner of movies, including drama, crime, Westerns and even romance. In itself, this was another painstaking art form that has died and which few of today's moviegoers are even aware.

Despite their varying backgrounds and individualism, did the music these composers produce differentiate between one movie to the next? Probably it did not differ all that much. Hans J. Salter's bombastic tones announcing the arrival of the *Creature from the Black Lagoon* are echoed in James Bernard's opening ear-blaster from *Dracula*, which in turn is mirrored in Paul Sawtell and Bert Shefter's 61-second belter of a title theme in *It! The Terror from Beyond Space*. Remember, these hard-hitting arrange-

Universal's "musical director" Joseph Gershenson (left), with studio guitarist Bob Bain

ments were solely aimed at grabbing the attention of an audience on tenterhooks. It was no good musically pussyfooting around when you were shortly to be confronted by the gill-man, a vampire count or a stowaway Martian intent on wiping out a spaceship's crew. Scores for horror movies had to be simple and direct, not cerebral. However, there *were* significant variations in flavors, in leitmotifs, that reflected a particular director's musical leanings. Only by listening to a great many soundtracks over a number of years can these subtle differences be discerned, even to those with very little aptitude in the tonic scale. If a soundtrack is distinctive enough, it will be remembered. It's as easy as that. Reviewing certain composer's works will reinforce that belief.

Hans J. Salter never received the credit he deserved for his 30-year stint with Universal-International, especially his work in the 1950s. You won't find his illustrious name listed on the credits of *Creature from the Black Lagoon*, *The Mole People*, *The Creature Walks Among Us*, *The Black Castle* and *The Incredible Shrinking Man*. It *is* shown on a handful of Universal Westerns from this period, but not on the company's fantasy/horror outings. In 1940, Russian-born Joseph Gershenson became head of Universal's music department. From 1949 onward, his name appeared as "Musical Director" or "Musical Supervision by" on the rolling credits of the company's horror roster; Salter was pushed to the sidelines, and he wasn't the only one. Gershenson was adept at tinkering with arrangements written by others, combining Salter's strident orchestrations with those of Herman Stein, Henry Mancini, Irving Gertz and Frank Skinner to form a sort of composite Universal horror score, unique to the company. It's this mix-and-match score that can be heard in *This Island Earth*, *Tarantula*, *The Monolith Monsters*, *Monster on the Campus*, *The Strange Door*, *It Came from Outer Space*, *The Land Unknown*, *Revenge of the Creature*, *Curse of the Undead*, *The Thing that Couldn't Die* and even the *Abbott and Costello Meet* flicks. Those with a fine ear will even detect its refrains in a few Audie Murphy Westerns as well, *Tumbleweed* (1953) being a good example. Gershenson, some musical purists might say, even had the gall to use Mancini's complete title theme from *Tarantula* as the title theme to *Showdown at Abilene* (1956), as blatant a piece of replication that anyone will ever come across. And where have you heard those decidedly non-Western notes that are played during the opening sequences in 1951's *Cave of Outlaws*? Correct—it's the title score from *House of Dracula*, stretched out to cover the initial 10 minutes of action, another instance of Gershenson taking liberties by awarding himself a misplaced musical credit.

It now seems unforgivable to many that Hans J. Salter, the unsung hero behind a string of memorable, semi-classical musical arrangements for Universal in the 1940s for which he *did* receive a composing credit (*The Mad Ghoul*; *Frankenstein Meets the Wolf Man*; *House of Frankenstein*; *Man Made Monster*), was never rewarded as such for his virtuoso efforts in the 1950s (Gershenson wasn't averse to using snippets from Salter's '40s scores in many of Universal's monster movies). Why this happened we shall probably never know.

This state of affairs didn't exist elsewhere; composers were included on the credits of most other companies' horror pictures, often in big bold lettering. Paul Sawtell (he had scored *The Mummy's Curse* in 1944) first met Russian Bert Shefter in 1957. Sawtell was the more prolific of the two, having contributed many Western themes for Warner Bros. and Columbia (Randolph Scott's *Tall Man Riding* [1955] is one of his best). Their first joint collaborations, in that year, were on *The Black Scorpion* and *Kronos*. They were later to stray into big-budgeters such as *The Fly*, *Return of the Fly* and 1960's *The Lost World*, but fans remember the pair for their work on *It! The Terror from Beyond Space*. *It!*'s title theme is 61 seconds of pulsating raw power, dragging the viewer into the action (and that forbidding Martian landscape), and the remainder of the orchestration (a refinement of the *Kronos* soundtrack) is just as riveting. Edward L. Cahn's space thriller may well have been a B movie, but the score by Sawtell and Shefter was class A, a worthy contender for the decade's finest sci-fi soundtrack.

Some composers chose to stay with one company rather than freelance their talents to all and sundry. One such composer was Mischa Bakaleinikoff, who worked almost exclusively for Columbia, writing not only fantasy scores but arranging music for their entire *Jungle Jim* series of B features, plus many Westerns (the Western was a much-favored second string to a composer's bow). Bakaleinikoff's specific musical signature was founded on a recurring, four-note leitmotif played on brass woodwind— "dah-dah-dah-dah." Speeded up or slowed down, it can be heard continually in *It Came from Beneath the Sea* and *Earth vs. the Flying Saucers*, a cue used to announce the arrival of something dreadful, such as the giant octopus or attacking UFOs. The music to both films is rather coarse and basic, detracting from Ray Harryhausen's eye-catching effects. Bakaleinikoff toned this phrasing down considerably in *20 Million Miles to Earth* and came up with a fairly low-key accompaniment to Harryhausen's rampaging Ymir, all the better for not drowning out the creature mayhem. He also perfected a two-note theme, used extensively in *Earth vs. the Flying Saucers*, to add menace to the UFOs' appearances. Bakaleinikoff's top arrangement for a horror movie is reserved for

Composers Paul Sawtell and Bert Shefter are best remembered for their music score for *It! The Terror from Beyond Space*.

1956's *The Werewolf*. Shrugging off those dirge-like "dah-dah-dah-dahs," he manages to produce a stirring (if scant) title theme, followed by a suitably ominous undercurrent, the perfect background to Steven Ritch's agonized wolf man. *The Werewolf* is without doubt Bakaleinikoff's finest Columbia horror hour by far, but one that is not often recalled today.

B-movie composer supremo Albert Glasser is one of the greatest names of all in the '50s lineup of horror/fantasy film composers, his scores always loud and in your face, unrefined and unsubtle, just how the fans liked them. His soundtrack to *Indestructible Man* is quintessential Glasser—brash, full-throttle throughout, complementing Chaney's equally bulldozing performance. Just as pulverizing is the opening theme to Richard Cunha's *Giant from the Unknown*, downright deafening if you turn the volume up on your home cine system, as is his speaker-rattling music in *Monster from Green Hell* and *The Neanderthal Man*. Bert I. Gordon, among a host of directors, appreciated Glasser's rough-and-ready artistry and hired him to score a number of his pictures, including *The Cyclops*, *War of the Colossal Beast*, *Earth vs. the Spider* and *Attack of the Puppet People*. Here was a classic example of music overriding the effects; with Glasser's arrangements thundering merrily away in the background, we could easily overlook those back-projected insects and model cars of which the director littered his pictures. This is probably why Gordon took him on in the first place! Glasser even managed to make Roger Corman's *Viking Women and the Sea Serpent* moderately presentable by sheer musical muscle alone, the mark of a true maestro.

At United Artists, Gerald Fried's music was instantly recognizable by the crowds, a stomping, almost semi-marching series of notes noisily played on woodwind instruments, the best example of his particular craft being *I Bury the Living*. *The Vampire* also featured Fried's brand of thumping notation, notably in the scenes of John Beal loping through the streets looking for victims. He embellished *Curse of the Faceless Man*, *The Fantastic Disappearing Man*, *The Flame Barrier* and *The Lost Missile* with his idiosyncratic soundtracks—certainly, no other composer's melodies sounded like his.

Paul Dunlap is a less-familiar name among aficionados, but he was yet another composer who brought a high degree of excellence to the low-budget horror movie. His title themes for *Blood is My Heritage* and *Frankenstein 1970* are what scores of this time were all about: short, sharp and catchy, oozing "X" certificate intimidation. Equally haunting was his soundtrack to *I Was a Teenage Werewolf*; even *Teenage Frankenstein* benefited from Dunlap's imaginative notes, as did *Target Earth*, while his score for Lippert's *Lost Continent* is nothing short of magnificent. His other composing credits include *The Angry Red Planet*, *How to Make a Monster* and *Invisible Invaders*.

In the 1950s, Roger Corman tended to use Ronald Stein to boost his B-monster-movies. Stein is another highly imaginative composer who could tone it down (*It Conquered the World*), beef it up (*Attack of the Crab Monsters*) or make it eerie (*Day the World Ended*). Stein's fantasy output mostly emanated from AIP and Allied Artists in such diverse pieces as *Invasion of the Hell Creatures*, *Not of this Earth* and *The She-Creature* and typified the expertise these composers brought to the genre: Whatever the subject matter, be it giant land crabs or a 50-foot woman (yes, he wrote the music to *Attack of the 50 Foot Woman*), Stein knocked up a believable score to underlie with élan what must have been on occasions the most tawdry of productions!

Composer Paul Dunlap brought *Teenage Frankenstein* (notice the Brit "X" rating) to life.

One-offs, or two-, three- or fou- picture dabblings into fantasy abounded in the 1950s when said composers were not busy working on mainly Westerns. David Buttolph produced two splendidly symphonic scores for Warner Bros. in *The Beast from 20,000 Fathoms* and *House of Wax* (he also scored many of the company's Westerns). Carmen Dragon's boisterous horror tones brought force and energy to *Invasion of the Body Snatchers*; John Seely's insidious music for *The Hideous Sun Demon* was much plagiarized in American TV dramas. Who could ever forget (perhaps many would like to!) Hoyt S. Curtin's crashing, guitar/piano score, which was as freakish as the picture it was backing—the infamous *Mesa of Lost Women*? Louis and Bebe Barron's electronic tonalities imparted an air of alien threat in *Forbidden Planet*. Disney's *20,000 Leagues Under the Sea* contained a rousing, nautical soundtrack by Paul Smith. Darrell Calker's pumped-up jungle music for *From Hell It Came* and *Voodoo Woman* had to be heard to be believed! Josef Zimanich did his utmost to liven up *Man Beast* and *The Incredible Petrified World*. Les Baxter's scores for *The Black Sleep*, *Pharaoh's Curse* and *The Bride and the Beast* were exemplary, given what he had to work with. Heinz Roemheld's archetypal theme for *The Monster that Challenged the World* is a great piece of '50s monster music. Henry Vars livened up *Gog* and *The Unearthly*. *The Tingler* crawled around to the refrains of Von Dexter, who also spooked-up William Castle's *House on Haunted Hill*. Manuel Compinsky's music was about the only worthwhile point of interest in *Killers from Space*. *The Man from Planet X* arrived via Charles Koff's interplanetary warblings. Ralph Carmichael was used on *The Blob* and *4D Man*; the phantom skulls in *The Screaming Skull* performed to the music of Ernest Gold. *Curucu, Beast of the Amazon* unveiled itself to the South American melodies of Raoul Kraushaar. And Leith Stevens provided a cracking outer space soundtrack for *World Without End*, the equal of any in this decade.

Which science fiction movie of the 1950s can lay claim to having 13 different composers contributing to the soundtrack? The answer is 1958's *I Married a Monster from Outer Space*. In 1958, Hollywood experienced a musician's strike, meaning

James Bernard's title credit for his most memorable score, *Dracula* (aka *Horror of Dracula*, 1958)

that companies either had to look outside America and Canada for the right person to score their pictures or resort to what Paramount did on this singular occasion—raid the vaults. *I Married a Monster from Outer Space*'s soundtrack is a humdinger, seamlessly knitted together by rerecording extracts from existing music written by the following: Lyn Murray, Leo Shuken, Ray Livingston, Nathan Van Cleave, Roy Webb, Mack David, Victor Young, Walter Scharf, Leith Stevens, Franz Waxman, Hugo Friedhofer, Daniele Amfitheatrof and Aaron Copland. As expected, all 13 names are omitted from the picture's list of credits! You would never, in a million years, notice the musical joins present in Gene Fowler, Jr.'s moody alien takeover thriller, so praise must go to Paramount's backroom staff that created the ultimate composite soundtrack without anyone, and certainly not the paying customer, knowing it.

Across the water, British fantasy films relied on classical composers such as Malcolm Arnold (Royal College of Music) and Muir Mathieson (Royal Academy of Music) to carry the plot; the horror film composer wasn't born until James Bernard came along and scored *The Quatermass Experiment*, followed by, more importantly, *The Curse of Frankenstein*. Bernard hit a peak with *Dracula*, his soundtrack so influential that it still reverberates down through the years. He would never top it, although his title score to *The Stranglers of Bombay* comes pretty close. But Bernard didn't have it all to himself; Frank Reizenstein's peerless music for *The Mummy* ranks as one of the finest Hammer scores of the '50s, on par with the best of Bernard (Reizenstein also co-wrote the music to 1960's *Circus of Horrors* with Muir Mathieson). Hammer also employed multi-talented Richard Rodney Bennett (Royal Academy of Music), nominated for several prestigious awards and knighted in 1998, to score *The Man Who Could Cheat Death*; Bennett tended to steer clear of the cinema, applying his dexterity to concert work. Lower down the ladder, Scotsman Buxton Orr's rasping tones could be heard behind *First Man into Space*, *Fiend Without a Face*, *Grip of the Strangler* and *Corridors of Blood*. Edwin Astley was another composer whose over-embellished scores guarantee partial deafness upon leaving the cinema; witness *Devil Girl from Mars* and *Behemoth the Sea Monster*. Television regular Stanley Black took time off from the small screen to work on *Blood of the Vampire* and *The Trollenberg Terror,* and Clifton Parker's music for *Night of the Demon* is a fantastic English-piece of orchestration that piles on the shocks and supernatural thrills in equal measure.

Stock scores consisted of excerpts from musical passages either composed by a variety of arrangers or taken from one arranger's spectrum of works, all of which formed a mosaic that was slightly ill defined but still effective. Take *The Fiend Who Walked the West*. Leon Klatzkin's stirring title theme is embellished by a few seconds of Bernard Herrmann's score from *The Day the Earth Stood Still*. The remainder of the soundtrack is a mix (used prudently in this particular film) which is difficult to pin down to one composer, although incidental tracks from a few of Klatzkin's TV Westerns and his themes in the *Adventures of Superman* television series are in there somewhere. The stock score was a musical soup of sorts, used extensively throughout 1950s cinema, especially in Westerns and crime thrillers.

So a myriad of composers worked minor miracles on their pictures, injecting tension, suspense, humor and credibility into what otherwise might have turned out to be a routine production. Their combined genius created a solid foundation to underlie the visuals, able to excite an audience as much as the director could. In an age where the cinema-going public pays money to see a film but not necessarily to hear the music behind the action, each and every one of the composers named in this chapter proves beyond doubt that music in films *does* matter. Their contributions now seem like lost art, those vibrant title themes that contribute to a movie's "Wow" factor, thereby becoming part of cinema's long history. The 1950s was the heyday of men like Bernard, Dunlap, Salter, Sawtell and Shefter, Fried and Glasser, their soundtracks blessed with a dynamism that failed to carry over into the 1960s and beyond. This expansive body of work should never be banished from the minds of fantasy lovers and must not be forgotten. And as long as there are fans who hold this decade dear to their hearts, it never will be.

We finish with a top-20 list of essential fantastic film soundtracks from the 1950s, taking into consideration title theme, incidental music and overall score. If the themes to *It! The Terror from Beyond Space* and *The Thing from Another World* can still electrify the senses and transport us back to when we first viewed these pictures as children over 50 years ago, then they have earned the right to immortality:

The Beast from 20,000 Fathoms—David Buttolph
The Creature Walks Among Us—Hans J. Salter
Dracula—James Bernard
Eyes Without a Face—Maurice Jarre
Forbidden Planet—Louis and Bebe Barron
Frankenstein 1970—Paul Dunlap
From Hell It Came—Darrell Calker
House of Wax—David Buttolph
Indestructible Man—Albert Glasser
Invasion of the Body Snatchers—Carmen Dragon
It! The Terror from Beyond Space—Paul Sawtell and Bert Shefter
Journey to the Center of the Earth—Bernard Herrmann
The Mummy—Frank Reizenstein
Night of the Demon—Clifton Parker
The 7th Voyage of Sinbad—Bernard Herrmann
Tarantula—Henry Mancini
The Thing from Another World—Dimitri Tiomkin
This Island Earth—Herman Stein
20,000 Leagues Under the Sea—Paul Smith
The War of the Worlds—Leith Stevens
Just missed out…
The Werewolf—Mischa Bakaleinikoff

Chapter 5
Let's Take Another Look: Part One

Derided, scorned, dismissed airily as "rubbish," laughed at and treated with contempt: The movies discussed under this heading do not warrant such treatment! Thought: If *Behemoth the Sea Monster*, *The Cyclops*, *Curse of the Faceless Man*, *Daughter of Dr. Jekyll*, *Day the World Ended*, *The Fiend Who Walked the West*, *The Land Unknown*, *The She-Creature*, *The Thing that Couldn't Die*, *The Vampire*, *Varan the Unbelievable* and *The Werewolf* were really *that* bad, why is it that they played for years and years in England, never off the circuits, always pulling in a fair-to-full house? Were *all* those customers truly blind to the fact that what they were paying to see was the cinematic equivalent of throwaway trash? How come many people I knew then, including myself, sat through the likes of *Frankenstein 1970*, *The Disembodied*, *The Mole People* and *Attack of the 50 Foot Woman* several times over and enjoyed, nay *lapped up*, every single minute, never got bored and waited in anticipation for their next arrival at one's local theater? Why do we keep going back to these pictures time and time again, greedy for their corny delights? Nostalgia? Seeking something more primal? Where does the appeal lie in something as hokey as *The Man Who Turned to Stone*? The simple truth is that the above movies, and countless others of their ilk, had an endurance, a longer shelf life as it were, quite unknown to modern-day audiences; fundamentally, they possessed the ability to entertain the public over a space of several years, long before the advent of mass marketing and hype within the cinema industry. Example: *The Land Unknown*, released in 1957, was still being screened in England in 1969, usually with *The Deadly Mantis*, and *still*, after 12 years, managing to draw a sizeable crowd into a movie theater. What monster movie can lay claim to that nowadays? The short answer is none.

One should seek out the positive in these pictures, not always plump for the negative. Superficially, they may appear juvenile fare but scratch the surface and quite often you come up with something much deeper. This chapter, the first of three, will rethink and re-examine 32 much-loved, but much-ridiculed, horror, sci-fi and fantasy films, to pinpoint that elusive "pulling" factor. Let's take another look and decide who was right—the critics or the fans. Each synopsis will end with an adverse comment, taken from a number of sources, to prove my point!

One-Eyed Alien Terrorizes the North Pole

Allied Artists' *The Atomic Submarine* (1959) is a fast-paced sci-fi actioner that never received a wide showing in the United Kingdom and tends to get passed over in many film compendiums. Directed in pseudo-documentary style by Spencer G. Bennet, this tells of an alien furtively hiding inside a flying saucer in the vicinity of the North Pole; the saucer is destroying ships and submarines, recharging its atomic reactor by tapping into the Pole's magnetic waves, causing radioactivity. U.S. atomic sub *Tiger Shark* is assigned to seek and destroy, to prevent any further disasters in the area.

The main point of interest in *The Atomic Submarine* is the ingenious set design by Jack Rabin, Irving Block and Louis DeWitt. Yes, *USS Tiger Shark*, the mini-sub *Lungfish* and the UFO are obvious models, but combined with artistic underwater scen-

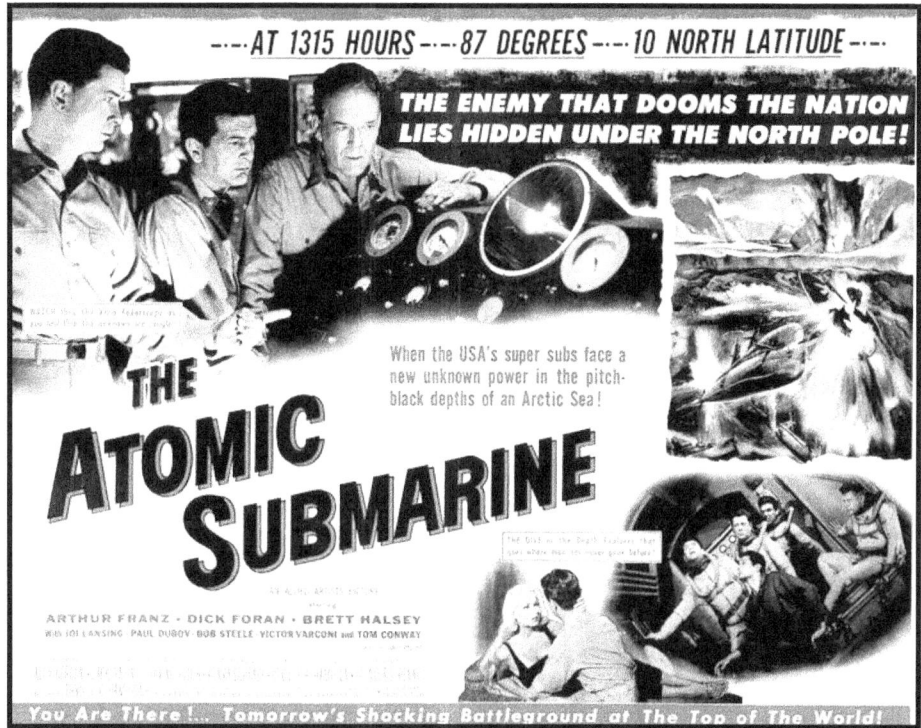

ery and the tentacled, Cyclopean alien occupying a globe situated within the sparsely furnished saucer, the effect is one of wonder rather than derision. Alexander Laszlo's "Electro-sonic" music also heightens the mood and suspense. True to form, the being is from a dying world and states, in sonorous Shakespearean tones, that Earth is suitable for colonization. The alien communicates by ESP and fries with radiation those who oppose it. Even when Arthur Franz shoots its eye out, the alien regenerates another. A missile fired from the sub destroys the UFO as it takes off for its home planet, and the Arctic shipping lanes are now safe.

Producer Alex Gordon assembled a better-than-usual cast of B movie regulars (Franz, Brett Halsey, Tom Conway, Dick Foran, Paul Dubov) to add weight and delivered an amusing script ("An underwater flying saucer!" "Little green men? Little green fish!") so no one would get restless over the 72-minute running time. Very much end-of-'50s in looks and ideas (the colorful '60s was just around the corner), Bennet's movie came across as a last-ditch reminder of what the decade was all about. Within the space of the next two years, films of this type (and caliber) would cease to exist.

"Only comes to life in the final 10 minutes."

$50 Million Heiress Turns into a Giantess and Gets Nasty

A spaceship resembling an oversized glowing balloon; a 30-foot bald alien dressed in a gladiator's outfit; a huge plaster cast hand; an even bigger rubber hand; and see-through 50-foot Allison Hayes wrecking the joint—yes, Allied Artists' *Attack of the 50 Foot Woman* (1958) has come to represent, over the years, the very heart and soul of the '50s B-horror movie and all that the genre stood for, where budgetary constraints

were no handicap to producing trashy, enjoyable fodder for the masses. Impoverished effects, risible dialogue, brief running time (66 minutes), exaggerated dramatics, outlandish poster and kooky title; the picture is far more cherished now than it was on first release. In the United Kingdom back then, amazing though it may now seem, the movie was deemed unsuitable for children, despite the preposterous content. Nathan Juran's laughable and loveable companion piece to *The Amazing Colossal Man* was awarded an "X" certificate from the British censor.

Ronald Stein's splendid title music gives way to reports of a UFO seen all over the globe. Heiress Hayes, married to two-timing slob William Hudson, who is carrying on right under her nose with kittenish Yvette Vickers, bumps into a globular satellite one dark night, inside of which is, according to her, a 30-foot giant. Nobody believes her, Hudson reckons she's going mad ("She was in a nuthouse for a while.") and needs to be committed to an asylum and Vickers sets her sights on the Star of India diamond that Hayes wears around her neck. But the large alien also wants the sparkler and the giant steals Hayes' pendant when she drives out to investigate the UFO further with Hudson ("It's real! It's real! I'm not crazy!"). Back in her villa, genetically contaminated by the alien's touch, Hayes turns into a 50-foot giantess ("Something's happened to Mrs. Archer!" screams the nurse, seeing that massive fake hand for the first time). Doctors are called out, Hudson and Vickers start making plans for *their* future and the action, plus Mark Hanna's marvel of a script, reaches new heights of irrationality as in the following scenes:

Doctor Roy Gordon, discussing remedial treatment for Hayes: "Forty gallons of plasma. And an elephant syringe?"

Deputy Frank Chase, on seeing a massive footprint in the flowerbeds: "Wow! What is it?" Sheriff George Douglas: "I dunno. But whatever it is, it wasn't made by a Japanese gardener."

"More morphine! More morphine!" shrieks the nurse as Hayes, now converted from a brunette to a blonde and wearing a fetching bed sheet bikini, crashes through the roof, then, "She's loose!"

As Hayes, transparent one minute, solid the next, walks into town, Gordon looks up at her: "She'll tear up the whole town until she finds Harry."

Chase: "Yeah, and then she'll tear up Harry!"

"I can't shoot a lady," cries Chase as Douglas orders him to open fire. Hayes demolishes the town's hotel and Tony's Bar, Vickers is crushed under falling masonry, Hudson is picked up by his colossus of a wife and she's electrocuted on power cables, toppling to the ground dead, her philandering husband, gripped in one enormous hand, dead also. The last word is left to Gordon: "She finally got Harry all to herself."

Attack of the 50 Foot Woman is a one-off; the fatuous 1994 remake conclusively showed that you cannot replicate what has gone before, not even with more money to play around with. Allied Artists' archetypal monster thriller was, like the Bert I. Gordon films it closely resembles (especially in the abysmal effects), conceived in an age where audiences were quite happy to put up with crudely constructed model hands, rock-bottom spacecraft, inferior superimposed shots of Hayes marching across the countryside and an alien who looked as though he was up for a bit part in *Spartacus*. It didn't matter then and shouldn't matter now, but this movie is living testimony to the fact that, while it's a chore to sit through a great many feature films classed as average, most average feature films from the fantasy genre *can* be enjoyed time and time again. You can quite easily forgive their inadequacies, because, deep down, they were made with passion. And *Attack of the 50 Foot Woman* proves it.

"Dismal. Only famous for its title."

The Incredible Shrinking Agar

Bert I. Gordon's *Attack of the Puppet People* (1958) usually ran in Britain as *6 Inches Tall*; along with *The Cyclops,* it showed that on occasion Gordon's work could hold its head high and compete with the best. Although nowhere near as polished as Universal's *The Incredible Shrinking Man*, Gordon's tale of a deranged puppeteer reducing humans to six-inch dolls because he cannot bear to see them walk out on him ("There's nothing worse than loneliness.") owed much more to Paramount's 1940 production of *Dr. Cyclops* in design and execution than Jack Arnold's seminal masterwork. John Hoyt starred as the owner of Dolls Incorporated; perky June Kenney applies for a secretarial position since the last woman to hold the job is now six inches tall and living in a cylindrical jar. John Agar, Hoyt's salesman, quickly turns on the charm, sensing that Kenney is slightly scared of her new boss *and* those eerily life-like mannequins standing silent in glass cylinders. When the two decide to marry (Agar proposes at a drive-in that's screening Gordon's *The Amazing Colossal Man*), her fiancé unexpectedly vanishes. After Hoyt has shown her Agar in one of the canisters, Kenney reports his disappearance to the Missing Persons Bureau ("He made Bob into a doll," she tells incredulous cop Jack Kosslyn). She then discovers Hoyt's dark secret. Blacking out in his workshop, she wakes to find herself shrunk like the others; the puppeteer's ray machine has turned her into a doll, to perform at Hoyt's leisure. What follows is an attempt by the little people to change themselves back to normal height and expose Hoyt to the authorities.

Aided by Albert Glasser's brash score, Gordon handles the miniaturized optical effects with a degree of aptitude, placing his cast in oversized sets and utilizing his much-favored split-screen technique to create illusory composite shots. The one scene guaranteed to set the teeth on edge is when Hoyt commands one of the six-inch people to sing "My Living Doll" to her companions, but this being an AIP '50s movie aimed at a young audience, what can you expect? Taken to a theater by their captor and asked to perform on a miniature stage, the cast disobeys and revolts ("Look at this monster [referring to a marionette in a hideous mask]. But not half the monster you are," one of them shouts at Hoyt). Agar and Kenney escape back to the laboratory, running past back-projected streets and chased by a rat. They return to normal size and walk away from the forlorn Hoyt who wails, "Don't leave me. I'll be alone."

The reason for Hoyt's disturbed frame of mind is never looked into but, in this context, it doesn't really matter. Gordon eschews the psychological for the visual, creating a 79-minute fantasy that never sags and always captivates, its tongue set firmly in its cheek. Whereas some of the director's other features lacked wit and charm, *Attack of the Puppet People* has both in equal measures. And John Agar was always worth the price of a ticket, whatever he appeared in.

"Inferior *Dr. Cyclops* retread."

Awakened by H-bomb Blast, Prehistoric Beast Heads for Home

As Ray Harryhausen's Rhedosaurus lies dying amid the burning ruins of Coney Island's roller coaster, spare a thought for the technicians who labored long and hard to bring Ray Bradbury's short story *The Fog Horn* to the big screen, establishing the basic formula for the atomic bomb-activated monsters which followed. Sticking closely to the "let's slag off (or bad mouth) the '50s" syndrome, many critics have never had a kind word to say about Warner Bros.' *The Beast from 20,000 Fathoms* (1953). "An interminable wait for the beast's appearance" and "Risible monster hokum" are just two of several unjust judgments passed on what is, after all, a key genre movie, and a classy one at that.

Fair enough, leading man Paul Christian and token love interest Paula Raymond don't exactly set the screen alight. Horror stalwart Kenneth Tobey has a secondary role as (once again!) a military officer; it would have been better all 'round if he had been given the lead. Tobey was an underrated actor not really given a great deal to do in the 1950s; his five-star performance in *The Thing from Another World* bore out the fact that he could carry a picture, and *Beast* would have greatly benefited from his brusque screen persona. It was left to veteran Cecil Kellaway to steal the acting honors as a crusty paleontologist, gobbled up in a bathysphere after 50 minutes. Despite those comments from the critics, *The Beast from 20,000 Fathoms* is Harryhausen's show; along with *20 Million Miles to Earth* and *The 7th Voyage of Sinbad*, it illustrates his best '50s work.

No, we don't have to wait an "interminable" length of time for the monster to appear, as that critic wrote. Nine minutes into the film the beast shows up in the Arctic with a bang, roaring its head off on an ice ridge and nearly burying scientist Christian in an avalanche. This scene is closely followed by the attack on the fishing boat and, shortly after that, the demolition of the lighthouse. In between, Christian has a hard time convincing the skeptics that the 100 million-year-old Rhedosaurus is alive and well and heading toward its ancestral home in the Hudson River Basin. After Kellaway is killed, the monster emerges in New York and goes on a rampage, meeting its end in the Coney Island Amusement Park.

Eugene Lourie's direction is workman-like, content to let the effects speak for themselves, and for 1953, these are astounding; you can see every bump, scale and ridge on that reptilian skin, each blink of the eye, as Harryhausen's stop-motion creation stalks the panic-stricken streets in bewilderment, crunching cars underfoot and in its jaws, plowing through buildings and swallowing a policeman (a scene cut from the *Beast*'s British TV premier). The creature also spreads a plague on the populace, caused by its diseased skin tissue. David Buttolph's bulldozing score matches the documentary-style monster action perfectly to add impact, and the fiery climax evokes sympathy for the beast in its death-throes—after all, it was only returning home after a deep sleep and never expected this kind of a welcome!

The movie was an unexpected success for Warner Bros. but was rarely screened in England, popping up in London in 1967 on a double "X" bill with *Rebel Without a Cause*. Harryhausen's string of colorful Arabian Nights and Greek Mythology features in the '60s and '70s have had the adverse effect of pushing this groundbreaker into the background. It should be recognized as the master's first-ever solo effort and the film that started the "monster-on-the-loose" ball rolling, the motivating force behind Toho's *Godzilla* and countless others. *The Beast from 20,000 Fathoms* is an enduring testimony to one man's singular talent in a unique branch of special effects. Bearing in mind that some initial prints were tinted in sepia and green, a colorized version is long overdue.

"Interminable wait for the Beast's appearance ... inferior trick work."

Giant Mexican Arachnid on the Loose

Three tremendous sequences highlight Edward Ludwig's *The Black Scorpion* (1957): Richard Denning and Carlos Rivas' descent into a vast volcanic cavern, the scorpions' lair, lasting 13 minutes; the scorpions' all-out attack on a passenger train (four

minutes); and the explosive climax in Mexico City's bullring when the biggest scorpion of them all takes on the military (five minutes). Willis O'Brien and Pete Peterson cooperated on the imaginative stop-motion effects and the rough-around-the-edges, almost primeval, look that distinguished this production over many others. O'Brien's smoking volcano could have been taken from any one of his *Lost World*–type ideas that he often sketched out in the 1940s, and the same could be said of the crevasse Denning lowers himself into; Gustave Doré's fantasy backdrops spring to mind in this rather extraordinary (for a '50s monster movie) and very atmospheric segment.

    A Mexican volcano erupts, unleashing a group of gigantic scorpions onto the populace. Geologist Denning has just enough time to start romancing dark-haired ranch owner Mara Corday before he's called upon to descend into a deep chasm in the crater's side with Rivas, where not only the scorpions lurk but also a 30-foot worm with claws and a huge crab-like spider. Dynamiting the cavern's entrance isn't successful—the monsters find an alternative exit, launch an attack on a train and human victims are gobbled up by scorpion Number One. The colossal arachnid heads toward Mexico City, meeting his end in one of monsterdom's most exciting finales, Denning firing a 600,000-volt electrified dart into the monster's throat after the creature has smashed up tanks and helicopters in the city stadium. In the closing seconds, Carlos Muzquiz turns to the departing Denning and Corday: "Hank. Senorita Alvarez. We have not yet finished." "Neither have we," grins Denning, obviously thinking about more pressing matters, now that the monster has been defeated!

    A carefully gauged buildup was the name of the game in '50s monster flicks (wrecked buildings, trashed vehicles, farms flattened, cattle eaten, a cop's body, weird sounds), to raise audience expectation to a fever pitch; just what was causing all this havoc? The question is answered in the 33rd minute, a close-up of a scorpion's drooling face looming into view, signaling the start to the arachnids' assault on men repairing telephone lines. Paul Sawtell and Bert Shefter were one of the decade's finest composing collaborations for B-horror movies, the pulsating score (their first joint effort) underlines the action where necessary. Along with the cavern interlude (which includes the obligatory pesky kid getting under everyone's feet), the derailment of the train is a nightmarish slice of expertly crafted monster mayhem, as the massive scorpions pick off the fleeing passengers with their pincers. Very dark passages such as this forced the British censor to award mandatory "X" certificates. This kind of bleak fare was certainly *not* kiddy-friendly, and the alarming aura given off in many of *The Black Scorpion*'s scenes was adjudged to be fitting for adults only. B-movie regular Denning always turned in a believable performance, which he did here; Corday appeared slightly uncomfortable in trousers, boots and shirt (as opposed to her all-white sexy image in *Tarantula*) and the authentic Mexican locations, with that omnipresent volcano, lent the movie an air of somber horror fantasy. *The Black Scorpion* is noisy, gritty, hard-hitting monster fodder of a kind that vanished from cinema screens a lifetime ago. Long may it be remembered for the pleasure it gave thousands of underage punters as it went the rounds year after year in English cinemas and as a testament to the skills of *King Kong* creator Willis O'Brien. This movie is monster entertainment *par excellence*.

"Poor monster movie … inept effects…"

Teenage Vampire on Campus

I Was a Teenage Frankenstein c/w *Blood of Dracula* was a big draw on the American drive-in circuit during the late 1950s. In Britain, promoter Samuel Z. Arkoff's X-rated teen-horror double-bill was also a popular crowd-pleaser on the Sunday circuit (no drive-ins in the United Kingdom—the unpredictable weather was against this outdoor method of viewing), playing as *Teenage Frankenstein* c/w *Blood is My Heritage.* Herbert L. Strock directed both movies for American International in 1957, but the vampire feature is the better of the two; *Teenage Frankenstein* is flatly directed, although enlivened by some graphic (for its time) laboratory sequences and an energetic performance from Whit Bissell as a descendent of Baron Frankenstein. Strock shot *Blood is My Heritage* in moody black-and-white, at a galloping pace, and of the proliferation of teen horror movies to have emerged from America during that period, this probably remains the worthiest of the lot.

Rebellious teenager Sandra Harrison, upset at her father's forthcoming second marriage, is offloaded onto Sherwood School where her fiery temper attracts the attention of science teacher Louise Lewis. Lewis has a theory that "there is a power strong

enough to destroy the world buried in each of us," a "natural weapon," and sets out to prove it by hypnotizing Harrison with an ancient Carpathian amulet. Regressing the girl into a vampire state, Harrison turns into a bloodsucker if anyone gets on her nerves and she slaughters three students before a final showdown with her demented teacher; during a struggle, Lewis is strangled and Harrison the vampire falls backward onto a broken table leg, expiring and changing back into her human form. "There is a power greater than science that rules the Earth and those who twist and pervert knowledge for evil only work at their own destruction," intones the head teacher as she stares down at Harrison's body, a warning to those who wish to tamper with age-old forces.

Twenty-seven minutes into this spiffing little vampire thriller, we are entertained (to use the word loosely) by partying-on bobby-soxers jiving to the strains of Jerry Blaine's "Puppy Love." A lot of teen horror movies felt the need to include a sub-rock 'n' roll sequence to cater to the younger audience (*Frankenstein's Daughter* and *I Was a Teenage Werewolf* had similar interludes). This was okay if you were in your late teens, but if older, they grated and held up the action, even if the music only lasted a few minutes. Elsewhere, Paul Dunlap provided an eerie score and Harrison's shivery vampire transformation scenes, incorporating time-lapse photography, batwing eyebrows, Lugosi peak, ragged fangs and dissolves, earned the movie, in the United Kingdom, that "Adults Only" certificate. In many ways, *Blood is My Heritage* is the female counterpart to *I Was a Teenage Werewolf*, female teen angst replacing male teen angst, a much-frequented theme in these low-budget pictures. The troubled Michael Landon appears in the teen werewolf flick, as its counterpart finds Harrison as the misunderstood student in the vampire movie, and in this respect, the young actress turns in a sensitive performance of unbridled intensity against budgetary odds. Science versus supernatural folklore—it was a much-favored motif in '50s horror cinema, but put over with a certain degree of panache in Strock's noteworthy cut-price horror show.

"Minor teen horror thrills."

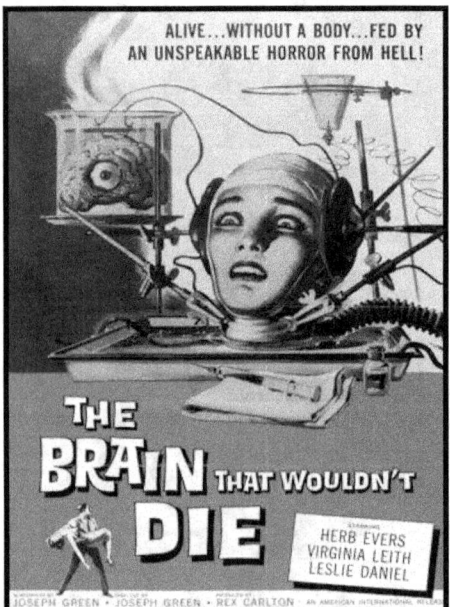

Wanted: New Body for My Fiancée's Decapitated Head

No, gore-freaks, the splatter genre *didn't* start at the end of the 1960s/early 1970s. It commenced right here, in 1959, with Sterling and Carlton's *The Brain That Wouldn't Die*, an overheated frightfest based on *Donovan's Brain* (1953), knocked out in 13 days at a cost of $62,000, banned for a few years and issued by American International in 1962. Director Joseph Green had a hand with the script, a veritable mishmash of horror clichés that was totally in tune with the movie's blood-drenched exploitative content. *The Brain That Wouldn't Die* may indeed be 82 minutes of appalling garbage (as one critic wrote), but this is one mad doctor, pseudo-*Frankenstein* howler that has "brainless cult classic" etched into every single sprocket hole. Shall we find out why?

The film opens with father and son surgeons (Bruce Brighton and Herb Evers) operating on a dying man. He expires (there's a view of an exposed brain), but Evers brings him back to life. "The human body isn't a jigsaw puzzle to experiment on," warns Brighton before disappearing from the scenario. In the basement of the family mansion, Evers, an expert in limb transplants, has created a monster from amputated body parts, locked up in a closet and tended by Leslie Daniels whose left hand is a withered, disfigured stump. Out for a drive and putting his foot on the pedal, Evers hits a crash barrier, his fiancée Virginia Leith is decapitated in the accident. Wrapping her head in a coat, Evers takes it back to the lab and rigs it up to laboratory apparatus. Result? A bandaged head nestling in a tray of blood that thoroughly objects to being there. "She's back. She'll live and I'll get her another body!" cries Evers, while Daniels stares at the head and mutters, "An experiment of horror!"

Virginia Leith, decapitated, is kept alive in a tray of blood in *The Brain That Wouldn't Die.*

The head has only 50 hours to survive, so Evers combs strip clubs looking for an acceptable body. Glamour model Adele Lamont, posing for five ogling photographers, fits the bill, so Evers persuades her to visit the mansion on the pretext that he'll remove that unsightly scar from her left cheek and make her more attractive to men, even though, deep down, she hates them. Back at the lab, Leith's head is communicating with the "something" in the cupboard by telepathy, complaining like mad. "We've got to stop him. He has no right to bring me back to this," she storms, adding to her gurgling, grunting companion behind the door, "I've got to see your hideousness. You've got to see mine. A head without a body. Can your horror match mine?" Goading the yet-to-be-seen creation into action ("Kill him!"), the thing rips off Daniels' right arm just as Evers turns up with Lamont. Giving the girl a drugged drink, he covers Daniels' bloody corpse and prepares to sever the model's head, stating to Leith, "I told you I'd bring you a body. A beautiful one. I want you as a complete woman, not part of one." But Leith isn't happy with the arrangement and gets her revenge—commanding the thing in the closet to prevent Evers from operating on Lamont, it grabs the doctor through the hatch and bursts out, a lumbering pinhead mutant who takes a chunk out of its creator's neck, killing him. The lab goes up in flames, Evers' version of the Frankenstein Monster strides off with Lamont in its arms and Leith's head laughs hysterically as the flames consume her.

Cut to 70 minutes on initial release but later restored to its full 82 minutes, *The Brain That Wouldn't Die* is pretty cheap-looking, no doubt about it, the all-over-the-place score looted from a dozen other movies. But it's a fun-packed experience, like a trashy stage play, piling on the gore and what passed for '50s titillation with gay abandon. In making

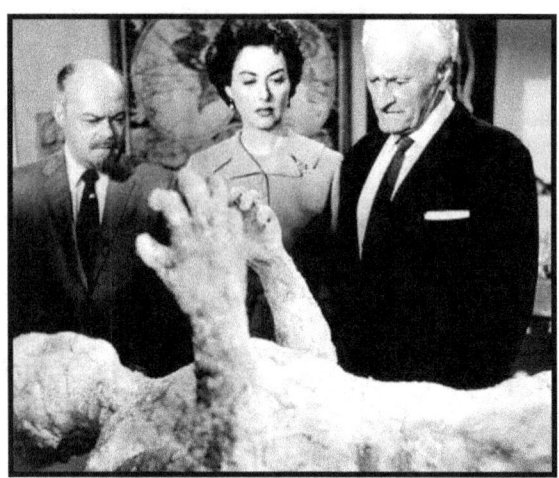

Luis Van Rooten, Elaine Edwards and Felix Locher confront the calcified 2,000-year-old gladiator, in *Curse of the Faceless Man*.

it, the producers appeared to have thumbed their nose at big-budget horror and said, "Here it is. Take it or leave it." Fans of the "so bad it's good" should take it to their hearts; this is hammy surgical hokum made with appetite, right up there alongside Richard Cunha's *Frankenstein's Daughter* in the topmost schlock-horror stakes.

"Atrocious ... derivative ... rock-bottom."

Stone-Encased Slave Searches for Lost Love

United Artists' *Curse of the Faceless Man* (1958) was originally released as a co-feature with *It! The Terror from Beyond Space*, both movies directed by the prolific Edward L. Cahn. Less remarkable than *It!* (Cahn and producer Robert E. Kent's finest hour), this 66-minute tale of 2,000-year-old gladiator slave Quintillus Aurelius, dug out of the ashes of Pompeii, only to revive and pursue his centuries-old love, comes across as a hybrid mix of *The Mummy* and *The Golem*. It's to Cahn's credit that he surmounts certain disadvantages to emerge with an eerie little chiller that in some scenes tingles the spine: Lead player Richard Anderson (scientific curator at the Naples Museum) is as stone-faced as the calcified Bob Bryant, wearing a perplexed expression throughout. Elaine Edwards (Anderson's girlfriend) and Adele Mara (Anderson's ex) do little else but scream their heads off as Bryant, bit-by-bit, comes to life. Gerald Fried's busy score is a little too overpowering at times and spoils the mood.

A medallion's inscription tells of a curse placed on a senator's family by Aurelius when he was forbidden to marry the family's daughter. Edwards just happens to be the spitting image of the daughter and, hypnotized, she regresses back 2,000 years to a past existence, reliving the flesh and blood drama in which the slave was caught. Heavy-footed Bryant staggers off his plinth and lumbers after the terrified woman, eventually carrying her off to the Cove of the Blind Fisherman, re-enacting the eruption of Vesuvius and the destruction of Pompeii. As he wades into the sea, the man of stone dissolves into dust and Anderson rescues Edwards, although this still isn't enough to bring a smile to his face.

Amid the constant hollering, Fried's discordant music and the implausible sight of Edwards, quick on her feet, unable to escape the clutches of slow-moving Bryant, Cahn manages to conjure up a few sinister sequences: A truck driver unaware of a pair of clutching hands reaches through the rear cab window, encircling his neck; Edwards sketches the stone figure, gradually becoming aware that it is moving, inch by inch; and Anderson, Mara and Luis Van Rooten enter the gallery, only to be confronted by the lurching Bryant. Cahn's extensive repertoire of B movies was characterized by purposeful direction that spurned unproductive fluff; they didn't hang about, and *Curse of the Faceless Man* is no exception. Dim performances from the leads notwithstanding, it's a nifty, low-budget shocker, a perfect reminder of how to make a bog-standard '50s second feature on limited resources and come up trumps.

"Tedious rehash of *The Mummy* and *The Golem*."

Valley of the One-Eyed Giant

BIG his initials may well have been—but big his films most certainly were not! Writer/producer/director Bert I. Gordon was the undisputed master of the rear-screened monster/giant bug movie during the 1950s, his cheapskate method of filmmaking the high (or low) point of such B-classics as *Beginning of the End*, *King Dinosaur* and *Earth vs. the Spider*. His productions were populated by B-list actors and greatly enriched by the talents of composer Albert Glasser. Gordon was a competent-enough director and even his scripts were pretty snappy. What let the proceedings down were the man's legendary and at times totally inept effects, incorporating split screen, back-projection, assorted props, toy models and superimposed figures: The supersized locusts crawling over photographs of buildings in *Beginning of the End*, the giant hypodermic syringe in *The Amazing Colossal Man*, the dinky toy trucks in *War of the Colossal Beast* and the fact that in many of the process shots we could see straight through from one image to the next. Did the man *ever* make a decent picture? Well, *Attack of the Puppet People*, as we have seen, was quite imaginative (shrinking

his cast to six inches tall instead of blowing them up into giants), but perhaps the most all-rounded Gordon effort is 1957's *The Cyclops*, his only '50s picture given an "X" classification in Britain—the remainder of his output were A-rated. *The Cyclops* has pace, believable acting, a loud Albert Glasser score and, by Gordon's own standards, if not by anyone else's, more or less adequate effects.

In Mexico, Gloria Talbott hires three disparate men to fly her to the Tarahumaro Mountains and help in locating her air pilot fiancé, who disappeared in the area three years ago. Once there, uranium prospector Lon Chaney discovers what he believes to be untold quantities of the ore and promptly demands they turn back so he can file his claim, missing airman or no missing airman. In fact, Chaney turns out to be a real crybaby, constantly moaning that he alone wants to leave but no one else does ("When are we gonna get out of here," he whines, over and over again). Nice-but-wooden James Craig is in love with tomboy Talbott and pilot/biologist Tom Drake seems to be on the trip simply to make up the numbers. After the director's parade of back-projected, magnified creatures is over and done with (a hawk, a rodent, two lizards and a spider),

Craig deduces that radiation in the valley is causing cells to mutate and multiply, leading to gigantism in animals. Forty-five minutes into the action, the team find parts of the wrecked aircraft in a cave and 25-foot-tall Dean Parkin makes his appearance as the missing pilot, one bulbous eye staring out of a shattered face, communicating in grunts and growls (Parkin's make-up is almost identical to the role he played in *War of the Colossal Beast*). Talbott doesn't at first twig that the giant is her fiancé; after the ever-complaining Chaney is killed and the giant wrestles with a massive python, Craig thrusts a flaming spear into Parkin's eye and the surviving three escape in their plane. It's only then that it finally dawns on Talbott that her boyfriend was the demented, disfigured giant, last seen lying comatose on the valley floor.

The Cyclops gets many a fan's seal of approval as Gordon's most hard-edged '50s horror show (hence that "X" rating), the trick photography marginally more accomplished, although in two clumsily worked instances we can see right through Parkin's superimposed figure. Chaney's grumpy, heavyweight presence adds necessary gravitas, Gordon's script is lucid, Glasser's music blasts away gleefully in the background and the film doesn't wear thin throughout its 75-minute running time. The most popular Bert I. Gordon effort to run in England during the early 1960s, *The Cyclops* is probably one of the best he ever produced, and although embracing many of his questionable trademarks, it displays a tad more adult imagination than others on his roster.

"Lacks credibility … paucity of special effects."

"Let's Send a Rocket to the Moon!"

Eagle Lion's *Destination Moon* is a landmark film: astronomical paintings by Chesley Bonestell; script by sci-fi author Robert A. Heinlein (from his novel *Rocketship Galileo*), Rip Van Ronkel and James O'Hanlon; production by whiz-kid George Pal; Leith Stevens' somber score; and winner of the 1950 Oscar for Best Special Effects. This movie, the 1950s first major sci-fi outing, visualized in methodical detail a manned flight to the moon, adding a mandatory anti-communist warning by way of a "we've got to get there before they do" message in its narrative. All things considered, Pal's seminal groundbreaker, shot in bright Technicolor, should by rights be up there with the '50s greats, but in some circles, it's not. Why is that?

Well, the factual, semi-documentary approach works against it; in a 91-minute movie, it's nearly an hour before John Archer and colleagues board the rocket and that opening hour includes the infamous Woody Woodpecker segment whereby the anarchic cartoon character presents to a crowd of potential backers the concepts behind rocketry in animated form. Leads Warner Anderson, Archer and Tom Powers involve themselves (but not, directly, the audience) in the intricacies and pitfalls of space travel while goofy Dick Wesson's semi-comic turn is, in fact, a turnoff. All four blast off in a hurry when the military arrives to prevent the trip from taking place; the government is scared stiff of radiation leakage from the rocket's engines, another dose of atomic neurosis thrown in by Pal, Heinlein and director Irving Pichel. We are treated to an uncannily accurate space walk, the problems of weightlessness and space sickness and views of the Earth and moon from space, before the rocket lands on Bonestell's garishly realized lunar surface. But instead of taking advantage of the forbidding surroundings in which the crew finds itself, *Destination Moon* then begins to flag; Wesson acts the clown, uttering one stupid line after another in a thick Brooklyn accent, while Archer scratches his head,

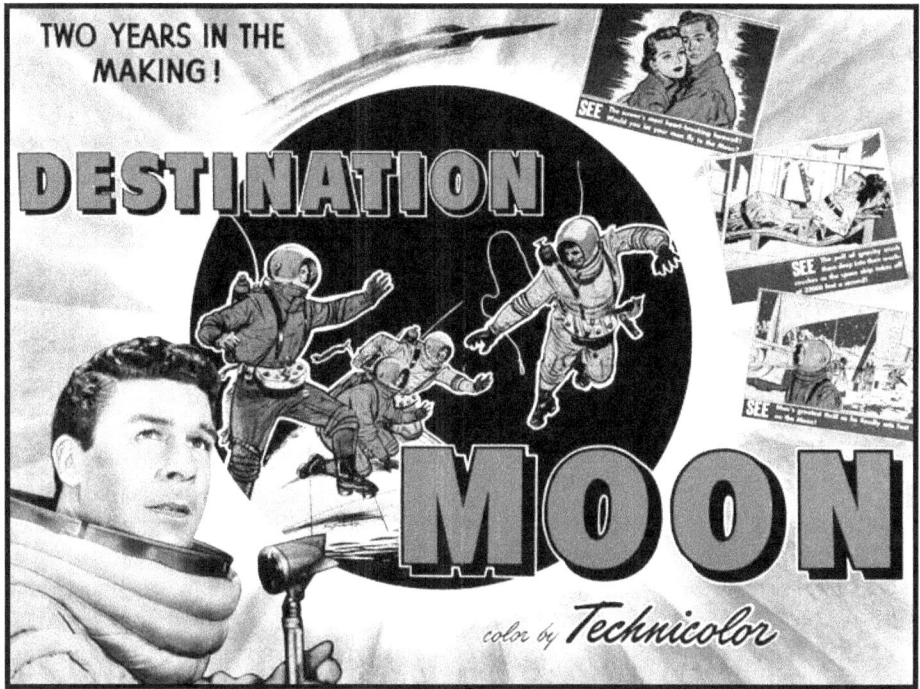

trying to figure out a way to get back to "Oith" (as Wesson calls it) on a less-than-full tank of fuel. Jettisoning non-essential items overboard is the answer—Wesson decides to stay behind by electing to become the sacrificial lamb, but they relieve him of his spacesuit (inside the rocket) and, strapped to his bunk, he heads back with the others.

Destination Moon has aged badly and in many ways is less fun to watch than Kurt Neumann's similar *Rocketship X-M* (see chapter eight), which was cheekily rush-released into theaters one month ahead of Pal's opus. The relentless quest for realism sought by Pal and his team, allied with a steadfast resolve to avoid the space operatic shenanigans represented in the old *Flash Gordon* and *Buck Rogers* serials, pushed the screenplay's inherent dramatic possibilities into the background. Compared to, say, *The Day the Earth Stood Still* and *The Thing from Another World*, two other early '50s classics, *Destination Moon* seems old hat and pedestrian to today's viewers. But make no mistake about it, this picture, flaws and all, is a very important step in the evolution of the serious, special effects-laden science-fiction motion picture that reached its peak with Stanley Kubrick's 1968 masterpiece, *2001: A Space Odyssey*. Kubrick and countless other fantasy filmmakers owe an enormous debt of gratitude to the pioneering skills of all those technicians who worked so hard to bring *Destination Moon* to the big screen over 60 years ago. Remember that, all ye who scoff.

"Juvenile space opera."

I Put a Spell on You!

Ex-model Allison Hayes romps through *The Disembodied* like a vamp in heat, attired in a number of revealing (for 1957) outfits, dagger tucked in belt, exuding the kind of sultry passion that would drive many men insane with desire. So there you have it—Hayes, most critics state, is the one and only reason to watch yet another 1950s

Allison Hayes casts an evil spell in *The Disembodied*.

voodoo melodrama where natives knock out continuous thumping beats on their drums in a mock African jungle setting. And we know Hayes is an evil piece of work even as the credits are rolling: She's seen pulling a cord tight around a doll's neck, as her husband, Doctor John Wengraf, almost chokes to death outside in his Jeep. But *is* she the only reason? Compared to Karloff's *Voodoo Island* and Edward L. Cahn's *Voodoo Woman*, *The Disembodied* ain't all that bad, even though the risible situations stretch one's incredulity at times: After all, Hayes, a self-styled voodoo queen named Tonda, blessed with supernatural powers, could have finished off Wengraf, the man she so detests, by reel one. Instead, she casts spells left, right and center to achieve her aim over a period of 66 minutes, only to fail and end up stabbed in the neck by Eugenia Paul.

What led up to the fatal stabbing? Craven hussy Hayes is seen by Paul smooching with her husband, Dean Fredericks, who is later found dead with his heart missing from the body ("His heart's cut out." "No lion could do that." "No. Only a human being."). When three white men arrive at Wengraf's house, one (Robert Christopher) mauled by a lion, Hayes cures the wounds by witchcraft but turns him into a zombie-slave who eventually wanders off and is cared for by Paul. The scheming Hayes then turns her attentions to Paul Burke, trying to cajole him into murdering her husband by offering herself on a silver platter, but Burke, doing his best to avoid Hayes' flashing eyes, ample cleavage and shorter-than-short skirt, refuses to have a hand in her devious plotting. Fuming at his rejection of her charms, Hayes stabs Wengraf in the stomach; it doesn't finish him off, so she attempts to smother her unfortunate spouse with a cushion. Finally, still burning with rage at Burke spurning her advances, she sets him up as a voodoo sacrifice, to cast a spell of death on her husband. Christopher lumbers dazedly on set, knife in hand; he's about to knife his buddy in the heart when in steps Paul. After Hayes is stabbed in the neck and dies, the various spells woven by the voodoo queen are broken. Christopher reverts to normal and Wengraf recovers.

The plot of *The Disembodied* is fairly involved for a B effort, undermined somewhat by Walter Grauman's pedestrian handling of his material, an ear-splitting Marlin Skiles score and dull performances from the leads, except, of course, Hayes; this is her show and she carries it off with style. Fondly remembered for *Attack of the 50 Foot Woman*, the actress tragically died at age 47 but left her everlasting legacy with these prototypical X-rated Allied Artists' movies. *The Disembodied* and *Attack of the 50 Foot Woman* may not indeed be high art, but they *have* ensured that Hayes' name, like so many others from this classic period of fantasy filmmaking, lives on in the eyes of the fans.

"More yawns than thrills."

Chapter 6
Godzilla and Rodan:
Japan vs. America

Godzilla and *Rodan*—twin Japanese colossi of '50s monster cinema—ushered in the start of the Kaiju Eiga (Monster Movie) cycle. Released in 1954 under the non-Japanese title of *Godzilla, King of the Monsters*, the first of Toho's rubber-suited creations to wade through miniature model cities took the horror world by storm, the titular protagonist propelling itself into iconic fantasy history. The follow-up, 1955's *Godzilla Raids Again* (more commonly known as *Gigantis the Fire Monster*) was a relative failure, forcing the company to rethink its strategy, which they managed in spectacular style. The following year, Toho's first monster movie in color, *Rodan*, proved to be as successful as *Godzilla*, maybe even *more* popular from a financial point of view, becoming unquestionably a big hit with genre buffs. In England, *Godzilla* had a sporadic release history, appearing infrequently at selected theaters and conventions. On the other hand, *Rodan* was never *off* the circuits, playing continuously from 1956 to 1968, an old favorite you could rely on to indulge yourself in 70-odd minutes of brash, lively monster action (and, if you were lucky, you would get *The Deadly Mantis* or *Tarantula* as second-helpings!). Comparing the films today, it doesn't take a genius to figure out *Rodan*'s popularity factor over *Godzilla*. It's faster-paced, has two completely different types of monsters, is presented in vibrant color and contains more incidents, with a little less in the way of issues in the script department—exciting, no-frills monster frolics. A fondly remembered audience-grabber from those halcyon days of the late '50s/early '60s, *Rodan* would, without a single doubt, be an essential choice on any fan's personal top-20 list.

In recent years, the original Japanese versions of both movies have surfaced on DVD, side-by-side with their Americanized counterparts, giving fans the opportunity to experience both pictures as they were originally intended to be screened in their native country, uncut and subtitled. But which versions are better—the Japanese originals or the edited, dubbed Americanized releases?

Japanese horror flicks suffered appallingly at the hands of foreign distributors in the 1950s, and quite often what we saw bore little or no resemblance to what the Japanese themselves had sat through. Apart from the atrocious dubbing, pivotal scenes were either cut or altered, sequences were shown out of context, continuity went all to pot as a result and American actors were brought in to promote box-office appeal to a non-Japanese audience; fresh scenes were added to the original film, and what you ended up with was a confusing clash of ideas that quite often didn't gel. *Half Human* (1955), Japan's entry into the Abominable Snowman celluloid market, was a victim of such tampering, the ubiquitous John Carradine roped in to play a scientist, which had the effect of making punters think they were watching two separate movies, such was the shoddy state of his poorly conceived intervals. But, in a way, they were! Worst hit was *Varan the Unbelievable* (1958). Myron Healy was the token American in this, one of Toho's most underrated monster pictures, a tale of a gigantic reptile emerging from a saltwater lake and stomping all over Oneida City. *Varan* was altered so drastically from one country to the next that several differing versions exist, none bearing much of a similarity to

Godzilla (1954) finds the monster surrounded by tanks and fire power, but the beast is not easily beaten.

the full-length Japanese original which, after many years of waiting, has now become available on DVD (chapter 15 deals with this film in depth).

Godzilla and *Rodan* were not immune to this studio interference, but was it to their detriment or advantage? Let's examine the facts in detail.

Godzilla (*Gojira*) in its true form has a running time of 97 minutes. A reverberant, clanging thump, followed by a deafening roar, is the curtain raiser, Akira Ifukube's insistent score drones menacingly behind the title credits. The opening few minutes show a freighter sunk by a mysterious glowing undersea explosion. Other boats meet an identical fate. Inoshiro Honda directs in a semi-documentary fashion to impart a sense of urgency and alarm. Godzilla, 400-foot-high, appears 22 minutes into the storyline, his scaly head looming over the brow of a hill on Odo Island where he has become a much-feared local legend. The monster has absorbed radiation from atomic bomb tests and thirsts for revenge. A counter-Godzilla headquarters is set up, 17 more ships are lost and, after 44 minutes, we get the first of Godzilla's two attacks on Tokyo City, lasting three minutes. A state of emergency is declared, a barricade of electrified pylons hurriedly erected around the city and, seven minutes after the first attack, our senses are assaulted by another blitz which stretches to a whopping 14 minutes. Godzilla's prolonged second nocturnal rampage through Tokyo must surely count as one of the greatest, if not *the* greatest, slices of monster mayhem ever presented on the big screen, almost too authentic for comfort. Like a sequence from a silent movie (apart from the sound effects, there is a lack of incidental music), this towering giant lumbers slowly through the streets and buildings like a reptilian nuclear holocaust, causing mass panic, smashing pylons, breathing fire, incinerating people, toppling towers, crushing the fleeing crowds underfoot, trampling on trains, upending bridges, blowing up gas tanks, coming under attack from the military and reducing the city to flames and ashes. The parallel with the horrors sustained at Hiroshima is only too evident in this powerfully riveting segment (effects: Eiji Tsuburaya; cinematography: Masao Tamai). Godzilla becomes a product of the atomic bomb, the misery he causes mirroring the pain and anguish of the populace during the final days of World War II—Armageddon revisited. The Oxygen Destroyer, a device that strips his flesh to the bone, eventually vanquished the monster. This funereal climax is exquisitely underscored by Ifukube's doom-laden music, as though a great and powerful god has been conquered. The picture ends with a dire warning of future nuclear tests reawakening another Godzilla.

The cut-down Americanized *Godzilla* comes in at a miserly 81 minutes, of which only 60 minutes has been lifted from the original; granted, this length was the '50s norm for monster fodder, but Toho's monochrome *piece de résistance* is no ordinary monster flick. The fervent antiwar message is ruthlessly ditched in favor of straightforward monster pandemonium (U.S. conscience over the dropping of the H-bomb?) and in comes Raymond Burr as a foreign correspondent who gets caught up in the events following the monster's first sighting on Odo Island. Sequences from the original cut were juggled around and inserted out-of-synch (the opening shot shows Tokyo in smoking ruins, a scene that, in the original, occurred *after* Godzilla's second attack). Other deviations: Dubbing replacing subtitles; new footage spliced in; key scenes discarded; body-doubles of Japanese cast members (viewed from the rear, speaking to Burr); Ifukube's ominous soundtrack conspicuous by its absence; and Godzilla's mighty 14-minute destruction of Tokyo (appearing 48 minutes in) reduced to 10 minutes, ruining the mood of dread set by this awesome interlude by inserting a pointless 20 shots of Burr standing at a window, reporting on the carnage; a couple would have been sufficient ("The prehistoric monster the Japanese call Godzilla has just walked out of Tokyo Bay. He's as tall as a 30-story building."). The ending is muted, no mention made of the bomb or the possibility of another Godzilla. At times, Burr (who mostly played heavies in the 1950s) seems to be a party pooper in the picture, as though he was never meant to be there in the first place, which, of course, he wasn't! This was the *Godzilla* made for the international market, the one we all paid to get in and see, as the original was very rarely shown outside of Japan.

The main characters in *Godzilla* are composed of the trio Akira Takarada, Akihiko Hirata and Momoko Kochi. The two males are both in love with Kochi; Takarada is her boyfriend, but she nurses an affection bordering on hero-worship for the eye-patched, troubled Hirata, inventor of the Oxygen Destroyer. When Hirata kills Godzilla, he cuts the breathing pipe to his diving suit and dies, sacrificing himself in order to preserve the couple's fragile relationship and to take the secrets of his invention to the grave. Subtly hinted at in the original, Burr blithely narrates that Kochi is in love with Takarada but was engaged to be married to Hirata and still has feelings for him, and leaves it at that. Kochi's father sympathizes with Godzilla and wants to save the behemoth for study, not to destroy it; this is also cast aside, as is the distress and heartbreak felt by various individuals in the aftermath of Godzilla's attacks, and other nuances present in the script. Another

An original Japanese poster for *Godzilla*

faux pas is this: How does Burr manage to leave Odo Island after it has been wrecked (including the helicopter) and then reappear as part of the Odo Island research team? And a common mistake in *both* films is that trilobites existed in the Jurassic Age and said Jurassic Age was two million years ago. Wrong on both counts!

So no contest here. Inoshiro Honda's first monster feature is a very dark allegorical anti-nuclear fantasy, standing head and shoulders not just above the clumsily edited American *Godzilla* but also Roland Emmerich's bloated 1998 CGI-created juvenile adaptation. A stark warning of what could be unleashed if man continues with atomic bomb testing, Toho's X-rated somber masterpiece should be viewed in all of its original glory.

Rodan, believe it or not, represents a different kettle of fish altogether. There is a strong case here for the Americanized release, the one that kept us glued to our seats many decades ago, being the superior and more complete of the two versions. The Japanese print is 82-minutes in length, compared to the Americanized 72 minutes. If we deduct the opening, tagged-on, three minutes of Pacific H-bomb testing footage (the reason for disturbing the monsters) in version number two, *not* included in the Japanese cut, the original, in reality, is 13-minutes longer than the better-known picture. (Rodan's appearance *is* attributed to nuclear bomb testing in the original, but only after 54 minutes). Moreover, several later sequences in *Rodan* number one are shorter than in *Rodan* number two, principally in the dynamic daylight attack on Sasebo (Fukuoka in number one) that is over a minute less, and the repeated confrontations with fighter planes. In effect, this means that *Rodan* number one has a great deal more padding than in the other version (mostly in the first 40 minutes), is slower in pace and differs in some significant areas:

1. In *R1* (let's call it that), at 55 minutes, one Rodan appears from the volcano and takes off, causing a Jeep to crash. In *R2*, at 49 minutes, *two* Rodans emerge; one zooms away, the second lingers and then shoots off, and it's this second monster that causes the vehicle to come off the road. In *R1*, we only get to hear about the second flying reptile at the end of the attack on Fukuoka.

2. In *R1*, there is far less footage of the monsters attacking jets than in *R2*; many of these aerial shots have been rearranged in *R2* to give maximum impact.

3. Conversely, *R1* shows a lot more of the giant bug Meganuron, plus repeated comings and goings in the flooded mine tunnels, than in *R2*.

4. *R1* doesn't contain a brief scene showing Americans on Wake Island; *R2* does (at 32 minutes).

5. The military barrage on Mount Aso begins at 74 minutes in *R1*; in *R2*, 62 minutes. (The climax in both versions is quite moving, the creatures perishing in the flames of the erupting volcano.)

6. In *R1*, Rodan's wingspan is 270 feet; in *R2*, 500 feet.

7. In *R1*, the monster flies over a young couple on the volcano; her dead body, skirt rucked up to the waist, is seen. This shot was cut for U.K. release by the censor's office.

8. Rodan is a species of Petranodon in *R1*; in *R2*, the monster is a Pterosaur.

9. In *R1*, the opening takes place in the "flooded west pit." In *R2*, it's "number eight mine."

But the major comparison must be in the overall execution, the dexterous manner in which *Rodan* was specifically tailored to suit a Western audience and pull in the crowds.

Inoshiro Honda directed *Rodan* at an almost leisurely pace, the early part lacking momentum, and Akira Ifukube's bombastic score is strangely subdued; in fact, many scenes contain no music whatsoever, lending the production a curious flatness. Even the monster's squawk over the opening credits isn't as ear shattering as in the American version. The upshot of all this means that the picture's most extraordinary sequence, one that left an indelible impression on my memory (I first caught *Rodan* as a 14 year old) is impaired by a few degrees. In *R2*, Kenji Sahara (37 minutes in) remembers stumbling into a vast cavern containing not only hordes of the carnivorous insects but a single, colossal egg. Ifukube's score rising to a crescendo, Sahara stares in mounting horror as the shell cracks open and baby Rodan makes its eye-boggling entrance, filling the cavern with a series of ear-splitting squawks. In *R1*, at 45 minutes, the scene is slightly shorter (bats are spotted; there's less of the monstrous chick) and, to the detriment of the atmosphere conjured up in this stupendous subterranean setting, the music and Rodan's roar is toned down. It leaves one with a sense of anticlimax, particularly after sitting through *R2* several times over in as many decades.

The colossal egg cracks to reveal the baby monster from *Rodan*.

The King Brothers successfully streamlined the picture ("X" certified in Britain) for global consumption (as they would with *Gorgo* in 1961). By a process of judicious but sympathetic editing, they gave *Rodan* the required punch it lacked in the original, thus delivering a quicker pace (the action moves like an express train), an all-round tightening up of the storyline and, just as important to Toho, big profits at the ticket office. Ifukube's soundtrack was expanded and amplified to underscore the full-blooded action and the picture shrewdly eliminated a lot of the early discussions and general chat, concentrating much more on the two Rodans in the second half than *R1*, which dwelt at some length on the Meganurons in the first half. Thankfully, the production team didn't feel the need for an American actor to hold up the action; a voice-over narration (delivered by Paul Frees and George *Star Trek* Takei) repeatedly emphasized the terror felt by the characters: "A feeling of uneasiness in the air." "A strange tension." "Afraid of the darkness." These unnerving words, together with the scenes inside the gloomy, flooded mine passages. make *R2* a far more dramatic monster outing than *R1* turned out to be. Yes, this is probably one of only two instances whereby the Americanization of a Japanese horror film has actually worked *in* its favor, instead of against it (the other being 1955's *Godzilla Raids Again*). The original Japanese cut of *Rodan* is, for long-standing addicts, a must-have edition to the collection, but for sheer no-holds-barred monster thrills, *Rodan* in its honed-down form is a '50s vintage treasure from sci-fi's golden age that has very few equals.

Chapter 7
Fifty Fabulous Lines of Dialogue from The Fifties

There is no escaping the fact that memorable lines of dialogue in modern-day horror, sci-fi, fantasy cinema are few and far between. Like the much-loved soundtrack, the scriptwriter's art seems to be on the wane, filmmakers putting all their efforts into CGI, pyrotechnical special effects and little else. This wasn't the case with the output of the 1950s. Producing incisive, intelligent pages of speech mattered, whether it was highbrow (*The Incredible Shrinking Man*) or lowbrow (*The Hideous Sun Demon*). This was the era of the spoken word. What's more, we heard every single quick-witted, expressive one-liner as clear as a bell, so much so that when we exited a cinema, those one-liners would stick in the memory for a long time afterward, to be quoted off pat among friends and fellow addicts. Lines were delivered with clear pronunciation, the diction fully audible; technicians managed to achieve the right sound balance between score and dialogue, where the former *didn't* drown the latter. Nobody ever walked out of a cinema in the 1950s and said, "I couldn't hear a word they were saying."

In addition, '50s fantasy features didn't contain only one or two sparkling snippets of conversation; they were chock-a-block with them! Take RKO's *The Thing from Another World*, for example. Charles Lederer's renowned script crackles with challenging comments, quick-witted exchanges and amusing rejoinders; it would be no trouble at all to write down a score of great lines from this one movie alone. The sequence where Kenneth Tobey and team troop down to the UFO buried in the ice brims with descriptive prose, drawing the viewer into what *they* are experiencing on the big screen (*Invasion of the Body Snatchers* is another classic in the script department); simply mouthing "Wow!" and "It's awesome" would be a very poor substitute indeed. The screenplay, and what the actors said, was of paramount importance in conveying the plot intricacies to an audience and fully involving them (as was the soundtrack which we broached earlier); on occasions, the obvious was stated and the results trite ("There's a monster coming!"), but mostly the dialogue summarized to perfection the essence of the picture we were watching. The following 50 lines spotlight the ingenuity of those scriptwriters in the 1950s who strived for some kind of refinement in their chosen field, from a grade A classic (*House of Wax*) to a grade Z no-hoper (*Phantom from Space*). "Oh my God," "It's awesome," "Go, Go, Go," "Cool," "That's not real, man," "It's so not true," "You've got to be kidding," "Fantastic," "Aaaarrgh!" and "Wow," today's regularly used figures of speech, are notable by their absence!

The Atomic Kid
Elaine Davis to Mickey Rooney: "I always pictured my perfect man as being tall, dark and handsome. And then you came along. Short, red-headed and radioactive."
Atomic Submarine
One-eyed alien to Arthur Franz: "So Commander Holloway, as you Earth inhabitants would express it, we meet face-to-face."
Franz: "That's a face?"

The Black Castle
Stephen McNally to friends: "Teresa won third prize today in shooting the biggest boar. Quite a feat for a woman, don't you think."
Paula Corday, witheringly eyeing her detested husband: "I don't know. I seemed to have got one without even firing a shot!"

The Bowery Boys Meet the Monsters
Leo Gorcey to Huntz Hall: "Well, I see you're back to your subnormal self again. Believe me, the udda way was an extinct improvement!"

Devil Girl from Mars: "I will select some of your strongest men to return with me to Mars."

Bride of the Monster
Victim in lab: "What are you doing to me?"
Bela Lugosi: "You will be soon as big as a giant. The strength of 20 men. Or, like all the others, dead!"

The Cyclops
Lon Chaney to Tom Drake: "You didn't get paid to be eaten by prehistoric animals, did ya?"
Drake: "That would be a novel death. Lee Brand—swallowed by dinosaur!"

Day the World Ended
Paul Birch, talking about the three-eyed mutant: "That thing was created to live in a poisoned world."
Lori Nelson: "Man created it and God destroyed it."

The Deadly Mantis
Alix Talton: "You mean this cute little bug?"
William Hopper: "Yeah, that cute little bug. In all the kingdom of the living, there is no more deadly or voracious creature than the praying mantis."

Devil Girl from Mars
Patricia Laffan: "Meanwhile, I will select some of your strongest men to return with me to Mars."
Hugh McDermott: "And if they don't want to go with you?"
Laffan: "There is no 'if'."

Earth vs. the Flying Saucers
Hugh Marlowe, on how to get rid of UFOs: "Of course! We cut the ultrasonic wavelength into the circuit and knock them down like clay pigeons."

Enchanting Shadow
Betty Loh Ti: "Mr. Ning. Maybe you've already found out the truth. To be honest, I'm not human. I'm a spirit."
Chao Lei: "In that case, we definitely have nothing in common to talk about."

House of Wax: "I'm going to give the public what they want—sensation, horror, shock."

The Fantastic Disappearing Man (Return of Dracula, U.S.)
Norma Eberhardt to vampire Francis Lederer: "Don't you want any dinner? Mother made a wonderful blueberry pie and the doctor's so anxious to meet you."
Lederer: "I have already dined."

Frankenstein 1970
Boris Karloff, delighted that the film crew staying in his castle will provide him with a fresh supply of body parts for his new creation: "Mr. Row, I'm becoming reconciled to your presence here. Your coming here may well be the solution to all my problems! (Laughs hysterically)."

Frankenstein's Daughter
Love-struck Donald Murphy to Sandra Knight: "Trudy, you know who I am. I'm not just Oliver Frank, I'm Oliver Frankenstein!"

The Gamma People
Paul Douglas, looking at Wolf Rilla's imposing castle: "Sinister looking dump, isn't it."

Gog
Constance Dowling: "In space, there's no such thing as the weaker sex!"

The H-Man
Gangster Makoto Sato to terrified hostage Yumi Shirakawa: "Don't scream. Come with me. Or would you rather be eaten by the H-Man?"

The Headless Ghost
American Richard Lyon, unable to fully appreciate the historical character permeating Jack Allen's English Gothic castle: "What's so impressive about a heap of old stones surrounded by a shallow ditch? Now take the modern skyscraper…"

The Hideous Sun Demon
Robert Clarke, annoyed that two doctors aren't taking his predicament (changing from man to sun demon) seriously enough: "It's all very well for you to joke about it. It's not very funny to me."

House of Wax
Vincent Price, detailing his plans to an interested partner: "With the help of my pupils, yes, I'm rebuilding my exhibition from the ground up. I'm going to give the public what they want—sensation, horror, shock. Send them out into the streets to tell their friends how wonderful it is to be scared to death."

House on Haunted Hill
Alan Marshall: "I'm interested in your reasons for this, er, party, besides some pleasant company."
Vincent Price: "Ghosts, Doctor. I think everyone wonders what they would do if they saw a ghost. And now my wife is giving us all the opportunity to find out."

I Married a Monster from Outer Space
Sam Dexter: "I'll say one thing for humans. They may not be very bright and their bodies fall apart in a ridiculously short time, but they do manage to enjoy themselves."
Tom Tryon: "You celebrating 'Be Kind to Humans' week?"

The Incredible Shrinking Man
Grant Williams to Randy Stuart: "Didn't you tell them who you were married to? The incredible Scott Carey, the shrinking freak!"

Invasion of the Body Snatchers
Kevin McCarthy to Dana Wynter: "This is the oddest thing I ever heard of. Let's hope that we don't catch it. I'd hate to wake up some morning and find out that you weren't you."

It Came from Beneath the Sea
Faith Domergue fends off Kenneth Tobey, who is getting too up close and personal for her liking: "When you're driving that atomic submarine of yours, do you have much time for romance?"
Tobey: "Huh, well, even if I did and had the time, where would I find the opportunity? You know, women aren't allowed on board a submarine."
Domergue: "Poor boy. I thought the Navy was, er, equipped for every emergency."

Kronos
TV newsreader, showing a picture of the 100-foot-tall alien robot to the camera: "Here's an artist's conception, drawn after Dr. Gaskell's description. Pretty scary looking, isn't it? Perhaps a gift from another world to ours."

The Land Unknown
Jock Mahoney: "Few things I can be romantic about."
Shawn Smith: "Name one."
Mahoney: "Well, women."
Smith: "Oh?"
Mahoney: "For example, although I know basically women consist mostly of water and a few pinches of salt with metals thrown in, you have a very un-salt like, non-metallic effect on me."
Smith: "I knew it! Let's talk about diesel engines, shall we?"

Lost Continent
Hugh Beaumont, staring down at a giant footprint: "I've seen tracks like these before."
Cesar Romero: "Yeah? Where?"
Beaumont: "In a museum. They're Brontosaurus tracks."

The Mole People
John Agar to Hugh Beaumont, realizing that their flashlight ran out of energy: "It's dead." Beaumont, knowing full well that their "cylinder of fire" will no longer protect them from the Sumerians: "And so are we!"

The Mole People (John Agar to Hugh Beaumont after their flashlight dies out): "It's dead!"; "And so are we."

Monster on the Campus
Judson Pratt: "Lieutenant Stevens speaking."
Richard Cutting: "This is Tom Edwards, Forest Services."
Pratt: "Yeah?"
Cutting: "I've just seen the monster."
Pratt: "What? You saw it?"
Cutting: "With my own eyes. Half man, half ape!"

The Monster that Challenged the World
Tim Holt: "Talk sense! What's down there?"
Casey Adams: "I don't know. I never saw anything like it before."
Hans Conried "Like what?"
Adams: "A creature. A giant creature!"

Mother Riley Meets the Vampire
Bela Lugosi: "This is the robot control. I intend to build 50,000 robots."
Philip Leaver: "50,000?"
Lugosi: "Yes."
Leaver: "But how many have you built so far."
Lugosi: "Er, one."

The Monster that Challenged the World: **"What's down there?"**

Not of this Earth
Jonathan Haze to Beverly Garland, realizing that Paul Birch might be an alien: "You mean the boss is some kind of man from Mars?"

Phantom from Space
Victim in police station: "How would you feel if somebody with a crazy helmet with pipes sticking out of it came at you in the dark. Now look, I know this sounds, er, crazy, but there wasn't any head in that helmet."
Harry Landers: "No head. No head at all?"
Victim: "It's the truth."
Landers: "I think you need some coffee."

The Quatermass Experiment
Jack Warner: "You see Mister Quatermass, I'm an old-fashioned sort of chap. I don't know much about rockets or traveling in space. I don't read science fiction. I'm a plain simple Bible man. I have a routine mind and I have to do routine things."
Brian Donlevy: "Such as fingerprinting an unconscious man?"
Warner: "When three men take off in a rocket and only one comes back, in our reckoning that leaves minus two, and minus two puts us in the embarrassing position of having to investigate plus one, whether he's conscious, unconscious or a gibbering idiot."

Quatermass 2
Percy Herbert: "What's in those domes, mister?"

John Rae: "Yes, what is it? Tell us!"
Brian Donlevy: "Inside those domes are creatures from outside this Earth."
The Rocket Man
Spring Byington to young George Winslow: "You like girls, don't you?"
Winslow: "I don't like any kinda girls! What good are they?"
The 7th Voyage of Sinbad
Kerwin Mathews: "Drop anchor. We go ashore at the first light of dawn. May Allah grant that we find food and water."
Helmsman: "And may Allah grant that we find nothing more."
Stolen Face (aka *The Scar*)
Everley Gregg to surgeon Paul Henreid, voicing what every woman knows: "A time comes in every woman's life when her mirror tells her that she looks a lot older than she feels."
Henreid: "A common complaint!"
The Strange World of Planet X
Hardly a scintillating final line from the scriptwriters.
Alien Martin Benson: "Goodbye."
Gaby André: "Will you come back?"
Benson: "Who knows."
Tarantula
Distraught Leo G. Carroll to John Agar and Mara Corday, surveying the wreckage of his laboratory: "Oh, you should have seen them. You should have seen them. You should have seen them before the fire. They lived on nothing but our nutrient. Rats eight times normal size. Guinea pig big as a police dog. Tarantula (arms open wide) ... lost. All lost."
Agar: "What about the tarantula?"
Carroll: "Burned. All burned."
Target Earth
Richard Denning: "The army must be doing something."
Richard Reeves: "Yeah, only in the meantime, we gotta play hide and seek with a bunch of zombies from Mars, or wherever they come from."
The Thing from Another World
Robert Cornthwaite, impatiently waiting for the thermite bombs to detonate and reveal the flying saucer: "A few minutes from now we may have the key to the stars. A million years of history are waiting for us in that ice."
Timeslip (aka *The Atomic Man*)
Faith Domergue: "What is it?"
Gene Nelson: "They took some X-ray pictures of that guy."
Domergue: "And they were fogged?"

The Thing from Another World: "A few minutes from now we may have the key to the stars. A million years of history are waiting for us in that ice."

Nelson: "Fogged? They didn't even come out. The guy's a living A-bomb!"
Tobor the Great
Reporter to Professor Taylor Holmes, staring at Tobor the robot: "Are you trying to tell me that this pile of tin could actually pilot a spaceship?"
20 Million Miles to Earth
Frank Puglia: "A strange animal has escaped."
William Hopper: "A strange animal? Like something you've never seen before?"
Puglia: "Like something *no one* has ever seen before."
The 27th Day
Patrons in a bar watch Arnold Moss on TV as he announces: "People of Earth. I am an alien from outer space."
Woman: "What's he selling. Flying saucers?"

The World of the Worlds: **"Welcome to California!"**

Untamed Women
Mikel Conrad, viewing the parade of prehistoric animals passing him by: "Looks like a zoo—about 100 million years ago."
War of the Colossal Beast
Roger Pace to distraught Sally Fraser who thinks her husband, the 60-foot colossal man, may still be alive: "Believe me, it's impossible. I was in charge of the search for him and I know. The medical authorities all agree, no man, no matter what his size, could take those two bazooka charges and a drop of over 700 feet and come through it alive."
The War of the Worlds
A local, seeing the Martian death ray swivel round to face him and his friends: "What are we going to say to them?"
Friend: "Welcome to California!"

I make absolutely no apologies for including an abundance of other fine examples of '50s scriptwriting in further chapters. They really are too good to ignore!

Chapter 8
Atomic Age Underdogs

1950 may well have heralded the dawn of the new wave of science fiction, fantasy and horror movies, with big budgets to match, but at the lower end of the market, the B movies still existed side-by-side with their more illustrious bedfellows, primarily from 1950 to 1956 and tailing off somewhat up to 1959. Yes, we all remember *The Thing from Another World, The Day the Earth Stood Still, The War of the Worlds, Forbidden Planet, Destination Moon, Creature from the Black Lagoon* and countless other top-notch productions. But who now remembers minor effects like *The Golden Mistress, Project Moonbase, The Rocket Man, Tobor the Great, The Flame Barrier* and *The Devil's Hand*?

If the first six films represent the icing on the cake, then the latter six represent the cake itself. Often shown as a co-feature or screened on a Sunday only, the '50s low-budget fantasy picture is fast receding into cinema's twilight zone, revered by a handful of buffs that wish to preserve their memory, no matter what. In their own basic fashion, they are just as important to the genre as their big brothers, all part of that rich tapestry mentioned before. Independent film companies put a great deal of time, effort and blind faith into their productions, working like Trojans on minimal funds. The '50s simply wouldn't be the same without *Flight to Mars, Captive Women* or *The Lost Missile* to titillate the tastebuds and liven things up. Even taking into account that many such films represent the lower-end of fantasy filmmaking, but that's all part of the fun! These lesser-known movies have big hearts and should never be forgotten, many inhabiting a cinematic nether region as far as obtainability is concerned. One can gain as much satisfaction from watching *Rocketship X-M* to any number of big-budget space operas manufactured by the major studios. In the following selection of cheapies but goodies, I've concentrated on the hard-to-find and little-seen. A clutch of titles from 1958/1959—*The Cosmic Man, The Gargon Terror, Beast from the Haunted Cave, The Brain from Planet Arous, The Brain Eaters, The Astounding She-Monster, Demons of the Swamp*—plus *Monster from the Ocean Floor, The Phantom from 10,000 Leagues* and *The Hideous Sun Demon*, have been thoroughly documented in other movie books and can be readily purchased on DVD. Let's hope that the rarities under discussion in this chapter, most of which are *not* available on official discs, will whet the appetite and make one realize that there is more to cinematic fantasy life than repeated viewings of the classics cranked out by Universal-International, Allied Artists and United Artists, however great *they* are.

1950

The 1930s and 1940s were the heydays of the cliffhanger serial, the majority knocked out by Republic that bestowed upon the '50s one of the very last of its type, *Flying Disc Man from Mars*. The 12-to-15-chapterplay format came to a close around 1953. In 12 chapters spread over 167 minutes, arch Martian villain Gregory Gay attempts to become supreme ruler of Earth with ex-Nazi John Craven (reprising his role from 1945's *The Purple Monster Strikes*). They bombard the planet with atom bombs but are thwarted by action man Walter Reed, boss of Fowler Air Patrol. Chapter One, "Menace from Mars,"

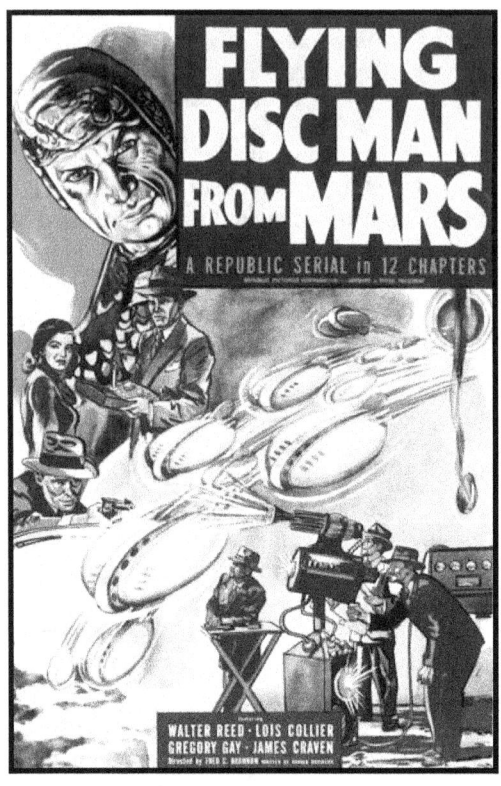

ran 20 minutes. The remaining chapters came in at 13 minutes 20 seconds: "The Volcano's Secret," "Death Rides the Stratosphere," "Execution by Fire," "The Living Projectile," "Perilous Mission," "Descending Doom," "Suicide Sacrifice," "The Funeral Pyre," "Weapons of Hate," "Disaster on the Highway" and "Volcanic Vengeance."

Gay (called Mota, or atom spelled backward!) arrives on Earth in a UFO shot down by Craven's atomic ray gun. Using the crater of an active volcano as a base to construct nuclear warheads, the Martian agrees to share his power with industrial scientist Craven in return for uranium stolen from Argosy Metals. These will be dropped from his disc-cum-rocket. It's not until chapter eight that Reed finally twigs that Craven is in cahoots with Gay; the duo have obtained $250,000 in ransom money by threatening to destroy a bridge using an aerial torpedo armed with a nuclear bomb. Following the blanket bombing of buildings, bridges and dams, the inevitable showdown takes place inside the volcano. During a fracas in Gay's laboratory, a quantity of bombs topples into the active volcanic vent. The volcano erupts, submerging Gay, Craven and their henchmen in molten lava. Reed plus secretary Lois Collier escape in Gay's disc-rocket that explodes in midair, the two parachuting to safety.

Moving as swiftly as Gay's chubby little rocket, each chapter had at least two fistfights, one gun battle, one car chase, several explosions and climaxed with the apparent demise of Reed who, as the next installment unfolded, had bailed out of his plane/car in the nick of time (in chapter five, he's ejected from the disc's bomb hatch, only to land in a pile of straw!). Gay's Martian costume was filched from *The Purple Monster Strikes*, his semi-disc machine from *King of the Mounties* (1942) and footage was incorporated from not only these two serials but from *King of the Rocket Men* (1949) and *G-Men Versus the Black Dragon* (1943). Howard and Theodore Lydecker were responsible for the wobbly effects and cardboard hardware, and Fred C. Brannon energetically directed, as he had done on previous Republic serials and would do on the two that followed in 1952: *Radar Men from the Moon* and *Zombies of the Stratosphere*. Gay pinched the acting honors, Reed came across like a cut-rate Clark Kent, Harry Lauter's one-dimensional heavy was a hoot and we were left wondering how, during all those countless fistfights, no one managed to lose their hat!

Missile Monsters was a 75-minute condensation of the series, given a sporadic cinema release in 1958/1959. As expected, with 92-minutes edited out of the original chapterplay, it took on a disjointed look but in some ways benefited from the ruthless scissorsjob, moving at a blinding pace. It is difficult to lay your hand on a copy of this now extremely rare picture—the original *Flying Disc Man from Mars*, though, *is* obtainable in all of its thrilling, hokey glory. (Note: *King of the Rocket Men* was also re-edited and issued as a 65-minute movie in 1951 under the title of *Lost Planet Airmen*. As at the time of writing, this remains commercially unavailable.)

Early '50s paranoia, linked to both a possible invasion by Russia and the Roswell UFO sightings of 1947, formed the basis to Colonial's *The Flying Saucer*, starring Mikel Conrad (who also produced, directed and co-wrote the script). But this saucer (previous films had referred to them as discs) wasn't from outer space—it was built by scientist Roy Engel and housed under a shack in deepest Alaska, emerging once in a while to swoop over American cities and cause panic headlines in the papers. Playboy Conrad is assigned to track the saucer down before the Russians lay their hands on it and use the vessel to drop atom bombs. Pat Garrison tags along as his "nurse," under the pretext that the guy is ill and is off to Alaska to recuperate.

Filmed in Alaska around Juneau, Spring Lake and the Taku glacier, Conrad's Cold War sci-fi yarn spins out its flimsy plot over a 75-minute running time; yes, the Alaskan scenery is splendid, but there's too much of it and little in the way of action. Scenes of Conrad staggering from one bar to the next in Juneau are drawn out to the point of tedium, and there's a "will they, won't they" Conrad and Garrison love angle inserted. Only in the final 10 minutes does the pace quicken. The whole cast fight it out in a tunnel under the glacier and Engel's saucer takes off with double-crossing assistant Denver Pyle at the controls, only to explode in midair as one of the CIA agents planted a bomb on the craft beforehand. Darrell Calker's melodious score amplifies the frosty,

breathtaking landscapes, but even fans of early '50s obscure science fiction will have their patience tested in this patently unexciting picture. And what is the significance, if any, of that elderly woman screaming her head off in the opening seconds?

On June 27, 1950, George Pal's *Destination Moon* was premiered in New York, detailing in semi-documentary fashion the first manned flight to the moon. But a month earlier, on May 26, Kurt Neumann's *Rocketship X-M* beat Pal's expensive opus to the post; it too told of an expedition to the moon, the difference being that the crew ultimately landed on Mars. Therefore, in cinema's own version of the space race, *Rocketship X-M* can lay claim to being the first postwar space adventure.

In June Lippert Productions rushed their low-budget space epic into the cinemas on general release, while Pal's movie went the rounds in August. *Destination Moon* is the film most buffs identify with from the outset of the 1950s, but in some ways *Rocketship X-M* is the more enjoyable experience. Pal's groundbreaker trod a shaky line between realism and jocularity, whereas Neumann went for a space opera approach; it was easier on the eye and stands up well today, easily comparable to its more celebrated neighbor.

Four men and one woman blast off from Earth toward the moon in the X-M rocket. They quickly lose power, avert a meteor storm (all '50s outer space flicks had to include a meteor storm), black out when a burst of power increases the ship's velocity, by-pass the moon and land on Mars. Photographed in red/sepia tints by Karl Struss and filmed in California's Red Rock Canyon (as was Richard Cunha's *Missile to the Moon*), the Mars sequences are successfully realized; Lloyd Bridges and crew stumble across a domed structure in ruins plus a metallic mask buried nearby in the sand. Those Martians that have survived a nuclear war have reverted to Stone Age savagery. The blind, bald humanoids with radiation scarring react to the newcomers' presence by hurling boulders at them. Professor John Emery and Noah Beery, Jr. are killed, but Bridges, Osa Massen and wounded Hugh O'Brian make it back to the rocket. Unusually for the period, the film ends on a fatalistic note; the rocket runs out of fuel and, with Bridges and Massen in each other's arms, crashes to Earth. "Tomorrow we start construction of the RX2," intones Morris Ankrum over the end credits. A pulp sci-fi classic of some standing, and, in its own way, an important genre picture.

1951

Five was one of the very first movies to deal with the after-effects of a nuclear war, a sober, doom-laden tale written, produced and directed by Arch Oboler and released through Columbia. From its opening shots of the atomic mushroom cloud spreading death to the world's major cities, to the disheveled Susan Douglas struggling up a deserted road and to the final scene of Douglas and William Phipps preparing to work the land, Oboler's stark end-of-the-world message is like watching Roger Corman's *Day the World Ended* minus the mutants. Pregnant Douglas, optimist Phipps, bigoted ex-Nazi James Anderson, nice black guy Charles Lampkin and elderly banker Earl Lee are the five sheltering in what in real life was Oboler's Cliff House, designed by Frank Lloyd Wright. Lee leaves the action early on, expiring from radiation sickness on a beach; Oboler then directs his efforts on the tension arising from the squabbling survivors. Phipps wants to set up house with Douglas and her baby, when it is born, and so does quarrelsome, work-shy Anderson, promising to take the woman to the abandoned city, ostensibly to search for her missing husband. In reality, he views the city as a looter's paradise, his for the taking. Lampkin looks on from the sidelines, playing referee.

Henry Russell's soundtrack builds on the silent deadness of this new world, creating a menacing aural backdrop to some startling images: A begrimed "Back in 5 minutes" note pinned to a store door; a newspaper reporting the world's annihilation dissolving from sight as rain spatters a dirty window; "Atomic Suds" washing powder; skeletal remains littering the vehicle-strewn streets and Douglas running hysterically through the woods clasping her dead infant to her breast. "How wonderful. Music. I've missed it so much," says Douglas wistfully as a generator brings electricity to the house, enabling them to play records. Douglas, Phipps and Lampkin reminisce about life before the holocaust. But all does not end well: Douglas discovers the rotting corpse of her husband seated in a hospital chair where he had gone to wait while she was in the X-ray room, a truly heartrending moment; Lampkin is stabbed to death by Anderson and the arrogant killer dies from radiation poisoning, after handing Douglas a tray full of worthless jewels. It is left to Phipps and Douglas to start a new life, whatever that life may be.

Radio scriptwriter Oboler (he detested TV so much that he made *The Twonky* in 1953, a semi-comical warning about the perils of television taking over people's lives) chose not to moralize in *Five*, focusing instead on humanity's struggle to regain its footing in a world destroyed by itself. By sparse use of the camera and tight editing, he produced one of the great post-apocalyptic films of his generation, but one that is seldom seen these days. Utterly devoid of pretentiousness, unlike so many of today's similar blockbusters, *Five* lingers long in the memory and, in its own unrestrained way, is a remarkable piece of minimalist cinema.

In complete contrast to the relative seriousness displayed in *Destination Moon* and *Rocketship X-M*, Monogram's comic strip *Flight to Mars* was lightweight and daft. We now had the first manned voyage to the Red Planet led by Arthur Franz, with reporter Cameron Mitchell, Virginia Huston (Franz's on/off girlfriend), John Litel and Richard

Gaines making up the crew. "Personally, I think this rocket is my coffin," states a worried Gaines as (yes, you've guessed it) the ship narrowly avoids collision with a meteor shower. Mars has black, monolithic towers reaching up into an orange sky—special effects aces Irving Block and Jack Rabin collaborated on a vast number of pictures in this decade (including *Rocketship X-M*) and are another pair of unsung heroes whose services to the sci-fi genre should never be undervalued. Their imaginative painted backdrops were the highlight of many a cheapo production, which is the case here. Unfortunately, as soon as the Martians appear, all sense of imagination goes out the window. They're just like us! Director Lesley Selander then takes us down the old tried and trusted avenue of a dying civilization living underground needing to populate (i.e. conquer) Earth as they are running short of natural resources. The Martians attempt to steal the rocket so they can reverse engineer their own invasion fleet, but Franz and company repair the ship and take off with feline Martian Marguerite Chapman on board; the girl's fallen for Franz and wants to play house with him on Earth, not on lonely old Mars. As a consolation prize, Mitchell gets Huston on the rebound!

It's not surprising that *Flight to Mars*, shot in 11 days, is now a forgotten '50s B movie. If any attempt had been made to portray an alien race as, well, *alien*, the film might have worked. By presenting the Martians as though they had just been flown in from the streets of New York was a big mistake; it means that Monogram's addition to the outer space adventure flick remains one of the worst Martian movies ever committed to celluloid. Even the bright Cinecolor photography can't save it.

The Atomic Age met up with the prehistoric age for the first time in Lippert's *Lost Continent*, a lively *Lost World* caper that can still hold its own as an exhilarating ration of '50s hokum. When an atomic-powered rocket goes AWOL in the South Pacific, Cesar Romero, John Hoyt, Chick Chandler, Sid Melton, Hugh Beaumont and Whit Bissell fly over the spot where it disappeared. An immense field of uranium on an uncharted island is causing anything that flies in the area to go off course—Romero loses control of the plane and it crashes in a dense jungle. Emerging unscathed from the wreckage, the men ascend a sacred mountain and, on the summit, discover not only the missing rocket but also a primeval forest populated by dinosaurs.

Director Sam Newfield and producer Sigmund Neufeld worked together on a number of '40s horror movies (*The Mad Monster*; *Dead Men Walk*; *The Monster Maker*), all released by bargain-basement outfit PRC, and their expertise showed on *Lost Continent*. In a way, the picture is an early ancestor of movies like *The Land that Time Forgot* and doesn't seem to have aged all that much over a 61-year period. Augie Lohman (he created *The Monster that Challenged the World*) organized the stop-motion effects (two Triceratops, a Brontosaurus and a Pteranodon); they're not up to Ray Harryhausen's high standards but adequate enough in this kind of setup. From the moment Romero and his team enter this cute-looking lost world, Newfield decided to shoot the sequences in a green tint to bestow an air of mystery, reverting to monochrome once the four survivors descended the mountain in an earthquake. Quite original for its day, the tinting still appears novel now and works for, rather than detracts from, the action. Another huge bonus is Paul Dunlap's stirring full-orchestral score, proof that even B movies benefited from a suitably rousing soundtrack. Two eight year olds sat through *Lost Continent*'s 83-minute running time without fidgeting once when this author put on a showing for them in 2011, loving every single minute. Enough said about the power to entertain that some of these old classics still retain.

Looking back on Edgar G. Ulmer's *The Man from Planet X*, it is very easy to snigger at Mid Century's primitive *Close Encounters of the Third Kind*-offering. Meccano set–type credits, plastic trees, too-obvious painted village backdrops, fake Scottish accents and a studio-bound setting (left over from 1948's *Joan of Arc*); Hollywood's answer to a Scottish moor is as far removed from the real thing as you could possibly get. So why set the action in Scotland at all? An alien from Planet X (so-named by astronomers) lands on those misty moors, his face an inscrutable mask behind a bubble space helmet. In a nearby broch (an ancient Scottish stone tower), reporter Robert Clarke, Margaret Field and scientists Raymond Bond and William Schallert are monitoring the planet's progress. The midget alien, communicating by modulated musical sounds from a chest speaker, has arrived on Earth in a ship resembling a large diving bell to replenish his dying, freezing planet with humans; he turns the local inhabitants into zombie slaves, planning to abduct them ("This is gonna be a village of zombies," mutters Clarke at one stage). Schallert wants the formula of the ship's heat-resistant metal so that he can cover himself in financial glory; he also fosters an unrequited passion for Field, but Clarke fancies her himself. Humanity proves to be as cold as the planet the alien has arrived from; his ship is bombarded by the military and blows up, taking the lonely visitor with it, and Planet X zooms harmlessly by into the far reaches of space.

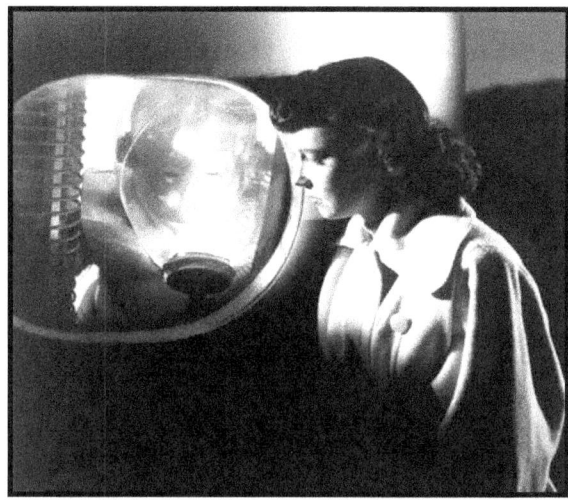

Margaret Field confronts the alien from *The Man From Planet X*.

Shot in six days, Ulmer's space outing hasn't aged well, and the very fact that it was "U" classified in Britain speaks volumes; compared to the X-rated *The Thing from Another World*, released the same year, it seems meek and mild, almost like an Ealing production with a cast of quirky characters. It also runs on similar lines to the Danzigers' *Devil Girl from Mars* but is nowhere near as good, while its inaccuracies (London's Scotland Yard, who arrive with the army, would have no jurisdiction in Scotland and its affairs) might irk many British sci-fi watchers. The photography is murky, the playing perfunctory and the effects rudimentary; it's the image of that rather endearing alien with the immobile face that has lasted over the years, the one thing from *The Man from Planet X* best remembered.

Christopher Reeve wasn't the first actor to portray Action Comics' Man of Steel (*Superman—the Movie*); 30 years earlier in 1948, Kirk Alyn donned those famous tights and outside pants in schlockmeister Sam Katzman's 15-chapter serial for Columbia, simply entitled *Superman*. In 1950, Alyn appeared again in *Atom Man vs. Superman* with the same team behind him, another 15-chapter saga from Katzman. The honor for the first feature-length *Superman* movie goes to *Superman and the Mole-Men*, released by Robert L. Lippert's own production company, with George Reeves in the title role. Originally touted as a chapterplay presentation to promote the character on TV, then issued as a feature and subsequently edited for inclusion in the teleseries, Lee Sholem's cheapo is a long way from Richard Donner's bank-busting epic, but it oozes charm over a running time of 62 minutes.

Clark Kent and Lois Lane (Phyllis Coates) are dispatched to the town of Silsby to report on the world's deepest oil well, 32,740 feet down and still counting. However, foreman Walter Reed has closed the well; he claims that they have struck dangerous radium deposits and that primitive organisms have been found on drill bits. Up from the bowels of the earth come two inquisitive Mole Men, looking like Munchkins from *The Wizard of Oz*—domed, baldheads, bushy eyebrows and claws. These peaceful creatures, leaving luminous footprints in their wake, just want to find out about the world above but mean and nasty Jeff Corey organizes a posse to hunt them down because "they're different." When one is shot, the other brings along two more of his kind, armed with a ray gun. In steps Superman to defend the Mole Men against Corey and his trigger-happy mob and ensure that they receive a safe passage back to where they came from.

Little in the way of special effects appear, the few on display shaky in the extreme. Superman's flying sequences are over and done with in a flash. Beefy Reeves made a likeable Man of Steel and Coates was just right as his feisty partner. Darrell Calker's score is also a delight. The Mole Men return to their home six miles down after sealing the wellhead with explosives, Coates' words echo the philosophical mood of the film: "It's almost as if they are saying—you live your lives and we'll live ours."

1952

Paramount's *The Atomic City* kicks off in fine fettle, with dire warnings on the misuse of atomic power, footage of the 1945 New Mexico bomb tests, scenes of devastated Hiroshima, imagery of the Russian threat to America's national security and the flip side of the nuclear coin—how the atom, if treated with respect, can save lives. Set in the stark atomic city of Los Alamos, the viewer might be duped into thinking that what follows is a Cold War thriller based on the H-bomb. Well, it begins that way: Lee Aaker, son of nuclear physicist Gene Barry (the actor's screen debut), is kidnapped by spies who want Barry's formula for the hydrogen bomb in return for Aaker's safe return. This act triggers a great deal of soul searching between Barry and wife Lydia Clarke. She admits to hating the place, surrounded as they are by barbed wire fences and shadowed by FBI agents, and she is terrified of the inherent danger lurking unseen in

In *The Atomic City*, the nuclear message becomes secondary to the inordinate amount of time spent on the FBI's complex undercover operation.

their industrial surroundings. She's also disturbed by the fact that their son continually says, "If I grow up" instead of, "When I grow up."

After that bleak opening section with its air of doom and gloom, director Jerry Hopper changes tack, devoting an inordinate amount of time on the FBI's complex and very thorough undercover operation to trap the spies, coupled with young Aaker's attempts to escape from his captors, who have kept him prisoner in ancient Indian cliff dwellings near Santa Fe. The "for and against" nuclear message becomes secondary to the plot and, as a result, the movie loses its potency, fizzling out as Barry and the Feds close in on the criminals' lair. Aaker is eventually rescued after the crooked scientist-cum-enemy agent has shot his two colleagues and surrendered. Like so many other movies featured in this chapter, *The Atomic City* is hardly ever recalled these days, submerged beneath more familiar genre heavyweights; if it had managed to maintain the momentum built up in the first 35 minutes, this would have been a nuclear thriller of some standing. As it is, it can only now be seen as a stepping-stone for Gene Barry to launch his career in George Pal's *The War of the Worlds*.

RKO-Radio's *Captive Women* (aka *3000 A.D.*) commences with four minutes of atomic bomb footage before the following hour plunges us into a nuclear devastated New York of the future populated by three races: The Norms (good), the Upriver people (bad) and the Mutates (ugly). There's a veritable clash of styles in this interesting, although not fully realized, post-holocaust flick: The Upriver people are dressed in *Siege of the Saxons* outfits; the Mutates look like cloaked devil-worshippers; Robert Clarke, pal Robert Bice and the male Norms, armed with bows and arrows, are dressed like Robin Hood and his Merry Men and the female Norms surely must have wandered in from the set of *Quo Vadis*. All speak in medieval English dialect and all three groups hate each other. Thank goodness then for Jack Rabin and Irving Block's imaginative design work depicting a New York in twisted ruins, black clouds casting an air of depression over the wrecked city. It takes our mind off the hammy acting and corny dialogue.

Bad-assed Upriver people leader Stuart Randall (he enjoys cutting off the sixth finger on Mutates' hands) gets invited to Clarke's wedding feast, but the whole shindig ends in chaos. Clarke's father is murdered, betrayed by Douglas Evans, who then makes a move for Clarke's double-crossing fiancée, Gloria Saunders. Randall's henchmen strangle Evans, while Clarke and Bice flee the scene to gather their thoughts over what to do next.

Meanwhile, Ron Randell (usually listed as Randall, but not in this movie to avoid confusion with Stuart Randall), the Mutate's leader, forms a raiding party: They require Norm women with which to procreate; the last baby born to them was an abomination. A successful foray sees the Norm girls shepherded away by the Mutates, while Randell falls in love with the best of the bunch, Margaret

Field. Clarke and Bice then join forces with Randell to drive out their common foe, the Upriver people. Scheming Saunders, switching from one side to the other when it suits her whim, is dispatched with an arrow and, in the final reel, Randall and his mob chase the Norms and Mutates through a booby-trapped tunnel under the Hudson; the roof supports are pulled loose and the tunnel collapses, wiping out the Upriver gang. The film ends with Randell, a Mutate, marrying Field, a Norm. There's hope for the human race yet!

Joint producers/scriptwriters Aubrey Wisberg and Jack Pollexfen did a much better job on *The Man from Planet X* than they managed here, but *Captive Women*, not seen for years, has a grimy aura commendable in a picture of such low origins. Yes, the acting is dumb, but Stuart Gilmore keeps things ticking over at a pace and the sets, particularly the weed-choked tunnel, water dripping ominously from the cracked ceiling, skillfully pull the viewer into the catastrophic, post-nuclear world that these oddballs inhabit. Cheap looking, but not bad for its type.

Together with *Red Planet Mars*, the early '50s reached a paranoid communist peak in American Pictures' *Invasion U.S.A.*, directed by Alfred E. Green. I use the term "directed" loosely—60% of Green's jingoistic "The Reds are Coming" docudrama, preying on people's Cold War anxieties and what life would be like living under the shadow of a nuclear conflict, was composed of newsreel footage taken from the Second World War. Combining this footage with Jack Rabin's model work (chiefly in the New York sequences) and Albert Glasser's tub-thumping score, Green drummed up a Soviet-invasion-of-America narrative verging on hysteria that, if it hadn't been so straight-faced in execution, would have turned out to be downright hilarious.

Five strangers in a cocktail bar are hypnotized by Dan O'Herlihy into imagining that they are all caught up in what amounts to a Third World War. Hundreds of enemy planes drop thousands of paratroopers; atom bombs rain down on cities; the Boulder Dam is destroyed; San Francisco is flattened; New York is reduced to rubble; the top brass of both countries meet and discuss and Gerald Mohr still has time to romance Peggie Castle ("War or no war, people have to eat and drink and make love.") before he's shot by soldiers who have broken into her apartment with one thing on their minds—rape. Heartbroken Castle jumps out of a window to her death and wakes up in the bar; the whole nightmare they have been living through turns out to be a vision of what *might* happen if America was to drop her guard. An all-out assault on the perils of communism, the movie at times is akin to watching the Pathé News that used to be a standard feature of cinema presentations in the United Kingdom. An inordinate proportion of stock footage is thoughtlessly edited (scenes of London's Blitz inserted as New York burns is one of several tactless mistakes) and the continual warnings concerning the dangers threatened by communism are rammed down the viewers' throat ad nauseam. It may well be a snapshot of the times, but *Invasion U.S.A.* is too feverish for its own good and becomes an effort to sit through. Perhaps it would have been more enjoyable as a political satire on relationships between two opposing world powers. Anyone remember the Marx Brothers' *Duck Soup*?

Never was there a more blatant piece of anti-communist propaganda issued under the guise of a sci-fi picture than *Red Planet Mars*, a grueling 87 minutes that preached one message, loud and clear: Don't let the Soviet Union take over the free world. No, Senator Joseph McCarthy (he of the McCarthy witch-hunt trials which took place between 1950 and 1954) didn't direct, although he might well have. Harry Horner (for Melaby Pictures) was behind this preachy, hypocritically solemn non-thriller. Peter Graves and wife Andrea King analyze television transmissions of the Martian surface, noting that an unknown intelligence is melting the mountains of ice to provide water for the network of irrigation canals. When coded communications from the planet are received in response to Graves' transmitted signals, several things happen: King frets and worries, gabbling on about bombs, a Martian war, the end of the world, Einstein and the fate of her two children; ex-Nazi scientist Herbert Berghof, holed up in the Andes, is ordered by his Russian bosses to intercept the messages and Graves' contact with Mars makes world headlines. Deciphering the codes, Graves ascertains that the Martians rely not on machines for day-to-day existence but cosmic energy which has eliminated the need to work; cue for Earth's wheels of industry to stop turning—factories and mines close, leaving millions unemployed. The movie then plummets into spiritual farce—it appears that Mars is a Utopian society presided over by a Godlike-being. ("The Sermon on the Mount—on Mars!" says King in awe.) A strong religious motif is introduced, Russian peasants digging up an icon and overthrowing the government, replacing it with priests, the whole world looking for some kind of divine intervention.

The final 10 minutes sees Berghof meeting up with Graves and King in their laboratory. He claims to have sent the messages all along, a treacherous plot to bring about the collapse of capitalism. But just as Graves lights a cigarette, a final message is intercepted, stating that the supreme authority on Mars is God himself; Berghof fires his gun at the transmitter and all three are blown to oblivion in a hydrogen explosion.

Explicit in its over-stated warning of Reds-under-the-bed, *Red Planet Mars* ranks as one of the '50s most boring sci-fi movies. Mahlon Merrick's lush soundtrack is more suited to a soap opera than this pompous anti-commie tirade; lacking dramatic narrative and way too talkative, even the most steadfast of aficionados will find watching this film akin to wading through treacle.

1953

Western? Crime drama? Or, film noir that contains psychotic overtones? RKO-Radio's Technicolor *Devil's Canyon* is hardly a conventional Western and no canyon exists in the movie as such. As will be seen with Fox's *The Fiend Who Walked the West*, psychopathic characters occasionally appeared in the Western genre as the lead role. Here, we had savage killer Stephen McNally holed up in Arizona's tough Territorial

Prison (the year is 1897), intent on breaking out, releasing the rest of the inmates so that they can run riot in nearby Yuma and putting paid to Dale Robertson. Ex-marshal Robertson has received an unjust 10-year sentence for gunning down McNally's two brothers, who came looking for him in a town that had outlawed gunfights. He knows that the tyrannical psycho, behind bars, is plotting his revenge. As for sexy outlaw girl Virginia Mayo—she's McNally's property but hankers after Robertson—she smuggles guns into the prison under the watchful gaze of brutal guard Jay C. Flippen.

Originally issued in 3-D, Alfred Werker's Western prison oater, complete with a blazing Gatling gun shootout that's straight out of a James Cagney gangster flick, is a fascinating curiosity, appealing to Western lovers and those with a penchant for tracking down rare screen loonies alike. Old hands Morris Ankrum and Whit Bissell put in an appearance, Mayo's ample breasts must have enveloped the front row in three-dimension and McNally snarls his way toward that bloody climax ("I told ya I'd getcha," he spits at Robertson. "I'm gonna splatter your brains all over that wall."); Robertson blasts him to death with a fusillade of bullets, forces the prisoners back into their cells and earns himself and Mayo a possible free pardon from the governor. To top it off, Russian composer Daniele Amfitheatrof supplies a menacing score that complements the hard-edged scenario. The movie becomes an A-rated psycho-Western that's certainly different in every sense.

Before Norman Bates and *Psycho*, there was Richard Barrie and *Edge of Fury*. The Hitchcock–type McGuffin here is a letter from the Willetstown State Hospital to Michael Higgins (playing Barrie) stating that until he finds the funds, his caseworker is unable to treat him for his "problems." Higgins is on a beach, painting; several armed cops close in, a scene repeated at the end, the letter floating away on the tide. What happens in between forms the framework to one of the earliest thrillers that, by and large, treated the subject of mental illness seriously without resorting to high-blown melodramatics. Moodily shot by Conrad Hall on desolate beach locations, directors Robert J. Gurney, Jr. and Irving Lerner take us on a 77-minute voyage into the twisted mind of a misogynist. *Edge of Fury* is not mainstream horror (hence the release being withheld until 1958 when United Artists, caught up in the horror boom, took a chance on it), but, as a study in madness (today, this would read bipolar disorder), it delivers quite a punch.

Boyish-looking Higgins, who works in the local library, befriends three women in a grocery store: Lois Holmes and her two daughters, Jean Allison and Doris Fesette. Finding a beach cottage for them all to rent after knowing the ladies for only three weeks, he develops a psychopathic hatred toward blonde, brassy Fesette, while fending off the sexual advances of dowdier Allison. Living in an adjacent shack, he spies on Fesette as she undresses, watches in disgust when the girl canoodles with her boyfriend and throws Allison roughly to the ground when she kisses him ("Don't ever do that again!" he snarls). Good-natured charmer one minute, short-tempered and jealous the next, he's finally tipped over the edge of reason when the three women plus two boyfriends leave his party early. Feeling rejected and humiliated, he goes berserk, running wildly around their cottage muttering, "You're trying to trap me! You tramp!" to nobody in particular (but aimed at Fesette), arming himself with rope, knife and ax and lying in wait for Fesette, who is out on a date. However, Fesette doesn't, as expected, end up a victim of Higgins' unbridled delirium. A delivery boy and Holmes are hacked to death, the bloodstained corpses discovered by Fesette on her return. We are then back at the start, Higgins seemingly oblivious to the surrounding police, the horrific murders he has committed and that damning letter.

Partly narrated, with voice-overs from the madman himself, *Edge of Fury* is compelling horror cinema, seldom heard of and little seen. Unfortunately, as at the time of writing, the movie remains unavailable on tape or DVD, a situation that needs rectifying; fans should be granted the opportunity of appreciating for themselves one of the '50s rarest of all psycho thrillers.

A third telling of Marie Belloc-Lowndes' novel *The Lodger* (filmed in 1926 and 1944) appeared in 1953. *Man in the Attic* is the one Jack the Ripper movie that gets overlooked in many mainstream film books, even though this Panoramic Productions' feature was released through 20th Century Fox. Other things going for it include fine photography and tense direction by Hugo Fregonese, authentic foggy Whitechapel set design, a tremendous score by Lionel Newman and villainous Jack Palance as the Ripper. Let's be honest, if you opened your front door to find Palance standing on the step with a little black bag, wouldn't *you* be afraid? Shot on a modest budget, Palance plays sinister Doctor Slade, renting rooms and an attic from Francis Bavier and Rhys Williams. Palance nurtures a pathological hatred of actresses, so he becomes distinctly agitated when he discovers that Constance Smith, a popular music hall star, also lodges there. The catalyst behind Palance's killing spree is his mother (isn't it always?). An attractive actress, her string of brazen infidelities led to his father drinking himself to death, so Palance's perverted mission in life is to butcher these stage harlots one by one. ("Jack the Ripper. What a stupid, revolting name!" he snorts in derision.)

Man in the Attic's one main weakness lies in the support cast. Everyone pales into insignificance beside Palance's reptilian countenance and disquieting performance; when he's not around (which isn't often), the proceedings drag. Also, the lengthy musical number with Smith and her troupe appears anachronistic; Newman's score is straight out of a 1920s flapper vehicle. And the murders are bloodless to say the least. Needless to say, Palance can't control his raging passions over Smith—he loves and loathes her in equal measures. Like most Ripper excursions, the film ends on a speculative note (it has to as the identity of the killer still remains in doubt); chased by the police after getting amorous with Smith and then threatening to slit her throat when she gives his advances the cold shoulder, Palance walks into the River Thames and disappears, presumed drowned. Good, but this picture has been pushed into the background by better Ripper interpretations, Mid Century's *Jack the Ripper* (see chapter 25) being one such feature.

W. Lee Wilder's *Phantom from Space* (Planet Filmways) is mentioned in chapter 14—the colorization makeover by Legend Films definitely makes this cheapo far more watchable than in monochrome. An alien lands in Santa Monica wearing a spacesuit and diver's helmet (a much-favored prop in '50s Z flicks). The helmet is the only way he can breathe Earth's atmosphere; when it is smashed, the being climbs up a gantry in an observatory where, exposed to ultra-violet beams, it sheds its cloak of invisibility, suffocates, falls to the ground and evaporates in a cloud of smoke. The *Invisible Man*–type effects are surprisingly well conceived (dig that floating helmet!), but the main leads (cop Harry Landers, scientists Lela Nelson and Rudolph Anders) are as stilted as the script, and the initial 25-minutes of communication cars searching for the alien's whereabouts drag interminably. But it's far, far better than that other movie featuring a diving helmet-wearing creature, also released in 1953, Phil Tucker's abominable *Robot Monster*.

Acclaimed sci-fi author Robert A. Heinlein co-wrote *Project Moonbase* (Lippert/Galaxy), a long-forgotten enterprise directed by Richard Talmadge, originally earmarked to be a TV series entitled *Ring Around the Moon*, but it never got off the ground. The author's vision of space travel in 1970 was expertly rendered to celluloid by effects technician Jacques Fresco. Rockets, a space station and the arid lunar surface all stand up to the best of what the early years of this decade had to offer. But the same can't be said of the space outfits: Donna Martell, Ross Ford and Larry Johns walk around in skullcaps, t-shirts, shorts and pixie boots, guns strapped to their waists, looking for all the world like Santa's little helpers.

The trio's mission is to orbit the moon in the Magellan spacecraft and photograph the surface to determine an acceptable site for a possible lunar base. Unfortunately, Colonel Martell has to land the ship in an emergency (sabotaged by Johns, a Russian agent), thus, by proxy, founding Moonbase Number One. Johns expires outside the Magellan, Martell and Ford are married on orders from the female President of the United States (it will bring in good publicity) and the movie ends on a fragmentary note, as if nobody quite knew what to do with all those loose ends.

Cordless phones (yes, Heinlein got that spot on!), signs in the space station's corridors stating: "Please do not walk on the walls," a nice outer space score by Herschel Burke Gilbert, a realistic moon walk and precision model work add up to a half-decent moon opera marred by two things—the script and Martell's lack of acting ability. Heinlein's characters nearly always possessed names with a double meaning—here, Martell is called Briteis, or Bright Eyes. The script is just as hammy—"Let's shove off in the Magellan" and "Bill, I muffed it!" These lines are examples of pulp fiction replacing scientific plausibility. As for Martell, if we can tear our eyes away from her capacious chest, it appears that the actress had difficulty in remembering her lines or investing them with meaning. Her permanently startled features run off the clichés with an agonized air, content to let her pleasing figure do all the talking. It's an inept performance, no two ways about it, but lends *Project Moonbase* a certain illogical drawing power. And the film doesn't drag its heels over 63 minutes—as a matter of fact, it's quick and enjoyable.

1954

One of a number of fantasy comedies made in 1954, Republic's *The Atomic Kid* starred Mickey Rooney as a prospector who, with pal Robert Strauss, wanders into a nuclear testing area in Nevada searching for uranium ("If we discover uranium, you'll be more famous than Liberace!"). An atom bomb is exploded after not-so-caring Strauss has driven away; Rooney, marooned in a house full of dummies, survives the explosion but winds up steeped in radiation, his head and hands glowing a lá Lon Chaney, Jr. in *Man Made Monster*. It follows that the communists focus on Rooney—if he could live through such a blast, they reason, he must possess unbelievable powers that could be used for their own corrupt purposes. Rooney's third wife (out of eight), Elaine Davis, supplies the love interest, while Whit Bissell and Bill Goodwin are doctors carrying out a series of tests on Rooney's radioactive body with a view to curing him.

Five-foot-two Rooney was already, by the mid-'50s, a veteran of countless movies and TV shows. Shrugging off his *Andy Hardy* image, he proved time and time again, later on in his career, that he could do straight roles as well as the rest of them: *Baby Face Nelson* (1957) and *The Last Mile* (1959) were powerful essays in gangster cinema, bolstered by Rooney's powerhouse star turns. In *The Atomic Kid* (produced by the man himself) he's a bundle of manic vivacity, acting everyone else off the screen (including co-star Strauss who strangely disappears for a

Mickey Rooney glows with radiation as he speaks to Elaine Davis in *The Atomic Kid*.

good part of the film's middle section) and rattling off his witty lines (story by Blake Edwards; script by Benedict Freedman and John Fenton Murray) with undisclosed glee. When Rooney jumps onto an electrified fence that has no effect on him, an FBI agent observes, "The atom bomb didn't kill him. This is kid's stuff." Later he says to the agent, "I don't smoke. Smoking and radioactivity don't mix." The chief commie spy wants Rooney because "he's a living nuclear chain reaction," but at the end, Rooney is successfully treated, the spy ring is busted, the pint-sized actor marries Davis and he and his bride inadvertently drive into another nuclear test site on their honeymoon, his vehicle screeching off into the distance as the bomb is detonated. Sadly, Mickey Rooney passed away in April 2014.

Director Leslie H. Martinson (he was behind 1966's *Batman*) wisely leaves his camera to focus on Rooney's high-octane clowning which, as we might expect, is carried off with consummate ease. It's light-hearted nonsense of course, pushing aside public concerns over the dangers associated with nuclear fallout, but Rooney makes us forget those issues in his magnetic and extremely professional performance. This is a sci-fi comedy that works.

The Bowery Boys Meet the Monsters, number 34 in a series of 48 Bowery Boy movies produced by Allied Artists between 1946-1958, featured two of the bunch, Leo Gorcey and Huntz Hall, with Bernard Gorcey making a fleeting cameo and the others only seen briefly at the beginning and closing minutes. Gorcey and Hall visit Gravesend Manor on Long Island where they hope the owner (John Dehner) is amenable to the local kids using his property to play baseball. Unfortunately, Dehner's brood parallels The Addams Family: He's a mad scientist, as is his brother Lloyd Corrigan; Vampira look-alike Laura Mason is a vampire; aunt Ellen Corby owns a six-foot-tall man-eating plant and lanky butler Paul Wexler looks as though he's just crawled out from underneath a tombstone. The madcap plot, reminiscent of an Abbott and Costello movie but rougher around the edges (Gorcey resembles in many ways Lou Costello and Hall plays the straight man), involves Corrigan's plans to place a human head on his robot Gorog, while Dehner wants to put a human brain in his pet gorilla Cosmos. The two visitors

from Manhattan might just be the answer to their prayers, although a tacky robot sporting Hall's dopey features and a man in gorilla suit mouthing Gorcey's infamous malapropisms doesn't bear thinking about! Chuck in a potion that, when drunk, converts Wexler and Hall into hairy fiends wearing goofy monster masks and we have 66 minutes of farce statically directed by Edward Bernds, where humans, gorilla, robot and hungry plant all end up in a frantic tussle; very funny if you're a New Yorker, moderately so if you're from the United Kingdom. As horror comedies go, the giggles come in fits and starts. Gorcey's mangling of the English language is the real highlight, if the audience can decipher his thick Brooklyn accent: "I took the trouble of drawing this little diaphram," "Gentlemen, I'm very much infested with this scientific friction," "Dr. Cyclops, I regurgitate, we're leaving," and "We depreciate this invective very much" are just four examples of Bernds and Elwood Ullman's wonderfully scatty script.

Originally issued in 3-D, United Artists' *Gog* has been unavailable for years in its original color format, prints were generally issued in monochrome. Long before Kubrick's HAL 9000 computer decided that it had a mind of its own, Ivan Tors' NOVAC, housed in a laboratory deep under the New Mexican desert, began killing off scientists with the help of experimental robots Gog and Magog. Scientific investigator Richard Egan arrives at the facility after two scientists have perished horribly in a low temperature unit (the film's one and only truly frightening sequence). Ex-girlfriend Constance Dowling is on hand to ensure Egan's thoughts are on her fulsome figure as well as finding out who, or what, is behind a spate of deaths caused by either a saboteur or an apparent computer malfunction (a woman poisoned by radiation in the chemistry lab, two volunteers dying from heart attacks on a centrifugal machine and high frequency noise destroying a worker). Is NOVAC's inventor, John Wengraf, responsible? He doesn't believe it possible for man to venture into space. According to him, only robots are capable of withstanding the physical demands met by space travel; humans are, to his way of thinking, a waste of time. And what is that object flying overhead—a UFO or a plane from "the other side" on a spying mission?

Typical of all his other productions, Tors spends far too much time exhaustively spelling out the techniques used in each and every scientific program in progress, including the construction of a scaled-down space station and how solar mirrors can harness the sun's energy to provide unlimited power. This, together with Herbert L. Strock's pedestrian direction, doesn't make for exciting sci-fi; the action only livens up when Gog and Magog embark on a rampage. Gog kills Wengraf and Egan, armed with a flamethrower, disables Magog. It's then discovered that NOVAC (nicknamed "The Brain") is being controlled by a rocket plane made of fiberglass; the computer was built in Europe and enemy agents planted a receiver in its works that could be used to their own advantage. The good old USAF blasts the rocket out of the sky, Gog is brought to a standstill and Egan finds time for some lip action with Dowling in hospital.

Robots go wild as Gog kills actor John Wengraf, his character the inventor of NOVAC, from *Gog*.

Gog does have its good points: The color photography is beautifully rendered in '50s pastel hues, the script witty in places ("A baby space station! Nothing will take us by surprise again."), the early techno set design imaginative in concept and the acting passable. The Cold War/anti-commie message is as plain as the nose on one's face, while moviemakers would never get away with that opening scene involving Pepe the monkey these days. Animal activists would be up in arms. *Gog* was perhaps Tors' best '50s shot at entertaining the masses, more so than the movie that succeeded it, the uneventful *Riders to the Stars*.

Universal-International horror stalwart John Agar starred in a lively, long-lost jungle-cum-voodoo flick from RK Productions/United Artists with ex-model Rosemarie Bowe entitled *The Golden Mistress*, a colorful, exotic actioner shot for the most part around Port-au-Prince's bustling waterfront in Haiti. In a convoluted storyline guaranteed to baffle most reasonably intelligent moviegoers, Agar played the debt-ridden captain of a boat, spending his days treasure hunting with his one and only crew member, a native boy (Jacques Molant). Itinerant Abner Biberman (he directed under the pseudonym of Joel Judge) steals part of an idol and a jewel-encrusted gold skeleton during a voodoo ceremony. With a vengeful high priest on his tail, he persuades daughter Bowe to approach Agar with a view to charter his boat in order to seek out the legendary treasure (which is linked to the skeleton and idol) of a tribe called The Untamed. At first, Agar declines the offer, having been on the wrong end of business deals with crooked Biberman in the past; he also believes the treasure (The Golden Mistress of the title) to be a myth. But when he sets eyes on the skeleton, dollar signs flash and he changes his mind; with Bowe, he heads off to find both the treasure and Biberman, who has disappeared with the idol.

Like a Saturday matinee cliffhanger serial, *The Golden Mistress* crams in one incident after another over the course of 83 minutes, and it's not too scary for the kids

to watch, either. Biberman falls to his death in shark-infested waters after the priest stabs a figurine inside his hat, but the idol is recovered; a young native priest, André Narcisse, is roped in on the treasure hunt; Agar saves Narcisse's son from sharks after his foot is caught in a giant clam and the team travels to a ruined palace where a second idol is located inside a wall. The two halves of the idol, when joined at a specific site on a fortress, point the way to a secret island where the treasure lies. During the night, Narcisse dies from voodoo magic, and on locating the remote island, Agar and Bowe dive into an underwater cave, surfacing in a river flowing swiftly between high canyon walls. In the island's swampy interior, the pair is captured by warriors of The Untamed and subjected to a voodoo ritual after they discover a lake whose floor is covered not only in gold skeletons but the skulls of victims speared to death in voodoo ceremonies. One of the natives throws Agar's oxygen tank into a fire; it explodes, setting the village aflame, the escaping couple leaves the treasure behind but finds romance instead, Agar counting his lucky stars that, in compensation for the loss of the gold skeletons, he has the ravishing Bowe on which to feast his eyes.

Haiti's National Folklore Theater troupe was hired to perform the native dances and William C. Thompson's bright photography heightened the Caribbean outside location work beautifully—you can almost feel the heat and smell the tang of salt air on the breeze. Galling for Agar collectors, this sunny picture, almost like a travelogue in parts and augmented by Raoul Kraushaar's bouncy score, is difficult to obtain, the original tape fetching exorbitant prices on the market. It deserves a DVD release, just to prove to doubters how versatile Agar could be when not combating the gill-man, the mole people or a certain giant tarantula! And ex-beauty queen Bowe (Miss Montana 1951), resembling a young Lauren Bacall, is as gorgeous as the scenery.

Science fiction in the '50s, once it started finding its feet, fell into two camps: those concerned with the technical aspects of space travel and "what was out there," and those featuring a monster from another world. Producers George Pal and Ivan Tors' space movies belong to the first grouping, appearing labored because these particular filmmakers tended to concentrate on scientific detail at the expense of plot. *Destination Moon, Conquest of Space* (1955) and *The Magnetic Monster* (1953), all worthy dramas of their kind, are nevertheless not as diverting as *It Conquered the World, Forbidden Planet* or even *The Man from Planet X* because of this "nuts and bolts" obsession. They're a tad too earnest and lack wit. (Pal ditched the jargon in *The War of the Worlds* and came up with an X-rated action

classic, which is more than can be said for his other '50s works.) United Artists' *Riders to the Stars* is a case in point. Man is trying to find a way of combating harmful cosmic rays to make space travel less hazardous. The Office of Scientific Investigation hits upon the idea of capturing a meteorite and bringing it back to Earth. By studying its minerals, scientists hope that this discovery might point the way to the invention of an artificial heat-resistant substance that could be used in rocket research. Four volunteers are chosen out of a group of 12, each to man a rocket and go trawling for meteorites. One quits ("It's a suicide mission!"), leaving William Lundigan, Richard Carlson and Robert Karnes to blast off in three rockets and rendezvous with a meteor shower in the hope of snaring one each.

Carlson chose to direct this wordy Tors effort (written by Curt Siodmak) that takes a full hour to get into gear, leaving just 22 minutes of space action. The men are put through a series of rigorous checks to ensure their suitability for the task ahead, which doesn't make for riveting cinema. Once up above Earth's atmosphere, Carlson engages the throttle. His milksop character panics, as the rocket shoots off into the unknown; Karnes' ship is hit by a meteorite and explodes. Lundigan succeeds in capturing a baby meteorite, crashing back on Earth but emerging in one piece into the loving arms of Martha Hyer. The space sequences are effectively staged and add a touch of color and excitement, but by then *Riders to the Stars* is dead in the water, having not recovered from that monotonous opening 60 minutes. It's true what some critics stated: Science fiction was a darned site more interesting than science fact! And *Riders to the Stars* provides the ammunition to back up this claim.

Panoramic Productions' *The Rocket Man* will strike a nostalgic chord with all those baby boomers that, like myself, were around seven years old, George Winslow's age, in this cozy family sci-fi comedy. In those days, young 'uns play-acted, living out their private fantasies away from the world of adult interference, be it cowboys, Indians, knights, soldiers or, in this case, spacemen. When Winslow is given a ray gun by a mysterious astronaut (wearing Michael Rennie's spacesuit from *The Day the Earth Stood Still*), he finds that the weapon, when fired, can not only halt objects in their tracks but force people to tell the truth—what an ideal toy for an over-imaginative child to possess! In a "good versus evil" plot designed for youngsters, Justice of the Peace Spring Byington and her daughter Anne Francis take Winslow into their care, acquiring him from an orphanage. That's the good. The evil comes in the shape of Emory Parnell, who wants to buy the orphanage, raze it to the ground and construct an oil well on the site. Charles Coburn plays Byington's persistent suitor and John Agar steps into the fray as a solicitor acting for Parnell in a bidding war who, by and by, sees his boss for the crook that he is and changes sides. Besides, Francis is a much more attractive prospect than working for Parnell. Winslow, forever yelling "Blast off," manipulates the whole affair to his own advantage with his magical gun; Byington gets to buy the orphanage and, to add icing on the cake, starts her own oil well as a bonus.

This, like *The Golden Mistress*, is another curio from Agar's extensive repertoire. It's something of a novelty to see the amiable actor in a role that doesn't, for a change, involve him combating a monster from the Universal prop department, but Agar never let the side down and he's a joy to watch. None other than satirist Lenny Bruce penned the script, while Oscar Rudolph directed in Saturday-Morning-picture-fashion to allow for plenty of hollering from lusty young voices. In the technological age where we now live, the world of the pre-teen as rendered in *The Rocket Man* will mean absolutely nothing to today's generation; for this reason, the film will probably never be issued commercially. A pity—childhood times were much more innocent and pleasures more simple back then, as this delightful little movie, over the space of 79 minutes, goes to show.

The decade's most beguiling mechanical man carries Billy Chapin in its arms, from *Tobor the Great*.

Republic/Dudley Pictures Corporation's *Tobor the Great* was another kiddy-friendly sci-fi movie with a slightly harder edge than *The Rocket Man*. This was the first picture to deal with the relationship between a boy and a robot—Richard Eyer was to continue in this vein in *The Invisible Boy* when he was teamed with *Forbidden Planet*'s Robby the Robot. Tobor actually gives Robby a run for his money as the decade's most beguiling mechanical man. Okay, he doesn't possess speech like Robby, but he's an endearing creation all the same. Professor Taylor Holmes has invented him; a robot is better suited to withstand the rigors of space travel than man, so Tobor, who can be controlled by telepathy, is earmarked as the first sentient being to be blasted off in a rocket and pilot the ship to other planets. Eleven-year-old boy wonder Billy Chapin ("Gadge" to his friends) forms a close bond with Tobor ("Gee, Tobor. You're beautiful!") while foreign spy chief Stevan Geray is ordered to steal Holmes' formula so that his country can create an army of robots to take over the world. When the agents hold Chapin and Holmes prisoner in a planetarium, Tobor picks up the professor's thought commands and comes crashing to the rescue in a blood-and-thunder climax.

Lee Sholem directs with oodles of verve while Howard Jackson's grand score is a revelation considering the movie's humble origins and subject matter. The script is also witty (Holmes to reporters: "Meet Tobor. [He's a] Childish joke of mine. Robot spelt backwards."). Other clever touches include Holmes relaying via speakers the sounds of fighting from *Sands of Iwo Jima* to scare off Geray and his gang, and a moving climax when Chapin, with Holmes, gazes up at the rocket shooting skyward with his metal buddy handling the controls and says wistfully: "Goodbye Tobor, and good luck." A strong candidate for the title of the '50s most engaging robot picture, *Tobor the Great* deserves a proper issue on DVD because it still has the power to entertain the youngsters—even today's under-10s will enjoy it.

1955

"Once upon a time, about two billion years ago, there lived no one, nowhere." This was the funereal opening line to Warner Bros.' 82-minute *The Animal World*. The movie was in Technicolor, had a fine Paul Sawtell score and was producer/director Irwin Allen's personalized rip-off of Disney's *The Living Desert* (1953); same jokey script, narrated by John Storm and Theodore von Eltz, same semi-documentary wildlife approach and, like the Disney flick, a box-office failure. Why has it been included in this chapter? Because 14 minutes in, Ray Harryhausen and Willis O'Brien produce a 10-minute segment showing various dinosaurs at work and play in the Jurassic Age.

Any modern-day Harryhausen fan may well be totally unaware of this picture, or of the great man's involvement. The stop-motion animation sequence was shot in eight weeks on a bench top against painted prehistoric dioramas, Harryhausen and O'Brien using ball-and-socket jointed models and large-scale mechanical heads for close-ups. A Ceratosaurus, Brontosaurus, Allosaurus, Triceratops, Stegosaurus and T. Rex put in an appearance, the dino-action kicking off with the Brontosaurus gobbling up a caveman. But the mechanical heads were a complete disaster and really, apart from the novelty factor of seeing the animators' work in color (and it was far less fluid than their other releases), the only worthwhile shot was of the Allosaurus leaping into the frame off-camera. Originally running at 15 minutes, the British censor ordered cuts to some of the bloodier moments (the Ceratosaurus tearing the flesh from a Stegosaurus), deleting five minutes of footage and awarding the film a "U" rating, not the more restrictive "A" about which Warner Bros. were kicking up a fuss. This was to be the last time the two giants of this highly specialized form of cinematic special effects were to collaborate together.

The author fondly remembers purchasing a miniature movie projector in 1958 (in America, a View Master) that contained inside its red plastic case two minutes of flickering black-and-white footage taken from the Harryhausen/O'Brien segment in *The Animal World*. By turning the film strip via a small crank, this archaic method of viewing 8mm celluloid was the nearest a schoolboy could get in those days to owning, however small, a piece of the real thing. How times have changed!

Dementia is a gripping psychoanalytical essay into a twisted, tormented mind that dates from 1953. Originally running at 61 minutes, the picture was considered too strong for public consumption, re-cut to 56 minutes and released in America in 1955 under the alternate title *Daughter of Horror*—this is the movie that is showing at the local theater in *The Blob* as the gelatinous alien squeezes out of the projection booth. In Britain, it was banned for several years and eventually screened in 1957. John Parker directed under his own production company, or should that have been Bruno VeSoto,

who played a rich playboy? Were Parker and VeSoto one and the same? We will never know for certain.

Encompassing certain surreal cinematic traits to be found in the works of Orson Welles and Luis Bunuel, *Dementia* is without dialogue, the avant-garde music of George Antheil standing in for speech, augmented by some fine choral work from Marni Nixon (the singing voice of Maria in *West Side Story*). This is a one-woman *tour de force*, taking place over a single night: Adrienne Barrett (one of only two films she ever starred in), alone in a seedy hotel room on skid row, grabs a switchblade and ventures out of the lobby, passing a police officer arresting a guy who has just beaten up his girlfriend. Walking through the desolate streets, she runs into winos, pimps, bent cops and assorted sleaze balls. In a misty graveyard, she has visions of her abusive father whom she knifed to death after he had shot her slut of a mother; she's then picked up by overweight VeSoto, taken to his swanky pad and offered money to sleep with him. In revulsion, she stabs him; he topples out of a window, grasping her necklace. Outside, she hacks off his hand, still clutching the necklace, and is pursued by two cops. Entering a jazz club, the cops close in and she wakes in her hotel room. Has it all been a nightmarish dream? No! In a drawer is a severed hand, a necklace entwined around the stiff fingers. The camera slowly pans away from her begrimed window, leaving the woman locked in her own self-delusional world.

Enough psychological reference points exist in this impenetrable movie to get all those would-be psychiatrists reaching for their notepads. Barrett runs from waves pounding on a beach. The woman-beating incident comes to mind near the start. The lascivious attitude of men toward women brings on a feeling of repugnance (or sexual repression?) in Barrett whenever he faces physical intimacy. Also, the close-ups of leering, unattractive faces and men portrayed as slovenly, greedy, hard-drinking no-hopers who view the female of the species as nothing but objects to satisfy their lustful urges reinforce that attitude. The newspaper's headline "Mysterious Stabbing" keeps floating into view. And Barrett herself, slyly demure one minute, is screwed up with madness the next. A decade ahead of its time in technique and ideas, *Dementia* is bleak fare, a sick fantasy exploring mental illness and paranoia that has very few equals. It's also completely different from anything else that has been made on this particular subject. Maybe Roman Polanski's harrowing study in sexual inhibition, *Repulsion* (1965), comes closest to it.

1957

Although featuring Robby the Robot, MGM's *The Invisible Boy* wasn't, strictly speaking, a follow-up to *Forbidden Planet*. Producer Nicholas Nayfack quit MGM after *Forbidden Planet* was released, set up Pan Productions, persuaded writer Cyril Hume to fashion a story with Robby in the central role and came up with another take on *Tobor the Great*. Richard Eyer (the genie in *The 7th Voyage of Sinbad*) played the 10-year-old son of computer geek Philip Abbott, and the boy's uneasy relationship with his disciplinarian father paralleled that with Robby; both Abbott and the robot were megalomaniacs, forcing Eyer to disobey the pair of them at times. *The Invisible Boy* was a mix of adult sci-fi and children's adventure, director Herman Hoffman not quite pulling it off. When Robby and Eyer are up to their childish pranks, it's enjoyable, but in the lengthy section dealing with "who's been taken over by the super-computer," the pace slows to a crawl.

Abbott has created an intelligent computer that comes alive, motivated by survival; it plans to disassemble itself and reassemble on board a satellite (launched on a rocket), where it will dominate the Earth by dropping bombs on major cities. ("The revolt of the machine," states Abbott.) Eyer rebuilds Robby, only to have the computer take control of the robot's brain; it also implants electrodes in a chosen set of scientists led by General Harold J. Stone to ensure its plans are carried out. Robby makes Eyer invisible for a time and faces the might of the military in a full-blooded showdown, stomping toward the rocket with instructions to torture interfering Eyer, who is hiding on the control deck. But the lad also has influence over Robby and restores order by instructing his robotic pal to smash the rogue computer. In doing so, the world is saved and Eyer finds himself on much better terms with his father. As for Robby, he ends up as the family pet.

An amusing touch, and a nod of gratitude to *Forbidden Planet*—a faded photograph of Robby stepping off a starship; according to Abbott, he's from 300 years into the future. *The Invisible Boy* has some far-reaching notions on how powerful, and possibly dangerous, computers can become in the wrong hands, particularly the hands of "our friends across the Pole," as they guardedly refer to the Russians. The film is an unusual addition to '50s sci-fi, but maybe a little too deep for its subject matter; *Tobor the Great*, in a less flamboyant way, is the much more entertaining picture, and better fun as well.

United Artists' *Man on the Prowl* hasn't been seen for years, last screened in England in 1962 on a double bill with *It! The Terror from Beyond Space.* Another in a long line of lost psycho movies, James Best starred as a mentally unstable mommy's boy, in and out of psychiatric hospitals, first seen murdering a woman who has spurned his advances. Almost hitting Mala Powers and her young son on his motorbike as they cross a street, he inveigles himself into Powers' household by fixing her washing machine, wooing her because of her unhappy marriage to Jerry Paris—he's neglecting her, putting business before pleasure. Powers is happy to go along with Best's romantic overture to begin with, but when he forces her to kiss him at a motel, she begins to have second thoughts. Best's cranky mother (Vivi Janiss) later visits Powers, warning her off her son because of his instability—suffering from a psychotic illness. He's been in her care for five years and she knows all about his crimes and isn't going to squeal to the cops or his doctor. But Best witnesses the meeting; consumed with anger and jealousy, he nearly kills Paris at his car workshop (an engine falls on him), beats his mother to death and breaks into Powers' house where she's babysitting. After trying to rape her, the sociopath is stabbed in the stomach by Powers, who is armed with a nail file. Staggering to a window, Best is shot dead by a police marksman.

Art Napolean directed this 86-minute *noir*-style psychodrama, now seemingly consigned to cinema's forgotten past. It should be resurrected as a reminder to fans that darker-than-dark thrillers of this nature once existed long before Hitchcock terrified audiences in 1960 at the Bates Motel.

Columbia's *The Night the World Exploded* is one of the company's lower-grade '50s efforts, a 64-minute take on Universal's superior *The Monolith Monsters*, released the same year. Flatly directed by Fred F. Sears, the expanding crystals from outer space in John Sherwood's mini-classic become black stones from the Earth's center containing Element 112 in Sears' unexciting potboiler; they too expand (when exposed to air), absorbing nitrogen from the atmosphere, emitting gas and exploding, causing cataclysmic earthquakes. And like the crystals in *The Monolith Monsters*, water is the rock's nemesis (although not mixed with salt). The pressure generated by continuous earthquakes has left the Earth with a three-degree tilt, so the end of the world is nigh. Seismologist William Leslie, who has invented a machine that can predict earth tremors ("Once those lines jump, a million people face possible death."), advocates the flooding of lowland areas to neutralize the element, blowing up a dam near the end to prove his point and saving the planet from destruction.

A custom-made Sam Katzman quickie, *The Night the World Exploded*'s patchy plot slogs its way through one stock situation after another, with too much emphasis on news footage depicting earthquake disasters. A prolonged spell in a studio mock-up of the Carlsbad Caverns has Kathryn Grant freezing in fear on a 90-foot descent to view the lethal rock particles floating in a pool. Really, the only watchable thing in this picture is Grant, a sultry, dark-haired beauty who married Bing Crosby the year this film came out—and her looks were put to much better use the following year in *The 7th Voyage of Sinbad*.

Yet another dish of '50s opposition to Russian propaganda was served up in Columbia's *The 27th Day*, a movie that was often found sharing the bill with *20 Million Miles to Earth* on U.K. circuits during the early 1960s. Although the grim warnings of Soviet world domination were over-dramatized to the point of obsession, this enterprising sci-fi offering from William Asher intrigued from the start. Five disparate Earthlings picked at random are beamed aboard Arnold Moss's UFO (a snippet from *Earth vs. the Flying Saucers* is inserted for a few seconds): Reporter Gene Barry; English rose Valerie French; German scientist George Voskovec; Chinese agitator Marie Tsien and Russian soldier Azemat Janti. Alien Moss gives each a box housing three capsules; these capsules collectively contain enough radiation to wipe out all human life on Earth (but not animals or plants). Moss is from a dying planet; his people want to populate Earth but abhor harming intelligent life forms. So he's leaving it to the five to destroy mankind in a dignified manner ("Practice peace—or die!"). However, after a period of 27 days, the capsules will become ineffective, as they will be on the death of their owner; only the recipients of the boxes can open them by telepathy and, by reading out map coordinates, unleash the destructive power harnessed within the capsules. Armed with this appalling information, all five are beamed back to where they came from, with one thought on their minds: What do I do now?

What their reactions are to the unimaginable power they hold in their hands makes for fairly riveting viewing. As news of the alien and his five captives leaks out, French tosses her box into the sea and sets off for America to join forces with Barry, where they end up hiding from the authorities on a derelict army base. Tsien commits suicide, her capsules, placed on a shrine, turning to dust; Voskovec keeps quiet about the capsules' secret to his inquisitive scientific colleagues and Janti is bullied and tortured by ruthless General Stefan Schnabel into allowing the Soviets to use the capsules to dominate the world. This is where the picture overplays the Iron Curtain threat, Asher zeroing in on newspaper headlines screaming doom and gloom, worldwide panic the result of all the scaremongering. Eventually, Barry, French and Voskovec give themselves up; Voskovec deciphers cryptic etchings on the remaining capsules and reads out a series of longitudes and latitudes, thereby releasing high frequency sound waves that kill all those enemies of human freedom. Janti, in the meantime, has been shot in the back for trying to escape his torturers, so his capsules amount to nothing.

The payoff, Voskovec communicating with Moss and informing the alien that his race are free to find sanctuary on Earth and establish a new society based on peace and love ("People of Earth. We accept your invitation."), is simplistic in its arrant precept of how to achieve world harmony by refusing to allow those interfering commies to mess things up (was this film ever released in Russia?). Barry and French make a delightful American/English pairing and John Mantley's script, from his own novel, is intelligent and, at times, witty (French to Barry on hearing a group on the radio: "What's that?" Barry: "Rock 'n' Roll music—almost."). Rarely screened these days, *The 27th Day* may be one of Columbia's lesser movies from the mid-'50s, but it's interesting nonetheless and doesn't falter over its 75-minute running time.

1958

Director Irving Lerner and his leading man Vince Edwards, who scored a minor hit with Columbia/Orbit's X-certified *Murder by Contract* in early 1958, reunited for *City of Fear*, an Atomic Age *noir* thriller, again produced by independent outfit Orbit. Steven *The Werewolf* Ritch (he had a bit part in *Murder by Contract*) co-wrote the script and also stars as a doctor whose expertise is the atom. Edwards plays a brutal killer, escaping from San Quentin and intent on making a million bucks by selling what he believes to

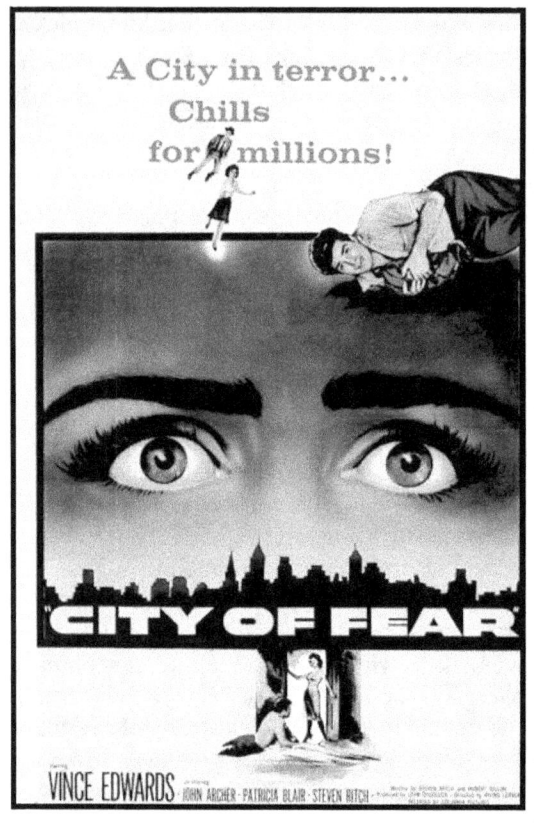

be a steel canister full of heroin ("One pound of snow."). Trouble is, that canister contains a granular form of cobalt 60, guaranteed to kill anyone who comes into contact with it within 84 hours. So when Edwards arrives in Los Angeles to take up where he left off with girlfriend Patricia Blair and ex-partner Joseph Mell, he's already a dying man but doesn't know it. The cops (Lyle Talbot and John Archer) don't want him anywhere near the city. ("He's a man holding the lives of three million people in his hands. That Ryker's loose with a cylinder of death that could wipe out a city.") They are desperate to track him down, almost going along with Ritch's extreme suggestion that lead suits and Geiger counters should, as a priority, be handed out to the public. With talk of mass evacuation and whether the mayor informs the public, the race is on to prevent Edwards, already developing a worrying cough and sweating profusely, from unknowingly contaminating millions with deadly radiation.

Lerner handles the action in typical '50s *noir* fashion: Jazzy score (Jerry Goldsmith); close-ups in shadow; terse dialogue; spare sets; a fast-talking dame; the introduction of seedy characters and gritty love scenes. If presented in a non-*noir* format, *City of Fear* would have been more borderline horror than police drama as the film treads a fine line between both genres. As it stands, it's an interesting hybrid that successfully gives out a dire warning of the perils to be faced by society if atomic radiation ran riot, bolstered by a mean performance from Edwards. After Blair succumbs to radiation poisoning and Mell is brutally murdered by Edwards, the cops close in on the criminal. Fatally sick and still refusing to believe that what he is carrying isn't heroin ("No! It's worth a million. It's a lie!" he cries, unable to break open the canister), Edwards is finally surrounded by the L.A. police force and dies in the gutter, a blanket thrown dispassionately over his corpse with a sign stating, "CAUTION. HIGH RADIATION." The final shot of this sign carries quite an impact, a fitting image that rounds off a tense, little-known atomic-based chiller.

Hack director William A. Berke, after spending years working on Westerns, war movies and seven *Jungle Jim* features, graduated to sensationalistic crime/social dramas, directing and producing a quartet of outstanding, largely undiscovered, genre examples between 1957 and 1958—*Four Boys and a Gun*, *Street of Sinners*, *Cop Hater* and *The Mugger*. All were distributed in England by United Artists and given "X" certificates.

Cop Hater is included here because of its psychotic overtones and realistic *noir* feel. The first adaptation of an Ed McBain novel, Berke's unflinchingly violent thriller, set in a city (New York? It's never mentioned) during a heat wave, had the whole of the 87th precinct mobilized in an effort to track down a psycho who is gunning down police officers out of hand. ("His crazy brain wants cops, cops, cops.") In a pared-down production where you can almost smell the sweat and cigarette smoke, Robert Loggia, engaged to deaf-mute Ellen Parker, investigates one petty loser after another, hampered by interfering reporter Gene Miller. When Loggia's partner, Gerald S. O'Loughlin, becomes the third victim (a fourth cop is killed by a gang in a related incident), the officer gets drunk and unwisely confides in Miller, criticizing the department's handling of the case, which Miller decides to publish. Following the damning newspaper headline, smarmy killer Hal Riddle enters Parker's apartment and is on the point of raping her at gunpoint when Loggia bursts in and, in a disturbing scene that wouldn't be allowed today, beats a confession out of the nutter—he's acting on instructions from another mental case, O'Loughlin's nymphomaniac wife, played with sluttish glee by Shirley Ballard. Upon her arrest, she declares her hatred of all cops, feels little remorse for her husband's death and blames the precinct for her unhappy marriage and lousy life.

A lost 75-minute gem, *Cop Hater* trounces by a mile many bigger-budgeted crime/psycho productions released in this decade. Berke's sleazy vision of an urban jungle inhabited by all kinds of losers and wanton dolls out for a good time may come across as trashy, exploitative fodder (Albert Glasser's smoky score is a great mood piece) but, for its time, this was brave filmmaking indeed from a minor talent, with its over-emphasis on police brutality and upfront sexual attitudes. United Artists issued many fine, hard-hitting X-rated (in Britain) dramas of this type during the 1950s (*Big House, U.S.A.*; *Black Tuesday*; *Baby Face Nelson*; *The Last Mile*); like *Cop Hater*, most haven't been seen for years. Fans don't know what they're missing: For instance, Edward G. Robinson's electrifying star turn as an insane killer breaking out of Death Row in *Black Tuesday* is the psychotic killer personified, yet this brilliant movie has never been afforded a digital release. Why?

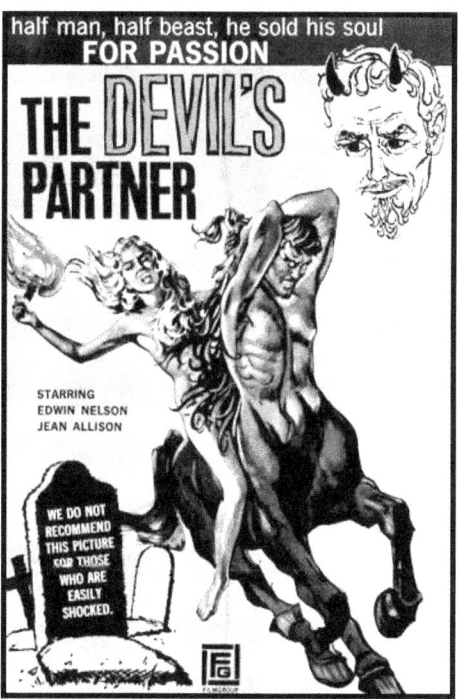

Not surfacing until 1961 through Roger Corman's Filmgroup, Huron Productions' *Devil's Partner* was a low-budget take on the Faust legend, starring B regular Ed Nelson as the man in league with the Devil. Nelson is a crippled hermit living in a rat-infested shack. One night, he slits a goat's throat, spreads blood on the corners of a hexagon and covers the carving with a goat's skin. The inscription "I Give My Soul for 2 Years" materializes on the skin and a clawed hand reaches out to the hermit who faints.

Next we see clean-cut Nelson exiting a bus in the town of Furnace Flats, letting on to everybody that he's the hermit's nephew. We know differently, of course—sweltering heat doesn't bother him, he calls himself "Nick" and he possesses the ability to bend animals to his will. People he takes a dislike to are disfigured (Richard Crane receives a jagged scar across the face when his dog attacks him), killed in a road accident (the plastic surgeon on his way to repair Crane's features crashes into a stray cow) or trampled on by a horse (Byron Foulger, an interfering old loner). Devilish Nelson also takes a shine to Jean Allison, Crane's fiancée, but she's sticking by her man, scar or no scar. After a reasonably sinister 73 minutes in which director Charles R. Rondeau, assisted by Ronald Stein's spooky score, moves matters along at a nifty pace, we are treated to a double transformation scene: A rampaging horse is shot by the sheriff; the horse, dying, morphs into Nelson; and Nelson, drawing his final breath, changes into the werewolf-looking hermit. The devil-worshipper gone to meet his maker, Crane's livid scar disappears.

None other than grizzled screen veteran Edgar Buchanan has a part in this picture, playing the town's doctor, but you won't find *Devil's Partner* listed on his filmography, or in many film compendiums, come to that. Another minor '50s production that remains unknown to most fans, this is an interesting little foray into the world of the satanic, ably acted and competently directed, with a neat line in sardonic throwaways, "I'm really the Devil," Nelson tells the sheriff. "Gets kinda hot down there!" It has "American International" stamped all over it, which is no bad thing!

The Monster That Challenged the World, *The Black Sleep*, *The Four Skulls of Jonathan Drake* and *I Bury the Living* are just four examples of the fine, and much underrated, output from United Artists that filled auditoriums in English cinemas on a Sunday afternoon. But *The Flame Barrier*, on the same company's roster, very rarely showed up. Although directed by Paul Landres and produced by Jules V. Levy and Arthur Gardner (the same team behind the excellent *The Vampire* and *The Fantastic Disappearing Man*), *The Flame Barrier* is a substandard "blob" jungle movie bearing an odd resemblance to Regal's *The Unknown Terror* and *Space Master X-7*. In fact, if shot in widescreen, the movie would have been perfectly acceptable as a Regal International production. But as part of the United Artists stable, it fails to impress.

Kathleen Crowley arrives in Mexico and hires warring brothers Arthur Franz and Robert Brown to track down her missing husband. After a satellite, launched from Rocket X117, crashed to Earth, Crowley's husband disappeared when searching for it in the Yucatan jungles. Three native bearers join the team; the skeletal remains of two others are found later on in the undergrowth. And 45-odd minutes into the picture, Crowley gets to smooch with Franz (she's obviously forgotten all about her wealthy husband). Thirteen minutes later, a cave is discovered, at the rear of which is the wrecked satellite coated in a protoplasmic goo, the head of Cowley's husband pokes up incongruously from the mass. The glowing alien entity shoots out deadly rays, stripping bodies of flesh and reducing them to skeletons, and it is doubling in size every two hours. In other words, it's on a course to conquer the Earth! Franz ascertains that the satellite is positioned across two metallic lodes; by connecting conductors from a solar battery to the rock walls, he can electrocute the organism. Brown slips into the blob after fixing a terminal and gets fried; Franz flips a switch and destroys the thing, leaving the cave arm-in-arm with Crowley.

Landres builds up some suspense in the jungle scenes, helped by Gerald Fried's pumping score, but in a 70-minute feature, just over 10 minutes dedicated to monster action simply isn't enough to rouse the interest. A-rated in Britain, *The Flame Barrier* ranks as one of United Artists' poorest sci-fi outings from the 1950s, and least-remembered by buffs.

Years before moviemakers hit upon the idea of creating motion pictures built around the theme of an object from outer space colliding with Earth and causing widespread catastrophes, William A. Berke Productions' *The Lost Missile* had an alien missile doing just that. Traveling at 4,000 miles per hour at low altitude and radiating a million-degree heat, this sleek vessel from regions unknown leaves a scorching path in its wake, melting snow on mountains, destroying jet fighters, turning oceans into steam, setting forests ablaze and incinerating humans. Ottawa is on the brink of total destruction, with New York next on the missile's list. Can scientist Robert Loggia devise a method to stop the missile in its tracks *and* keep fiancée Ellen Parker happy at the same time? ("Well, marry your hydrogen warhead!" she storms at him.) The impatient lass wants to get married pronto, end of the world or no end of the world (the two had starred together in *Cop Hater*).

Berke himself was to direct but died of a heart attack on the first day of shooting, at age 54. Son Lester W. Berke took over the reins to complete what would have been his father's one and only science fiction movie.

At least 25% of the film's 72-minute length is taken up by stock footage, but as a low-budget forerunner to all those '70s disaster epics, *The Lost Missile* passes muster; the effects are minimal but they pack a fair punch, the documentary approach (Lawrence Dobkin narrates the events) drums up a real sense of impending destruction and there are

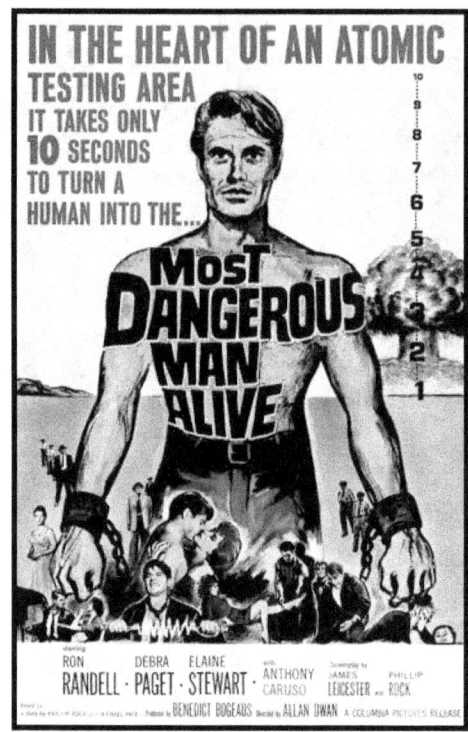

some satisfying human touches inserted to raise the fear factor (children evacuated; people taking shelter in subway tunnels; a man desperate to be with his wife who has just given birth). And no happy ending for hero Loggia, either—he perishes from radium poisoning after inserting a miniature hydrogen bomb into a rocket's warhead; the rocket blasts off, launches the bomb at the missile and blows it out of the sky, saving New York after Ottawa has been reduced to ashes. Containing an unusually laid-back score from Gerald Fried, *The Lost Missile* may appear antique by today's standards, but those million-dollar blockbusters had to get their inspiration from somewhere—perhaps it could have been from barnstorming little actioners like this.

What a shame that veteran director Allan Dwan's swansong should turn out to be so dull that it was shelved until 1961 (for U.S. release) and 1963 (for U.K. release). The man who brought us such treasures as the silent version of *Robin Hood* (1922), *Rebecca of Sunnybrook Farm* (1938) and *Sands of Iwo Jima* (1949) floundered with his very last picture, Trans-Global's *Most Dangerous Man Alive*. Basically an inferior retread of Lon Chaney's invigorating *Indestructible Man*, Ron Randall plays a gangster on the run that wanders into a nuclear test area. A cobalt bomb explodes but Randall somehow survives the blast, radiation (from Cobalt Element X) causes his tissue to gradually mutate into steel; full of hate, he goes after slimy business partner Anthony Caruso, who framed him for murder. Debra Paget and Elaine Stewart are the two dames in Randall's life, the ubiquitous Morris Ankrum (looking grumpier than usual) is the token cop while caring scientist Tudor Owen wants to help the gangster by finding a method to halt his unforeseen transformation. ("10,000 volts of electricity wouldn't kill him. He's more steel than human!")

It's a promising scenario, although tackled many times before in this decade (*The Amazing Colossal Man*; *The Hideous Sun Demon*), so where exactly does *Most Dangerous Man Alive* go wrong? The movie is stagnant in places, Dwan's direction lacks urgency; in a couple of scenes, notably the police roadblock set up to trap Randall, who is driving a truck loaded with dynamite, dramatic thrust lapses to such an extent that it's almost like watching an outtake of the film destined for the cutting room floor, not the film itself. Randall, hardly the most charismatic of actors, staggers around in a torn shirt and tie, absent a lot of the time as Dwan dwells on Caruso and his cronies' buffoonish attempts to evade their bulletproof ex-colleague. One or two bursts of amusing dialogue ("I'm not flesh anymore, I'm steel. You understand? Steel!") and a lively final five minutes (Randall throws Caruso over the edge of a quarry and is reduced to dust by flamethrowers) fail to ignite the spark. Even Columbia, who distributed the movie, couldn't save it from being one of the poorest "man affected by radiation" outings of the 1950s. A turgid mix of sci-fi and mob melodrama simply doesn't hold the interest of viewers.

Hitchcock's personal favorite, *Shadow of a Doubt* (1942), resurfaced as a remake in 1958 under the guise of *Step Down to Terror*. Harry Keller directed one of Universal's least-known thrillers, Charles Drake starring as a mother-fixated schizoid who murders wealthy widows for their money and diamond jewelry—and all this two years before Anthony Perkins in *Psycho*! For Norman Bates, substitute Johnny Walters; Drake was a little on the bulky side to successfully pull the role off but still managed to switch from nice guy to heartless killer with a certain amount of aplomb.

After an absence of six years, Drake turns up at his mother's house, makes himself at home and focuses his attention on his brother's attractive widow (Colleen Miller). Mum (Josephine Hutchinson) frets over her boy and his repeated headaches while Miller's seven-year-old son, Ricky Kelman, starts to bond with him. But why does Drake, on the surface a mild-mannered guy, fly off the handle at the least provocation? The ring that he gives Miller ("It always bothers me when I see beautiful stones on undeserving fingers.") is inscribed "RD to JD." Who are those people? Where does all that cash come from he's stashing in a bag? What was so important about that article he tears out of a newspaper? And who exactly is Rod Taylor, supposedly conducting interviews into American suburbia ("Typical street, typical town.") but keeping one eye firmly fixed on the shifty Drake? These are the enticing morsels Keller drops into the viewer's lap as Miller begins to wonder what kind of a monster Drake really is. Her concerns appear to be well founded when Drake runs over Kelman's new bike on purpose (he had an accident on one when he was a child) and she reads the missing article in the library that screams, "The Traveling Murderer at Large." He also informs Miller that all women are "stupid parasites dripping with diamonds," not the kind of comment designed to get her into bed.

Over the space of 76 minutes, Keller raises the suspense level by cramming in every kind of stock psycho twist and turn fans might concoct: Miller tells Drake to get out of the house, convinced he's the killer; Drake switches his interest from Miller to a neighboring jewel-encrusted widow; Taylor is a cop, on Drake's tail; Drake tampers with the outside wooden staircase, almost causing Miller to tumble to her death and finally, the nutter spikes his sister-in-law's milky drink but she survives, thanks to hunky Taylor who has fallen hook, line and sinker for her dark-haired charms and reckons she's safe from Drake's predatory instincts inside the house. ("He can't make a fuss in front of his mother. He loves her.") Drake finally meets his comeuppance in a car crash after he drives off from the house and swerves to avoid hitting a child on a bike. At his funeral, Hutchinson still holds the opinion that her son was a

sweet-natured soul who didn't possess a bad bone in his body, even though *we* know he murdered in excess of three women. And Taylor gets Miller all to himself.

Note: Astute soundtrack listeners will twig that producer Joseph Gershenson used short passages from *Tarantula* in the early scenes to heighten the tension. It works for anyone who hasn't seen Jack Arnold's giant spider classic; if you have (and most have!), you'd half expect to see John Agar, Mara Corday and Leo G. Carroll wander on set at any moment!

"Filmed in Psycho-Rama! The Fourth Dimension!" screamed the posters when Howco International's *Terror in the Haunted House* (aka *My World Dies Screaming*) made it onto the British circuits in late 1961, playing second feature to the King Brothers' monster movie *Gorgo*. This sub-*Rebecca* psychological potboiler was unique in using subliminal images throughout its 78-minute running time (the uncut print is 84 minutes) to get its message across; a devil face, a bug-eyed face, a skull (in red), a cobra head and the message "Scream Bloody Murder" were flashed up at intervals, a persuasive technique banned in the United Kingdom from 1962 onward. Because of the possible effect of this mental-imprint on young children's minds, the movie was given an "X" rating.

An opening subjective chat with a psychiatrist in which Cathy O'Donnell tells of her recurring nightmares involving an old mansion lays the plot foundations. Following a whirlwind courtship, Gerald Mohr takes his bride, O'Donnell, to a rented house in Florida upsetting the girl no end; this is the identical place she's had visions of since meeting Mohr. In particular, O'Donnell is terrified at the thought of what lies behind the door to the attic. ("Death awaits me in its most hideous form at the top of those stairs," she wails.) Grizzled old caretaker John Qualen, resembling Adolf Hitler's long-lost father, mooches about the Gothic edifice, knowing more than he lets on, while owner William Ching comes and goes, appearing increasingly nervous on each visit. A falling chandelier almost crushes O'Donnell, leaving us wondering whether or not Mohr is trying to drive his young wife insane and, if so, why? And who pushed Qualen down the stairs to his death? After a lot of verbose head-to-heads relating to convoluted family secrets, and O'Donnell passing out every few minutes from fright, it transpires that the poor girl knew Mohr when they were children living together in the house (their initials are carved on a tree). When seven, she witnessed the axe murders of her entire family in the upstairs attic by Qualen. Traumatized, O'Donnell subsequently spent years in a sanitarium. Mohr has brought her back to use shock tactics in the hope that this will unblock her mind; when madman Ching attempts to slaughter her and Mohr with an ax in the attic, her memory returns. Ching falls on the ax-head and dies, leaving the newlyweds to walk away from the accursed place and start a new life.

As downbeat as the worry lines on Mohr's morose features, *Terror in the Haunted House* is blessed with an excellent performance from O'Donnell as the screwed-up bride. Along with Darrell Calker's score, blasting away at every given opportunity, it's a psychodrama that, although indifferently directed by Harold Daniels, is worth a look, if only to see how it was all done without the aid of copious amounts of Technicolor blood and gore that signified the psycho thrillers of the upcoming decades.

Ib Melchior's garishly distorted vision of the Red Planet is a treat for the eyes, from *The Angry Red Planet*.

1959

Rocketship MR1 has returned from Mars and is orbiting Earth. Scientists, worried that their repeated messages to the ship have met with no response, bring it down in Nevada. ("That thing up there. It's a flying coffin," states a soldier.) Traumatized Nora Hayden appears unsteadily in the rocket hatchway; Captain Gerald Mohr is carried out on a stretcher, a green slime coating his right arm, while the other two members of the crew (Les Tremayne and Jack Kruschen) are missing. Was director Ib Melchior's *The Angry Red Planet* trying to ape *The Quatermass Experiment* in this long opening sequence? It's an intriguing appetizer to an intriguing end-of-the-decade sci-fi actioner that is a bit more wacky than most, containing startling images guaranteed to please the fantasy brigade.

Given a drug to restore her memory, Hayden recounts the mission's story from her hospital bed. After dodging a meteor (it doesn't prevent the girl from dabbing perfume behind her ears, a nice human touch amid all the shipboard activity), the MR1 lands on a Martian surface bathed in a red/pink light, perfectly matching Hayden's flaming locks ("Shall we go out and claim the planet in the name of Brooklyn?" asks Kruschen). Outside in a weird jungle, green, three-eyed Martians, giant man-eating plants with tentacles and a huge alien aberration combining the characteristics of a bat, a rat, a spider and a crab ("King Kong's big brother.") greets the astronauts; an ameba-type monster with rotating eyes skulks in a silvery lake while, in the distance, strange buildings reach into the sky. Shot in Cinemagic (or New Eastman 5250), Melchior's garishly distorted vision of the Red Planet is a treat for the eyes; composer Paul Dunlap astutely keeps his score to a minimum, allowing the unique effects to take over and work their magic. Kruschen is gobbled up by one of the Martian blobs and absorbed into its see-through stomach, and Tremaine suffers a fatal heart attack. Blasting off with a Martian warning ringing in her ears, Hayden makes it to Earth, along with Mohr who is coated in goo from the ameba, which is where we came in.

Mohr's alien infection is successfully treated, enabling him to play house with Hayden who lets her hair down in the closing minutes, and although the ship's tapes were wiped clean by the Martians, one is left intact with a stern message: "Do not return to Mars. We will destroy you." No wonder no Man has ever set foot on the planet since the date of this diverting little space opera! Released in late 1959, *The Angry Red Planet* has a definite '60s feel to it; not surprising, really, with the new decade (and a new way of presenting fare such as this) looming on the horizon.

Paramount's *Destination Space* is included here because it forms part of John Agar's '50s repertoire of fantasy/sci-fi pictures, even though it was developed as a pilot for a television series that, figuratively speaking, never took off. Coming in at just under 52 minutes and using a great deal of special effects footage from *Conquest of Space* to save on costs, Agar's role was secondary to that of Harry Townes as a billionaire entrepreneur supervising a rocket launch to the moon on board a space station dubbed the "BB" after the billions he has spent on it. When a meteoroid glances across the station's hull, causing serious damage, the launch is aborted; Townes has to return to Earth to convince a cynical Senate committee that the space program, despite expensive setbacks, is vital in promoting America as the world leader in space technology. "The space station isn't a white elephant," he states emphatically, pleading his case.

Showing insufficient signs of promise, this production has all the hallmarks of a TV space opera with nowhere to go. After the lengthy inquest into what went wrong with the rocket launch, we have a wordy spell in a restaurant with Townes, fiancée Whitney Blake and Gail Kobe; Kobe blames Townes for keeping her husband up in the station for too long and then, when Blake goes to powder her nose, states that's she's fallen in love with him. Back on the station with a Senate observer in tow, launch number two is also postponed when ice causes the rocket's nuclear drive to overheat, almost resulting in the first atomic explosion in outer space. "More delays," yells Agar, snapping his pencil in frustration, a cue for the movie to come to an abrupt end, leaving enough loose threads to spin a cobweb.

Joseph Pevney's direction is superficial to put it mildly, old-timer Cecil Kellaway stands around pulling faces and doing very little and fan favorite Agar's talents are definitely *not* put to good use (the usually affable actor looks distinctly fed up with the whole business). The only excitement to be had is watching clips from *Conquest of Space* in black-and-white, not color. It's hardly surprising, on this showing, that Paramount and CBS pulled the plug on the teleseries. This is of historical interest only to diehard fans and Agar-watchers.

William J. Hole, Jr., the man behind drive-in favorite *The Ghost of Dragstrip Hollow* (1959), also directed the virtually unknown devil cult quickie *The Devil's Hand* (Crown International). The film was mothballed until 1961, subsequently given a desultory release in the United Kingdom in 1962 on a double bill with Roger Corman's *The Undead* (1956). Almost like a Corman production, a small cast acts between four sets (an apartment; a hospital; a shop; a crypt); this is an undiscovered treasure that deserves wider acclaim. The director involves the audience from the outset and never lets up over 71 minutes: Robert Alda (Alan Alda's father) is troubled by repeated dreams of a blonde woman (Linda Christian) in a diaphanous gown, giving him the come-on. Lured to a doll boutique by Christian's "mental projections," he finds a doll of her on display, together with a doll of his fiancée, Ariadna Welter. The shop's owner, Neil Hamilton (Commissioner Gordon from the *Batman* TV series) sells Alda the blonde-haired doll and sticks a pin in the other, causing Welter to suffer a heart seizure, whereupon she's hospitalized. Alda meets the bewitching Christian, becomes infatuated with her and soon finds himself enrolled as a member of a cult worshiping Gamba the Great Devil God. The satanic ceremonies take place during the full moon in a crypt under loony Hamilton's shop—he's the self-appointed High Executioner and newcomers have to undergo a *Pit and the Pendulum*-type ordeal to prove their loyalty, a spinning wheel with eight sheaths slowly lowered onto their bodies, one of which contains a knife. As a test of Alda's loyalty, Welter is abducted from the hospital to be the next sacrificial lamb. Breaking free of Christian's spell, Alda rescues his girl, Hamilton is knifed to death by his own fiendish device and the house goes up in a blazing inferno. But as the couple drives off into the night, High Priestess Christian is still around; she loves Alda and wants to get her claws back into him.

Granted it has economical production values, but *The Devil's Hand* has a polish about it that many low-budget thrillers of this type don't possess, and it doesn't hang about, either; it's surprising that in the annals of horror movies, this engaging little black magic outing seems to have disappeared off the face of the earth. And although not really fitting in with the action, the surf instrumental played over the opening credits is extremely catchy.

Chapter 9
Chaney, Karloff and Lugosi in the 1950s

In 1950, Lon Chaney, Jr. was 44 years old, Boris Karloff, 63 and Bela Lugosi, 68. All three horror icons suffered from health issues: Chaney nursed a drink problem, Karloff relied on drugs to ease a lifelong battle with back pain and Lugosi was dependent so much on morphine and methadone to alleviate sciatica that he was now classed as an addict. The glory days for these premier horror actors were well and truly behind them, their string of '30s and '40s classics fast receding into the twilight zone as the new decade's array of X-rated monsters born of the atomic bomb loomed on the horizon. Lugosi had been released from his Universal-International contract (Karloff and Chaney were still with them, just) so all were free to lend their talents to any interested party, if there were any out there. But apart from their famous names, impeccable horror credentials and box-office reputations, what could these stalwarts bring to the atomic-powered stage that was getting rapidly underway with the likes of *The Thing from Another World*, *Destination Moon* and *The Day the Earth Stood Still*.

Of the three, Chaney was far more suited to the '50s Atom Age manifesto than Karloff and Lugosi were, and, in his favor, was a few years younger as well. Many viewed Karloff and Lugosi as being somewhat old hat, their shadowy antics belonging to another era, not fitting in with the contemporary, fast-developing method of fantasy filmmaking, a defining shift away from how things *used* to be done. Chaney wasn't as subtle an actor as the other two could be; his bruising, menacing persona was more than adequate in efforts like *Indestructible Man* and *The Alligator People*, two films that Karloff and Lugosi would never have been asked to appear in. On the other hand, Chaney lacked the versatility to handle the dexterity evident in Karloff's *Grip of the Strangler*, a film that confirmed just how much an underrated actor the Englishman was. And Lugosi, ignored by the major studios (and even the independents) and hampered, some said, by a thick Hungarian accent, wouldn't have featured in *any* of these pictures, a forlorn, washed-up has-been criminally neglected by Hollywood producers, content to take whatever crumbs were offered to him (mostly from Ed Wood) for meager wages, however small the role.

So as the 1950s beckoned, their collective talents spread out into television as well as the cinema; Chaney and Karloff, in particular, made a prodigious number of forays into the world of the small screen. In this respect, Chaney is probably best remembered for his role as Chingachgook in 39 episodes of *Hawkeye and the Last of the Mohicans* (1957). The two also starred in suspense dramas, Westerns, mystery shows and crime thrillers, often cast as the heavy. However, between 1950-1959, the horror output from all three, weighed up against the previous two decades, was minimal. Chaney starred in seven horror films, Karloff also appeared in seven, with Lugosi limited to only five (or seven if you include *Glen or Glenda?* and the elusive *Lock Up Your Daughters*). The films involved ranged from the excellent (*Grip of the Strangler* and *The Black Sleep*) to the good (*The Cyclops* and *Frankenstein 1970*) to the poor (*Plan 9 from Outer Space* and *Voodoo Island*). By the end of the decade, ready to enter the 1960s, Chaney was appearing in a lot of low-budget fare, a hulking brute saying very little, while Karloff was still going strong, showing up in any number of foreign horror features (and earn-ing mega-bucks in the process) and Lugosi, having spent so much time portraying one of the dead and a pale shadow of his former self, had passed on in 1956. So what did these three former "Titans of Terror" actually achieve in the 1950s? In the previous 20 years, they had been the standard-bearers of their generation—but not any longer. Could any of what they appeared in be perceived as worthwhile? Let's take a closer look.

The uncomfortable looking Lon Chaney in his police uniform, along with old crone Gisela Werbisek, from *Bride of the Gorilla*

Most film fans would admit that Lon Chaney, Jr. was not the most flexible of actors, but this lack of range didn't prevent him from being continually in work; he was much in demand during the 1950s, turning up in a phenomenal amount of TV programs as well as a handful of classic non-horror features—*High Noon*, *The Indian Fighter*, *Springfield Rifle*, *I Died a Thousand Times* and *The Defiant Ones* are just five of the many high quality pictures that can be included on Chaney's extensive résumé. His employment in '50s horror movies got off to an inauspicious start; he was cast, against type, as a police commissioner in Curt Siodmak's silly man-into-ape potboiler, *Bride of the Gorilla*, filmed over seven days and released in 1951 by low-rent producers Realart Pictures. In a risible plot that was played commendably straight by all concerned, barrel-chested Raymond Burr starred as the roughneck manager of a rubber plantation, in love with the owner's (Paul Cavanagh) wife, blonde bombshell Barbara Payton. Following an argument, Cavanagh is punched to the ground by Burr and dies from a snakebite. This leaves Burr free to marry the not-so-grieving widow but, unbeknown to him, Cavanagh's death has been spotted by native medicine lady Gisela Werbisek. In revenge, the old crone spikes Burr's wedding drink with a potion made from deadly leaves, casts a spell and before you know it, Burr is undergoing a transformation from hunk to huge ape, running off into the jungle and leaving behind a very bemused Payton. After much coming and going amid the lush vegetation, the couple is shot dead by Chaney and Tom Conway, Burr changing back to human form.

Chaney looked uncomfortable in police uniform and was no doubt hired for his name, the film echoing the supernatural jungle dramas of the 1930s and 1940s. Utilizing the same jungle settings that appeared a year later in *Bela Lugosi Meets a Brooklyn Gorilla*, *Bride of the Gorilla* is put together with a certain amount of dash by Siodmak and keeps the action going over its short 65-minute running time, but it's hardly top drawer horror fodder and one wonders why Chaney ever bothered with it.

Universal's *The Black Castle* (1952) appears now to be a last-ditch effort to revive their cobwebby Gothic melodramas of the 1940s and to hammer home the point, musical plagiarist Joseph Gershenson included passages from *Frankenstein Meets the Wolf Man*, *House of Frankenstein* and the *Mummy* movies in the soundtrack. Chaney, mute (what

Boris Karloff plays the kindly phsycian, holding the catatonic-inducing drug, from *The Black Castle*.

was it with the actor and scriptwriters? This was his fourth non-speaking part in the '50s), played Gargon, Count Stephen McNally's chief henchman. Richard Greene (soon to star in England's long-running *Robin Hood* TV series) infiltrates the sadistic McNally's castle under an assumed name to make him pay for murdering two of his best friends in a "hunt for humans" game (as in *The Hounds of Zaroff;* aka *The Most Dangerous Dame*). Greene promptly falls head-over-heels in love with the Count's unhappy wife, Paula Corday. When Greene's ruse is finally let out of the bag and he's incarcerated in a dungeon with Corday, kindly physician Boris Karloff devises an escape plan: He administers the *Romeo and Juliet* couple a drug which places them in a catatonic state. McNally, thinking the two are safely out of the way, opens Greene's coffin to make sure he's not alive and is shot dead. As for Chaney, he meets his fate by tumbling into a pool full of alligators; Karloff is stabbed to death.

Secret passages, torture chambers and gloomy dungeons appear in *The Black Castle*, plus the film features an Edgar Allan Poe sting in its tail. But it seems like a throwback to the previous two decades, a dusty, worn-out Gothic genre that both Hammer and Roger Corman successfully revived in Technicolor much later. A-rated in Britain, Nathan Juran (his directorial debut) could have injected a bit more spice into the stodgy mix and upped it into the "Adults Only" category to make the picture more gripping. As it is, *The Black Castle* is too talkative and unexciting; Chaney's brutish character is instantly forgettable, particularly when offset against Karloff's shadowy performance as the benevolent doctor. It was in this year that Chaney parted company with Universal-International to seek greener pastures with other studios.

His next four horror pictures fully demonstrated the no-nonsense Chaney style of acting: coarse, blustering and forceful, basic heavy stuff with no frills attached. Chaney's very name, in the eyes of the fans, related to X-rated horror and this quartet proved to be popular hits partly *because* of that name. *Indestructible Man* is the only '50s movie to give him star billing and his ability to portray the kind of person you wouldn't want to meet down a dark alley was put to good use in this fast-moving thriller (reviewed in chapter 13). In the film, his character (a gangster brought back from the dead), apart from a short dialogue at the beginning, was mute. He was mute again in *The Black Sleep*, playing Mungo, a former doctor who, thanks to Basil Rathbone's experiments in unorthodox brain surgery, had been turned into a half-mad strangler, controlled by Phyllis Stanley. Staggering around on set like Quasimodo minus his hump, with an unhealthy penchant for directing his homicidal tendencies toward his own sister, Chaney had little to do but to put on a menacing stare, ending up strangled to death by one of Rathbone's deviants. But he did receive third billing (above Lugosi, which didn't go down too well between the pair), proving once again that his name alone was synonymous with horror and would guarantee fans paying to see the flick, whether it was good, bad or indifferent. Notwithstanding unfavorable comments in some quarters, *The Black Sleep* is solid mad doctor fare, illustrative of '50s Gothic with a dash of the '40s about it, despite the trio of Chaney, Lugosi and John Carradine being way past their prime. (Ironically, Carradine himself took star billing as a mad doctor in Republic's *The Unearthly* [1957], a cheaper copy of *The Black Sleep*. This counted as one of the actor's best '50s horror performances.)

The Cyclops (reviewed in chapter five) had Chaney playing a bullish prospector, on the hunt for uranium deposits in Mexico. Once he discovers them, all interest in searching for Gloria Talbott's missing fiancé goes out of the window, and he spends most of his screen time bellyaching over the fact that *he* wants to go back to civilization while the rest of Talbott's party don't. It was an unsympathetic part, but it suited Chaney's belligerent acting method; to be honest, when his character was finished off by the one-eyed disfigured giant, the movie fell flat, which says a lot for his on-screen charisma, if you could call it that.

Fox's X-rated *The Alligator People* (1959) served up a tasty dish to young horror buffs in the late 1950s— it was directed by Roy del Ruth in pin-sharp CinemaScope, had imaginative man-into-reptilian creatures, an involved plot and a good score by Irving Gertz. Attractive Beverly Garland played the damsel in distress, the requisite eye-candy to many under-16-year-olds who had managed to sneak into a cinema and catch it. Furthermore, Chaney as a grizzled, alligator-hating, hook-handed, alcoholic hick who lusts after Garland turned in a marvelous over-the-top-performance, one of his best from this period. Chaney also loathes Richard Crane, Garland's missing husband, who is the subject of George Macready's radiation-based experiments in limb-replacement. "I'll kill you, Alligator Man," he roars, after Crane has rescued Garland from his clutches. "Just like I kill any four-legged 'gator. You hear me? I'll kill ya!" But the tables are turned in the explosive climax; Chaney bursts into Macready's laboratory just as Crane emerges from the steam sporting an alligator's head, and the bumpkin, shocked at Crane's transformation, is electrocuted on cables.

Chaney's final '50s horror flick was a real oddity, Mexico's *La Casa del Terror* (1959). Many Mexican horror/sci-fi movies contain a chaotic comedy element and this was no exception to the rule—funnyman Tin Tan (aka German Valdes) was roped in to supply the zany interludes in a story concerning a mad doctor (Yerye Beirute) pinching corpses in an attempt to resurrect the dead. A portly looking mummy (Lon Chaney,

A Mexican lobby card from *La Casa del Terror*, released in 1964 as *Face of the Screaming Werewolf*.

light years away from his 1940s Kharis) is spirited from an exhibition and pumped full of blood and electricity in Beirute's laboratory; when revived, Chaney, the former mummy, turns into a wolf man. During the full moon, the monster embarks on a rampage in the city, savaging several women and carrying off Tin Tan's girlfriend, Yolanda Varela, to the lab. Tin Tan confronts the werewolf and, in a tussle, Chaney and Beirute perish as the laboratory, which in time-honored fashion, goes up in flames.

La Casa del Terror is like a proposed production of *Abbott and Costello Meet the Wolf Man* minus the talents of Abbott and Costello! Baseball-cap perched over constantly mugging features, Tin Tan's silly antics patently fail to hit the funnybone and become tiresome; Beirute bears an uncanny resemblance to a young Boris Karloff; Chaney's werewolf make-up is similar in design to Jack Pierce's legendary Wolf Man; and what on earth are snippets from *Forbidden Planet*'s soundtrack doing in the laboratory sequences? Throw in references to Universal's '40s horror output, *House of Wax* (Beirute's "failures" are housed in a wax museum) and even *King Kong* (Chaney scrambling up the sides of buildings with the damsel in distress draped over his shoulders) and you have a ragbag of ideas filched from all manner of genre classics. Whether it works as a pastiche or not is open to conjecture and one's like, or dislike, of horror comedies. Cut out the Tin Tan bits and you would have an above-average Mexican parody of an American werewolf movie (the metamorphosis effects are first-rate). Even Chaney looked ill at ease in his wolf man role, realizing he was never going to repeat the success of his beloved Lawrence Talbot. (Note: None other than Jerry Warren laid his hands on this film, restructured [i.e. butchered] it and released his chopped-up product as *Face of the Screaming Werewolf* in 1964. Avoid at all costs!)

To sum up, Chaney's '50s output is fitful to put it mildly; *Indestructible Man* was Chaney incarnate, his low-budget winner, where he could put to effective use his three primary acting traits: puzzled, dim or angry. Despite his limitations, he seemed sadly underused in many respects during the '50s. Producers had little regard to his classic '40s *Wolf Man* and *Mummy* series and bypassed him in favor of a new breed of more natural (and younger) horror actors such as John Agar, Richard Carlson and Richard Denning. His main body of work in this decade lies in television and non-horror pictures. Seven horror outings over nine years is a lean return for a man who once thrilled audiences as the cursed Lawrence Talbot, loping through five Universal-International *Wolf Man* classics (including *Abbott and Costello Meets Frankenstein*)—Chaney's "baby" as he once termed the part; none of what he appeared in during the 1950s could ever be classed as such.

King Karloff fared much better in the '50s; his seven horror features, although a varied bag, all contained worthwhile performances, but then Karloff was one of those highly accomplished actors who very rarely turned in a below-par show whatever he appeared in. Authoritative, reliable, his mellifluous tones edged with a slight lisp, Karloff was a more consummate reader of character than Chaney and Lugosi, bringing hidden depths to his roles; moreover, his *Frankenstein* association and glowering screen presence stood him in good stead with the upcoming generation of horror filmmakers, so in a way it's surprising that he starred in only seven horror pictures between 1951 and 1958. Like Chaney, his television work-rate was incredible; he also lent his services to Italy in the seldom-seen oddity *Il Mostro dell'isola* (*The Island Monster*, 1953) that could *almost* be classed as an eighth Karloff excursion into the unnatural. More on that later.

Boris Karloff (left) and Charles Laughton pose for a publicity shot from *The Strange Door*.

In 1951, still allied to Universal, Karloff starred in *The Strange Door* alongside another cinematic heavyweight, Charles Laughton, a long-winded dollop of overripe Gothic-type theatrics encompassing Edgar Allan Poe themes in its setup. In this adaptation of a Robert Louis Stevenson story, Laughton hammed it up to the hilt, a deranged 17th-century nobleman keeping his brother (Paul Cavanagh) locked in the dungeons for marrying the woman they both loved. In revenge, he plans to marry Cavanagh's daughter, Sally Forrest, to ne'er-do-well Richard Stapley, hoping the girl becomes tainted and loses her innocence. However, the couple falls in love, so out of spite, Laughton imprisons them in the same cell as Cavanagh, the walls narrowing inch by inch on all three when the madman's waterwheel contraption is set in motion. Karloff, the creepy servant, comes to the rescue; Laughton is crushed in the wheel's mechanism and Karloff, dying from stab wounds, manages to throw the cell key to Stapley who unlocks the door seconds before the walls crash together.

Like *The Black Castle* which came immediately after it, Joseph Pevney's hokey costume drama attempted to resurrect the Gothic potboilers of the 1930s, throwing in an imposing castle complete with dungeons, hidden panels and a remarkably constructed Poe-like device used for torture (it wouldn't have looked out of place in one of Roger Corman's '60s Poe pictures. In a modest way, *The Strange Door* is a prototype for Corman's Poe thrillers). Although atmospheric in parts, it failed to work with both critics and the public for the simple reason that science had now replaced folklore. *The Strange Door* was a horror anachronism, a slice of Gothic fakery belonging to another time and place; it didn't sit comfortably with the newfangled type of monsters unleashed by the atom bomb or appearing from outer space in flying saucers. Laughton, resembling a blond, overweight cherub, hogged the camera to such an extent that everyone else melted into the shadows, even Karloff as the ghoulish dungeon keeper, Voltan. This was Laughton's show; Boris was reduced to bit player, although, to his credit, he did his best to create an interesting character out of virtually nothing. On the plus side, the black-and-white photography was diamond hard and, for soundtrack buffs, the refrains to Hans J. Salter's semi-classical *House of Frankenstein* score could be discerned, artfully overhauled by Joseph Gershenson to provide a stirring musical backdrop. But, for a 1951 semi-horror movie, it still looked old-fashioned.

The Black Castle was also old-fashioned Grand Guignol, with Karloff content to skulk in the castle's recesses, a doctor who assists lovers Richard Greene and Paula Corday in escaping from Stephen McNally's castle. He gives the moonstruck couple a potion that places them in a state of near-death and smuggles their bodies out in coffins. Stagy and rather dull, with too much dead weight in the middle section, this is one of the low points of Karloff's '50s career in horror movies (although there was little horror on display to raise the goosebumps). It's also one of Universal's low points—no wonder the company's executives ditched further plans to produce Gothic melodramas of the '30s/'40s variety and Jack Arnold's *It Came from Outer Space* and *Creature from the Black Lagoon* (both in 3-D) were just around the corner, ready to revive the company's flagging fortunes. Old-time Gothic thrillers these were not; new-age science fiction they most certainly were. The former King of Horror wasn't to figure in Universal's legendary run of monster-laden motion pictures that would stimulate audiences for years to come; *Abbott and Costello Meet Dr. Jekyll and Mr. Hyde* (1953) gave Karloff equal billing with the popular pranksters, but as far as Universal-International went, that was it.

Universal cast the funny men in a series of horror comedies, of which Charles Lamont's *Abbott and Costello Meet Dr. Jekyll and Mr. Hyde* was the second-best (*Abbott and Costello Meet Frankenstein* remains the tops). Karloff had joined forces with them before, in *Abbott and Costello Meet the Killer* (1949); in this latest confrontation, Karloff juicily took on the role of Dr. Jekyll and made it his own, the transformation scenes, utilizing Bud Westmore's make-up, were first-rate. In fact, the sequences were so frightening (at the time) that they forced the British censor into slapping an "X" certificate on the picture, banning young Abbott and Costello fans from seeing it. Bud and Lou play two inept American cops assigned to Scotland Yard; a killer known as "The Monster" terrorizes London and the duo hope to impress their new boss by bringing him to justice. The resulting slapstick action is slowed down by the inclusion of a romance between reporter Craig Stevens and Helen Wescott, but there are some hilarious moments in the film: Costello receiving a dose of Karloff's potion and waltzing into a pub sporting a giant mouse head; a frenetic interlude in a wax museum housing effigies of the Frankenstein Monster and Dracula and that anarchic final shot when five cops all change into monsters. English audiences squirmed in their seats at the Americanized London accents that rang false, but this didn't detract from a lively, enjoyable offering. If the movie had been brave enough to omit the comedy trappings, it would have made a vintage Jekyll and Hyde vehicle, even bettering Spencer Tracy's 1942 effort which was a bit too earnest for its own good.

In between finishing the Universal flick and 1957's *Voodoo Island*, Karloff undertook a raft of television work and made room for one foreign film, *The Island Monster*, in his busy schedule. Shot in the latter part of 1953, this tale of a sadistic drug baron and his gang smuggling illegal substances out of the Isle of Ischia (sister island of Capri) can hardly be termed horror, even though Karloff was mean and nasty, abducting and manhandling a young girl with such unhealthy relish that the British censor, without doubt, would have had raised eyebrows and reached for his scissors. The dubbing was atrocious (Karloff's voice was overlaid by a Karloff impersonator complete with lisp, the results hilarious) and the rest of the acting substandard, but in compensation, the Italian locations were ruggedly attractive and composer Carlo Innocenzi provided a stirring, somewhat out-of-place, soundtrack (Innocenzi was responsible for the atmospheric score in *Mill of the Stone Women* in 1960). For Karloff purists only, *The Island Monster* patently lacks *any* kind of monster and wasn't seen in England until 1962.

Boris Karloff, as a television hoax-buster, and Rhodes Reason from *Voodoo Island*

Director Reginald LeBorg and Bel-Air/United Artists, having used Chaney and Lugosi in *The Black Sleep*, hired Karloff for *Voodoo Island*, a mundane voodoo thriller filmed on location in Hawaii. Karloff was cast as a television hoax-buster who is hired by a rich industrialist to investigate three missing members of a survey party; the fourth (Glenn Dixon) has returned from scouting out possible sites for a luxury hotel on an island, but is in a trance-like state due to a supposed voodoo curse, to which Karloff scoffs. Once on the island, Karloff, ice queen Jean Engstrom, Elisha Cook, Jr., Rhodes Reason, Beverly Tyler, Murvyn Vye and the zombie-like Dixon trek through the jungle, shadowed by two natives. Apart from the natives, the place is home to one other obstacle—man-eating plants. Engstrom takes a dip and is strangled by inflatable leaves sporting suckers while Tyler is attacked by something resembling a cross between a Triffid and a Venus fly-trap. Dixon expires, scared to death, Cook, Jr. falls to *his* death from a bridge and Tyler surrenders herself to Reason's masculine charms. Vye, witnessing a small girl gobbled up wholesale by one of those rubberized Venus fly-traps, goes into catatonic shock, winding up like Dixon at the beginning. As for Karloff, he and the remnants of his party are allowed to leave the island by the native chief as they have been persuaded that voodoo's supernatural power exists.

One or two moderately scary scenes (Dixon's right eye twitching, the prelude to various disasters; needles thrust into dolls' heads) do nothing to alleviate the boredom felt in watching this flabby excuse of a voodoo movie. Karloff, as usual, is excellent, bringing zip to a far-from-riveting role, and Reason also shines as a boat captain with a past. But the climax simply peters out, as though all concerned had held up their hands and shouted, "Enough is enough!" *Voodoo Island* is, without question, Bel-Air's worst '50s horror feature; only Karloff's energetic playing saves it from sinking without a trace, a true mark of the man's screen magnetism, where he alone could rise above

Boris Karloff at first investigates the Haymarket Strangler but then discovers that he is the fiend, from *Grip of the Strangler*.

derivative material and hold a film together. This magnetism reached fruition in the next three X-rated pictures he made in 1958, *Grip of the Strangler*, *Frankenstein 1970* and *Corridors of Blood*, a highly regarded trio constituting the zenith of Karloff the Uncanny's roster of horror films produced in the 1950s. Perhaps none reach the monumental standards set by his '30s and '40s classics (an impossible task), but they make darned good horror viewing in any fan's book. The first two were hugely successful in England, playing for years without interruption on the horror circuits.

Karloff was 70 years old when he starred in *Grip of the Strangler* (U.S. title: *The Haunted Strangler*), the part so strenuous that it would have finished off an actor half his age. Part Jekyll and Hyde, part murder mystery, part Jack the Ripper—Robert Day's mesmerizing chiller was blessed with a coherent plot, authentically grim 1880's Victorian atmosphere, titillating dancing girls, a fine Buxton Orr score and convincing acting. Karloff plays a doctor investigating the notorious Haymarket Strangler case following a series of brutal slayings in London's backwaters. He is convinced that the wrong man was sent to the gallows. Against the orders of the police, he exhumes the victim's body, discovers a surgeon's knife among the bones and then undergoes a transformation, from kindly doctor to insane, murdering fiend. An outbreak of fresh killings ensues, young women stabbed and strangled to death, and we are left wondering whether Karloff is the original strangler, or someone else.

The transformation sequences in the film, executed with little make-up and no trick visual work, are astonishing, given the actor's age: His left arm twists in paralysis, as do his features, lank hair flops over maniacal eyes, lending him the appearance of a developmentally challenged psychopath. When Karloff, in a cell, morphs into his alter-self and breaks out of a straitjacket, audiences of the day sweated as much as Karloff obviously did in shooting the scene! The denouement, that Karloff was the mad strangler all along, the rediscovered knife triggering long-buried homicidal desires, comes as something of a surprise and the picture ends with him replacing the knife in the wrongly accused man's grave before dying from police bullets.

The doyen of horror showcased one of his strongest-ever latter-day performances in Day's superior shocker; he was just as good in Allied Artists' *Frankenstein 1970*, eternally remembered for its terrifying opening minutes in which a young girl is pursued through dark woods by a variant of Universal's Frankenstein Monster. Karloff, a descendent of the iniquitous Baron, was now the creator, the rudimentary laboratories of old replaced by atomic energy-based hardware, his seven-foot blind creature swathed in bandages lumbering around the set like a giant mummy. Limping, scarred, blond hair cut *en brosse* style, Karloff chewed the scenery, his rascally performance, delivery of acid dialogue and expressive features bely his age and puts the rest of the cast to shame. Although condemned by many critics and fans as being inferior fare, there is much to recommend in Howard W. Koch's addition to the ongoing *Frankenstein* cycle: Imaginative set design (the castle's ornate Gothic vaults are sublime); Paul Dunlap's resounding score; a different-than-normal monster; Karloff in full flight and gleaming black-and-white CinemaScope photography. It was a very popular film in England for a number of years; many fans caught the picture several times over, fidgeting through the second feature it was nearly always shown with (the tedious *Macabre*), simply to experience, on the high, wide and handsome screen, Karloff's delicious antics as he slices up a movie crew and uses their body parts to create his new super-being in an atomic reactor. *Frankenstein 1970* is a meaty chunk of late '50s horror, nowhere near as bad as some people may think.

The final film in Karloff's 1958 trilogy, *Corridors of Blood*, found itself shelved for a lengthy period and not screened in England until 1962, released with the indifferent *Nights of Rasputin*. Karloff, once again in top form, plays a distinguished surgeon trying to concoct a formula that will alleviate the agonizing pain felt by his patients as they undergo amputation. Anesthesia hadn't been invented, so compassionate Karloff prepares a compound from opium and various other chemicals, experiments with the gas on himself and winds up addicted to dope. Christopher Lee is a pockmarked scoundrel, smothering down-and-outs in Francis de Wolff's public house and selling their corpses to the local hospital; Lee and burly de Wolff eventually blackmail the doctor into signing forged death certificates. In the frantic climax, Lee stabs Karloff to death, but not before a jar of acid is hurled into his face. Son Francis Matthews is left to carry on his father's work with the aid of his diary.

Corridors of Blood wasn't a great success because it fell awkwardly between two slots: A surgical-cum-horror Gothic drama on the one hand, a semi-serious historical document of London's slums circa 1840 on the other, a brew that didn't please everyone. Robert Day's forceful direction, faultless production design and sharp monochrome cinematography reproducing London's bawdy Dickensian lowlife are exemplary, and that also goes for the ensemble playing. But horror fans (after all, they were the target audience) required something more straightforward for their ticket money, not a sermon on the rights and wrongs of surgery without some form of drug. And once Karloff becomes addicted to opiates, the movie

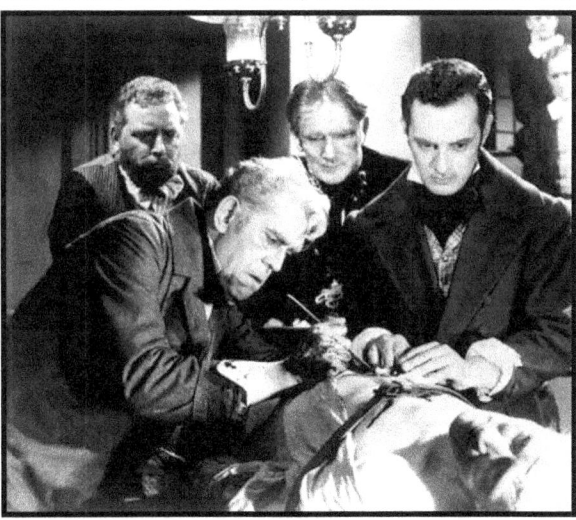

Boris Karloff plays a compassionate surgeon who becomes addicted to his cure for pain and Francis Matthews plays his son, in *Corridors of Blood*.

quickly goes off the boil, content to dwell on repeated scenes of gruesome surgical procedures and little else. The going becomes turgid, the plot fails to maintain the interest, the suspense drains away and even Karloff wears a look of disheartenment. Buxton Orr's commanding score strives to keep up the momentum in a feature that is now viewed in a better light than it was 50 years ago. But Karloff weathered the storm; his rock-solid status remained intact and he coasted into the next decade, continuing to flourish in the world of horror cinema, in England, in America and in Europe.

On October 29, 1951, work began on Bela Lugosi's first picture of the new decade, (*Old*) *Mother Riley Meets the Vampire*, also titled for American audiences *Vampire over London* and *My Son the Vampire*. Edward D. Wood, Jr. wasn't the first male cross-dresser that Lugosi ever encountered—drag artist Arthur Lucan had been successfully playing Irish washerwoman Old Mother Riley since the 1920s (on radio, in the music halls and in films), alongside wife Kitty McShane as his man-hungry "daughter" (it's doubtful whether such a slightly perverse double act would be allowed in today's sensitive cinematic climate). The hyperactive comedian had already made screen history by being the first man to figure in a picture dressed as a woman for its entire length. This was his 17th appearance in a role stretching right back to 1936 and was to be his last (McShane wasn't in it, the couple having separated), his pairing with the aging *Dracula* legend counts as one of the most bizarre collaborations in British cinema but one that, oddly enough, worked.

Lugosi was 69, Lucan 66, when filming commenced with John Gilling at the helm; neither could be classed as spring chickens but Lugosi looked sprightly enough, as did the manic Lucan. Lugosi plays Doctor Von Housen, a mad scientist operating in London under the guise of a vampire; his plan is for world domination via a race of mentally controlled robots. The picture opens with the abduction of a scientist's daughter who may possess knowledge of the whereabouts of rich uranium deposits in South America; Lugosi needs the ore for his atomic experiments. When a crate containing a prototype robot inadvertently ends up in the hands of Lucan, who is in severe debt and awaiting inheritance money from a recently deceased uncle, Lugosi commands the robot to his gloomy old mansion, bringing the hapless Lucan with it. The stage is now firmly set for slapstick farce, culminating in several frenetic chase scenes as Lugosi, assistant Philip Leaver and their goons head for Tilbury docks, Lucan in hot pursuit.

Released in Britain in 1952, (*Old*) *Mother Riley Meets the Vampire* was a moderate success (incorporating topical issues such as food rationing and unscrupulous rent collectors into its scenario), delighting Lucan's legion of fans, the comedian carrying on the tradition of vaudevillian tomfoolery perfected by George Formby, soon to be continued by Norman Wisdom. But there were not enough sequences showing Lugosi and Lucan interacting off each other, like an alternative variation on Abbott and Costello; Lucan's admittedly popular Old Mother Riley character took center stage for most of the movie's second half, shunting Lugosi to the sidelines. Outside of the United Kingdom, broad British farce was a genre that few non-English citizens could entirely relate to; there were plans to trim some of Lucan's scenes and re-shoot further sequences with Lugosi, issuing the movie in other countries as *King Robot*, but the actor was in such ill-health that these plans failed to materialize. Fascinating as a period piece (especially seeing Dora Bryan, Hattie Jacques and Richard Wattis in their younger days), (*Old*) *Mother Riley Meets the Vampire* now seems like a museum relic from a distant age;

conversely, it was the only feature Lugosi made in the 1950s where he looked reasonably fit and well, and for that, we must give thanks to independent producers Renown and Fernwood for hiring him in the first place.

Lugosi's next flick must count as his oddest of the '50s, the infantile *Bela Lugosi Meets a Brooklyn Gorilla*. Shot over a nine-day period in May 1952 for the sum of $50,000, this corny South Seas semi-horror romp concerned two Americans, Duke Mitchell and Sammy Petrillo, marooned on a tropical island and at the mercy of mad Doctor Zabor (Lugosi) who has invented a man-into-ape serum ("I'm Dr. Zabor. Welcome to my creepshow!"). Jealous of the attention his native girlfriend (Charlita) is giving to smooth operator Mitchell, he injects his rival with the serum, turning him into a huge, shaggy gorilla that goes on a mini-rampage. However, the whole sequence of events turns out to be a dream. The Americans wake up in a dressing room to find themselves nightclub entertainers playing themselves; Lugosi, in reality, is the joint's owner.

Director William Beaudine's rehash of *Zombies on Broadway* could easily have been titled *Bela Lugosi Meets Dean Martin and Jerry Lewis*; Mitchell and Petrillo's all-too-accurate impersonation of the popular duo's act had Martin, Lewis and boss Hal Wallis consulting lawyers to ensure that it would never happen again on screen. Lewis, incensed at Petrillo's spot-on imitation, even tried to prevent the film from being shown, but it was eventually given a sporadic release and did brisk business. In a tired plot dating right back to the 1930s, a graying Lugosi doesn't put in an appearance until 22 minutes have crept by; when Mitchell breaks into song, performing his Dean Martin cabaret act, the movie almost grinds to a halt. Lugosi played it straight, as he had done in *Abbott and Costello Meet Frankenstein*, compensating for Petrillo's constant mugging and Mickey Mouse delivery ("Don't mind my friend. He has a one-syllable brain," says Mitchell to Lugosi at one point, referring to the rubber-faced Petrillo). When the only entertaining character in a picture (apart from crazy-but-cute Petrillo; his partner, on the other hand, lacked charisma) turns out to be a performing chimp (Ramona), fans might have some idea of what sheer purgatory it is to sit through a large part of this wacky jungle balderdash. However, it *is* endowed with a sense of naïve absurdity and, as horror-comedy goes, is harmless, goofy fun for the kiddies. Many people find it a hoot. Others hate it with a vengeance.

Full marks to an actor of Lugosi's horror pedigree for taking on this contrived nonsense and acting as though he was cast in a far more serious piece of work, even to the point of self-parody. His morphine addiction limited him to a three-day shoot, so it's a miracle he actually made it on set. Apart from his stern-faced performance, a few amusing moments and the delectable Charlita doing a passable send-up of Dorothy

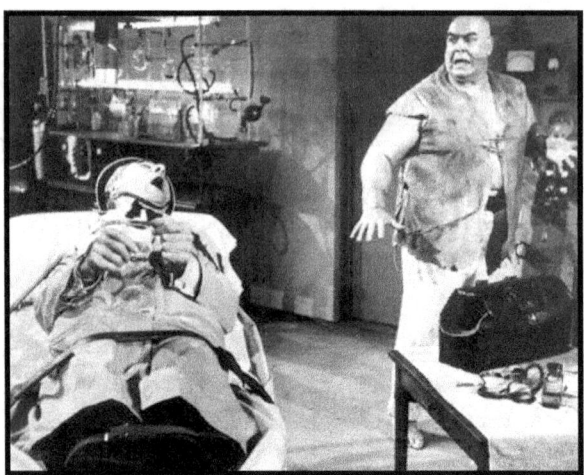

Bela Lugosi, strapped to a table, is about to get zapped by Lobo (Tor Johnson) in *Bride of the Monster*.

Lamour (Bing Crosby and Bob Hope would have been right at home with this kind of material to lampoon), *Bela Lugosi Meets a Brooklyn Gorilla*, now classed in some departments as a cult classic of sorts, is dumb and stupid with limited appeal, even compared to the low standards set by one Edward D. Wood, Jr. who stood in the wings, ready to throw the aging, out-of-work star a lifeline. This was to become Lugosi's own Last Chance Saloon period in his epic career in horror films.

Film fanatic Alex Gordon shared an apartment in Hollywood with Ed Wood, a young ambitious moviemaker bursting with offbeat ideas, anxious to make his mark in the industry. Wood, like so many others, harbored aspirations to become the next Orson Welles, but lacked the one vital ingredient in his lofty ambitions—talent. He also lacked finances, so when Gordon introduced Lugosi to the cross-dresser in 1953, Wood saw that the old horror legend could be bought for peanuts and promptly hired him to become a bemused member of his retinue of eccentrics and weirdoes. Lugosi was, in Wood's fervent eyes, the ace in his pack, his major selling point to distributors of conveyer-belt trash, as would John Carradine be to Jerry Warren in a couple of years' time. Lugosi's role in Wood's first-ever attempt at filmmaking, *Glen or Glenda?*, was the narrator, acting as the link in a series of almost deviant sketches representing Wood's ramshackle homage to transvestites. Seen most of the time sitting in a big easy chair, Lugosi spouted a succession of incredulous, illogical monologues with an intensity born out of sheer desperation to work, elevating this pseudo-documentary rubbish to the absolute pinnacle of bad film production values. The reviewers uniformly savaged the picture but that didn't deter Wood or his entourage one iota; he wasn't finished with Lugosi yet—he had more in store for his principal asset, planning to allow the actor to express himself carte blanche in his next hare-brained opus, *Bride of the Monster*.

Alternatively produced under the titles of *The Atomic Monster*, *The Monster of the Marshes* and *Bride of the Atom*, *Bride of the Monster*, wrapped up in March 1955 after a three-week shoot, may well be the best all-round film Lugosi and Wood completed in the 1950s. Granted, it's a microcosm of all of the director's infamous trademarks and gaffes: shaky sets, hand-painted backdrops, overstated acting, rubbery monster (an octopus), woolly script (courtesy of Wood and Gordon) and lumbering Tor Johnson playing second fiddle to Lugosi's mad Doctor Vornoff. But it *does* possess a degree of continuity and plot; this, together with Frank Worth's lively score and Lugosi (now a very sick man, looking tired) turning in a credible performance, makes *Bride of the Monster* (X-rated in Britain) a standard '50s horror movie with a smidgen of merit to its name.

Okay, Lugosi goes through the same old routine he had done so many times before: crackpot scientist experiments with radiation, hoping to produce a race of atomic-powered supermen to enslave the world, and, as a by-product, creatures (the octopus) evolve into carnivorous giants. But Wood seems to have put a great deal more effort, enthusiasm and even emotion into *Bride of the Monster* (as does Lugosi), determined to promote his pet project on a grade -B level rather than a grade Z, and the result is passable—just. And stop to think about it. There were far lousier horror pictures churned out in the 1950s than *Bride of the Monster*; *Teenage Monster* and *Robot Monster* are two examples of amateurish, shoddy filmmaking, tons more third-rate in every way possible to Wood's mad scientist effort.

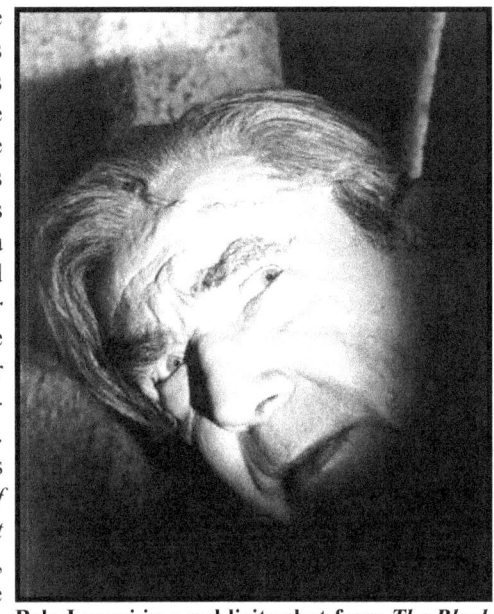

Bela Lugosi in a publicity shot from *The Black Sleep*.

With offers of work dwindling, Lugosi must have thought he was back in the big time when, in late 1955, Bel-Air/United Artists contacted him regarding a role in their new horror vehicle, *The Black Sleep*, a full-blooded surgical-cum-Gothic thriller with Basil Rathbone in the lead, playing a ruthless doctor experimenting in illegal brain surgery. If so, his high hopes were dashed; Lugosi was principally hired because of his name alone which the producers reckoned still had box-office clout. He was cast as a mute servant, his total screen time amounting to less than three minutes (as opposed to Lon Chaney's six and a bit). The veteran horror star felt humiliated in the non-part and pleaded with director Reginald LeBorg to be allowed a few lines of dialogue; much to his chagrin, the request was brushed aside on the grounds that the character had no tongue. (Paradoxically, this anonymous cameo mirrored the one Lugosi had played in Universal's *Night Monster* [1942] where he was a near-silent manservant hovering in the background, doing very little. But then, the actor was in his prime.) Looking thin, drawn and stooped, this was to be the great man's final full-length piece of acting, albeit a minor, unsatisfactory one; all he really does is shuffle across the set to let people in and out of Rathbone's Gothic mansion. He tries valiantly to invest the part with some dignity but it's a thankless task. Besides, Rathbone's dominating turn dwarfs not only Lugosi's performance but everyone else's—*The Black Sleep* was practically a one-man show as far as he was concerned. It wasn't a particularly happy shoot either: Rathbone was haughty, looking down on his fellow actors with disdain (see Greg Mank's *Lugosi and Karloff*), even one of Lugosi's stature while Chaney, harboring both a drink habit and an almighty grievance over Lugosi's disparaging comments about him being unsuitable for the part of *Son of Dracula* (according to Arthur Lennig's *The Immortal Count*), engaged in roughhouse antics with the far-from-well thespian and had to be told to calm things down.

The Black Sleep was the most expensive picture Lugosi appeared in during the '50s. Although his salary was standard flat rate, his compensation was a small reward when we consider that United Artists saw fit to give him fifth billing on the posters to pull in the crowds. Certified "X" in the United Kingdom, the movie was a perennial fixture on England's horror circuits during the early 1960s, allowing fans to catch a broken Bela near the closing stages of his long, fruitful career, at a low ebb, a shambling figure that bore little resemblance to the once handsome, celebrated stage performer whose commanding portrayal of Bram Stoker's vampire Count would forever be linked with his name.

In July 1956, Ed Wood shot some footage of Lugosi (now penniless and beset with marriage problems) outside Tor Johnson's house; Lugosi, dressed in his black Dracula cape, emerges from the doorway in dazzling sunlight, picks a flower, lets it drop and walks off camera. Further scenes were filmed in a graveyard, where Lugosi spreads his cape like the fabled vampire of yore. On August 16, 1956, Lugosi died in bed, at peace, finally, after years of drug dependency and being treated with indifference by the industry he so loved. But Wood was determined his two-minutes plus of footage wouldn't go to waste; it was integrated into his next "epic" and the one film that the poverty row director would go down in history for—*Plan 9 from Outer Space*. This cheapjack portion of grade-Z schlock kicks off with Lugosi standing by an open grave, attending the funeral of his brother. The scene outside Johnson's house quickly follows, and then, for the remainder of the picture, a stand-in replaces Lugosi, appearing briefly in cape after Lugosi dies and is resurrected by aliens. Wood entered his name on the credits as "Guest Star" which Lugosi, perhaps looking down from on high and blessed with a wry sense of humor, would have found quite amusing (in all probability, had Lugosi lived, he might have appeared in Wood's next work of non-art, *Night of the Ghouls* [1959], a topsy-turvy exercise in the supernatural, performed to the best of their ability by the director's stock company of sham actors). All in all, a sad end to an illustrious career in the motion picture industry which spanned nearly 50 years and totaled some 110-feature films.

Mystery surrounds *Lock Up Your Daughters*, an obscure Lugosi compilation that now appears to be lost. That notorious producer of B quickies, Sam Katzman, apparently cobbled together this collection of scenes from the actor's Monogram efforts either in 1951 (when Lugosi was in Britain, touring in a stage adaptation of *Dracula*), 1956 (immediately after his death) or 1959. Surfacing in the United Kingdom in February 1959, it was passed uncut and given an "X" rating by the British Board of Film Censors, released by New Realm and the E.J. Fancy organization and screened in local flea-pits in some parts of England on a double bill with *The Neanderthal Man*. This author caught it teamed up with Karloff's *The Boogie Man Will Get You* in October 1966 at the Palace cinema in Truro, Cornwall where it was shown A-rated. The disparity in ratings can easily be explained: Local councils in England had the power to impose their own certifications on films if need be, and *Lock Up Your Daughters* may have been trimmed for viewing outside of London, although at a running time of 51 minutes, this doesn't really seem feasible. Also, the movie was composed of scenes from *Invisible Ghost, The Ape Man, Return of the Ape Man, Voodoo Man, Spooks Run Wild, The Corpse Vanishes* and *The Corpse Vanished* (Lugosi didn't appear in this last movie, known as *Revenge of the Zombies*—John Carradine was the star); each of these

Monogram potboilers was A-rated in England, so even with "new" footage of Lugosi playing a mad doctor conducting experiments on a young woman, why would the film have been passed as an "X," given the gimcrack production values on display? The other spanner in the works is that *The Ape Man* was also known under the similar title of *Lock Your Doors*, which confuses the issue even more. Comments that unused footage of Lugosi was filched from Ed Wood's *Glen or Glenda?* can be discounted as pure speculation. Some listings quote The Bowery Boys in the "cast" as well as Polly Ann Young, both appearing in *Spooks Run Wild* and *Invisible Ghost* respectively. It could well be that only a limited number of prints were made of *Lock Up Your Daughters*, none of which survive today, something which has occurred many times before with ultra-rare feature films. That it *did* exist seems beyond doubt; maybe one day it will be unearthed from the vaults and thus allow Lugosi aficionados to see for themselves what they have been hankering after all these years.

As far as the 1950s are concerned, Lugosi is usually remembered for his collaboration with King of the Awful, Edward D. Wood, Jr., a collaboration that Tim Burton brought so vividly to life in 1994's aptly titled *Ed Wood*. Apart from *The Black Sleep*, Lugosi inhabited cinema's equivalent of grade-Z land, his output patchy at best, living on past glories, his golden years a fading memory. But his name, in the arena of horror cinema, will live on forever, and will always be associated with, more than any other actor who has portrayed him, the immortal Count Dracula. So forget Lugosi in the '50s—the decade treated him badly and did him no favors whatsoever. Bela Lugosi's film legacy belongs to the '30s and '40s and it is the treasures he made in those two decades that we will return to again and again.

In contrast to the output from the three old pros of horror, the three new kings to the throne didn't fare much better in the 1950s: Peter Cushing starred in seven horror movies, Christopher Lee in eight and Vincent Price in seven. Even the output from the challenge led by the new generation of American upstarts was around the same figure. As an example, John Agar was in eight (nine if you include the 1959 TV pilot *Destination Space*), Jeff Morrow four and Richard Denning five. Chaney, Karloff and Lugosi didn't rule the roost as they had done previously; their names were included with so many others as cinemas in America and Britain were deluged with atomic-themed horror, science fiction and fantasy movies featuring a whole host of unfamiliar actors. So, no, perhaps the threesome's 1950s inheritance shouldn't be bracketed side-by-side with *The Wolf Man*, *Frankenstein*, *Dracula* and many other venerable, ageless classics, all of which forged their standing in this field. But it's far from disposable; in re-evaluating their body of work from the 1950s, nuggets can be found amid the rubble, lasting proof that Chaney, Karloff and Lugosi, three former giants of fantastic cinema, will live eternal in the minds of those with a genuine love for horror movies and the actors who starred in them.

Chapter 10
Gill-Man Number One!

Released in 3-D in 1954, *Creature from the Black Lagoon* became a box-office smash on both sides of the Atlantic and over the years has gained the deserved reputation of being the 1950s quintessential creature-feature, a highly influential production imitated in countless other films since. It provided Universal-International with much-needed funds and the fans with an iconic monster, an "advanced amphibian" on a par with King Kong, the Frankenstein Monster and Godzilla. Needless to say, a sequel was called for and *Revenge of the Creature* appeared hot on its heels a year later, followed by the last in the trilogy, *The Creature Walks Among Us*, in 1956. But over the years, opinions have tended to differ as to which, out of these three pictures, is the best. Viewing the movies over 50 years later, it could be argued that *The Creature Walks Among Us* may well lay claim to being the finest, most all-rounded and complete gill-man feature, even though most film compendiums would beg to differ, as would many buffs.

It doesn't help the issue that I caught all three films in reverse order to the years they were made: *The Creature Walks Among Us* in July 1961 (on a double bill with *Tarantula*), *The Revenge of the Creature* in November 1961 (with *The Mad Ghoul*) and the original *Creature* flick not until July 1967 (teamed up with Lugosi's *Dracula*). During that period, *The Creature Walks Among Us* was by far and away the most popular of the trio on the English horror circuits, with *Revenge of the Creature* a close second. The first film was given a major airing in the United Kingdom in early 1955 but oddly, unlike the other two, wasn't a regular feature in theaters afterwards. And when I caught it, I was mildly disappointed which, in turn, brought on guilt feelings *about* being mildly disappointed! After all, this was the archetypal creature-feature horror outing that had kick-started the whole "man-in-a-rubber-suit" genre. So why was it I felt the way I did, even though admittedly I was entertained and excited in equal measures (even more so when I caught it in 1978 in a reissued 3-D version). Well for starters, my judgment had been clouded to a certain extent by sitting through the second and third movies several times over; I was used to seeing the gill-man in a built-up setting, pitted against the cops and scientists, treated like a freak of nature. Here, the action was confined to the still waters of the Black Lagoon where the creature dwelt and the overall mood felt at times as claustrophobic as the jungle settings, and as a result less thrilling. But let's examine all three movies more closely before we jump to any hasty conclusions.

Jack Arnold's forceful direction, combined with Hans J.

Salter's bombastic soundtrack, was what really made the first offering rise above its B-movie trappings, plus, of course, Bud Westmore and Jack Kevan's sublime amphibious gill-man, the '50s most photogenic creature by far. After Salter's title score blasts away over the credits, Arnold grabs the audience's imagination in the third minute as we see a real life claw, the mirror-image of the fossilized one seen dug out of the clay, slide off the riverbank, the composer's strident music assaulting the eardrums, raising the hackles and nailing those few seconds in the minds of a generation of horror fanatics, never to be forgotten. The attack on the native in the tent is the stuff of nightmares, and then the pace becomes unhurried as Richard Carlson, Richard Denning, Julia (Julie) Adams, Whit Bissell and assorted crew head up river in the direction of the creature's territory, crammed together in Nestor Paiva's battered old craft. In this fairly long lull, Arnold not only focuses on the tensions created by the ever-lurking monster hiding in the atmospheric lagoon and man's elemental fear of what lies beneath the surface of deep water, but the ongoing rift between Adams, ex-beau Denning and current beau Carlson. At one point, the two men are out in a rowing boat, Denning armed with a rifle:

Denning: "Come on! Come on!"

Carlson: "You talking to me, Mark, or something else out there?"

Denning: "Both, David."

This short snippet perfectly encapsulates the animosity the men feel toward each other and, in Denning's case, toward the creature; he regards both as sworn enemies, to be defeated at all cost.

Once the gill-man commences its assaults on the hunters, things heat up and become more frenetic, although a touch repetitive. Arnold orchestrates a number of well-staged, frenzied showdowns that culminate in the creature being gunned down, his body drifting toward the camera and filling the screen.

Arnold was behind the helm of the violent follow-up, *Revenge of the Creature*, also originally screened in 3-D, the gill-man a much more savage protagonist, up against man in an urban environment totally alien to him. Captured by dynamiting the Black Lagoon, the creature is taken to Miami's Ocean Harbor Seaquarium where it is put on display in a massive tank, to be studied not only by the public but also by Professor John Agar and dishy ichthyologist Lori Nelson. There is an alarming piece of action when the gill-man is lowered into a pool and revives, creating havoc, but what follows is rather draggy. Agar begins romancing Nelson (as does the creature, who finds her sexually alluring!) while attempts are made to communicate with the gill-man, and it's a long, talkative 30-minutes before Arnold revs up the pace by having his avenging demon

The gill-man is captured, chained and put on display in *Revenge of the Creature*.

break free from its restraints, the monster clambering out of the tank into the dazzling Miami sunshine, the crowds running in terror. The most striking image in the flick has to be a beautifully composed shot showing the back view of the gill-man, glistening wet, emerging step by step from the water at night onto a jetty like a black, scaly devil, just as Agar and Nelson stroll into a jazz club; the scene where he walks in on the jazz party is a scream in more ways than one! After abducting Nelson, the gill-man is again shot by the cops and sinks beneath the waves.

Arnold didn't take up the option to direct the third in the series; John *The Monolith Monsters* Sherwood took over the reins. In hindsight, Sherwood did a good job, his direction more measured than Arnold's and needed here because this picture had a more involved plot than the other two. *The Creature Walks Among Us* is almost a different movie altogether, part of the series but somehow separate from it, having a more contemporary feel. The picture doesn't sag in the middle, is composed of three sections (the hunt, the gill-man's conversion from amphibian to land animal and the imprisonment/escape), has three main locations (the Everglades, at sea and San Francisco) and, as a bonus, presents us with *two* different monsters; the gill-man and the changed gill-man. The pairing of Jeff Morrow and Rex Reason is a blinder, following their successful partnership in *This Island Earth*: Tetchy Morrow is portrayed as a modern-day Frankenstein-type figure, altering the gill-man's genetics (after it has been burned with kerosene) to create another being, his very own monster, regardless of scientific ethics; Reason plays the compassionate scientist with a conscience, firmly against Morrow's stubborn idealism. "The stars or the jungle," is his personal analogy, questioning constantly the good and the bad of what they are doing. Making up the cast is slinky Leigh Snowden, trapped in a loveless marriage to Morrow, and beefcake Gregg Palmer who lusts after her—yes, like the first *Creature* film, *The Creature Walks Among Us* has a messy *ménage a trois* included in the layout to appease adult audiences of the day; in England, the movie, like the other two, was rated "X."

Morrow's cold-hearted nature not only reflects itself in his contemptuous attitude toward Snowden but toward the unfortunate creature also:

Morrow: "We are changing a sea creature into a land creature."

Reason: "We'll only use what nature offered. The lungs were there. We didn't make them."

Morrow: "Huh, you'll see, Doctor Morgan."

Reason: "Just don't move too fast trying to change him."

Morrow: "Are you afraid of unknown things?"

Reason: "I'm only afraid of misusing what I do know."

Later, at a celebratory party, Morrow states, "Change the metabolism and man will change," labeling his wife, "worthless, useless." In fact, Arthur Ross' thoughtful script sizzles with acerbic exchanges, mostly between the two leads, Morrow's marital problems mirroring his dispassionate dismissal of any feelings the hapless gill-man might possess:

Morrow: "You mean return kindness with kindness?"

Reason: "I believe it."

Morrow: "You think that's always true, doctor? You think that if I give kindness, I can always get kindness in return?"

Reason: "How do you mean?"

Morrow: "Oh come now, Doctor Morgan. You're a very perceptive man."

Reason: "I'd rather not talk about it. It isn't any of my concern."

Morrow: "Then clinically as a scientist you should be interested. Imagine how often love is returned with hate and loyalty is returned with infidelity."

The acting in Sherwood's final *Creature* entrant is of the same high standard as the other two: Morrow and Reason are the match of Denning and Carlson, while Agar, although not really having a sparring partner to bounce ideas off, was always a reliable leading man. As for the girls, I'll leave you to decide who was the most alluring: Dark-haired Adams, a little on the innocent side; blonde Nelson, kittenish and a bit naïve and platinum blonde Snowden, the toughest and sexiest of the three (but certainly not the "cheap little tramp" Morrow accuses her of being.)

There are several splendid sequences in the third *Creature* movie: The gill-man attacking the boat in the Everglades, going up in flames as kerosene drenches his body; the reshaped creature staring inquisitively at his captors as the bandages are removed from his altered features; the hulking monster, attired in sackcloth, emerging from the darkened back of a truck into harsh sunlight and slowly walking down the ramp, warily eyeing the nervous humans on guard with rifles and a tremendous climax, easily the most enthralling of the series, in which the monster escapes from his electrified pen and smashes his way through Morrow's house, hurling his tormentor to his death from the verandah. And the final minute showing the gasping, bullet-ridden creature standing atop a sandbank, looking longingly at the sea before lurching down the slope to a certain death, is one of Universal's most telling, almost moving, fade-outs, evoking sympathy for the gill-man and his plight.

Mention must be made of Hans J. Salter's modified *Creature from the Black Lagoon* score, revamped here to give maximum impact to the pared-to-the-bone proceedings. Salter never received a composer's credit for his brilliant work on these films, arranger Joseph Gershenson stealing the glory, an act of criminal negligence, some might say. A soundtrack that delivers in all the right places; the low-key but effective screen chemistry of Morrow and Reason; that literate script; Sherwood's competent direction and one of the '50s most menacing, yet charismatic, monsters, in two guises. Five persuasive reasons why *The Creature Walks Among Us* makes for 78 minutes of classically essential creature hokum, a superbly structured, fast-paced horror film. Scene-for-scene and frame-by-frame, Sherwood's effort beats the previous two *Creature* movies in practically every department (albeit in an unassuming, less showy fashion). *The Creature Walks Among Us*, after years of being looked upon as minor league fodder, unreservedly qualifies for the title of Gill-Man Number One in this fan's book, an underrated crowd-pleaser from the Universal catalogue that deserves further recognition.

Chapter 11
Cahn's Sci-Fi B-Movie Par Excellence

The 1950s became a breeding ground for low-budget science-fiction movies and among the countless turned out was United Artists' *It! The Terror from Beyond Space*. The film tells of a rocket returning to Earth from Mars, the crew terrorized by a monster that requires human blood and tissue to sustain it, leading to cellular collapse in its victims. It's a picture that's mentioned a lot in this book, and not without due cause; here is the one production that transcends its budget limitations to take on the mantle of "The Decade's Finest Sci-Fi B Thriller." Everything about *It!* screams "Archetypal Classic!" Once in a while, a group of filmmakers get their heads together for a singular idea, everyone pulls his weight and the end result is an artistic triumph for all concerned, making, in a way, their own personal statement. *It!*, in terms of '50s commodity, represents one such golden moment and holds its head up well 54 years on. But to find out why, let's analyze the picture's various components to see how those components, welded together, form a deeply satisfying whole.

Director: Edward L. Cahn; Cinematographer: Kenneth Peach

Cahn directed a fair number of horror thrillers in his time, but none to match *It!* After the title credits have leapt out of the screen in mock 3-D, almost knocking you back into your seat, the camera pans across a forbidding Martian landscape to a sleek spaceship, waiting to blast off. Cahn then segues effortlessly into a two-minute prologue: A Washington spokesman explains to the press that Colonel Marshall Thompson, sole survivor of the Challenge 141 Mars expedition, is being brought back to Earth for court martial on the grounds that he killed nine colleagues for food and water after the rocket crash-landed (a neat device to relay the plot to the audience). Returning swiftly to Mars, Captain Kim Spalding prepares for takeoff. On the five-minute mark, Cahn allows the viewer a glimpse of a silhouette, certainly *not* human, and large reptilian feet padding the deck, accompanied by a throaty, growling noise—but *only* for a few seconds. *We* now know there's a monster aboard, even if Spalding doesn't. The ship shoots off into a starlit space and Cahn takes things easy, introducing the characters, their relationships and Thompson's own version of events. At 15 minutes in, having racked up the tension and expectancy levels, the mood and tempo changes: Thom Carney hears banging and crashing beneath his cabin; Cahn shows a three-digit claw rummaging along a shelf and another fearsome silhouette, and a roar breaks the silence. Investigating two decks below, Carney walks through a doorway to his death. Cahn depicts his savage demise at the hands of the stowaway in shadow to keep audiences on the edge of their seats. From here on in, the director ups the pace to fever pitch, ably guiding his camera around the ship's cramped, utilitarian interiors, subtly photographed by Kenneth Peach: galleys; storage compartments cluttered with crates, drums and cabinets; narrow corridors; metal stairways and the flight deck; blinking, flashing analog instrument panels; inky black corners set off by brightly lit foregrounds; faces/bodies in half-shadow—visually, Gothic sci-fi at its most intriguing.

In a publicity pose, Ray Corrigan as "It" carries an unknown victim across his back.

It!'s most mesmerizing section commences at 25 minutes and demonstrates magnificently the merger of Cahn and Peach's talents, both going for the jugular. The monster's face comes into view inside the air duct, the crew deciding to dispatch it with grenades, rigging them to the ventilation hatch's grill ("Get outta here! Get a lead start," yells Thompson, realizing they're too close to the thing for comfort). As the monster bursts out of the exploding grill, smoke forcing it to breathe heavily in the oxygen-depleted air, Cahn tracks along a line of worried faces, the crew listening to the bedlam over the intercom system. Spalding and his men, carrying guns, descend the stairs and tentatively approach the battered door to C compartment. The buckled door opens, then jams, the lights flickering and short-circuiting. Paul Langton, rifle at the ready, peers through the murk. The monster emerges half-seen from the smog, grabs Langton's weapon and bends it in half, twisting the edge of the door in anger. As Spalding and company open fire, the thing, a dark menacing figure, advances toward camera, filling the frame; still blazing away, the crew retreat through the connecting hatch. Cahn's forceful approach, combined with tight editing and Peach's imaginative lighting, brings this riveting sequence of events to heart-racing life, one of sci-fi's most memorable eight minutes of alien monster pandemonium.

117

As "It" breaks through to each level of the space craft, the suspense and fear is amped up.

The Cahn/Peach partnership remains consistent throughout the movie and never slackens. Cahn shoots the baggy-suited alien from above, looking down from deck hatches as it drags its lifeless prey through the smoke left by gas grenades, Peach shrouding some scenes in a near-blackness. His use of masking light against shade really comes to the fore in the parts where the monster is trapped in the ship's nuclear reactor, and when Thompson electrifies a stairway. Much of *It!*'s footage is just plain dark, period! Cahn also inserts, at regular intervals, views of the rocket drifting through space (the same views, judging by the three stars to the right of the vessel!) to segment the action, and only the '50s could get away with a space walk created by tilting the camera to one side, filming the actors in slow motion, and making it work. So Cahn plus Peach become the perfect sci-fi marriage, both director and photographer complementing the other to exhilarating effect.

Composers: Paul Sawtell and Bert Shefter

It!'s title theme (mentioned in chapter four) is one of the '50s greatest, 61-seconds of seat-shaking power that rolled over packed audiences in the early 1960s and left their ears ringing. And that's only for starters. The remainder of the soundtrack is just as spellbinding. There's the mournful, out-of-key wailing that is the accompaniment to the rocket falling through space, the views of Mars becoming musical cues for new scenes; the rumbling, menacing overtures announcing the snarling arrival of the monster; the prolonged aural assaults during the confrontations between crew and alien and the softer, incidental snatches when the crew discuss life-threatening injuries or Marshall and Shawn Smith begin to bond. And Cahn isn't afraid to dispense with music altogether in some interludes, thereby heightening the suspense—silence often speaks louder than music. Make no mistake, Sawtell and Shefter's arrangements for this film are in a class of their own, the B-movie soundtrack elevated to stratospheric heights; the music still resonates in the ears of fans decades later.

The Actors; Scriptwriter Jerome Bixby

Marshall Thompson, Kim Spalding, Shawn Smith, Dabbs Greer, Ann Doran, Paul Langton, Robert Bice, Richard Benedict, Richard Hervey and Thom Carney act with a total belief in what they are doing (and so does Ray Corrigan as "It"), doing full justice to Jerome Bixby's terrifically wry script. There's not a moment where we think, "What are they going on about?" or spot a hammy performance because hammy isn't part of *It!*'s manifesto. Let's indulge ourselves in a selection of juicy morsels from Bixby's sparkling screenplay:

Spalding to Thompson, convinced he's a murderer: "What are you thinking about? Those nine men you left down there?"

Thompson: "Yes. But I didn't kill them."

Spalding: "Still sticking to your story of the mysterious creature. Do you expect a court martial to believe it?"

Thompson: "Those men were killed by something—not me."

Later, when Spalding points out a bullet hole in a skull found on the Martian surface, he states to Thompson "There's only one kind of a monster that uses bullets." "By the time we get to Earth, I'll have his confession on tape," he tells his team before dark-haired Smith, his girlfriend, tells him to back off from Thompson; besides, she's already got her sights trained on the colonel, the only one around to not discount his story.

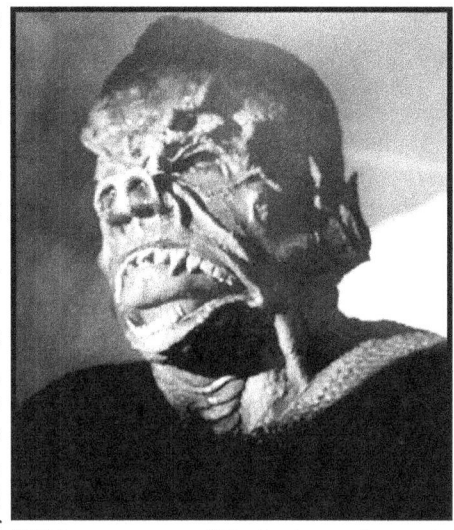

"It" becomes one of the best man-in-a-rubber-suit monster ever created.

Greer, on receiving no response on the intercom from missing Carney: "If this is one of his jokes, I'll make him walk home."

On discussing the monster, Greer asks: "How could that thing have gotten aboard, and why?"

Spalding: "Just to kill us?"

Thompson: "What is the usual reason an intelligent creature kills."

Smith: "It's hungry? What makes you so certain it's intelligent, Colonel, not just an animal?"

Thompson: "It opened the door to C compartment."

Greer, hearing the monster crashing around via the intercom, sums up their predicament to perfection: "It has to kill us or starve, and we've got to kill it or die."

Thompson, as he wires up a stairway: "There's enough voltage in these lines to kill 30 human beings. The only drawback is, the thing isn't human."

Spalding, dying from an alien infection, observing Thompson and Smith tactlessly holding hands and making eyes at one another: "You and him, just out of nowhere."

Thompson to audience, as the monster batters its way up through the hatches toward the survivors: "We are in the top level of the ship. This is either where we die, or it dies."

The final word is left to the Washington spokesmen who informs the press at the end, "Another name for Mars is death."

Bric-a-brac

William Glasgow, Herman N. Schoenbrun and Bixby were responsible for the functional set design: Overhead pipes, conduits, electric wiring, interconnecting stairs and fuel tanks, resembling the Arctic base's drab Quonset huts in *The Thing from Another World*. Cleverly added to the serviceable hardware were the day-to-day sounds:

Continuous whirrs, hums and beeps emanating from the ship's console boards. Fanciful gave way to realism—swanky this spaceship wasn't!

The action, set in 1973, demonstrates that producers in 1958 were a little too overly optimistic regarding man's dreams of reaching other planets by the 1970s.

The monster is suffocated to death by the opening of outside hatches to let the air escape. In actuality, this would cause the rocket to implode. Instant annihilation would be the result as well with grenades detonating on a spaceship, as well as two bursts from a bazooka.

Paul Blaisdell designed the alien suit but didn't receive a credit listing.

It! runs at 69 minutes and not a single frame of those 69 minutes is wasted.

As we all know, Ridley Scott's *Alien* was more or less structured on *It!*'s basic storyline.

In England, X-rated *It!* shared the bill most of the time with *Curse of the Faceless Man*, but could also be found with United Artists' *Man on the Prowl*. The author was lucky enough to catch it in February 1964, co-featured with *Horrors of the Black Museum*. You don't get value for your money like that these days!

Chapter 12
Bring on the Girls!

Each and every one of the films described in this chapter is a gold-plated guilty pleasure—for men! How could they not be, with catchpenny titles like *Bowanga Bowanga*, *White Sirens of Africa* and *The Wild Women of Wongo*. Wives and girlfriends can busy themselves with making tea or coffee—let the male of the species sit back and enjoy a host of scantily attired young females cavorting around in Stone Age swimwear or Space Age jumpsuits. We're not talking quality here—we're talking male titillation. The ladies have John Agar, William Hopper, Rex Reason and Richard Denning. We men can make do with Laurette Luez, Dana Wilson, Doris Merrick and Jean Hawkshaw. View on!

Long before *The Clan of the Cave Bear*, *One Million Years B.C.* and *Creatures the World Forgot*, there was *Prehistoric Women* (1950). Not to be confused with Hammer's 1966 film of the same name (aka *Slave Girls*), Alliance Productions' 74-minute interpretation of what life was like 10,000 years ago in the Stone Age is so utterly daft that it will have audiences laughing their socks off, if in the right mood for it. Voice-over narration stands in for grunts as we are told of the origins of Laurette Luez's all-female tribe of '50s glamour girls after witnessing a three-minute orgasmic dance performed to what sounds like Sandy Nelson belting out a rhythm on his drum-kit. In Luez's mascara-enhanced eyes, men are pathetic weaklings not worthy of her attention. Anyway, they would only mess up her expensive hairdo and carefully applied lipstick. To prove her point, her tribe ambushes a number of males by felling them with slingshots. They haul the defeated men back to camp, where the captives, judged to be possible husbands, are forced to become submissive sex slaves in the women's treehouses, with a touch of S&M and bondage on the let's-play-naughty-games menu. Allan Nixon, the men's virile leader and resident male chauvinist, comes to their rescue (if they want to be rescued, that is!), decides to show Luez and her pals who is the boss around here and is of the opinion that these fiery wenches would make good mating material. He introduces everyone to the mechanics of making fire (two stones rubbed together), defeats a troublesome nine-foot giant (Johann Petursson), burns to death a marauding turkey (no, that should read flying dragon—but it *is* a turkey!), dribbles at the mouth in the joys of eating roasted meat and ends up marrying Luez. With his warriors in tow, all paired with the willing females, they return to Nixon's camp to propagate for the continuation of the human race.

Surprisingly directed with a modicum of flair by Gregg C. Tallas, *Prehistoric Women* is kitsch with a capital K. The tongue-in-cheek script is worth a King's ransom: "Engor and his tribesmen are amazed to see that they've been attacked by members of the weaker sex," intones the narrator, and when Luez has a catfight with Mara Lynn over Nixon's manly magnetism, we get, "It seems that women were women in those days, too." "Cooked meat goes on the menu for the first time," the voice-over states as Nixon sinks his perfect white molars into a juicy steak, while apparently "Romance solves any problem" is the cause of the men and women realizing, in fact, that unbridled lust solves everything. Luez is one foxy, leggy chick in a very revealing animal skin (the actress appeared in the *Bomba the Jungle Boy* TV series in 1952). She and her vixens look as though they've just stepped out of a Los Angeles beauty salon; any wonder Nixon's men aren't in a hurry to leave those treehouses! May I add a word about Raoul Kraushaar's outlandish music or, to be more precise, musical effects (he also scored *Bride of the Gorilla* and *Invaders from Mars*)? It roars when an elephant, tiger or panther appears, it slithers with the snakes and it gurgles during the water scenes; it's a cacophony of ceaseless noise using every note in the book—and it works! Like everything else in *Prehistoric Women*, it's designed to be so wildly over-the-top that the end result defies any kind of sensible critique or analysis. The movie is an uproarious hoot because it refuses to take itself seriously and, as an added plus, the Cinecolor photography is a wonder to behold. But what renowned anthropologists Louis and Mary Leakey (who discovered the earliest hominid remains in East Africa) would have made of it all doesn't bear pondering.

Lex Barker starred in five *Tarzan* movies, but a different actress played Jane alongside him in all five productions. His second outing in the role was RKO-Radio's *Tarzan and the Slave Girl* (1950) that had the Lord of the Jungle up against a tribe of Egyptian-looking warriors called the Lionians, ruled by Prince Hurd Hatfield. Hatfield's race suffers from a mysterious disease, leading to a lack of children, so the warriors, headed by Anthony Caruso, venture from their lost city and abduct native maidens for breeding purposes, keeping the skimpily dressed gals in a slave-bride harem straight out of an Arabian Nights fantasy. As if these concubines weren't enough to get the male juices flowing, Vanessa Brown (Jane) and sultry blonde bombshell Denise Darcel (who would simply *love* to get into Barker's loincloth) are also captured by the Lionians—and they're as scantily attired as the other women! Six-foot-four Barker, Cheetah, Robert Alda and Arthur Shields march off toward the city in pursuit, dodging poisonous darts fired from blowguns by a tribe called the Waddies, who camouflage themselves as trees. In the city, baddie Caruso has imprisoned Brown and Darcel in a tomb, viewing them as enemies. He's also extremely disgruntled at the scar that Barker gave him on his left cheek in a fight. In a lively climax boosted by Paul Sawtell's even livelier music, Barker rescues the girls with the aid of his pet elephant, the maidens are set free, Caruso falls into a lion pit, Cheetah joins in the fray and Shields and Alda cure Hatfield's sick young son..

Filmed on RKO's jungle backlot, *Tarzan and the Slave Girl* is 74-minutes of good, clean fun, director Lee Sholem ensuring that there's not *too* much female flesh on display to upset the censor (the picture was U-rated in England). Barker, in hindsight, made a great Tarzan and certainly possessed the athleticism and physique required for the part; as for that mischievous chimp, Cheetah manages to get drunk in one scene guaranteed to have the kids (and a few adults) in paroxysms of laughter.

Continental Pictures' 1951 release *Bowanga Bowanga: White Sirens of Africa* (aka *Wild Women*) is one step below *Prehistoric Women*'s production values, if that's at all possible. Although not in color, it bears two similarities: The Amazonian female tribe uses slingshots for weapons; and Gordon Zahler's score, like Raoul Kraushaar's, crashes away nonstop in the background, trying desperately to fill in the plot's numerous incongruities and lapses in taste. Director Norman Dawn uses a hell of a lot of stock wildlife footage in the opening half to pad out the 61-minute running time (and validate the $100 budget!) as big game hunters Lewis Wilson, Mort Thompson and Don Orlando run into the Ulama, a tribe of Hollywood starlets in leopard-skin bikinis inhabiting a remote African plateau ("You get all the blondes and I'll get all the redheads," says Thompson with a cheesy grin). A momentarily glimpsed man in a gorilla suit fails to materialize (a pity—this is one movie that could have benefited from a man in a gorilla suit), one of the Ulama women ("A vision of womanly loveliness.") abducts weedy Orlando and shots of an orangutan are inserted at five-minute intervals, but for what purpose is anyone's guess.

Once Wilson and Thompson rejoin their diminutive, dumb Italian comrade, the hilarious dialogue, spoken in truncated English, kicks in. Apparently, these savage babes are after strong men; any undernourished specimens are sacrificed to their Fire God. "Me talk white man talk. What name are you?" barks Dana Wilson, the tribe's leader, and to Orlando, "You're weak man. You're no good. We burn you." More gibberish follows. "Where you come from?" she asks Wilson. "America." "Not hear of such place." Thrown into a cave to await their fate ("What a charming bunch of chicks."), Thompson has to fight one of the women but is defeated. More male prisoners are shown, with a warning: "Husband try to run away. Get big spear in back. Queen wants big white husband—quick!" Then it's Wilson's turn to prove his manliness, which he does, overthrowing his opponent. He's then told, "You husband for Queen!" Kindly Charleen Hawkes eventually helps the trio escape after the sexually frustrated tribe stage a revolt, turning on their Queen for grabbing every suitable male beefcake for herself ("You take all husbands. We take nice man."). Singing an Italian ditty, the three men and their blonde native benefactor waltz off into the sunset, arm-in-arm, thus bringing to a close one hour of total cinematic jungle madness; you'll either laugh until you drop, or switch off the TV in derision. They certainly don't make confections like this anymore!

Jewell Enterprise's *Untamed Women* (1952) was one of many feature films made in this period to filch passages from Hal Roach's eponymous *One Million B.C.* (1940). That's not surprising—Roach's canny use of live lizards and other animals (plus a man in a dinosaur suit), set against pictorial prehistoric dioramas, was a template for the prehistoric adventure movies of the '50s and '60s. *Untamed Women* contains a great deal of footage from Roach's innovative classic and just as well—the remainder of the action veers from ineptness to unintentionally farcical to pure corn; director W. Merle

Connell and his technicians knocked this out in a week, and it shows. Bomber pilot Mikel Conrad tells the events in flashback. Conrad and his crew of three are shot down over the Pacific (the action takes place during World War II); taking to a dinghy, they land on an island populated by prehistoric monsters and a tribe of savage (but sexy) women led by High Priestess Doris Merrick. Their tribe descended from the Druids. Speaking in Olde Worlde English ("Thou sayest thou can fly like a bird."), Merrick at first wants to try the male interlopers and sacrifice them but then has a change of heart. After all, it's not often that all-American hunks visit her island abode! And when Conrad and his crew thwart an attack by the Hairy Men, a race of primitive warriors from the Stone Age (where do *they* originate from?), the women look upon their saviors in a new light. The return of the Hairy Men in the frantic climax coincides with a volcanic eruption which destroys the whole island; Conrad escapes in a raft, is picked up and we are back at the start of the picture where he shows a doctor a metal necklace of Druid origins, just to substantiate his story.

Not as bad as one might expect, *Untamed Women* is harmless *Lost World*–type fun containing snatches of female titillation, plus a few monsters to excite the youngsters. But it's ruined by one factor—Richard Monahan's irritating performance as the bomber crew's resident joker. Every line he speaks (in a thick Brooklyn accent) is either too comical or he tells a too silly tale; what a pity that giant armadillo didn't gobble him up when he took refuge in a tree from the creature halfway into the picture. And can anyone explain why the leader of a tribe stuck on an island in a prehistoric age is called Sandra? That just about sums up this supremely silly, 70-minute excursion into male-fantasyland; who wouldn't want to be washed-up on an island occupied by sex-starved women wearing next-to-nothing?

Astor's *Cat-Women of the Moon* (1953) may have been as lifeless as the lunar surface, but the company still saw fit to remake it in 1958 as *Missile to the Moon,* which is the better of the two, especially in its colorized incarnation. Arthur Hilton's direction is as static as Victor Jory's performance—he's the captain of a rocket that lands on the moon after a prolonged run-in with a meteorite. Jory and his three male colleagues are led by female crewmember Marie Windsor into a system of caves where the air is breathable. The team is attacked by two of the ropiest giant spiders ever to hit the big screen (suspended in midair on wires) before they stumble across Moon City, situated on the border of the light and dark side of the moon, inhabited by a bevy of females ("The Hollywood Cover Girls") all wearing black leotards with black wigs to match. These winsome gals use thought control to manipulate Windsor, Jory and company, hoping to hitch a lift back to Earth on the rocket where their goal is to rule the world by telepathy. But internal wrangling among them, mostly over the men they hanker after, means that Jory and the others, minus one of the crew who has been stabbed in the back after discovering gold, leave the caves in a hurry and blast off for Earth.

The Cat-Women of Moon City, played by "The Hollywood Cover Girls," from *Cat-Women of the Moon*.

Originally released in 3-D, Hilton's bargain-basement moon monstrosity is one of the '50s all-time slip-ups, bereft of a single redeeming feature. Correction: The painted backdrops of the moon's rugged pockmarked surface lend a slight air of desolate mystery, but that's about all. Jory, Sonny Tufts and Windsor look embarrassed in their roles, those rubber spiders inspire giggles, the script is clichéd, the rocket's flight deck was formerly used in a submarine movie and the Moon City resembles a temple left over from a biblical epic dating from the silent era. No doubt about it, Richard Cunha's 1958 update, although itself a camp-filled B romp, is marginally more watchable than this stinker—at least it is genuinely funny in places. *Cat-Women of the Moon*, over the course of 64 minutes, is totally devoid of *any* humor whatsoever.

Bring on the International Beauty Contest Winners of *Missile to the Moon*: Miss Florida, Miss France, Miss Germany, Miss Illinois, Miss Minnesota, Miss New Hampshire, Miss New York State and Miss Yugoslavia. Mincing on set like models on a catwalk, the girls fail to cut it as glamour pusses; trouble is, under all that greasepaint, and wearing less-than-flattering costumes from a pantomime production of *Ali Baba and the 40 Thieves*, they don't look all that prepossessing. *Missile to the Moon* was the third of Richard Cunha's quartet of films made for Astor in 1958 and the Moon Maidens were played by this list of lovelies. As mentioned, the movie was a superior (if that term can be used!) rework of *Cat-Women of the Moon*, worked along similar lines. Michael Whalen blasts off for the moon with Richard Travis, Cathy Downs and two escaped convicts, Frankie Avalon look-alikes Tommy Cook and Gary Clarke, on board. Whalen, apparently, visited the moon 20 years ago, so when he dies in an accident before touchdown (caused by that old stand-by, the meteor shower), the Maidens' half-blind leader, K.T. Stevens, thinks that Travis is Whalen because of a medallion he's wearing. Lustful Nina Bara also thinks the same, attempting by hypnosis to pry bemused Travis away from fiancée Downs and offering the Earth woman as sacrifice to a large hairy spider on wires known as the Dark One. The moon females want the rocket in order for them to populate Earth as the moon's oxygen (?) is running out; Cook covets the diamonds that festoon the subterranean caves and Clarke just wants to get the hell outta there. Finally, one of the rebellious maidens blows the lunar world to pieces; Bara knives Stevens in the back and perishes under a falling pillar. Out in California's Red Rock Canyon (sorry, the moon!), the six-foot slabs of foam known as the Rock Men close in on Cook and his diamonds; stepping into the sun's cosmic rays, the greedy delinquent is burnt to a cinder, the others heading off to Earth and safety.

Cunha's low-grade space opera is 78-minutes of undiluted schlock, still possessing the ability to entertain after several beers, notwithstanding the fake painted backdrops, toy-shop spiders, corny script and laughable acting. Legend's colorized restoration job (chapter 14) breathes more life into this cheesy production than maybe it warrants, but at least it makes those international beauties more attractive than they are in black-and-white!

Roger Corman's contributions to this ragbag collection of hot celluloid female flesh are the wonderfully titled AIP productions *Viking Women and the Sea Serpent* (1957) and *She Gods of Shark Reef* (1958). But the titles are the only wonderful things about these $50,000 reels of girly hogwash. The first (full title: *The Saga of the Viking Women and Their Voyage to the Waters of the Great Sea Serpent*) concerns a bunch of lovesick Viking babes (speaking in Norse/New York drawls), led by Susan Cabot and Abby Dalton, who go searching for their men-folk, who have been missing for three years. Narrowly avoiding being feasted on by a gigantic sea serpent (The Monster of the Vortex), the women are washed ashore in the land of the Grimolt (California's Bronson Canyon; film crews must have been tripping over themselves location shooting in this much-favored spot)), lorded over by King Richard Devon. Devon fancies Dalton; Dalton wants to rescue her beau, Brad Jackson, from slavery; scheming dark-haired Cabot also lusts after Jackson but sides with Devon; Devon's son, Jay Sayer, is a sniveling, prissy coward and pint-sized, flaxen-headed Jonathan Haze hurls himself into one fight after another, his eyes firmly set on June Kenney's shapely legs. Kirk Douglas and *The Vikings* this isn't! After 60 minutes of low-budget action, Devon and his mob pursue the women but are smashed to pieces by the serpent; Dalton, Kenney, Sally Todd and crew, together with their men (minus two-timing Cabot who has been savaged to death by dogs), reach their homeland as the sun rises.

Cabot, pouty and sexy, comes out tops in the acting honors, a couple of backdrops conjured up by Jack Rabin, Louis DeWitt and Irving Block look splendid, the serpent is so-so and the dialogue is suited to under-12s only. One man, and one man only, makes this film watchable—Albert Glasser. *Viking Women* is hoisted out of the mire by his clamorous score, a score that keeps going even when the pace flags. Like so many other badder-than-bad movies featured in this book, Corman's juvenile fantasy adventure benefits greatly from a worthwhile soundtrack that is a lot better than the picture it is backing. And color would have made all the difference as well.

On location in Kaua'i, Hawaii, filming the gangster thriller *Naked Paradise* (1957), Corman took full advantage of the island's spectacular scenery by drumming up a South Seas adventure whose paper-thin plot could have been written on a postage stamp (Corman was adept at shooting back-to-back movies; he achieved it again in 1963 with *The Raven* and *The Terror*). Two brothers (Bill Cord and Don Durant) on the run from the police (the opening murder of a cop is pretty brutal) are shipwrecked on a tropical island inhabited by sarong-clad women ruled over by a crusty middle-aged queen, Jeanne Gerson, ranting and raving like the Wicked Witch of the West. Cord falls in love with dark-haired Lisa Montell; gunrunner Durant wants to hightail it out with a bag of stolen pearls; Cord, Durant, Montell and Gerson end up on a reef; Durant is torn apart by the smallest killer shark in the history of the cinema and Cord plus Montell sail away, leaving Gerson and her girls to carry on worshiping the god Tanga Roah—the deity's stone head lies on the ocean floor, guarded by sharks.

Corman retained the services of cinematographer Floyd Crosby and composer Ronald Stein from *Naked Paradise*, but *not* (unfortunately) Richard Denning and Beverly Garland. Crosby's lush Pathecolor is lost on current DVD issues, while the crashing surf drowns out Stein's score (and much of the dialogue). And talking of dialogue: Robert Hill and Victor Stoloff's script is totally devoid of priceless interchanges—a dumb movie with no dumb lines to match. All those nubile goodies remain firmly under wraps—among the films included in this chapter, there's less for the voyeur to slaver over, a dire omission by Corman who should have stuck to the exploitation side of things, given the South Seas material and all that it stands for. With hunky dudes Cord and Durant embarrassingly wandering around in micro-sarongs to cover up their modesty, add a couple of hip-wiggling dances, Gerson constantly flagging messages to "The Company" (whoever they are), the microphone boom clearly visible in one shot, Gerson tossing coconut husks on a fire as an offering to the gods and Cord rescuing Montell on a surfboard, *She Gods of Shark Reef* must go down as Corman's worst-ever '50s feature, regardless of those gorgeous Hawaiian locales. Praise be to Tanga Roah that it's only 63-minutes long.

Once upon a time, 10,000 years ago, there were two islands: Wongo and Goona. Nature had not been kind to these Stone Age people—the drop-dead gorgeous women of Wongo were lumbered with brutish men-folk; on Goona, the handsome men-folk were cursed with scraggy/overweight women whose top priority was a good shave. An impending invasion of ape men (well, two to be exact) throws the warring tribes together and, would you believe it, the sex-starved hussies from Wongo fall in lust with the men from Goona, while the men from Wongo, for reasons known only to themselves, salivate at the thought of playing house with those unwholesome females from Goona. The male leaders of both tribes sport blue rinses, there's a cardboard temple built to worship the Dragon God (a large crocodile), the hunks from Goona look as though they've stepped out from the pages of a men's gay magazine, semi-pornographic dances abound and every so often, a talking red parrot butts in with a few knowing asides. Filmed around a theme park in Florida in bright Pathecolor, *The Wild Women of Wongo* (1958), as its title suggests, is a screwy prehistoric romp that surely has to be included in the Golden Turkey awards as one of the most inept caveman/cavewomen flicks ever committed to celluloid.

Full marks to a ludicrous script that is crammed full of 20th-century speak; not a grunt in earshot! "This reminds me of a dream I once had," coos Jean Hawkshaw as she ogles Johnny Walsh's well-honed pecs, her pals giggling like a bunch of overexcited schoolgirls. As they gaze into each other's eyes, in comes the parrot: "Oh no, here we go. Break it up. Break it up." Hawkshaw wanders off with Walsh (he's from Goona, as if you hadn't guessed), they kiss and get down to some nookie, after which she brazenly announces to her father that she wants to marry the stud. "No" is the short answer. Banished to the temple for their carnal thoughts, two beefed-up guys in loincloths, representing the ape men invasion, attack the girls. Pushed into a morass by the spear-wielding damsels, the wimps are eaten by the big croc ... end of invasion.

Returning to their village, they find it deserted. "Although my father is the King of Wongo, I am his daughter," shouts Hawkshaw, stating the blindingly obvious in trying to exert her authority. They then decide to head to Goona ("You wanna live here for the rest of ya life without any men at all?") and meet the local women ("You come in peace—with spears!" they yell before shrieking and running away). Walsh and his buddies, skinny-dipping in a lake, are lassoed one by one by Hawkshaw and company for the purpose of choosing mating partners ("This one's mine; he's cute!"). Marching their captives back to Wongo (cue for the parrot to squawk: "Left right, left right; left, two three, four, left, two, three, four"), they're taken to the Temple of the Dragon God, unbound, paired off and married by the campy High Priestess. Then the men from Wongo march in with the unkempt lasses from Goona and they're married! The final shot? All those muscle-bound dudes take it in turns to wink at the camera. "Well, how about that," says the parrot, echoing the sentiments of those watching this shiny piece of garbage and, as a consequence, saving itself from a long-overdue neck wringing.

Director James L. Wolcott, producer George R. Black, writer Cedric Rutherford, photographer Harry Walsh and Jawall Productions should be truly mortified at having the audacity to inflict 72 minutes of no-holds-barred dross onto a paying audience. Having said that, it is without doubt a scream to sit through and, as is the case with most guilty pleasures, warrants a second taste! But only a second!

Film is like a blank canvas, waiting for ideas to be formulated and committed to celluloid. Unfortunately, *Island of Lost Women* (1959) remains blank throughout its mercifully short 71-minute running time. Warner Bros. (this surely has to be their most rickety release of the 1950s) could have had so much fun with this familiar scenario if the production team had decided to throw caution to the wind and ham it up. Two guys (Jeff Richards and John Smith) land their crippled plane on a remote Pacific Island where they find nuclear physicist Alan Napier and his three ripe-for-the-plucking daughters: Urana (Diane Jergens), Venus (Venetia Stevenson) and Mercuria (June Blair). "They come in threes. Yeah man!" slobbers Smith, eying up the tunic-clad beauties. Napier, horrified at the devastation caused by the H-bomb on Hiroshima, has turned his back on civilization, creating a secret Garden of Eden. Anybody getting too close to the island is blasted to death by an atomic flamethrower; also built in Napier's cave laboratory is a reactor fed on uranium isotopes that ensures interlopers will be swiftly dealt with; he doesn't want the scientific world to know where he resides. As expected, sex rears its ugly head—the trio of Vestal Virgins have all read about men in magazines (where did they get those from?) but have never seen one in the flesh. Now two all-American studs have appeared out of the blue, like manna from heaven, and the girls' hormonal juices are in full flow! Stevenson grabs Richards, Blair digs her claws into Smith and young Jergens has to be content with reporting every kiss and suggestive innuendo back to her father. Enraged at his chaste daughters' unseemly behavior, he blows up the aircraft, forcing the men to build an escape raft.

Director Frank Tuttle sorely needed an injection of humor in the script department to give us the odd laugh or two: One cannot present this kind of material straight; it just doesn't work. Apart from the inane opening line, when Smith, flying over an island, turns to Richards and states, "Look over there. That's an island. Let's check it out," the dialogue is as flat as the action. *Prehistoric Women* and *The Wild Women of Wongo* were hilarious for all the right reasons. Warner Bros.' flop is as miserable as the expression on Napier's face. The scientist's laboratory ends up as a mushroom cloud in the end, flames triggering a chain reaction; a plane appears soon afterwards, ready to whisk all six (unharmed by radiation fallout) to a better life in the United States. The only thing lively about *Island of Lost Women* is Raoul Kraushaar's noisy score; for the rest, read a capital B for Boredom. A guilty pleasure it ain't!

Chapter 13
Let's Take Another Look: Part Two

Pretty-Boy Psycho Stalks the West

In 1966, Robert Evans became boss of Paramount Pictures. Back in 1958, as one of Hollywood's up-and-coming retinue of young actors with a reputation for being difficult on set, he was offered the role of Felix Griffin in *The Fiend Who Walked the West*, an unusual rehash of Henry Hathaway's *Kiss of Death* (1947), taking over the part first played to such chilling effect by Richard Widmark. Widmark made his name as gangster Tommy Udo, a giggling psychopath who in one scene (cut by the British censor on first release) hurls an old lady in a wheelchair down a flight of stairs. Evans was told that this was the part that would make *him* hit the big time and, let's give the actor his due, he turned in a career best performance in a movie that was misunderstood at the time but has grown in stature over the years, if you have been lucky enough to catch it. The movie has only been screened once on British television, in 1972. And its issue on DVD has been sporadic.

Originally roughed out under the working labels of *Rope Law*, *The Hell-Bent Kid* and *Quick Draw*, the film's title (and, as a consequence, its marketing strategy in the eyes of the distributors) was changed when Fox decided to jump onto the popular (and moneymaking) 1950s horror bandwagon by altering their promotional publicity to give it an individualistic horror/Western slant. This obviously did the trick—when I first saw it in May 1963 (double billed with *She Devil*), I was under the impression that what I was about to experience was some sort of monster movie set in the Old West. In thinking this I was wrong, but that didn't prevent me from enjoying what was essentially a dialogue-driven psycho-Western molded in *film noir*-style, with Evans' standout turn holding the interest throughout. He was totally unlike any other Western villain I had ever come across. Being in CinemaScope was another big bonus. It may well have been talky, but *The Fiend Who Walked the West* was a popular enough draw on the U.K. horror circuit during the 1960s, more often than not teamed up with Toho's *Rodan* or Regal's *Kronos*.

Hugh *Wyatt Earp* O'Brian, receiving a stiff 10-year sentence in a federal prison for his part in the Aureate City Bank robbery, finds himself sharing a cell with Evans, a young cowpoke-cum-sadist nursing a boat-load of psychological hang-ups. Befriending Evans, he lets slip with details of the robbery, a big mistake. When Evans is released after a few weeks, he immediately sets off to get his hands on the loot, and woe to anyone who gets in his way. He fires an arrow into an old lady in a wheelchair, blasts her son with a shotgun and even O'Brian's pregnant wife (Linda Cristal) receives an unwelcome visit, suffering a miscarriage as a result of Evans' sexual depredations. When sheriff's deputy Ron Ely is gunned down after getting on the wrong side of Evans, the authorities have had all they can take; they decide to fake O'Brian's prison escape in the hope that, as the only person to get remotely close to the madman, he can prevent any further murders and bring Evans to justice. After more killings and twists and turns, there's a final confrontation in a saloon where O'Brian empties his revolver into the psychopath and is reunited with his wife.

X-rated in Britain, Gordon Douglas' Western-with-a-difference was banned in Sweden and other parts of Europe because of its violent content (Evans continually beats up girlfriend Dolores Michaels and ends up strangling her) and intimidating script. The film is underlined by a spare but edgy soundtrack from Leon Klatzkin; his symphonic title score is a treat, with elements of Bernard Herrmann's music for *The Day the Earth Stood Still* added to give a fantasy effect to the proceedings (the composer specialized in scoring TV Westerns: *Have Gun, Will Travel* and *Rawhide* among them). Harry Brown and Philip Yordan's incisive script, based on Ben Hecht and Charles Lederer's celebrated screenplay for *Kiss of Death*, fizzes with menace, as befits the

material. *The Fiend Who Walked the West* takes as its central theme the tense, mistrustful Evans/O'Brian relationship, the pair circling each other like a couple of rattlesnakes, knowing full well that one wrong move will end in a killing. In three pivotal sequences, artfully choreographed by Douglas (he directed *Them!*), Evans' sneering, cunning delivery, creating a series of half-truths, blind alleys, threats and self-deluded flights of fancy, is the perfect foil to O'Brian's taciturn, patient demeanor, a man biding his time, waiting for the right moment to strike, as in the following exchange:

Evans: "I suppose they told you I'd kill ya if I caught on to what you were doin'."

O'Brian: "They didn't have to tell me that."

Evans: "I guess they didn't know that I'd kill ya anyway, though, for chokin' me the way you did."

O'Brian: "They mentioned that too."

Evans: "Ha, ha, they know me better than my own pa did. That's very funny, Sad Man."

Despite a bravura piece of acting from Evans, he wasn't taken seriously by the critics because his boyish looks were considered at odds with the role of a lunatic. Nonsense. His dark, matinee-idol features work for, rather than against, the character he is creating. Why have an ugly psycho when, against type, you can have a good-looking one! Besides, young James Dean-type "cool" actors with curling upper lips were making inroads into Westerns anyway. Nobody could ever accuse cowboy star Audie Murphy of being anything but cute (and even *he* played a couple of mean critters in his time!); James Best portrayed a giggling killer to perfection in Budd Boetticher's *Ride Lone-*

some; while every teenage girl's fantasy, Ricky Nelson, was a revelation in Howard Hawks' *Rio Bravo*. Evans plays the part to the hilt, and never did anything better—like O'Brian in the picture, audiences can't take their eyes off him for a second, a sure sign of a winning performance in any cinemagoer's book. Photographed in crisp black-and-white, *The Fiend Who Walked the West* is an underrated psychological thriller that takes place in a distinctive milieu that sets it apart from others; the movie deserves a full-blown DVD release to show fans just what they have been missing all these years.

"Violent and dull."

Radioactive Goo Threatens Tokyo

Released in 1958, Toho's *The H-Man* (*Bijo to Ekitai Ningen*) represented a change in direction for Inoshiro Honda and his team. Temporarily casting aside their rubber-suited monsters, this Atomic Age-themed tale told of a cargo boat that passed too close to an H-bomb explosion for comfort, the ship's company changing into radioactive blobs that feed off human flesh. When the crew of a passing ship board the deserted vessel, all but two are liquefied; the survivors bring the contamination back to Tokyo, where the gelatinous ooze begins to prey on humans by dripping onto them. The residue is washed into the sewers by rainwater, where it proliferates, emerging through the drain covers to claim more victims. Intermingled with the horror hokum is Japanese *film noir*, concerning cops trying to bust a narcotics gang and giving protection to nightclub singer Yumi Shirakawa. Scientist Kenji Sahara reckons he knows who, or what, is responsible for bodies vanishing into thin air, leaving only their clothes, but the police have their doubts and it's up to Sahara to convince the authorities of the danger Tokyo finds itself in. And, of course, he fancies the vulnerable Shirakawa like mad.

The H Man, **Toho's most adult-oriented piece of horror hokum, climaxes in the sewer system.**

Shot in over-bright color and TohoScope, *The H-Man* was originally issued in a 97-minute length, cut by 10 minutes shortly after. The dubbed American version comes in at 79 minutes, a few minor edits implemented to quicken the pace. All told, this counts as Toho's most adult-orientated piece of '50s horror hokum. The contemporary gangster milieu/monster marriage works, based on an intelligent script and a lack of the usual histrionics that can blight quite a number of Japanese horror movies. Two scenes stand out. First, the sequence on the empty vessel when the boarding crew face their worst nightmares in the dingy passageways and, second, the fiery finale in the sewers, the military, armed with flamethrowers, pouring blazing gasoline into the tunnels to exterminate the creatures and almost setting the city ablaze in the process. Throw in a risqué (for 1958!) nightclub dance, bodies melting into bubbly gunge and the blobs appearing in glowing green human form, like fluorescent phantoms, and you have an excellent X-rated Toho picture that tends to get bypassed in favor of all those reptilian giants stomping across Japanese cities during the 1950s. Masaru Sato's marching-type score lessens the mood when it comes into play, which isn't often (most scenes are devoid of music), but that's the only downside to *The H-Man*, one of Toho's more persuasive pictures from this productive period in their highly acclaimed history.

"Garishly photographed nonsense."

Chaney's Finest '50s Horror Hour

After Lon Chaney, Jr. left Universal-International in 1952 to freelance, he lent his burly presence, and bankable name, to any number of movies and television shows throughout the 1950s, including telling cameos in *Big House, U.S.A.* and *High Noon*. From 1951 to 1959, the actor actually appeared in only seven horror films, of which *Indestructible Man*, released by Allied Artists in 1956, remains the best of the bunch, beating by a whisker his role in *The Alligator People*. There he played a hook-handed bayou loner who hated alligators and had the hots for Beverly Garland. But that was a supporting part—*Indestructible Man* gave Chaney, Jr. star billing and he made the most of it, carrying the production from start to finish, even though his dialogue was limited to the opening three minutes, a head-to-head argument with crooked lawyer Ross Elliott behind prison bars.

Chaney is "Butcher" Benton, a bruising thug, part of a four-man team who have stolen $600,000 in a violent robbery and left it for Chaney to stash away in the Los Angeles sewers. He's the only member of the gang to be apprehended and has been given the death penalty. Trouble is, Elliott, his double-crossing lawyer, doesn't know where the loot is hidden and Chaney, hours away from the gas chamber in San Quentin prison, is not letting on. His last words, spat out between gritted teeth to smarmy Elliott, are, "Remember what I said. I'm gonna kill ya. All three of you," words that will come to haunt Elliott in the days to come. Executed the next morning, Chaney's body is retrieved from the state penitentiary morgue and revived by two scientists who pump the corpse full of electricity as part of an experiment to find a cure for cancer. The killer comes alive, mute and impervious to bullets, determined to hunt down and eliminate the associates who put him behind bars. Eight slayings later (the two scientists, three cops, two ex-buddies and a car-owner), Chaney heads for the sewers and the cash, followed by cop Casey Adams and a posse of police. Getting his hands on the dollars, the "Butcher" receives a bazooka rocket in the chest and is fried by flamethrowers; his features horribly flayed and agonized with pain, he scrambles out of the drains onto a power station gantry and perishes trying to connect electrical cables in an attempt to give himself more strength, thus leaving Adams to continue his not-quite-off-the-blocks affair with peroxide blonde Marian Carr.

Writer/producer Jack Pollexfen only directed three pictures in his career, which comes as something of a surprise, as the brash *Indestructible Man*, a blend of police and horror thriller, moves at a cracking pace, shot in the semi-documentary tabloid style honed to perfection in the popular television series *Dragnet* (1951-1959). It's a fact that *Indestructible Man* strays into *cinema vérité* territory at times, so stripped to the bone is Pollexfen's style of shooting. Photographed in grainy black-and-white, the movie successfully portrays a feeling of doggedness and a steely edge lacking in other films of this nature, and the murders committed by Chaney are quite brutal. The only trifling irritant is the number of times the director insists on inserting into the framework a close-up of the actor's squinting eyes. Ably bolstering Pollexfen's horror/crime outing is Albert Glasser's bombastic soundtrack, not letting up for a second but never an intrusion. Glasser is one of a select band of film composers who specialized in bringing B movies to life during this frenetic period; his integral work behind *Indestructible Man* symbolizes a form of artistry regrettably lost within the horror cinema sphere of today.

And what about Chaney himself? Let's be honest, he wasn't the world's most expressive actor, content to let his 6' 2", 220 lb. bulky frame and gruff persona do all the talking. But his name alone would guarantee many a fan seeing "Lon Chaney" on the billboards and think, "Hmmm. Maybe it's worth a look." He was without doubt a horror box-office draw, even now in the 1950s (based on his classic output from the previous decade), and here he played to all his heavyweight strengths, acquitting himself with honors. X-rated in Britain, *Indestructible Man* (a rehash of Chaney's own *Man Made Monster*: Even Adams states at one point that the "Butcher" is a "monster-made man!") was a firm favorite on the Sunday one-day circuit in the early 1960s, usually showing with *Invasion of the Body Snatchers* or *The Black Scorpion*. It somehow epitomized the gutsy approach given to mid-'50s horror movies and begs the question: Was this actually Chaney's finest hour in a 1950s horror movie (or, to be more precise, finest 70 minutes)? Without doubt, on reflection and compared to other performances in other films, it most definitely was!

"Lacks style ... star in poor form."

Victorian Explorers Plumb the Depths of the Earth

20th Century Fox's lavish *Journey to the Center of the Earth* (1959) remains the finest cinematic adaptation of Jules Verne's classic adventure novel. The movie features a seasoned director at the helm (Henry Levin); an expensive budget; Oscar-winning screenwriter Charles Brackett (*Sunset Boulevard*) teamed up with Walter Reisch (the two had collaborated on Marilyn Monroe's *Niagara*, 1953); beautiful DeLuxe Color and CinemaScope photography; James Mason's box-office muscle and Pat Boone's family appeal and a fabulous musical score by Bernard Herrmann.

So why is it that so many film compendiums and certain critics persist in giving this handsomely constructed fantasy the thumbs down?

Maybe it's that final scene: Arlene Dahl, resplendent in mauve attire and carrying a parasol, gives Professor Mason the come-on, ending in a clinch in front of thousands of students. "Sickly sweet" as one writer has described? Not at all, it's in keeping with the film's lighthearted nature, the culmination of a long-running verbal spat between the two in the manner of an old Spencer Tracy/Katherine Hepburn vehicle. Perhaps it's Pat Boone serenading Diane Baker in the opening few minutes with "My Love is like a Red, Red Rose," but Boone was a popular singer at the time and his crooning slot only lasted a couple of minutes anyway. "A lack of wonder" is how one critic puts it; this great-looking production has "wonder" by the bucket-load! The art direction is superlative (principal shooting took place in Carlsbad Caverns, New Mexico), conjuring up a subterranean world of crystalline grottos, dark forbidding tunnels, cathedral-sized caverns, a forest of giant mushrooms, a salt labyrinth, the ruined city of Atlantis, an underground ocean and flesh-eating dinosaurs. Punctuating it all is Herrmann's atmospheric soundtrack.

James Mason, Arlene Dahl, Pat Boone and Peter Ronson are taking *A Journey to the Center of the Earth.*

The revered composer was a master at creating the right mood and his contemplative score, performed predominantly on woodwind and brass, perfectly evokes the spirit of the underworld. Acting-wise, Mason is in top form as the tetchy Professor Lindenbrook (a part originally earmarked for Clifton Webb), Boone shines as Mason's star student and Dahl makes a formidable, flame-haired beauty. The attention to all things Victoriana is also beyond reproach, as is the sense of time and place. But the one thing above all others that truly lifts this picture into a different dimension is Brackett and Reisch's scintillating script, almost unique in the annals of fantasy filmmaking and worthy of closer scrutiny.

Mason, in response to Diane Baker's question as to how long it will take to melt the block of larva (inside of which is a plumb bob), brusquely replies, "A typically female question." The dialogue, at regular intervals, stresses the Professor's innate distrust of women and the fact that, in his eyes, he has to be resigned to being lumbered with Dahl on the expedition. It's in the edgy Mason/Dahl relationship that the script drips with waspish asides. "You can't come along. You're a woman!" he barks, followed by, "To burden myself with a woman is sheer stupidity!" Perched on the edge of a bottomless gulf, Dahl turns to Mason: "Poor Sir Oliver. Stuck with a woman. If only you could see your face." Mason testily responds: "That's my consolation, Madam. I don't have to look at it. You do!" As the exploration begins, Mason advises his colleagues to "use our canteens freely at the moment. There'll be plenty of mineral springs on the way." "As my husband's chart indicated," states Dahl. Mason, irritated, snaps back: "Is Professor Goteborg to be with us on our entire journey, Madam?" "Sorry!" is the curt riposte.

On retiring for the day, Dahl wakes up: "Someone is walking up there. I heard footsteps. Human footsteps."

Mason: "Madam, since the beginning of time, women have heard footsteps—up there."

Dahl: "My hearing is extremely acute!"

Mason, bluntly: "The hearing of all women is extremely acute."

Like a couple of sparring partners, this witty banter between the two carries on right up to the final scene in which Mason asks Dahl to stay at his house to help in writing his memoirs. She fakes shock/horror at such a suggestion, although secretly pleased that he made it.

Mason: "Well, er, what do you propose?"

Dahl, smiling: "Oh, that's not a word I bandy about, Professor."

Mason: "What did I say? Which word?"

Dahl replies: "I thought it would catch in your throat!"

Naturally, the couple embraces, but not before Dahl informs Mason, "I warn you. I'm wearing stays again."

Yes, a cracking screenplay; this film is as much a joy to listen to as well as to watch. The producers took a few liberties with Verne's novel and made some significant revisions. The scribe most definitely did *not* mention Gertrude the Duck! The picture also clocked in at a lengthy 132 minutes; it's 45 involving minutes before the explorers line up on the edge of Sneffels Yokull at the start of their journey, but that didn't bother audiences of the time. *Journey to the Center of the Earth* is a solidly crafted, majestically paced fantasy, a contender for the '50s finest and as enjoyable now as it was 53 years ago. Juvenile it isn't—exciting and wondrous it is! (Note: Eagle-eyed movie detectives with a penchant for unusual cine-facts and trivia should check out Universal's *Cave of Outlaws*. Filmed partly in Carlsbad Caverns, this lively Western contains many underground scenes that feature in Fox's fantasy, most markedly in the sequences in which Boone becomes separated from his companions in the labyrinth of salt tunnels. For Boone, substitute cowboy MacDonald Carey in the selfsame setting, an odd juxtaposition if ever there was one!)

"Juvenile ... lacks wonder."

Helicopter Crashlands in Mesozoic Valley

Years before *Jurassic Park* and CGI dinosaur effects, fans of the *Lost World*–type of monster-filled actioners gathered in droves on a wet Sunday afternoon, or at midnight in their local Odeon, to catch Universal's rip-roaring *The Land Unknown* (1957). A popular draw on England's horror circuit (usually paired with *The Deadly Mantis*), the movie had two big things going for it to guarantee catching a young fan's attention. It was shot in CinemaScope, an added extra for cinemagoers of that period used to seeing their fantasy fare on a normal screen size and it was X-rated, giving it far more bite than others of its ilk. Originally slated as an expensive A production to be filmed in color and 'Scope, with Jack Arnold directing, a series of internal wrangles ended with the picture relegated to B status, stripped of its color (but retaining the widescreen) and acted by a team of relative unknowns. Arnold bowed out of the project and Virgil Vogel, who had directed *The Mole People*, took over. Universal were none too happy with the results, especially the monsters, but viewed decades later, *The Land Unknown* can be treasured for what it is, a sprightly paced prehistoric opus which fills its 78-minute running time with all kinds of incidents and excitement.

Noteworthy in '50s design, the movie's limitless backdrops inside the hidden crater are stunningly realized, especially when viewed on the big panoramic screen in a cinema, a diorama of distant mist-shrouded cliffs, waterfalls, lofty, exotic trees and dense tropical jungle, imbuing the production with that crucial sense of awe. Okay, those monsters that Universal so disliked—the lumbering T-Rex is a man in a rubber suit, there are magnified lizards, a model Pterodactyl, a carnivorous plant and a fearsome Elasmosaurus (a large-scale replica was built). No stop-motion animation and *no* computerized effects, but somehow this rag-bag collection of primeval monstrosities (courtesy of Clifford Stine) fits in with the film's overall gritty look, and they were certainly savage enough in the British censor's eyes to warrant that "X" classification. Moreover, the paying public didn't criticize these creatures—they

The Land Unknown contained quaint special effects comprising men in suits and large scale models, but the prehistoric monsters were effective.

loved what they were being subjected to! So *The Land Unknown* has that necessary *Lost World* ambience in abundance to enthrall the fans and keep them pinned to their seats.

What about the cast? Hunk Jock Mahoney took the lead, soon to star in a run of *Tarzan* movies. Mahoney was sturdy rather than expressive, but in a picture such as this, overacting wasn't called for and he filled the role of a naval commander-cum-geophysicist perfectly. Ex-beauty pageant queen Shawn Smith, "Miss California 1940," starred as the token feisty female; Smith sported a blonde rinse (in stark contrast to her severe brunette countenance in *It! The Terror from Beyond Space*) and was a real head-turner, both on-screen and, apparently, off. "I always love to meet men, Captain," she coos at one point, gaining the admiration (and frank ardor) of Mahoney a little too quickly. The acting honors went to Henry Brandon, playing a half-crazed survivor of a previous expedition who had managed to survive in the lost valley for 10 years with only dinosaurs for company. Brandon turned in a menacing performance and added gravitas, capturing the inner turmoil of a man who is unable to figure out where he belongs in the scheme of things—in this prehistoric prison, alone or back among his own kind.

Mahoney, Smith, William Reynolds and Phil Harvey, investigating a warm water area in Antarctica, clip a Pterodactyl in their chopper and plummet into a primordial crater 3,000 feet below sea level. Once there they encounter a variety of prehistoric beasties plus the demented Brandon, who takes one look at the gorgeous Smith and decides that he wants her all to himself; the others can leave whenever they like, *if* they can repair their damaged helicopter. They manage it in the end, cannibalizing parts from Brandon's wrecked helicopter and rescuing the hermit from the jaws of the Elasmosaurus. Back on board ship, Mahoney gets a well-deserved clinch from Smith after she has hinted that she would like a baby, a heaven-sent proposition if ever there was one! Vogel directed this stylish caper with bags of vigor, showing far more zeal than he did in the rather sedate *The Mole People*, and the noisy action doesn't let up for a second, ensuring no clock-watching or fidgeting. Produced during Universal's golden age of monsterdom, *The Land Unknown* is a worthy reminder of how brilliantly produced this company's creature-features were in the 1950s and why they are still regarded with such high esteem by fantasy aficionados. And this is one black-and-white feature from the '50s that should be singled out for colorization forthwith, regardless of whether or not we think the colorization process is a gimmick best avoided. *The Land Unknown* in CinemaScope *and* color? Wow!

"Lacks the panache of *King Kong*."

You're Looking a little Gray-Faced Today

Columbia's *The Man Who Turned to Stone* (1957) is packed to the rafters with '50s B actors: William Hudson, Charlotte Austin, Tina Carver, Ann Doran, Frederick Ledebur, Paul Cavanagh, Barbara Wilson, Victor Varconi, George Lynn and Jean Willes. In addition, King of the Quickies Sam Katzman produced while the relatively unknown Hungarian Leslie (Laszlo) Kardos directed. Victor Jory, whose saturnine physiognomy didn't exactly radiate good will to all men, took top billing. Was this a blueprint for disaster? Not exactly. Although it could never be classed as a Columbia five-star horror production, *The Man Who Turned to Stone* is still a respectable X-rated mad scientist feature that rattles through its 71 minutes with the odd flourish here and there.

A group of scientists, led by Jory, were all born in the 1730s and met in Paris in 1780, determined to discover the secret of immortality and how to prolong life. By the use of bio-electrical energy transference, they found a method of siphoning the life force from healthy young women and have now attained the age of 220. However, if this force is denied to any of the group for a short interval, petrification and death is the sure-fire result. Jory has set up a laboratory in the grounds of the La Salle Detention Home for Young Women; over the space of two years, 11 mysterious deaths have occurred whereby apparently robust inmates have died from heart attacks. Jory's antiquated method of sustaining eternal life is to send out lanky Ledebur, who grabs the screaming girls in Frankenstein Monster-mode. Taken to the lab, the unwilling donors are submerged in a bathtub of copper sulphate solution and connected to electrical apparatus (all very 1930s in concept). Their bodily essence is then transferred to gaunt-looking Ledebur; he has a tiresome habit of turning to stone a lot faster than his colleagues and needs regular topping up with female life force to rejuvenate his more-or-less youthful complexion. Good-guy Hudson,

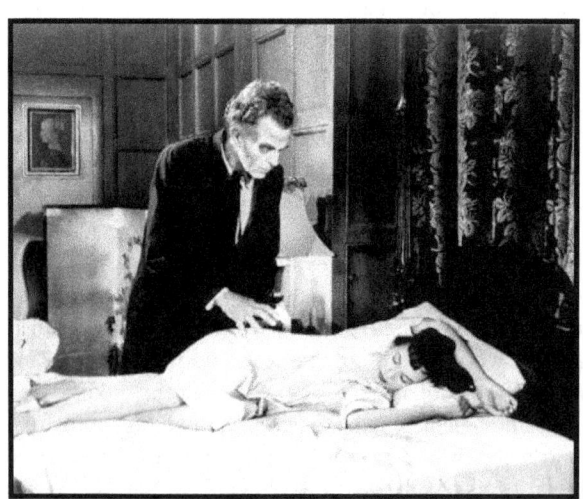

Frederick Ledebur grabs another victim, seeking a cure, in *The Man Who Turned to Stone*.

suspicious to a fault, is soon looking into missing death certificates, performing autopsies and needling Jory and his cronies at the risk of his own life and Austin's, whom he's fallen for big time.

Finesse is at a short premium here. Kardos, in his one and only horror outing, is content to allow the cast to react in front of a stationary camera in most scenes. Somehow, though, this brisk little movie overcomes these shortfalls. The effects showing skin tissue gradually changing to stone are basic but weird (dark shades circling the eyes, cheeks and brow wrinkled); Doran is particularly loathsome as the head of the reformatory, perceiving her argumentative, bitchy charges as nothing more than objects fit only to keep her and her gang of zombies going for another 100 years or so. There's an abundance of female flesh on parade, more in keeping with an exploitation flick; the script does its best to avoid the usual horror clichés; George Duning's stock score is used sparingly but constructively and Jory just about manages to chew the scenery. The picture climaxes in the customary inferno—a fire in a basement sets the mansion ablaze, Jory and Doran (finally exposed, their secret out) choosing to perish in the flames, Cavanagh and Ledebur having succumbed to the petrifying process. And yes, Hudson saves heroine Austin in the nick of time.

Cold-shouldered by critics, *The Man Who Turned to Stone* may not be on the same level as other Columbia '50s horror outings, but it's still an enjoyably put-together picture that holds its own, having a distinct '40s feel to it. Never broadcast on British television and appearing back in 1964 on the lower half of a double bill with *Creature with the Atom Brain*, Kardos' mad doctor effort embodied all the ingredients necessary for a 70-minute horror second feature. It's a lot better than many people give it credit for.

"Charmless ... lacks intelligence ... silly."

Biblical Rejects Control Warty Quasi-Humans

Universal's *The Mole People* (1956) is a fantasy adventure masquerading as a monster movie, more suited to a younger audience than the company's run of X-rated horrors during this time. Why is it a monster movie? It horrifies mainly because of the mole men themselves—with their knobbly skin, bulbous eyes, big claws and sackcloth clothing. These were less fearsome creations than, say, the gill-man, but rather endearing all the same. Anthropologists John Agar, Nestor Paiva and Hugh Beaumont meet up with them when they descend a shaft on the site of a ruined city in Asia. In galleries deep below ground, the 5,000-year-old Sumerian civilization is alive and kicking ("Gentlemen, we are in 3,000 BC," states Agar with a deadpan expression as they are escorted to the Sumerian

The pasty-faced ancient civilization meets John Agar and Hugh Beaumont (on the ground), from *The Mole People*.

city), its pasty-faced albino inhabitants masters of a quasi-human slave-race known simply as the beasts. Agar and company are, at first, regarded as spiritual beings (mainly because of their flashlight, the "cylinder of fire" or the "burning light") but then with suspicion; after all, what god would go to the aid of three of the beasts being fettered and beaten and then free them. Certainly not their god, Ishtar. Agar falls in love with Cynthia Patrick (the actor was blessed with a lot of attractive female co-stars in his Universal career), Paiva dies of a combination of madness and sheer exhaustion and the mole beasts revolt against their tormentors, slaying them to a man. Patrick makes it to the surface with Agar and Beaumont, only to perish under a falling pillar during an earth tremor.

"Quirky" is an apt description of some aspects of *The Mole People*. The opening five-minute pre-credits sequence has Dr. Frank C. Baxter presenting in glazed-over delivery a dissertation on the legendary wonders that *might* be found within the Earth's interior. Then there are the Sumerians themselves: With their farcical costumes, talcum powder make-up and Old Testament speech, we would have thought that this lot had wandered in from an adjoining Cecil B. DeMille set as extras on one of his biblical epics. And what about that odd four-minute dance, with pipe and drum backing, performed for the benefit of the three sacrificial virgins! The cast surely must have cracked up during this scene! The script is droll in places (Agar, lighting a pipe: "Did you ever hear of anyone smoking dried mushrooms?") and mild horror (the three sacrifices burnt to a blackened mess; the mole beasts whipped into servitude) sits more or less comfortably with the production's overt campiness. Once again, un-credited composer Hans J. Salter provided an atmospheric soundtrack, remarkable in itself considering the hokey material to work on, while Virgil Vogel directed at an undemanding pace, perfectly suited to this kind of storyline. With its imaginative subterranean backdrops, warty, rubbery villains and the unflappable Agar in the lead, *The Mole People* may well be classed in some quarters as one of Universal's lesser creature-features, but it entertains nevertheless and is quite fun to watch as a guilty pleasure.

"Thoroughly boring nonsense."

Killer Wasps from Outer Space

Among the more bizarre monstrosities to descend on Earth from the dark regions of space were the huge mutated wasps in Gross/Krasne's *Monster from Green Hell* (1957), a creature-feature distributed by DCA that often shared the bill with *Rodan* and *Plan 9 from Outer Space* in the early '60s. A raft of technicians were behind the film's special effects: Jack Rabin, Louis DeWitt, Irving Block and Jack Cosgrove created the scenic backdrops and models; Wah Chang and Gene Warren worked on the stop-motion (the pair collaborated on Universal's *Dinosaurus!* in 1960). Scientists Jim Davis and Robert E. Griffin are sending various animals (monkeys, crabs, lizards, guinea pigs) into space to test the effects of cosmic radiation on skin tissue. When one of their experimental rockets crashes in the West African jungle, a nest of wasps it was carrying is unleashed on the population in the form of gigantic flightless killer insects that begin to feed on human flesh. Davis and Griffin are dispatched to Libreville near the coast and prepare to embark on a 700-mile trek across the African plains to the village of Mongwa, situated in an area called Green Hell dominated by a smoking volcano. This is where the monsters, and dozens of corpses pumped full of poison, have been sighted.

Airily brushed aside as lukewarm fodder in some compendiums, Kenneth G. Crane's contribution to '50s monsterdom is, in fact, a well-constructed giant insect thriller that seems to go on a lot longer than its 71 minutes would lead you to believe. The reason for this is twofold: Crane's whirlwind pacing and the manner in which the plot development has been divided into manageable subsections designed to keep the punters happy—rocket base scene; first appearance of a monster (after 9 minutes); panic in African villages; a monster killing two porters (17 minutes); Davis and Griffin's 14-minute *Jungle Jim*-type safari, complete with wildlife footage; a prolonged native attack (lifted wholesale from 20th Century Fox's 1939 production of *Stanley and Livingstone*; you can spot Spencer Tracy at one point!); arrival at the village of Mongwa; a night assault by the wasps on Davis' camp, including a wasp versus giant snake battle (52 minutes) and the showdown with the queen wasp and her drones on the slopes of the volcano (filmed in California's Bronson Canyon), including a spell where the team become trapped in a cavern.

One of the mechanical giant wasps used in *Monster from Green Hell*.

When Davis and Griffin reach the hospital in Mongwa, Doctor Vladimir Sokoloff has perished while on a hunt for the big buzzing menaces, a poisoned stinger lodged in his neck. Daughter Barbara Turner, after hearing the news, appears to forget all about her deceased father pretty pronto, burying her elfin features in Davis' strapping chest every few minutes and deciding to join the party that hopes, with the aid of gelignite grenades, to destroy the nest near the active volcano. In some prints, the final eruption that buries the monsters under molten lava was shown in "Lava Vision," or color to be more exact. As for those monsters, in an early scene, when the wasp appears over the brow of a hill, it appears to be 10 times bigger than those enlarged, artfully designed heads that slowly emerge from the bushes in search of prey. The stop-motion work is unsophisticated compared to what Ray Harryhausen was coming up with, but, combined with models and composite shots, we are presented with an outlandishly different type of creature that typified the mid-'50s B monster movie. The script is stuffed with clichés ("Look! Footmarks of a monster!" "Monsters in Green Hell? Superstitious nonsense!") so credit must go to the cast for injecting a modicum of believability into it all. Complementing the action, Albert Glasser's racket of a stock score sounds like a locomotive about to come off the rails, becoming one more splendid example of this composer giving the audience its money's worth. Okay, this production may not have been in the *Deadly Mantis* or *Black Scorpion* class (it resembles both at some points), but if ever the word "cute" can be applied to a '50s monster flick, then *Monster from Green Hell* is cute!

"Silly offering ... routine direction."

Don't Lose Your Head!

Vanwick's *The Monster of Piedras Blancas* (completed in 1958, but released in 1959) was, in a roundabout fashion, partly financed by Universal-International. Jack Kevan, who had contributed toward the creature design work in *Creature from the Black Lagoon*, *This Island Earth* and *The Mole People*, set up Vanwick with Universal voice coach Irvin Berwick in 1958. Universal loaned Vanwick members of their own production staff to help out on the company's first picture (this was Berwick's directorial debut) while Kevan was given the go-ahead to pattern a new monster based on a few of Universal's tried and trusted creations. What Kevan came up with was a composite creature with the claws from *The Mole People*, the feet from the mutant in *This Island Earth* and the gill-man's torso, looking like a hybrid cross of the gill-man (from which it took its inspiration) and the Martian in *It! The Terror from Beyond Space;* Kevan himself wore the monster suit, along with stuntman Pete Dunn. Set around California's Point Concepcion area and the seaside community of Cayucos, this grisly outing told of a ferocious amphibian-cum-reptilian being inhabiting a cave system below a lighthouse. Crusty lighthouse keeper John Harmon, who has known all about the legendary monster for years, keeps the thing in check by feeding it daily on scraps; when its source of nourishment isn't forthcoming, the monster, attracted by raw meat, ventures into the town, tearing off the heads of those unfortunate enough to cross its path.

"Never saw anything like it in my life. Head ripped clean off." This line of speech from the opening scene of two decapitated fishermen discovered on a beach sets the grim tone, and the cast of zany characters fits the bill nicely: Les Tremayne, the town's seen-it-all-before medic; worn-around-the-edges cop Forrest Lewis; loud-mouthed storekeeper Frank Arvidson; Jeanne Carmen, Harmon's daughter; and biologist Don Sullivan, Carmen's all-American boyfriend. Like most minor-league horror films, we have to sit patiently through the teasers and wait for the blood-and-thunder final curtain: A claw reaching blindly for a tin of food (before the credits role), an arm fondling Carmen's clothes when she goes for a night swim, a crab crawling over a severed head and a monstrous silhouette on a wall. At 45 minutes, the monster's torso strides into shot, a bloodied head clutched in one claw; 17 more minutes pass before the action heats up, the slavering creature terrorizing Harmon, Carmen and Sullivan in the claustrophobic confines of the lighthouse. Sandwiched between the monster mayhem, the pace tends to lag in places as the surviving cast members debate at length on the beast's origins ("A Diplovertabron" expounds Sullivan). What holds the attention during the lulls is an appreciation by the cameraman of the rugged coastal scenery, some believable acting and snatches of priceless

dialogue. Sullivan: "If he can think, we're in real trouble." Small boy interrupting a funeral: "He was in his office, dead. And Mum, he didn't have any head." Lewis to Tremayne: "Doc. You don't think we've got a monster on our hands, do you?" Sullivan: "He's inhuman, nearly seven feet tall!" Carmen to Sullivan: "Hurry. The monster's in the lighthouse with Dad." And Berwick even chucks in a "kissing in the surf" sequence straight out of *From Here to Eternity*! The creature meets its end when Sullivan clubs it over the head with a rifle butt after the lighthouse beam has blinded it; senseless, the beast falls from the top of the building into the raging sea.

The Monster of Piedras Blancas wasn't released in the United Kingdom until 1963, on a double "X" bill with Mardi Gras' *The Dead One*. It was Vanwick's one and only horror film, a fascinating pooling of talents that produced a genuinely irresistible B creature-feature before fading from the limelight. Like a more violent cousin of Universal's own amphibian man, this particular rubber-suited monster is up there with the '50s best. A commercial DVD release would be very much appreciated.

"Crude horror film … little to recommend to the fans."

We're No More Intelligent Than Our One Million-Year-Old Ancestors

Global/United Artists' *The Neanderthal Man* (completed 1952, released 1953) has an impressive pedigree: Director Ewald André Dupont was one of the founding fathers of early German cinema, directing his first film in 1918; co-writer Jack Pollexfen was to end up with a string of horror screenplays under his belt; a young Beverly Garland was allowed to display her charms; composer Albert Glasser's tumultuous score threatened, at times, to swamp the action and veteran make-up artist Harry Thomas' list of credentials included *Frankenstein's Daughter*, *Night of the Ghouls*, *Killers from Space* and *Missile to the Moon*. But is the sum of all these parts equal to the whole?

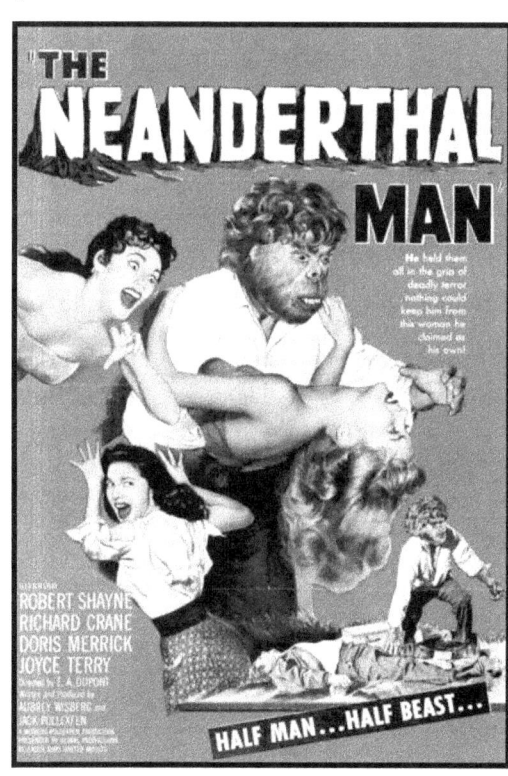

Predating Jack Arnold's similar *Monster on the Campus* by five years, *The Neanderthal Man* can lay claim to being the first '50s X-rated man-into-ape man movie. Filthy-tempered, misunderstood Robert Shayne, a professor in anthropology, is obsessed with the Stone Age, claiming that ancient man had the same intelligence levels as modern-day man. Scorned by his fellow scientists whom he dismisses as "stupid hypocrites," he injects himself with a serum that taps into his dormant, primitive cells, turning him into a murderous Neanderthal. After embarking on a couple of rampages in

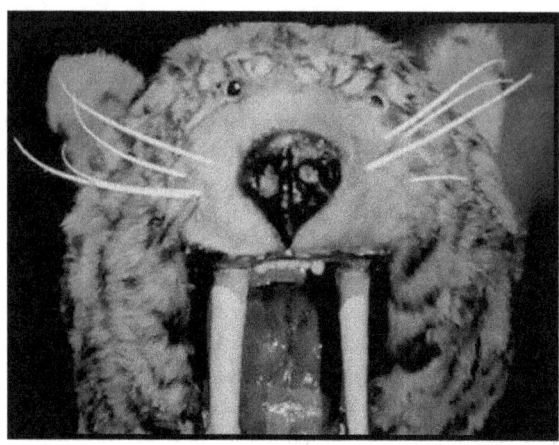

Make-up artist Harry Thomas incorporated elephantine tusks on the tigers, but not in a very threatening manner, from *The Neanderthal Man*.

the woods (not displaying much intelligence at all!), he's mauled to death by his own creation, a saber-toothed tiger.

A rough-cut template for what was to follow in this area of horror cinema, Dupont's outing has its ups and downs. The transformation scene (at 38 minutes) is short, carried out to the sound of a screeching cat: Shayne sweats, sprouts facial fuzz, his hands twist into claws; he then dons Thomas' Neanderthal Man mask, destroying all credibility. It's not the greatest example of workmanship to have originated from the decade, an inflexible facsimile unable to meld with the actor's own features to form expressions. Glasser's bulldozing soundtrack works wonders here, making this sequence more horrifyingly intense than it actually is. Thomas' make-up also incorporated the elephantine tusks on the tigers and deaf-mute housemaid Jeanette Quinn's ape woman get-up, shown in a series of photos (the actress was listed as Tandra Quinn in *Mesa of Lost Women*.)

Shayne's treatment of his character doesn't elicit the compassion it should, which becomes a major flaw. As though stuck in a 1940s melodrama, he hollers, bullies (fiancée Doris Merrick is ordered to pack her bags) and throws tantrums, a one-dimensional mad scientist deserving of everything coming to him. Elsewhere, good-guy Richard Crane paces through the motions, Joyce Terry (Shayne's daughter) is pretty but vacant and it is left to Beverly Garland to at least look as though she's enjoying herself in her role as a flirty waitress. Robert Long, the game warden, also acquits himself with a modicum of acting know-how. The script contains one or two jewels ("It was inhuman! More animal than man! He looked like a gorilla!" and "A cat? With tusks?"), while Dupont directs in short bursts, fading out scene after scene as was the norm in those days.

So, no, *The Neanderthal Man* doesn't add up to a fully accomplished package, hindered by Shayne's barmy performance and that fancy dress horror mask. Realistically, it should be looked upon as a low-budgeter that paved the way for the popular "X" certified man-into-monster genre; ratty around the edges, striving to reach a target of sorts but failing at the final hurdle. Like the Neanderthal itself, it's primitive but hokey fun.

"Wooden ... clichéd ..."

Chapter 14
To Colorize or Not to Colorize

The jury is most definitely out on film colorization, the process whereby black-and-white movies are imbued with color to present them in a pseudo-Technicolor format. Two-tone Technicolor has been around for a very long time (*Mystery of the Wax Museum* and *Doctor X* are two pioneering '30s horror flicks shot in early color), as has color tinting (*The Phantom of the Opera*; *Nosferatu*). Colorization, on the other hand, only came to the fore in the 1980s when William Markle, after experimentation in the 1970s (several '30s cartoons were issued in crude color), formed Colorization Inc., marketing a number of 1940s/1950s classics in the process, a process which in the long run turned out to be both costly and time-consuming. Turner Entertainment jumped on the bandwagon during the 1980s, but because of criticism in a lot of quarters (Turner's less-than-spectacular handling of colorization, above all others, was singled out by the unbelievers, their videos ridiculed in the press), the whole colorization deal blew itself out in the late 1990s. It still continues today in lesser form, with greater emphasis given to enhancing color via the computer, and can be used successfully in color recovery, the method of restoring faded prints to their former glory. A trickle of oldies-but-goodies are occasionally released as good quality, digitally spruced-up color issues, and many WWII documentaries and historical newsreel footage, as well as TV programs from the 1960s, have benefited from being screened in color, however unrealistic that color may still appear at times.

And that's the crux of the matter—is the premise feasible that manufactured-in-a-lab computer color is so realistic that it can better a black-and white-oldie? The short answer is that sometimes it can in places, and sometimes it can't. Take Howard Hawks' *The Thing from Another World* as an example of how colorization *used* to come across. Turner released the color version in 1988 on VHS. Some scenes work—the long sequence on the ice as the team investigates the buried flying saucer is visually dazzling; an icy blue/gray sky, a bluish ice cap and a deep blue UFO aerofoil with a greenish tinge, contrasting smartly with the brown snow suits worn by Kenneth Tobey and company. Brightly lit, these tones perfectly convey an impression of intense cold, more so than the monochrome print. But back inside the Quonset huts, the flesh-tones are the usual orange hues (the curse of colorization), the overall color-wash almost sepia, with a predominance of greens and browns, low contrast prevailing in the darker scenes. The images are fuzzy in some areas, and other shots remain firmly rooted in monochrome; briefly, perhaps, but they do.

Without doubt, it's a novel way to view the RKO classic, in

unaccustomed color, but is there any point to it all? Some may say it breathes new life into oldies and somehow modernizes them; others would argue that they shouldn't be meddled with, that color, in fact, destroys the atmosphere, impact and style built up in the original black-and-white production. Then there's that odd feeling of guilt. Should one actually *enjoy* watching a re-mastered color copy of a picture that has consistently entertained over a long period, but in monochrome (as the film's cinematographer intended). Is it indeed sacrilege to think, and even state, that a colorized classic is, in some instances, *more* watchable in this format than in its former medium. After all, *The Thing* wasn't earmarked as a color picture, so why go to all the bother of turning it into one. The arguments continue to rumble on, a conflict of differing thoughts and opinions on the subject; an act of cinematic vandalism on the one hand, a just reward for a movie that was originally intended to be made in color, on the other.

It's true to say that techniques in this field have advanced dramatically in recent years with the advent of digital technology. Skin-tones are now much more subtle, colors and contrast brighter (putting to bed that flat, wishy-washy, early '30s cartoon aspect, thereby adding depth), lighting more chromatically-corrected and fuzziness a problem dealt with effectively. The films look far more natural than they used to. However, the expense involved in color transference means that only around 150 colorized movies are out on the market, a figure that will not be greatly added to because of an overall lack of interest on behalf of the general public. Diehard buffs may welcome a colorized edition of Ed Wood's *Bride of the Monster* into their collection, but the majority of cinemagoers nowadays couldn't really care less (even if they have heard of the film in the first place). Among those 150-plus features, the majority are out-and-out classics—*Casablanca, All About Eve, It's a Wonderful Life, Angels with Dirty Faces, Way Out West, The Longest Day* among the list. Only a handful fall into fantasy/horror/science fiction, including the mighty Kong (and *King Kong* in color isn't the act of heresy that some people might imagine). Analyzing 12 of that handful will throw up some interesting observations and determine how these '50s pictures, ranging from the essential (*Invasion of the Body Snatchers*) to the distinctly non-essential (*The Killer Shrews*), have fared from colorization; shorn of their black-and-white origins, to be presented to fans in a drastically altered state. Have they been improved upon, or haven't they? Let's find out, and give them star ratings: One (poor), two (average), three (good), four (excellent) and five (exceptional.)

Note: Toho's *Godzilla* was given a color treatment of sorts by Italian director Luigi Cozzi in 1977. Cozzi got his hands on the Americanized print, added newsreel footage from World War II and used color gels a frame at a time to tint various sequences. Released in some parts of Europe as *Cozilla*, online snippets show Godzilla plowing through a red-lit Tokyo that still retains, amid flashes of garish greens, blues and reds, monochrome images. It's probably just as well for all concerned that this mockery has been unavailable for years.

RKO's *The Thing from Another World* has already been commented on. As of 2012, both the Turner colorized video (1988) and double DVD set (2007), which includes the Turner version, are no longer commercially available. A blue RKO logo gives way to the title lettering in fiery red (nice, this), but from the opening scene inside the Anchorage Officer's Club, it's apparent that the scourge of this process manifests itself in the uneven flesh-tones—the cast all sport brownish-orange faces, giving them a cartoonish appearance; Margaret Sheridan's green sweater looks swell, though. As previously stated, the "saucer on the ice" sequence really comes into its own—we can almost feel the penetrating Arctic cold emanate from the screen—and back at base camp, the alien is a sinister dark shape beneath the blue/green ice. Actually, the gloomy interior shots, although looking dingy with low contrast, probably suit the cramped settings more, the  darker corners merging from brown to black. Unfortunately, once or twice, the color gives up the ghost and we are back in monochrome land. James Arness is green-tinted (green seems to be the preferred color choice for aliens and monsters), his tattered suit a dark blue, and the vivid blue/white electrical bolts that fry him to ashes really stand out. Regrettably, the print is slightly ill-defined around the edges, particularly annoying if juxtaposed with the high definition re-mastered black-and-white copy. To sum up, it's an interesting exercise watching this legendary sci-fi production in a *kind* of color and if given a digital makeover, the results would have been dramatic to say the least. But this murky version doesn't really do the film any justice, and seasoned addicts will probably stick to the original monochrome version that they have treasured all these years, consigning Turner's effort to the backburner. Two and a half stars.

Turner did a real hatchet job on *Invasion of the Body Snatchers* (the 1988 video is now unavailable). The title lettering is the mandatory green (on a mauve background) and so are the alien pods, spewing out pink, foamy replicas. The general finish is crudely executed: Muddy greens, dingy blue skies verging on gray and brownish skin-tones (admittedly, Dana Wynter *does* look radiant in color). After 10 minutes, matters improve slightly, the night scenes almost approximate an early, unrefined Technicolor print, but again, a number of sequences have a habit of reverting to monochrome. The pivotal greenhouse segment, 42 minutes in, works well, the shiny green pods ejecting their frothy pink blanks, the greenhouse itself awash in deep mauves, but over the course of 80 minutes, Don Siegel's suspenseful thriller looks uniformly substandard in its colorized dressing. Thank goodness for Siegel's nail-biting direction, the ensemble playing, Carmen Dragon's fabulous score and that classic final line to keep us going: "'Course it's a nightmare. Plants from another world taking over human beings? Mad as a March Hare!" One and a half stars.

In 2007, stop-motion animation wizard Ray Harryhausen personally supervised the colorization of three of his mid-'50s movies for Columbia/Sony: *20 Million Miles to Earth*, *It Came from Beneath the Sea* and *Earth vs. the Flying Saucers*. With one of cinema's greatest special effects technicians at the helm, has the man himself made any headway in this process where others have fallen by the wayside? Let's see. The latter film commences with standard white lettering over a stormy blue background and while it's true to say that there are signs of real progress (flesh-tones are cleaner), the color appears very pale, almost "off," bright exterior shots giving way to duller interiors. It could simply be that the predominant color range in *Flying Saucers* is green, silver and steel gray anyway: Green for the lab, silver and steel gray for the aircraft and UFOs and gun-metal blue for the aliens. The effect is one of blandness, and even the saucers' attack on Washington doesn't look any better colorized. Not one of the master's more arresting achievements, *Earth vs. the Flying Saucers* is passable in black-and-white, a bit of a slog in color. Two stars.

The routine *It Came from Beneath the Sea* has never been declared a Harryhausen classic, hampered by static direction, a stodgy script and an inferior musical score. The fluorescent green lettering rolls and the stormy sea looks a treat in deep navy blue, contrasting nicely with the strong blue sky later on. The sub's interior, with its gleaming hardware, is also well done. Blood-red sunsets look almost perfect, the skin-tones are pinker and the colossal octopus is (you've guessed it) a shade of dirty green with pink suckers. The color sheen livens up what is basically a mundane effort from Columbia (the Golden Gate Bridge interlude *does* look splendid), although it was a big hit when first released. Yes, *It Came from Beneath the Sea* turns out to be far more entertaining as a colorized feature. Three stars.

The Venusian Ymir lies dead at the end of *20 Million Miles to Earth*.

20 Million Miles to Earth finally hits the colorized jackpot. Did Harryhausen put that much more effort into this one, more so than the other two? We all know that the picture is one of his particular favorites, as it remains with many lovers of animated monster movies, and we now learn that it was originally to have been filmed in Technicolor anyway. Whatever the reason, this tale of a Venusian reptilian creature rampaging through Rome is an outright winner in the colorized stakes, almost akin to watching a different film altogether. A lovely color-balanced Columbia logo sets the right mood, and then we have standard white lettering over a blue/gray background. The opening shots paint a picture of sunny Italian villages and seascapes set against a blue Mediterranean backdrop, the returning spaceship a gleaming silver dart plunging into a glittering aquamarine ocean. (Has anyone noticed how closely the opening credits to *20 Million Miles to Earth* resemble the opening credits to *The Quatermass Experiment*? Minimal, yet threatening, music, a cloud-filled sky and a rocket approaching Earth, bringing—what?) But the real bonus is the Ymir itself, now a vibrant, glistening green animal (its back ridges are gray, the skin stained brown in places) that leaps from the screen in mock 3-D (you won't need those glasses!). Harryhausen has done his number one creation proud, presenting us with a new concept of how, frame-by-frame, one of monsterdom's most mesmerizing '50s creatures would have appeared on the screen in color. It looks magnificent, the imagery pin-sharp. The beguiling hatching scene is quintessential Harryhausen, the baby Ymir clambering out of its green-tinged egg-sac in front of an alluring Joan Taylor, resplendent in pink cardigan and blue dress. The battle between gray elephant and green Ymir really does stand out, bringing a new level of excitement to this 50-year-old sequence, as does the scaly monster stalking William Hopper and company among the ancient brown stonework of Rome's Coliseum. *20 Million Miles to Earth* is a treat, glorious in its colorized edition, almost faultless, to the extent that fans will be reaching for a copy of this rather than a monochrome DVD when they next decide to watch it. An unqualified success—five stars.

House on Haunted Hill is almost as good. Legend Films have turned William Castle's popular gimmicky shocker into a somber-looking work of some distinction. Using state-of-the-art technology, the interior scenes (the entire action takes place at night) are saturated in deep mauves, browns and reds, with nigh-on-impeccable skin-tones, making the old Vincent Price vehicle shimmer like a 1940s sumptuously textured period drama. We can almost smell the mustiness and see the dust! Colorization adds to the picture rather than detracts from it, giving it a new lease of life. Four and a half stars.

And a new lease of life is what Legend has performed on Ed Wood's *Bride of the Monster*; whether or not audiences think Wood's low-rent horror farrago deserves this treatment is open to conjecture! But spruced up in color, *Bride* looks splendid, with its green title lettering, red/mauve octopus, gray-toned lab and richly dark night exterior shots lending it the muted, pastel air of an early '30s Bela Lugosi horror feature, which of course it is—only made 20 years later! Colorization makes it possible to overlook Wood's numerous shortcomings and say—"This ain't as bad as I thought it was," no mean feat indeed! Then it earns three and a half stars.

Legend has brought about a similar miracle with Wood's notorious *Plan 9 from Outer Space*. The ultimate in poor taste has now mutated into something we have all come to love over the past 50 years, probably because decrepit filmmaking of the Ed Wood variety no longer figures in today's super-glossy, ultra-polished and thoroughly sterile area of fantasy cinema. *Plan 9 from Outer Space* is living proof that *any* production can benefit from colorization, even movies such as this, Wood's lasting testament to self-deluded greatness. What a huge difference color makes: Now we can see Vampira's blood-red nails; the wires supporting the hub caps (sorry, flying saucers); the gray hair of the Lugosi stand-in (as opposed to Lugosi's legendary black peak); the gaudy purple space outfits; the red curtains in the saucer's cabin; the mauve mist in the cemetery and the *true* contrast between those badly edited day/night/day/night sequences. Yes, Wood would never have believed that his grainy old black-and-white vehicle has been given such a digitalized makeover that it elevates the picture from a grade Z to a grade B! It was popular enough to be a crowd-puller on wet Sunday afternoons in England circa 1962/1963. If presented in the expertly rendered job that Legend has bestowed upon it, *Plan 9* might even have been afforded a national run on the circuits! Four stars.

Richard E. Cunha's *Missile to the Moon* is the ideal vehicle for the colorization procedure, being as daft as a brush, similar to an elongated *Star Trek* episode minus Kirk, Scotty, Spock and Bones. The lurid blue/yellow titles are a portent of things to come: dark green spacesuits; green (again!) rock-men; the moon's bright blue sky; the aluminum-foil tunnel and the blue/green-skinned Moon Maidens. The Maidens' subterranean home is

The Moon Maidens of *Missile to the Moon* were perfect candidates for colorization.

decked out like Aladdin's cave, a riot of golds, pinks, reds and silvers, the women's outrageous sparkling trinkets and gravity-defying headpieces adding to the rich color tones. In fact, the colorization in this corny romp is positively gaudy! To cap it all, one of the decade's fakest of fake spiders comes trotting out of its lair on visible wires, black-furred and red-faced. Legend has pulled it off again, making Cunha's camp space opera a B movie of great satisfaction, rather than one at which to fire vitriolic darts. Four stars.

W. Lee Wilder's quickie from 1953, *Phantom from Space*, gets the ball rolling with yellow titles morphing into blue over a backdrop of blue swirling clouds, followed by grainy newsreel footage. A UFO (resembling a glowing white light bulb) has landed somewhere in Los Angeles and the authorities are anxious to track it down. When they do, the occupant is a humanoid figure dressed in a white spacesuit and wearing a diving helmet. Most of the movie's running time takes place in a green-tinted laboratory where the invisible alien attempts to communicate with Noreen Nash (auburn hair, pink scarf, yellow coat and navy blue dress). After cops and scientists chase the being into an observatory, it reveals itself under the mauve beams of ultra-violet lamps as a bald-headed, naked, white-skinned creature with green eyes and lips. Unable to breathe in Earth's atmosphere, it expires and vaporizes. A greenish color scheme seems to suit this long-forgotten cheapo, the earlier shots tinged in mahogany-brown, but it's a bit hit and miss in the colorization department (the original print's condition might have posed a few problems). Therefore, Wilder's 73-minutes of schlock sci-fi, featuring a few flashes of imagination in the "invisible alien" segments, gets a three-star rating.

Why has Legend felt the need to colorize *The Killer Shrews* and *The Giant Gila Monster*? These HPC releases from 1959 encompass the worst traits to be found in '50s B creature-features, both lacking in thrills, excitement, credible production values and up-to-standard monsters. Ironic, then, that in color, they look pretty cool. Both contain sharp exterior shots and faithful skin-tones, the pictures beautifully rendered in '50s pastel hues to fit in with the times (especially the hot rods in *Gila Monster*). *The Killer Shrews* has bright green/yellow titles, *The Giant Gila Monster* a mottled mauve/green/pink to match the skin of the magnified lizard. Unfortunately, audiences cannot ignore those lame beasties, color or no color (the oversized shrews are dogs covered in shaggy coats with fangs, and the giant lizard is a real lizard plunked amid model cars and buildings), so that, in a way, colorization becomes superfluous; no self-respecting fan would give either film a repeated look-in, however well they have been enhanced. Three and a half stars for both flicks, which, to be honest, they hardly merit.

Therefore, *20 Million Miles to Earth* emerges as the outright winner, with *Invasion of the Body Snatchers* the loser. Colorization of old movies will carry on, pandering to those who nurse an itch for something off the wall in their collection, allowing them to pick and choose on a title according to their fancy. Maybe it is a marketing shtick, a passing fad as many have suggested, but it certainly doesn't do any harm or dent a classic's reputation, despite what some critics may think, as can be seen with *20 Million Miles to Earth*. If handled properly with love and respect, the results can be astounding, propelling the picture into another dimension. And there's no escaping the fact that such altered movies are fun to watch, flaws and all. But, as the opening to this chapter read, the jury is still very much out on this issue.

Lastly, here's a list of 20 films I personally reckon would look tremendous in color (Digicolor? Compucolor?), if treated with due reverence:

The Alligator People
The Beast from 20,000 Fathoms
The Black Scorpion
The Black Sleep
Creature from the Black Lagoon
The Day the Earth Stood Still
The Fabulous World of Jules Verne
From Hell It Came
Frankenstein 1970
Godzilla
The Incredible Shrinking Man
It! The Terror from Beyond Space
Kronos
The Land Unknown
The Monolith Monsters
The Monster That Challenged the World
Night of the Demon
The Quatermass Experiment
Tarantula
Varan the Unbelievable

Up for consideration…
Unknown World

Chapter 15
Gigantis and Varan: Toho's Forgotten Monsters

Godzilla and *Rodan* are two undisputed giants of the Japanese Kaiju Eiga genre that remain the greatest of all Toho's rubber-suited creations from the 1950s. But two features dating from, respectively, 1955 and 1958, were never afforded the same commercial coverage as *Godzilla* and *Rodan*—*Godzilla Raids Again* and *Varan the Unbelievable*. Not screened in the United Kingdom until the early '60s in heavily doctored forms, these films have long been overlooked by fans used to seeing Godzilla in all his various later incarnations, unconscious of the fact that a distant cousin and lizard-like relative lurked around the corner. Now that original uncut Japanese versions have become available on the market for both pictures, Toho's least-seen monster flicks deserve reappraisal. Granted, they may have their faults, but both remain integral, important entrants in Toho's extensive back register of classical monster movies.

Following the worldwide success of *Godzilla*, Toho rush-released *Godzilla Raids Again* (*Gojira No Gyakushu*) in 1955 with a different director (Motoyoshi Odo, or Oda on some prints), different composer (Masaru Sato) and a different-looking Godzilla; smaller in build, sporting a newly designed head. The cast consisted of three main characters: flying partners Hiroshi Koizumi and Minoru Chiaki, with attractive Setsuko Wakayama supplying the female interest, all working for a fishery company in Osaka. On the lookout for bonitos (tuna), Chiaki's plane develops engine trouble and he's forced to land on barren Iwato Island. His colleague comes looking for him and lands alongside, the pair building a fire to stay warm. Then a roar is heard. Godzilla appears above a rocky ridge, in battle with another monster Angurus and, after the fight, the enemies tumble into the sea. Back in Osaka, scientists blame the hydrogen bomb for reawakening both monsters (an Ankylosaurus and a "second" Godzilla) and a state of emergency is declared. Footage of Godzilla destroying Tokyo (from the first film) is screened to the authorities as a warning of what Osaka might expect should the creatures get too close for comfort. Godzilla enters Osaka Bay 26 minutes into the picture, planes drop flares to steer him back into the ocean but when escaped convicts crash a stolen petrol tanker, the blaze attracts the monster and he returns, along with his spike-backed rival. After a titanic tussle in which Osaka is reduced to burning rubble, Angurus is defeated and Godzilla heads back out to sea. He is then located on another snow-covered island. The air force bombs the island and

Stampeding humans flee from the battle of the two titans, from *Gigantis the Fire Monster*.

the monster is buried under an avalanche of ice.

Compared to the mighty *Godzilla*, the follow-up seems colorless and sluggish. Sato's conventional, jaunty music jars with the more serious monster action, while Odo's static directorial style is simply content to allow actors/monsters to wander into shot. The film plays in three segments: the opening sequence, from protracted scenes of Chiaki and Koizumi flying over the ocean to the discovery of Godzilla and Angurus; the middle section, showing the combatants trashing Osaka and the overlong 18-minute finale depicting the bombing of the island and Godzilla's death. The special effects are impressive in that the "let's wreck the model city" was perfected by Toho yet let down by an absence of a stirring musical soundtrack. With lack of pace both in the opening and closing segments of *Godzilla Raids Again*, the only thing to hold the interest is the destruction of Osaka; this overall slackness probably accounted for the film's poor showing at the box-office. Such was *Godzilla Raids Again*'s critical and commercial failure that the producers of the first *Godzilla* movie took out a lawsuit against the picture's makers, the main reason for adjusting the title on subsequent Japanese and American prints—Warner Bros., who distributed the Americanized version outside of Japan, were unable to secure the rights to the Godzilla name because of this lawsuit, hence the switch to Gigantis.

Godzilla and Angurus destroy everything in their path, from *Gigantis the Fire Monster*.

The revamped *Godzilla Raids Again* surfaced in England in 1963 as *Gigantis the Fire Monster* (produced by Paul Schreibman in 1959), on a double X-rated bill with *The Gargon Terror*. Five minutes shorter than the original's 82 minutes, *Gigantis* kicked off with an atomic bomb explosion and footage of "deadly missiles and rockets" to explain the monster's manifestation; it cut down on the numerous fishing scenes, trimmed the prolonged climax by a couple of minutes and, in the final analysis, emerged a better, all-rounded feature film. *Star Trek*'s George Takei narrated (as he would do in *Rodan*) and no American actors appeared to throw a monkey wrench into the works. All references to the name "Godzilla" were excised from the print (even on revised versions that still contained the *Godzilla Raids Again* title!). Newsreel footage of Godzilla trampling through Tokyo shown to scientists was augmented by views of prehistoric life filched from other productions, stress laid on the fact that Gigantis (or Gigantus) was a "Fire Monster," with a ridiculous (and totally untrue) statement that dinosaurs hibernated underground during the Jurassic Age because of atmospheric radiation and lived in a world of fire. Also ludicrous was the dubbed speech ("Oh look, the monster's coming." "Gigantis is huge, he will destroy everything.") and the fact that Angurus sounded like an off-key air-raid siren. On the plus side, Sato's inappropriate music was replaced by

American producer Schreibman who utilized snippets of Paul Sawtell and Bert Shefter's title and incidental scores from *Kronos* and *It! The Terror from Beyond Space*, beefing up the action no end.

The tightened-up *Gigantis the Fire Monster* was much more of a success than it had been in its previous existence, even if it was only shown in independent cinemas, and, along with *Rodan*, is a rare example of necessary American editing triumphing over Japanese sloppiness. The same cannot be said of what American distributors Jerry A. Baerwitz and Jack Marquette performed on *Varan the Unbelievable* (*Daikaiju Baran*): The uncut Japanese original, now uncovered for the first time in pristine black-and-white and widescreen format, is a lost Toho masterpiece; the re-edited version is cinematic butchery taken a step too far.

Varan emerges from the sea, from *Varan the Unbelievable*.

Varan was released in England in 1964, teamed up with *The Demon Doctor* (*The Awful Doctor Orlof*). Baerwitz's severely cut 1961 rehash had Myron Healy and his Japanese wife (Tsuruko Kobayashi) holed up on an island, experimenting with a desalination chemical on a lake supposedly inhabited by a legendary monster feared by local natives. Thirty-two minutes into the movie (which only runs for 70 minutes in its shortened form) Varan appears ("Nothing can stop it. Bullets, shells—nothing!" screams an officer). The creature razes a village to the ground, is blasted by the military and attacks Oneida City. It then swallows a quantity of Healy's chemicals, lowered on parachutes, and falls onto a lorry loaded with explosives which blow up. Feeling groggy, Varan wades back into the ocean, presumably to die, although this isn't made clear, Healy stating at the end that, "Whether it's dead or alive, we won't have to worry anymore." A talkative start, clumsy editing, erratic continuity and crass dubbing notwithstanding, *Varan*, ragged-looking or not, was a hit with monster movie lovers in the early '60s; the film was in widescreen, the Toho effects were excellent (although darkly lit) and Varan himself was a corker of a monster. To be honest, punters of the time wouldn't have had the patience to sit through a Japanese-speaking horror flick with English subtitles. *Varan* in its chopped-up guise was what Western audiences were served and to which they became accustomed, appeasing their appetites, warts and all.

But now we are presented with the opportunity to see for ourselves what Inoshiro Honda and his team envisaged in the first place, the original conception of *Varan*. At last, we have confirmation that what we heard about many moons ago concerning the superior uncut Japanese edit being an entirely different beast to the truncated mishmash we sat through in 1964 turns out to be true. First released as *Daikaiju Baran* in 1958, Honda's forgotten classic comes in at 87 minutes, 17 minutes longer than the emasculated

Varan. Watching it is like being subjected to another movie altogether, so let's contrast the two, using the titles *Baran* for the original and *Varan* for the Americanized travesty.

Out of *Baran*'s opening 48 minutes, only around nine minutes of original Japanese footage has been cannibalized and included in *Varan*'s first 45 minutes. *Baran* opens with a shot of a gleaming rocket, pressing home the atomic significance in relation to the unfolding events. In the foothills of Northern Japan (the Tibet of Japan, *not* an island!),

A close-up of Varan eying an approaching airplane, from *Varan the Unbelievable*.

a gargantuan reptile lurking in a lake (the God of Baradagi) is worshipped as a deity, similar to *King Kong*. Akira Ifukube's marvelous music underscores the imaginative Gustave Doré–type scenic views of the lake, mountains and jungle backdrops to set the right mood. Two scholars searching for a rare species of Siberian butterfly in the Tohoku area hear a deafening roar and are killed by a rockfall, caused by something unknown. A research party (two men, one woman) investigates the deaths and comes under native suspicion, the leader of the tribe telling the trio to return to where they came from ("You cannot explore. Go back!"). Twenty minutes into the film, Baran emerges from the lake, walking both upright and on all fours ("That's an oversized lizard! It's unbelievable!") and smashes the native village to matchsticks. Back in Tokyo (*not* Oneida City as in *Varan*), scientists meet to discuss the monster's origins (a species of Varanopode) and the military plus news reporters converge on the lake that is shelled with chemicals. Baran, enraged at the disturbance, leaves his abode, comes under bombardment, traps two of the party (lovers Kozo Nomura and Ayumi Sonoda) in a cave and then, with the forest ablaze, flies off on membranous tissue situated between its four limbs.

Virtually every scene included in this long opening passage *never* made it into *Varan*; the complete butterfly scenario was omitted in favor of a specially filmed 30-minute sequence showing Healy speaking nonstop about his methods of removing salt from saline water. And to underline the ruthless (and thoughtless) editing: In *Baran*, at 22 minutes, the village leader dies, followed by, at 42 minutes, the monster menacing the scholars in the cave. In *Varan*, the leader perishes at 36 minutes, and only six minutes later (as opposed to *Baran*'s 20 minutes), Healy and his wife are inserted into the cave shots, the scholars (termed feature writers in *Varan*) having disappeared. So 14 minutes of monster footage has been removed in the modified version from this sequence alone. Moreover, in *Varan*, the monster is never seen airborne and his roar sounds strangely muted.

To continue with the original, Baran makes his way toward Tokyo (not, as stated, Oneida City) and, following several confrontations with battle cruisers (many of these

scenes don't figure in *Varan*), begins a night attack at 69 minutes. In *Varan*, at the same point in time, the movie is virtually done and dusted, the attack having lasted 11 minutes against the original's 15 minutes. Professor Akihiko Hirata (he invented the Oxygen Destroyer in *Godzilla*) has designed an experimental bomb and needs to detonate it inside the monster. In *Varan*, the beast staggers into the sea but whether it lives or dies is left open-ended; in *Baran*, it also staggers into the sea (after swallowing several of Hirata's bombs and toppling onto the lorry containing explosives) and blows up, almost certainly dead, leaving the cast standing on the shore, mourning its passing.

Varan the Unbelievable in its original cut is classic, well-mounted Toho, leisurely paced at first, the involved butterfly plot punctuated by well-staged monster antics, the acting a little less affected than the norm, the direction assured. Baran/Varan rampaging across Tokyo's airfields doesn't disappoint (okay, the model tanks are fairly obvious, as are the wires connected to the jet planes, but these are distinguishing features of Japanese monster effects and one almost becomes immune to them) and the finale is cohesive rather than the muddled mess apparent in Baerwitz's hatchet job. Photographed in the darker tones that catapulted *Godzilla* to godly status and in TohoScope, this X-rated '50s Japanese monster opus personifies Honda and his technicians' much-vaunted craftsmanship; it's a thrilling, well-crafted delight, more so when viewed against Toho's child-friendly, A-rated creations in color that proliferated during the 1960s. Yes, it was well worth the long wait—*Daikaiju Baran* counts as one of the company's finest, more adult, moments.

Chapter 16
Regal by Name—Not Quite By Nature!

Prolific low-budget filmmaker Robert L. Lippert struck a lucrative deal with 20th Century Fox in 1956 to finance and distribute his cheapo productions under the nomenclature of Regal Films. The movies would be shot using anamorphic lenses but marketed as RegalScope, Fox insisting that the company's flagship CinemaScope process be reserved solely for its own big-budget motion pictures. Between 1956 and 1966, Lippert produced 180 features under the Regal Films banner, mostly crime thrillers and Westerns, with a smattering of horror. Most were highly profitable for both Lippert and Fox. Only five horror/sci-fi movies were made by Regal in the 1950s: *She Devil* (completed 1956, released 1957), *Back from the Dead* (1957), *Kronos* (1957), *The Unknown Terror* (1957) and *Space Master X-7* (1958).

It should be noted that Hammer's *The Abominable Snowman* (1957) and Triad's *The Flesh and the Fiends* (1959), although respectively issued in RegalScope and DyaliScope, were *not* Regal Films productions. *The Abominable Snowman* was distributed through 20th Century Fox via Lippert, filmed in widescreen and released under Lippert's exclusive brand name based on the CinemaScope process; the movie's credentials could equally have been termed "in MegaScope" or even "in HammerScope" (both formats were employed in future Hammer features), and Lippert's association with Hammer (commencing in 1950; see chapter 25) was brief anyway. In *The Flesh and the Fiends*, DyaliScope was the promotional idiom used (as it was with many continental widescreen productions.)

The five true Regal Films formed part of the staple diet of many a fantasy fanatic, a mixed bag drawing in the crowds on Sunday afternoons, year in, year out, not for their content which, apart from *Kronos*, was ordinary to say the least, but because of their one saving grace; they were shown in widescreen. In the late '50s/early '60s, widescreen horror films that appeared in massive cinemas on larger-than-normal screens were a big draw for young fans who were probably bamboozled into thinking that what they were watching was somehow superior to standard screen aspect. It mattered not that *The Unknown Terror* was patently lacking in *any* kind of terror—it was up there on that all-enveloping screen, enabling audiences to participate in the action more so than standard format ever did (theaters were more cavernous in construction than those of today, built to hold audiences of up to 2,000, being perfectly adapted for projecting films in varied permutations of 'Scope). So those fungoid natives looked doubly scary, but not scary enough to warrant an "Adults Only" certificate; in the United Kingdom, *Back from the Dead* was the only X-rated flick among the five; the others were "A" classified.

The four "A" certificate Regal productions, when not presented as second features with more prestigious outings, were frequently screened as double bills, allowing under-14s (if accompanied by an adult) to have their first taste of lukewarm horror before they were old enough (16) to experience the real thing. *Back from the Dead* often went the rounds with assorted crime thrillers. In hindsight, they weren't all that bad; a lot worse existed out there on the circuits at the time. Let's take a look at Lippert's run-of-the-mill programmers and decide whether or not we wasted money on our tickets all those years

ago when getting in to see *Space Master X-7* c/w *The Unknown Terror*. In actual fact, do the Regal horrors in "stunning RegalScope" contain points of interest that have been scoffed at or ignored in the past?

Kurt Neumann, the man behind *Rocketship X-M*, directed the first of Regal's widescreen horror/fantasy efforts, *She Devil*, a Jekyll and Hyde–type melodrama of reasonable interest. Biochemist Jack Kelly and benefactor Albert Dekker invent a serum distilled from an extract of fruit flies. This, they reason, will cause wounds and ailments to heal themselves, much in the same way lizards are able to grow new tails after an injury. Requiring a human guinea pig on which to experiment, they inject tuberculosis sufferer Mari Blanchard with the potion. She recovers from the disease, but the cure has an unforeseen side-effect: Blanchard has undergone a drastic personality change; like a chameleon, she is able to will herself, in times of emotional stress, to transmute from a pleasant brunette into a manipulative, homicidal blonde predator. Kelly, who has an almighty crush on the femme fatale, turns a blind eye as Blanchard struts her stuff, thieving and flirting without so much as a single qualm. Things go from bad to worse when Blanchard meets filthy rich John Archer at a party. Hungry to lay her hands on his wealth, she strangles Archer's wife, marries the playboy and kills him in a car crash, emerging unscathed from the wreckage to claim her inheritance. Horrified at what they have created, Kelly and Dekker render Blanchard unconscious by pumping carbon dioxide into her bedroom, and they administer an antidote. The experimental serum is driven from her body, allowing the tuberculosis to return; in the final frame, Blanchard, in her brunette form, expires.

As an exercise in dual personality, a much-favored '50s theme, *She Devil* just about pulled it off, flawed by a hasty conclusion, Blanchard's clumsy handling of her twin roles and the too half-hearted Kelly, as the leading man. Paul Sawtell and Bert Shefter's score turned from menacing to smoochy whenever Blanchard in her Marilyn Monroe guise appeared, while Neumann would do far better with his second Regal movie, *Kronos*. Neumann and Carroll Young's script, though, sparkles with laconic exchanges to satisfy all dialogue lovers, mostly at Blanchard's expense:

Blanchard to Kelly and Dekker: "You created me and I'm your responsibility!"

Archer, seeing blonde Blanchard for the first time: "That is the most beautiful test tube I have ever seen."

Blanchard to her creators: "I'm immune to everything, afraid of nothing!"

Blanchard to lustful Archer: "Haven't you guessed? Dr. Bach and Dr. Scott simply materialized me out of a test tube."

Archer: "Of course, I should have known that anybody as lovely as you couldn't possibly be human."

Dekker to Kelly: "Did we create an inhuman being?"

And lastly, Dekker voices to Kelly what horror cinema addicts have known for decades: "You wouldn't be the first man to fall in love with his own creation."

Director of low-budget Westerns, Charles Marquis Warren had a stab at the supernatural genre with *Back from the Dead*, turning Catherine Turney's novel of reincarnation, *The Other One* (Turney wrote the script), into a jumbled occult potboiler.

A British Quad poster bearing the "X" rating for *Back from the Dead*.

Pregnant Peggie Castle visits the house her husband Arthur Franz shared with his first wife, who disappeared in mysterious circumstances six years back. Repeated shots of crashing waves, a ghostly voice chanting, "You can't get away from me" and Raoul Kraushaar's noisy, wailing soundtrack doesn't bode well for Castle; she suffers convulsions, loses her baby and is instantly possessed by the spirit of the long-dead woman, a devious seductress who sets out to cause trouble for everyone around her. If given the big-screen treatment, *Back from the Dead* could have been an absolute cracker on the heavily explored theme of dual identity, but Warren was obviously shackled by budget restraints and couldn't produce the goods to give the material the consideration it deserved. His inconsistent direction, coupled with too much dark photography, muddies the waters, the end result a turgid mess. Tied up in the confused plot is a black magic cult led by evil priest Otto Reichow; after what seems like hours showing the cast scampering from one house to another, Castle causing all kinds of mischief, the movie climaxes with a sacrificial ceremony in which Reichow attempts to drain the blood from Evelyn Scott, but for what purpose is never made clear.

Apart from Castle, Franz and Reichow, there's a lot of peripheral characters in the picture (Castle's sister; Franz's ex-in-laws; Franz's buddy and Reichow's female acolyte), perhaps one too many, a sign of over-ambition. The outcome is a frantic, dialogue-driven timetable of random occurrences, Warren relying a great deal on Castle's agitated and scheming possessed wife to satisfactorily carry the storyline. To her credit, the actress does surprisingly well (beating by a whisker Mari Blanchard's similar stint in *She Devil*); however, even at 79 minutes, the film, despite a couple of eerie moments, seems twice as long and is marred by that appalling score. The widescreen format rescues the movie from mediocrity but it sorely needed a surer hand at the helm; nevertheless, Warren was given another shot and was just as shaky in his next picture for Regal—the lackluster *The Unknown Terror*.

They may have appeared frightening to a generation of eight-year-olds, who first came across them in the hallowed pages of *Famous Monster of Filmland*, but in reality, on the big screen, those fungus-faced natives in Warren's second Regal feature weren't that frightening at all. Tacked onto an adventure-type scenario is a mild horror yarn concerning mad biologist Gerald Milton. Holed up on a Caribbean island, he's nurturing a fast-growing hallucinogenic fungus in the legendary Cave of the Dead where human sacrifices were once carried out. Local natives, due to be sacrificed to their gods, are used by Milton in his experiments with the fungus, turning them into mutants who inhabit the cave. John Howard, wife Mala Powers and crippled Paul Richards (he's in love with Powers; she was his sweetheart before Howard moved in) arrive on the island in search of Powers' brother; the scientist was searching for the cave and disappeared. The trio become embroiled with Milton and his native wife May Wynn, spending the last half of the picture inside the cave, warding off the mutant natives, the dripping fungus and crazy Milton. Wynn finally seals the cave entrance with explosives, Milton is killed in the blast, Howard dies after falling on rocks and Powers and Richards swim to safety, emerging from the sea in each other's arms.

The Unknown Terror is flat-footed and unconvincing; the oozing fungus resembles soapsuds cascading down the cave walls (and rumor has it that it was!), the fungoid natives *might* scare the pants off the nippers (and did, many moons ago!) while the B regulars go through the motions proficiently enough without stretching themselves. Warren slackly directs, resulting in a lack of suspense, surprises and shocks (he returned to television on completion of this movie). This program filler served its usefulness, introducing youngsters to the world of horror, however diluted that horror was.

One of the most bizarre spectacles in American sci-fi '50s cinema was the sight of 100-foot-tall Kronos ("A Metallic Vampire Stalking the Earth!" screamed the trailers) pulverizing its way across the Mexican countryside, thousands fleeing in its wake. Like a colossal hydraulic press with pistons as legs, this giant robot from another world had an electronic vocabulary all of its own; it beeped, it buzzed, it thrummed and it whirred as waves of pulsating light transmitted on electrical bolts radiated from its domed head. Yes, *Kronos* remains Regal's most celebrated fantasy achievement, a one-off event in terms of limited B-movie resources (the budget ran to $160,000 *not* preventing director Kurt Neumann and his crew of technicians from coming up with an absolute belter (Neumann made *Kronos* back-to-back with *She Devil*.)

Deposited on a Mexican beach by a flying saucer (termed Asteroid M47 by scientist Jeff Morrow), the robot's task is to suck up energy from Earth's power plants, an "accumulator" of sorts, and transport it to a dying planet where it will be converted into matter. Morrow, having to constantly defend himself from the advances of frisky Barbara Lawrence (sex in the lab seems to be the sole thing on *her* mind!), warns the military not to nuke the robot, but to no avail; a plane carrying the H-bomb crashes into Kronos, which feeds off the resulting explosion and increases in size. As the robot steamrollers its way toward a Los Angeles nuclear facility, frantic Morrow also has another problem to contend with, colleague John Emery. The alien force controlling the robot soon possesses Emery and he's giving information by telepathy to Kronos detailing the sites of key power installations. After Emery destroys himself in remorse at his actions, Morrow hits upon the idea of lowering a negative-charged bolt between Kronos' antennae to reverse polarity. A parachute drops the bolt successfully, Kronos absorbs its own incredible electrical force, implodes violently and ends up a pile of twisted metal.

Paul Sawtell and Bert Shefter's pounding music underlined the ingenious special effects (Jack Rabin and Irving Block) in a unique sci-fi offering, and if audiences think they've come across this soundtrack before, they'd be right; it was honed to perfection, speeded up and used to great effect in *It! The Terror from Beyond Space*. We have to wait a full frustrating half-an-hour for Kronos to appear, standing sentinel on a beach like a towering metal monolith, and Neumann's direction in that opening segment is pedestrian in places. But when the robot begins its rampage across fields and rocky terrain, the pace steps up a gear and never lets up. Neumann, aided and abetted by Karl Struss' crystal-clear widescreen photography, delivers some spellbinding scenes of mass destruction in a picture that is as good as the much-maligned B movie can get. Regal, in the sphere of science fiction, would do no better, not in the '50s *or* the 1960s; *Kronos* is a minor classic of its type, triumphing over budgetary odds, never to be repeated.

The final entrant in Regal's mélange of '50s fantasy efforts was the disappointing *Space Master X-7*. A space probe returns to Earth covered in alien fungus spores, termed "Blood Rust" by Doctor Paul Frees. A sample is taken to Frees' laboratory where the spores multiply at an alarming rate. Following a tussle with his mistress (Lyn Thomas) over the whereabouts of their son (he's in Hawaii), Frees is hit on the head, dripping blood over the fungus that quickly devours the doctor and spreads throughout the house. Bill Williams turns up from the space agency, fries the organism to death and, at that point, director Edward Bernds' *Quatermass*-type facsimile quite literally loses the plot.

Yes, after an encouraging opening 20 minutes, *Space Master X-7* goes off the boil, the producers having run out of ideas on where to go with the story. What makes up the remainder of the running time (50 minutes) is a protracted police hunt for Thomas, carrying the lethal spores on her body and in danger of contaminating the whole of America. Williams and the cops must prevent her from going to Honolulu at all costs, so Bernds pads out the action to interminable lengths and shoots in semi-documentary style in a futile attempt to generate some excitement. Thomas evades her pursuers by altering her looks and boards a flight to Hawaii, agent Robert Ellis on her tail. The director doesn't even finish his effort with a sucker-punch; turning back to the States, the plane belly flops on the Santa Barbara airstrip after the rubbery killer fungus has caused a spot of bother in the baggage hold. The passengers disembark to a de-contamination center (including Thomas) and that's it.

It goes without saying that if in normal screen size, this movie would have sunk without trace a long time ago. RegalScope presents the action in a more favorable light but *Space Master X-7* is an exceedingly dull sci-fi picture, in fact the weakest out of the five '50s Regal productions. It was fairly successful on the Sunday horror circuits solely because, paired with *The Unknown Terror*, younger buffs could experience *two* widescreen sci-fi/horror flicks in one sitting, a veritable luxury at the time. Which is why, as stated, these five pictures went the rounds year after year. Never was presentation over content truer than in Regal's run of oddball fantasy features that consistently pulled in the crowds, no matter how lame (*Kronos* excepting) they indeed were.

Chapter 17
Monster Number One: Life Before CGI

In 1993, Steven Spielberg's computer-generated Tyrannosaurus Rex crashed through a compound barrier in *Jurassic Park*; even dyed-in-the-wool monster junkies like myself, who had been subjected to every conceivable movie monster imaginable over a 40-year time span, were forced to sit up and take notice. From that day onward, the computer took a firm hold on the field of monster effects and hasn't let up since. But CGI hasn't worn well over the years. Which CGI monster has made any sort of impact on audiences since Spielberg's trumped-up "the dinosaurs are coming" opus was foisted upon us in a blaze of hype? Answer—none. Take *Godzilla*, for example. The Japanese original is etched into the minds of past generations of fans and has been the subject of 20-odd movies, cartoons and comic strips. Toho's creation is right up there with the gill-man, the Frankenstein Monster, Dracula, the Wolf Man and King Kong, forever enshrined as one of fantasy's key figures. But what about the 1998 incarnation? Nobody can remember it; Roland Emmerich's giant, computerized lizard is just that—a giant, computerized lizard, lacking personality and depth. And as with most modern-day CGI beasties, it's there one minute, gone the next. The camera refuses to linger on these "cooked up in a computer" creatures; a lack of faith in the end product, maybe? Legions of fans, if called upon, can roughly sketch Harryhausen's Ymir or the mollusk in *The Monster that Challenged the World* because these monsters were allowed an abundance of screen time. They were the stars of the show. Nowadays, they're not.

Blandness, sterility and lack of fright appeal have set in. Where once monster movies were "X" or "A" rated, nowadays, they're classified as child-friendly. More mature members of the cinema-going public have become increasingly blasé over the whole computer deal. Take CGI dinosaurs. They might well be aesthetically accurate in detail according to the geological age they inhabited, but frequently they look flat and pixilated. Compared to a solid stop-motion model, they're almost two-dimensional. CGI wizardry also lacks the one essential ingredient guaranteed to grab an audience—wonder. Wonder has virtually disappeared from monster effects. Everyone now knows, thanks to documentaries and magazines, exactly how these things are conceived, straight from the drawing board into the intestines of a computer. In this respect, computer monsters don't actually exist. That hairy spider on strings in *Missile to the Moon* existed, cheap looking or not; it was constructed by hand. A computerized creature is simply an ephemeral image composed of millions of pixels that, after usage, vanishes into the ether, unlike, say, a Harryhausen model that (if you had access to one) could be picked up, touched and moved into various positions. It's the difference, dear fan, between one holding this book and an e-book. School kids can now drum up a reasonable-looking monster on their laptops; what is the point in creating large replicates or manipulating intricate models inch by inch, photographed at a single frame at a time, when a computer can perform the task without too much fuss and bother.

CGI didn't exist in the 1950s; optical and mechanical effects ruled the roost, so it's somewhat ironic that during this decade, audiences were assailed by an arresting onslaught of mind-boggling monsters that lodged in the memory for a very long time afterward. Film companies had a capacity for making a thousand dollars spent on effects seem like a million bucks. And it didn't require an army of technicians to bring them to the silver screen—two to three at the most or, in Harryhausen's case, one. Nobody needed countless magazines telling them how such-and-such was made; the technician could quite easily work it out. We all knew that Bert I. Gordon placed his performers in front of back-projected magnified insects and lizards; that Jack Arnold's *Tarantula* was a real tarantula matted into the action; that the spider in *World Without End* was a furry dummy worked by wires; that the giant ants in *Them!* were specially constructed imitations worked by animatronics; that *Godzilla* was a man in a rubber suit

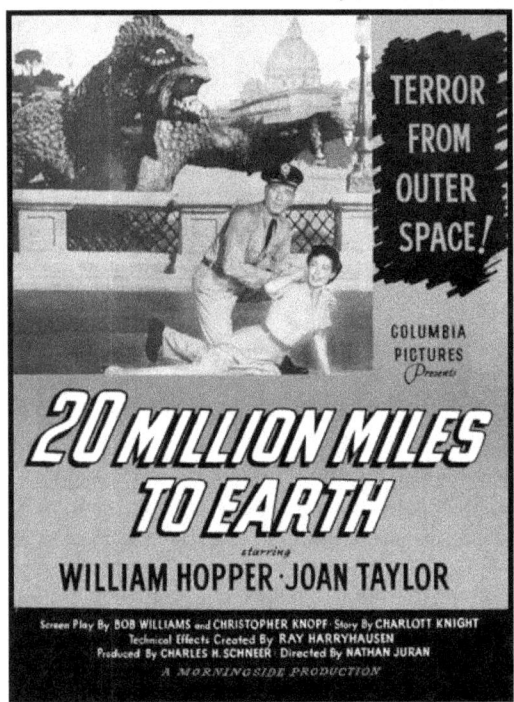

and that a filmmaker by the name of Ray Harryhausen *somehow* managed to combine his marvelous creations with live footage to stunning effect. Admittedly, on rare occasions, the not-so-special effects raised the eyebrows and provoked the odd titter. But remember—all were devised without the aid of computers; their imaginative conception wasn't impaired through lack of computer knowledge. Humans were responsible for their transference to the big screen, not machines. Spectacular results could be, and were, achieved pre-CGI: Godzilla's destruction of Tokyo and, skipping forward to the '60s, Gorgo's demolition job on London are classic sequences made in the days when computers had nothing whatsoever to do with the film industry. Both movies could *never* be bettered by digital tampering.

And that brings us to a very important question: Which particular monster, out of the veritable zoo that we were exposed to in those far-off days, tops the list of all-time greats? After a great deal of head-scratching, here is my top 10 list, in order of preference, of what I reckon are the 1950s pivotal monsters, the crème de la crème of monsterdom, if you like.

20 Million Miles to Earth—The Ymir, a giant Venusian reptile on the rampage in Italy. Judging by the number of years it ran in England, Columbia's feature has to be the most popular monster movie of the 1950s. From the monster's birth, crawling unsteadily out of a gelatinous egg-sac, to the escape from the cage, its capture and finally the final stand atop Rome's Coliseum, Ray Harryhausen manipulates his anatomical marvel with faultless expertise, imbuing his alien creature with emotional depth, savagery and pathos; he successfully created, in this modest production, a dynamic being to which mass audiences could identify. It wasn't family fare, either—in England, *20 Million Miles to Earth* received an "X" rating. One of the maestro's favorite movies—and colorized, it takes on a whole new perspective in big-screen entertainment.

Godzilla—Inoshiro Honda's titanic radioactive dinosaur was a stomping nuclear holocaust, trashing all before it, including the plot, which didn't really matter; the monster's prolonged wrecking of Tokyo is one of fantasy cinema's greatest segments of unadulterated monster-mayhem. Like a black behemoth, Godzilla roars, breathes fire, glows with radiation, crushes humans underfoot, demolishes buildings,

The Cyclops might just be Ray Harryhausen's finest creation, from *The 7th Voyage of Sinbad.*

tears up power lines, swats planes out of the air as though they were flies and gobbles up trains; no wonder the British censor slapped an "X" classification on the movie. Dark, violent scenes such as this will never again feature in today's watered-down monster fare.

The 7th Voyage of Sinbad—The Cyclops. Yep, Harryhausen again, but no one else could come close to what the man achieved in the 1950s; every fantasy filmgoer from eight to 80 can remember the impact that his cloven-hoofed, one-eyed horned giant, processed in Dynamation, had on them at the time when it strode from the mouth of a cave on the Isle of Colossa, bellowing its head off. It left an indelible impression on this writer as a 12 year old, and even my young son, seeing the uncut 1975 reissue, was mesmerized enough by the thing to suffer the odd nightmare. An extraordinary, exotic monster straight out of the pages of the Arabian Nights and a personal best for Harryhausen which, given his exceptional creative output, is really saying something.

Tarantula—Universal's effects ace Clifford Stine used two tarantulas for different setups in this superior monster show; never has a spider appeared so monstrous than in Jack Arnold's riveting giant insect thriller, shot mainly at night to convey an atmosphere of scientific experimentation gone horribly wrong. The scene when the townsfolk, laying down dynamite on a road, spot the gigantic spider crawling over a distant hillside straight toward them, goes to show what can be pulled off by using hard-won resources rather than cash to get one's ideas across—a fabulous platter of monster action, one of the company's defining moments.

The Monster that Challenged the World—Augie Lohman's mechanically operated giant mollusks-cum-caterpillars really leapt out of the screen, their big hypnotic headlamp eyes and drooling mandibles a favorite image with horror film poster collectors. The lengthy end sequence, when one of the articulated creatures attacks Audrey Dalton and her daughter in a laboratory, depicts Lohman's 20-foot model in all its glory, a one-off in a way, endearingly '50s in conception, although not so cute as to avoid a British "X" certificate when first released.

Rodan—True, in some scenes audiences can spot the wires hoisting Rodan and his mate over the city they are about to destroy, but so what? Toho's first monster outing

One of the Willis O'Brien/Pete Peterson-created giant scorpions from *The Black Scorpion*.

in color was a huge success for the company, running, like *20 Million Miles to Earth*, for an unbroken 12 years in England. Rodan, in young fans' eyes, was as terrifying as Godzilla, his dynamic battle with the military at Sasebo almost recreating the same level of urban destruction evoked in Godzilla's wrecking of Tokyo. And the mechanically operated caterpillar-like Meganurons were just as splendiferous. Without doubt, this becomes the second finest Japanese monster film of the '50s.

The Beast from 20,000 Fathoms—Ray Harryhausen's first solo effort proved to be, against all expectations, a big success for Warner Bros., perfectly displaying the man's unique talents for producing knockout effects on low finances. His animation of the Rhedosaurus, along with the Ymir and Cyclops, counts as one of the top three best pieces of stop-motion of the decade. Whether demolishing a lighthouse, capsizing a boat or stalking the New York streets, this striking, pebble-skinned dinosaur, tongue flicking, eyes blinking in the sunlight, is a creature of which audiences can relate. Which is why Harryhausen has acquired godlike status over the years; no other craftsman of his type (with the exception of Willis O'Brien) has invested so much blood, sweat and tears into bringing his eye-catching models to life. We fans are eternally grateful that he did.

The Black Scorpion—Which brings us to Willis O'Brien himself, Harryhausen's old mentor. Working in tandem with Pete Peterson, O'Brien fabricated, out of a standard monster-on-the-loose scenario, a vigorous horror flick of some note. Not only did we get a pack of oversized scorpions but a gripping sequence inside the depths of a volcano. This mid-section interlude probably arose from some of O'Brien's aborted storyboards dating back to the previous

A publicity shot of Craig Stevens and Alix Talton with *The Deadly Mantis*

decades; it has a distinct '30s look about it and was a tremendous, unexpected bonus for fantasy fans, featuring not only the scorpions but a worm-like creepy-crawler and a super-bug. The final confrontation in a Mexico City stadium, the military versus an extra large scorpion, is a climax ranking as one of the '50s most exciting. Underrated in some quarters, *The Black Scorpion*, 50 years on, comes across as one hell of an animated monster spectacle.

The Deadly Mantis—Another winner from Universal-International, Clifford Stine's marvelous effects as eye-opening as ever; a colossal, extremely ferocious, praying mantis thaws from an Arctic iceberg and causes problems all round for Craig Stevens and his men before flying down the Gulf Stream toward Washington and New York. The attack on the airbase and the final showdown in Manhattan's Holland Tunnel are just two acts of monster pandemonium that ensured a full house in British cinemas right up to 1969. Stine's large-scale model mantis is a beaut, a super creation very popular with buffs at the time.

Varan the Unbelievable—Try to obtain a copy of the original, uncut Japanese edit to fully appreciate what Inoshiro Honda and his team were trying to attain. Varan is a monster to be reckoned with, not given its due, in the heavily altered, and shortened, American print. The plot involves a gargantuan prehistoric scaly lizard that is forced out of its saltwater lake home; enraged at the disturbance, the monster heads toward Tokyo, trashing native villages and fighting off battleships en route. The picture has bags of monster action, filmed by Honda in the classic darker tones that highlighted *Godzilla*, and Varan is a formidable adversary in the grand Toho tradition. This picture is so good in its original form, and so rarely seen, that it has edged out of my top 10 the giant ants in *Them!* The fiery medieval devil in *Night of the Demon* and the towering crystals in *The Monolith Monsters* also came in for consideration. Apologies for this, but you can't list 'em all!

Chapter 18
A Monster of Foreign Delight—
and a Nod to Verne

Forget *Jurassic Park*, *The Lost World*, *One Million Years B.C.*, *The Animal World* and countless other segments of prehistoric life included in countless other movies. The only picture to *really* convey to an audience a literal translation of a world that existed millions of years in the distant past is Karel Zeman's enchanting *Cesta do Praveku* (Studio Gottwaldow 1954/1955). Variously released under the titles of *Journey to a Primeval Age*, *A Voyage to Prehistory* and, in its 1966 Americanized format, *Journey to the Beginning of Time*, Zeman's Czechoslovakian fantasy masterpiece remains the director's crowning triumph, all the more so when one considers that the marvelous effects on display were created some 40 years before the advent of computerized digital imagery.

A keen student of film, Zeman first became interested in the field of special effects in 1943 when he enrolled in Zlin's animation studios, tutored by Hermina Tyrlova, a pioneer in producing animated shorts. At around this date in his early career, Zeman also became fascinated by the prehistoric world; the paintings of noted Czech artist Zdenek Burian, integrated with the prose of eminent paleontologist Josef Augusta, captivated him, as did the novels of Jules Verne. The combination of Burian and Verne was the catalyst that spurred Zeman into producing a number of full-length fantasy pictures from 1954 onward, mostly based on the writings of Verne, in particular *Journey to the Center of the Earth*. Burian has the reputation of being one of the three greatest exponents of prehistoric art, bringing to vivid life on canvas Earth's distant geological ages; American Charles R. Knight and England's Maurice Wilson are the only two who can equal his work in this field. Burian's plates, captured in full glory in *Prehistoric Animals* (Spring Books 1956), show an astonishing eye for detail, both in his interpretations of long-dead animals discovered in the fossil records and the scenery in which they inhabited. His spectacular paintings portraying the jungles of the Carboniferous Age remain unsurpassed, limitless vistas of swamps, forests and exotic plants over which a crimson sky hangs heavy with smoke from volcanic eruptions. It was Burian's inspirational artwork, above everything else, that drove Zeman and his team of technicians to attempt something similar on celluloid, to recreate to the best of their ability those stunning primeval landscapes, to imbue their production with the crucial age-old atmosphere called for to carry the story. Stop-motion animation, mattes, animatronics, multiple exposures, model work, wildlife footage, split-screen and accurately rendered panoramic glass backdrops were the techniques used, all without the aid of a computer. In a way, it was a milestone in dynamic special effects, mirrored in the making of *King Kong* 21 years earlier.

The plotline in *Cesta do Praveku* is slight, but it was meant to be so. Zeman's intention was to approach his subject matter from a documentary point of view, rather than a plot-driven exercise in boys versus monsters, ultimately becoming a lesson in the evolutionary process. Narrated by Josef Lukas, first introduced poring over a battered journal, a trilobite in his hand, the opening few minutes stress the Verne and Burian influences, as well as showing photographs of fossil dinosaur bones in museums. Next we see Lukas, Vladimir Bejval, Petr Herrmann and Zdenek Hustak rowing a boat through a dark grotto, emerging into a sea of ice. We are now in the Ice Age and straight off, the four boys encounter a trumpeting mammoth on the riverbank, a snow-laden rocky mountain diorama adding to the sensation of brooding emptiness. ("A mammoth. A veritable mammoth. It's colossal. Quite colossal," whisper the youngsters, viewing the shaggy elephant through binoculars.)

Two prehistoric beasts approach one another in *Cesta do Praveku*.

This feeling of emptiness, of silence and of sheer solitude is prevalent throughout the film (E.F. Burian's score is used sparingly). These amazing creatures existed eons before Man arrived, in an unpopulated world, and this is one of the big success factors in *Cesta do Praveku*: No roaring, aggressive monsters here (apart from one sequence). These beasts are going about their business regardless, behaving naturally, man not yet figuring in the scheme of things, not for a very long time to come. (In a way, Zeman's picture predates BBC-TV's *Walking with Dinosaurs* [1999], whereby prehistoric life was recreated by computer and casually observed; creatures to study, not to interact with.) The four adventurers discover a cave crammed with bones and early human artifacts, see a tussle between two woolly rhinos and then, from the Ice Age, they make their way down river, drifting through swirling mist into the sub-tropical Tertiary period, the longest and most evocative section of the film. Using stop-motion animation throughout this segment, Zeman brings a whole array of prehistoric wildlife to the screen: pelicans, antelope, elephants (the Deinotherium), the Uintatherium, a saber-toothed tiger, giraffes, horses and gazelles, the humid air filled with the buzzing of insects, a dormant volcano soaring above the horizon. After an angry giant flightless bird, the Phororhacos, pursues Lukas, the explorers pass into the Mesozoic period, coming under attack from a swarm of Pteranodons, glimpsing a Styracosaurus and witnessing a twilight battle to the death between Ceratosaurus and Stegosaurus, all set against an arresting Jurassic backdrop. As well as stop-motion, animatronics breathe life into the Brontosaurus and Trachodon. A full-sized 20-foot model Stegosaurus enables the boys to clamber over its dead body like playful children, taking measurements and photographs.

No fantasy film to date has ever reconstructed the Carboniferous era; here, Zeman has conjured up a vista of lofty trees, thick jungle, massive shrubs and never-ending lagoons, populated by huge dragonflies (Meganeuras) and salamanders (Stegocephalians), a wondrous visualization steeped in primeval ambience in which the young cast are seemingly projected directly into the depths of a Burian masterwork. The adventurers lose their journal, but unruly Bejval, forever wandering off and causing trouble, retrieves it from the jaws of a warty amphibian and the four eventually end their journey down

The young explorers re-visit the ancient past in *Cesta do Praveku*.

the "river of time" at the dawn of creation, in the Silurian period, on a desolate shoreline where the lowly trilobite is the only living animal around (in actuality, they wouldn't have been able to breathe Earth's toxic atmosphere, but that's beside the point!). There's no account of how the boys manage to find a way back to their own time—the movie closes after two trilobites are found in the sea.

The original Czech cut of *Cesta do Praveku*, running at 92 minutes, was rarely seen in England, only screened at festivals and given a solitary showing on the U.K.'s commercial television channel in 1963, appearing as four 23-minute episodes. An 87-minute digitally restored version in pristine monochrome surfaced on a French video release in 1997 (with French subtitles) but is no longer available. Plans to have the full-length original issued on DVD in 2010 were curtailed because of various legalities. What fans of this little-seen fantasy have to make do with at present is the coarsely dubbed Americanized print, concocted in 1966 by William Cayton under the title *Journey to the Beginning of Time*; the producer wanted to jump onto the *One Million Years B.C.* bandwagon and capitalize on Hammer's successful prehistoric saga, so what better way of doing it than to restyle Zeman's magnum opus, adding new opening and closing scenes, a cast of stand-ins and tinting it in color.

Cayton's version does nothing to enhance the reputation of Zeman's original—in fact, it does its level best to sabotage the timeless quality and charm that makes *Cesta do Praveku* such a rewarding experience. Zeman's opening six minutes (continuing up to the point where the four boys row out of the cave into the Ice Age) is jettisoned in favor of a new 10-minute sequence showing four American youths crossing New York's Central Park. Inside the American Museum of Natural History, they peruse the skeletal remains of dinosaurs and inspect a model of a medicine man in an Indian canoe. Back in the park, they take a boat out onto the lake and discover a cave entrance. Rowing into the cave, the film *then* defaults to Zeman's original, tinted in ghastly shades of skuzzy color. During this opening 10 minutes, we never get to see the boys' faces in close-up (they're filmed from the rear), as to do so would show them to be the impostors they really are; it would be far too evident that what we have here are four Americans taking the place of the four young Czechoslovakian actors.

So basically, the bulk of *Journey to the Beginning of Time* is *Cesta do Praveku* with a tagged-on beginning and ending. But much dissimilarity occurs in this tampered-with version of the Czech classic. The pages of Josef Lukas' journal, detailing their journey and the ages they are passing through, have been edited out, as these would betray the movie's Czech origins. E.F. Burian's fine orchestral music (missing entirely from the garish credits) is used *too* much (augmented by a tuneless score added by Cayton), shattering the peace and quiet that highlighted the original. And the exact translation of the delightfully quaint Czech script (by Zeman and J.A. Novotny) has been completely lost, replaced by childish lines such as "Wow! Look at those mountains," "If that's an elephant, I'll eat my beret, pompoms an' all," "What an ugly monster. Is he very dangerous?" "Nah! He's a vegetarian," and "Why, if I brought a Stegosaurus home, Dad and I could go for long walks after supper with it." The dubbing is sloppy in the extreme; in numerous scenes, the lads are seen jabbering away while the American dialogue is completely out-of-synch with what they are saying. The dinosaur battle has growls and roars added while three vital minutes from the fantastical Carboniferous sequence are missing (the lads approaching the densely vegetated swamplands on their raft). The ending leaves out the discovery of the trilobites in the ocean; instead, we have footage

of an erupting volcano and odd, distorted images representing (one assumes) Earth's primitive life forms. Then the American actors wake up in the museum; their voyage has been a dream, each one hypnotized by the old shaman in the canoe. And coming in at 83 minutes, the picture is several minutes shorter than both the original and the French re-mastered copy.

Cesta do Praveku, completed in 1954 and screened at film festivals in Europe in 1955, is a haunting, at times poignant, journey into childhood desires, harking back to what most pre-teens at that time would have loved to set out to do, to explore a prehistoric world with all its stupendous sights, the ultimate big adventure. Innocent in many ways when set side-by-side with today's explicit cinematic and social climate, the overall power of this entrancing movie has not diminished one iota over a period of 50-odd years; we can truly soak up the primeval atmosphere so beautifully rendered by Zeman and his team. And if we must have it in color, someone should give the picture the painstaking care and attention that Ray Harryhausen performed so successfully on *20 Million Miles to Earth*; a digitally restored, colorized print of Zeman's *tour de force* would be very welcome indeed! [Note: A Czech color print sanctioned by the Karel Zeman Museum has now become available. In 1974, the British Museum of Natural History commissioned Invicta Plastics to produce a series of 1/45 scaled models of various prehistoric life

One of the fabulous dinosaurs crafted in Karel Zeman's *Cesta do Praveku*.

One of the retro-special effects sequences created for *The Fabulous World of Jules Verne.*

based mainly on the paintings of Zdenek Burian. These realistically sculpted figures, 23 in all, are still the preferred choice of experts and have become collectors' items.]

As a postscript to this chapter, Zeman's *The Fabulous World of Jules Verne* (*Vynalez Zkazy*; Studio Gottwaldow, 1958) is another fine example of the director's pictorial genius and obsession both with the classical works of the French author and the pioneering series of fantasy features concocted by visionary filmmaker Georges Méliès between 1896-1913, in particular *Under the Seas* (1907). Created in MystiMation, this is a remarkable evocation of Verne's prophecies, utilizing stop-motion animation (a giant squid), glass-painted backdrops, life-sized models, sea life footage, live action, puppetry, multiple exposures and incredibly detailed engravings within its rich fabric. Virtually every frame of film contains some form of trick effect, the entire 83 minutes dazzling the eye with a design uniquely different. Drawing its stimulus from *20,000 Leagues Under the Sea* and *Mysterious Island*, the simplistic plot has Professor Arnost Navratil and pupil Lubor Tokos kidnapped by megalomaniac Miroslav Holub and his pirate gang. Taken by submarine to a vast industrial complex housed within the crater of an extinct volcano, Navratil is ordered to construct a huge bomb packed with a new form of explosive; Holub plans to fire the missile from a massive cannon to demonstrate his intentions of dominating the world. The completed bomb slips from its cradle as warships approach, destroying the island base—Tokos manages to escape in a balloon with winsome Jana Zatloukalova, drifting off romantically toward the rising sun.

In terms of technical virtuosity and ideas, this movie was many years ahead of its time; *The Fabulous World of Jules Verne* exemplifies the work of one of cinema's least-known but most imaginative fantasy moviemakers. It's a must-see purchase for lovers of eccentric cinema.

Chapter 19
British Sci-Fi:
From a Duck to a Dinosaur

In 1950, man reached the moon (*Destination Moon*); in 1951, he came up against the Frankenstein Monster–type occupant of a flying saucer (*The Thing from Another World*) and the peaceful occupant of another (*The Day the Earth Stood Still*); and in 1953, *The Beast from 20,000 Fathoms* invaded New York at the same instant that Mars invaded the Earth in *The War of the Worlds*. Landmark productions, each and every one, but manufactured in America. Yes—while our cousins from across the Atlantic were being treated to Chesley Bonestell's astronomical backdrops of the lunar surface, alien James Arness stalking the company of an Arctic research base, Gort the Robot blasting the military with a laser beam, Ray Harryhausen's animated dinosaur rampaging through New York's thoroughfares and Martian fighting machines reducing Los Angeles to flaming rubble, we Brits were being fed ex-radio special agent Dick Barton on the trail of a stolen death ray (*Dick Barton at Bay*) and Douglas Fairbanks, Jr. lumbered with a duck that laid radioactive eggs (*Mister Drake's Duck*). Like the early British horror movie (chapter 25), early British sci-fi suffered from a lack of major studio financing and, as a consequence, appeared behind the times in comparison to U.S. product. Hammer's influential *The Quatermass Experiment* lifted the genre out of the doldrums, but not that much; British science fiction films continued to be made in black-and-white (*Satellite in the Sky* was the exception), budgets were kept to a minimum and American stars were shipped over to boost appeal (and, hopefully, box-office takings) on the international market.

Looking back, it's easy to see why critics have belittled movies like *Four Sided Triangle*, *Devil Girl from Mars* and *Stranger from Venus*. Scene for scene, they cannot hope to compete with the expensive glossiness brought to the big screen in *Forbidden Planet*, *Conquest of Space* and *This Island Earth*. They represent a time when British sci-fi struggled to match its American counterpart, but that doesn't mean to say that one has to continuously devalue these often unsophisticated pictures. They are not, as one writer once described them, "pale imitations of the real things." British sci-fi showed signs of marked improvement toward the latter part of the '50s when the industry, quite correctly, cottoned on to the fact that an "X" certificate was a sure-fire route to box-office success; *Quatermass 2*, *The Trollenberg Terror* and *First Man into Space* bore this out beyond all reasonable doubt, each picture successfully aimed fairly and squarely at the adult audience. Let's sort the wheat from the chaff and run through, year-by-year, what homegrown sci-fi fare offered to the great British public from 1950 to 1959.

1950

Between 1946 and 1951, *Dick Barton: Special Agent* was a nationwide "must" on the BBC's Light Program. At the height of its popularity, 15 million listeners huddled around their radios and tuned in to hear one of the most famous radio theme tunes of all time introduce the latest piece of derring-do from a character said to have been the inspiration behind James Bond. This was the perfect form of mass escapism for the

Don Stannard as the title character from *Dick Barton: Special Agent*

shell-shocked public in those dark days following the end of the war. Hammer Films specialized in knocking out feature films derived from radio plays and produced three movies based on the square-jawed hero's radio exploits, each around 70-minutes long: *Dick Barton: Special Agent* (1948), *Dick Barton Strikes Back* (1949) and *Dick Barton at Bay*. Plans for a fourth, *Dick Barton in Darkest Africa*, were shelved when leading man Don Stannard was tragically killed in a car crash on July 9, 1949 following an end-of-shoot party.

Let it be said that the *Dick Barton* movies are beyond criticism. They were made 60 years ago, and what passed as entertainment then would empty a cinema today! In *Dick Barton at Bay*, barely over an hour long, Stannard, zooming around a drizzly London in an open-topped sports car and wearing a white trench coat, is as stiff as his upper lip; the script is peppered with exclamatory, purely British, colloquialisms ("Great Scott!" "Crikey!" "By Jove!" "Darn It!" "For the love of Mike!"); the cartoon villain is a dastardly German; the death ray machine could have been constructed by a schoolboy in a backyard; and, upholding the BBC's own Dick Barton Code of Conduct, fights are strictly limited to the "sock 'em on the chin" variety. The plot? When megalomaniac German Meinhart Maur and his gang of ruffians steal Percy Walsh's death ray loaded with top brass military personnel to bring the planes down, Stannard and buddy George Ford track the mob down to the Beachy Head lighthouse. In a climatic fight, the machine is disabled (Stannard simply throws a gun into the works!) and Maur topples to his death from the top of the lighthouse. Director Godfrey Grayson's homage to the radio star is thrill-a-minute nostalgia, thick-ear stuff that a whole generation of families took refuge in from the harsh reality of life in those far-off, innocent times—and yes, Rupert Grayson's instantly recognizable theme music that lodges itself in the brain and refuses to let go remains intact.

The Americans weren't the only ones worried by the threat of a Russian nuclear holocaust. Set in a gray London still suffering from bomb damage sustained in the Blitz, London Films/The Boulting Brothers' *Seven Days to Noon*, produced, written and directed by Roy and John Boulting, told of a conscience-stricken scientist (Barry Jones) who threatens to detonate an atomic device, the UR12, at noon on Sunday in Central London if the government doesn't halt the manufacture of nuclear weapons. This was to be Britain's one and only '50s doomsday thriller and it's a superb example of filmmaking at its grittiest, blending good old-fashioned Englishness with Cold War menace. André Morell played the Special Branch officer on the hunt for Jones, aided by the scientist's colleague, Hugh Cross, and daughter Sheila Manahan. Shot in the documentary style that Val Guest effectively brought to the screen in his two *Quatermass* movies, containing stark images of the Capital courtesy of Gilbert Taylor, Jones flits from one location to another, carrying the bomb in a valise. Always one step ahead of his pursuers, he eventually hides out in brassy revue star Olive Sloane's room and holds her prisoner while the city is evacuated. The scenes of mass evacuation are reminiscent of those carried out during the war, leaving a London eerily deserted, troops combing the empty buildings as time runs out. With 10 minutes to go, Jones is tracked down to Westminster's ruined St. Stephen's Church, where we saw him at the beginning; running from the building screaming "Too late," he's shot dead by soldier Victor Maddern; Cross successfully disables the bomb with one minute left on the clock.

There's no disguising the anti-Russian feeling running throughout the film. With the Prime Minister withholding information up to the last second, rumor is rife concerning troop mobilization. Are the Russians about to invade? "We're so scared, we don't trust anyone," states one person succinctly. The mentally unstable scientist makes his feelings clear to Sloane: "It's better for a city to perish than the whole world." Some biting touches include the Crown Jewels, art treasures and museum valuables being ferried away from the 12-mile blast area while pets are left to perish; a man plays the "Atomic Racer" game in an arcade and Jones first hears the Prime Minister's radio broadcast of what is happening framed within the fossilized remains of a dinosaur. John Addison's fine score is perfectly tuned to the action, and the whole picture has a "matter-of-fact" air to it, including Morell's clipped performance. The U.K.'s sole '50s contribution to Cold War paranoia cinema is as suspenseful as anything to emerge from the States in the early years of this decade, but the film is very rarely seen nowadays.

1951

British sci-fi showed no signs of lifting itself out of its cozy rut with *Mister Drake's Duck*, a comic fantasy concerning a duck that lays eggs containing uranium. Val Guest, yet to make his mark with Hammer's two *Quatermass* thrillers, directed this perky, homey tale of newlyweds Douglas Fairbanks, Jr. and Yolande Donlan (Guest's wife), who take up residence on Greenacre Farm, left to them in his will by Fairbanks' uncle. On a trip to the local market, Donlan buys 60 Aylesbury ducks, one of which lays eggs with green uranium yolks. As soon as the news gets out, the British army appears in force—Operation Chickweed is underway. Soldiers, tanks, aircraft, armored vehicles and cannons arrive in droves; that duck, when it can be separated from the other 59, must be safeguarded to prevent an international incident! The Americans lay claim to the bird as theirs because Fairbanks is a Yank; predictably, the Russians also get in on the act. Eventually located, the radioactive duck is taken to Guy's Hospital in London, operated on to learn its secrets and dies. But was it the right duck? In the closing seconds, Fairbanks picks up an egg which, when tapped, emits a strange tone, just as the army returns. Is there a second duck laying uranium eggs? We will never know!

Intermittently funny, *Mister Drake's Duck*, a variation on the Goose that lays the Golden Egg parable and made by Fairbanks, Jr.'s own production company, is hardly cutting-edge cinema, and a running joke concerning an armored truck that continually flattens the farm's brick-built gate post wears a bit thin after a while. Fairbanks, the perky Donlan, country yokel Jon Pertwee and a cast of English eccentrics play their parts with a kind of manic energy as befits a farce of this nature. The film was popular at the time, but again demonstrated that compared to what was appearing from across the ocean, the British still had a very long way to go in the sci-fi genre. Guest's goofy movie, dealing with (but skating over) the possible effects of uranium poisoning, was a case of two webbed feet forward, one webbed foot back.

Ealing Studios cut down on the whimsy to produce a caustic satire on industrial relations in Alexander MacKendrick's *The Man in the White Suit*. Alec Guinness is a scatterbrained boffin who invents a revolutionary fabric that is impervious to dirt, wear and tear, thereby placing the whole of England's textile industry in jeopardy. As washerwoman Edie Martin grumbles toward the end of the film, "What becomes of me when there's no washing to do?" Chiefs of industry Cecil Parker, Michael Gough and Ernest Thesiger, scared stiff that Guinness' "everlasting thread" will bring about the collapse of their mills, plot to make sure the secret formula is suppressed and not leaked to the papers, as do the workers, afraid of losing their jobs. Ignoring huge financial bribes, Guinness is reduced to being a fugitive on the run, chased through the dark streets in his glowing white suit in the frenetic climax and finally cornered by the mob. But the cloth suddenly becomes unstable and disintegrates ("We're saved!" they all cry); the manufacturing industry is spared from ruin although in the dying seconds, the inventor *may* have another trick up his sleeve.

A warning of the dangers of scientific progress sounding the death knell for socialism and employment, *The Man in the White Suit* is a marvelous Ealing picture that hasn't aged at all. Apart from the great casting of Guinness, Gough, Parker and Thesiger, husky voiced Joan Greenwood plays Parker's vivacious daughter and busty Vida Hope is the worker nursing a passion for the disinterested Guinness. It's certainly more razor-edged than most of the company's '50s output, a fantasy farce minus the belly laughs and an important constituent of British cinema's golden age that rewards on repeated viewings.

1953

Along with *Stolen Face* (1952), Hammer's *Four Sided Triangle* occupies an important niche within the company's pre-1957 history. Terence Fisher directed both pictures and both exhibited various trademarks that were to appear in this company's future repertoire, but in diluted form (A-rated, not "X" certified). The pieces of the Hammer jigsaw were gradually coming together but lacked that one vital ingredient to coalesce the product into a complete whole. *Frankenstein in the English Countryside* would be a fitting title for Fisher's daring tale of two scientists (Stephen Murray and John Van Eyssen) who invent the "Reproducer," a machine that can replicate any object, inanimate or living. When Van Eyssen marries peroxide blonde Barbara Payton (the trio are all childhood friends), Murray, also in love with her, clones a duplicate for his own pleasure. Unfortunately for him, Payton Mark 2 comes complete with Payton Mark 1's memory banks; she, like her "twin," loves Van Eyssen, rejecting Murray after going away on holiday with him ("Even if I did let her go, what good would it do. Don't forget, there are two of them, in love with the same man."). In order that she might return his desires, Murray erases her memory ("an empty mind and a new beginning."). The result is a beautifully blank zombie. In a final conflagration (yes, a favored Hammer climax even then!), Murray and his creation are burned to death in the blazing laboratory; the original Payton survives, much to the relief of husband Van Eyssen.

Uncannily forecasting the likes of *The Fly* and *Frankenstein Created Woman, Four Sided Triangle* contained, in one form or another, traits that would crop up in countless Hammer Gothic productions that followed the unprecedented success of *The Curse of Frankenstein*, particularly in the laboratory sequences. In these, Fisher's expertise behind the camera shone through, borrowing heavily from *Bride of Frankenstein* (and *Man Made Monster*?). He cleverly set up the scenes as a montage of odd-angled close-ups, flashing bulbs and bubbling flasks, Malcolm Arnold's rising score imbuing feverish activity into Murray and Van Eyssen's experiments. Yes, Hammer *did* exist before Cushing and Lee appeared in gory Eastmancolor; *Four Sided Triangle* pictures an embryonic Hammer gaining, step-by-step, a foothold in the world of sci-fi/horror. It appears, now, to be slightly unfinished and dainty, peculiarly English in design (not helped by an avuncular James Hayter narrating the story and a cozy village setting), but it was the blueprint of what happened next. Fisher's first tentative sortie into Frankenstein territory must be looked upon as a movie of some considerable significance.

Fisher also directed *Spaceways*, dabbling his toes further into the sci-fi pool. Becoming yet another Hammer adaptation of a radio play, this talkative space opera attempted to cross-fertilize romance and postwar espionage with a "first man into space" storyline. Unfortunately, Fisher's much-vaunted fluid camerawork faltered at the first hurdle, the result being that *Spaceways* was hard going, even for early Hammer followers. Romance came in the form of Eastern European starlet Eva Bartok; she's in love with American scientist Howard Duff, whose bitchy wife (Cecile Chevreau), bored with life on a research station, plans to run off with lover Andrew Osborn, a spy who has stolen Duff's scientific blueprints. When the pair disappears, intelligence officer Alan Wheatley accuses Duff of murdering them and stowing the corpses on board a rocket that is orbiting the Earth as a satellite. To prove his innocence, Duff becomes the first astronaut into space, flying off in the AS1 with Bartok to show to the authorities that the bodies, presumed hidden on the satellite, aren't there. Wheatley tracks down the lovers near Brighton, Osborn shoots Chevreau before being arrested and Duff has the job of steering the AS1 back to Earth where presumably he will live happily ever after with Bartok.

Set in the world of Bakelite instrument panels, makeshift spacesuits and none-too-accurate technical jargon, *Spaceways* is very humdrum in execution and ideas. Fisher manages to breathe some life into the project in the closing sequences on board the AS1, staying in sharper focus and generating a degree of suspense, more so than what he established in the previous hour. The paltry budget couldn't match the ambitions of the makers and it showed. Compared to *The Quatermass Experiment*, produced two years later, *Spaceways* is like something from another age, showing the huge strides Hammer made in those two years, from run-of-the-mill programmer to an out-an-out classic.

1954

Lost in the mists of time, Merton Park's 84-minute *The Brain Machine* (released through RKO) opened in sci-fi/horror fashion, the initial scenes reminiscent of a forthcoming *Quatermass* film. To compound the effect, soundtrack addicts will detect Trevor Duncan's hackle-raising music from the BBC teleserial *Quatermass and the Pit* (1958/1959) used here as the main title theme. An insane criminal, responsible for murdering four people, is brought to Doctor Patrick Barr's mental health institution. Barr's wife, standoffish Elizabeth Allan, wires the psycho's head up to a machine termed an electroencephalograph to record his violent brainwaves. Then Allan ups and leaves Barr, moving to the North London Hospital. Her next patient (Maxwell Reed) is an accident victim suffering from amnesia—when Allan rigs him up to the machine, his erratic brain patterns, made worse by a blood clot, match those of the other killer's and she's sure that she's got another psychopath on her hands.

Director Ken Hughes, as he would do in *Timeslip* (1955), jettisoned the scientific potential of the ECG machine and instead put his foot on the gas, going flat-out for trashy *noir*; there's not an ounce of fat in this lean, mean production—it steadfastly refuses to ease up. British heartthrob Reed, playing against type, is mesmerizing as a vicious crook selling the control drug cortisone on the black market. Imprisoning interfering Allan (who still wants to treat his condition) in a lockup garage under a railway line, he decides to murder Gibb McLaughlin, the head of the racket; callous hit-man Edwin Richfield, hired by McLaughlin, strangles Reed's tramp of a wife but is shot dead by Reed in the lockup. After gunning down McLaughlin in a hail of bullets at the offices of Amalgamated Chemicals, half-crazed Reed is arrested and Allan walks off with husband Barr.

The Brain Machine crackles with helter-skelter energy—more could have been made of the sci-fi aspect, perhaps turning Reed into some kind of brain-fried monster. But that was the American way. The British way was to play it low-key, so Reed *is* a monster, but more of an off-the-rails one. Hughes' violent B thriller, seldom seen these days, needs rooting out for reappraisal.

Patricia Laffan as Nyah from *Devil Girl from Mars*

Danziger Brothers'/Spartan's wonderful *Devil Girl from Mars* (directed by David MacDonald) showed that it *was* possible to produce high-camp sci-fi on a shoestring budget and come up with something that would long be remembered with affection. Patricia Laffan played Nyah, a lofty female Martian on the lookout for healthy men to take back to her home planet in order to breed and, by doing so, preserve the Martian race, decimated by atomic war. All the males have perished, leaving a women-only matriarchal society. Landing her splendid flying saucer near a remote Scottish inn was probably *not* the best location in Britain to lay her well-manicured hands on prime specimens of British manhood, but that's what she does, accompanied by her pet robot Chani. Statuesque Laffan was alluring as the mad empress in *Quo Vadis*; here, dressed from head to toe in black PVC, she's positively mouth-watering! Any red-blooded male would be only too glad to get well away from those dreary Scottish moors and hitch a ride on her UFO but, no, reporter Hugh McDermott, Professor Joseph Tomelty and convict-on-the-run Peter Reynolds do their utmost to thwart Laffan in her plans to steal a required quota of human mating material. Also at her mercy are young Hazel Court and Adrienne Corri who Laffan despises as being weak examples of womanhood.

Take these ingredients (a force field preventing escape; Chani resembling a refrigerator on clumpy legs, blasting thunderbolts from his head; Laffan's laser gun reducing humans to ashes and a heavenly designed flying saucer) and add Laffan's hilarious monotonic recitation, rattling off her lines by rote, Edwin Astley's raucous score, a pseudo-scientific script that defies all logic and two English beauties in Court and Corri and we have an endearing slice of nonsense that is hugely entertaining, even today. And audiences know that this has "Made in Britain" stamped all over it when, in the middle of yet another bout of mayhem, the landlady announces to her regulars that there is, "nothing like a good cup of tea in a crisis." The censors were unusually lenient with this movie—*Devil Girl from Mars* is without doubt the scariest British "U" film ever released in the 1950s.

Like *Devil Girl from Mars*, *Stranger from Venus* took place virtually on one set, an English public house set in leafy countryside. A cut-price version of *The Day the Earth Stood Still* with Patricia Neal, who is more or less reprising her role from the Robert Wise film, American Burt Balaban's minimalist alien invasion tale had Venusian Helmut Dantine healing Neal after she had crashed her car, sustaining life-threatening injuries. Introducing himself to a nearby inn's residents, the suave-looking alien announces to politician Derek Bond, Neal's fiancé, that he has arrived on Earth to warn against the misuse of atomic weapons. If Earth's leaders refuse to listen to his message, the Venusian mother ship, due to release further crafts over a field, will burn off the atmosphere and annihilate the surrounding area. The army lays an electronic trap to destroy the UFOs but Dantine, in a fit of conscience, orders the fleet to head back to their home planet. Poisoned by Earth's atmosphere, he disappears in a melodramatic death scene, leaving Neal's scarf by the side of a lake—he loved her but was afraid to admit it.

Yes, a saucer *is* shown near the end, although not quite up to the standard of Klaatu's ship exhibited in the 20th Century Fox classic, and Neal displays the inner radiance that highlighted her performance in the earlier movie. The script is fairly witty in places ("These aren't the fingerprints of a human being." "Well, Arthur, let's see this monster of yours from outer space.") and Eric Spear's score is lush beyond belief, a little *too* overpowering given the low-budget ambience. Despite Dantine's remoteness, his scenes with Neal (she's infatuated with him) are quite moving, bringing a touch of humanity to the perennial theme of "first contact." There's nothing earth shattering in *Stranger from Venus*. Rather the film maintains a restrained edginess that keeps us watching and makes one forget the absence of any sort of up-to-the-minute special effects.

1955

Journalist Paul Douglas and photographer Leslie Phillips, traveling through Eastern Europe by train, are arrested in the small Balkan state of Gudavia for being possible spies. Released on orders from ruthless dictator Walter Rilla, who doesn't want to draw outside attention to his subversive activities, they discover that Rilla is experimenting with gamma rays on both adults and juveniles; a few child geniuses are produced that one day might control the state, but most adults are turned into mindless idiots called Goons who run through the streets and countryside like a herd of wild zombies, causing mayhem.

Directed by John Gilling for Columbia/Warwick, *The Gamma People* was a heavy-handed clash of styles, played for laughs in some scenes, played deadly straight in others. The anti-communist message wasn't fully developed, Gilling content to focus his attention on whether Douglas and Phillips can uncover Rilla's secret and escape from his army of Goons in one piece. Rilla's castle laboratory was well designed and the climax, in which both lab and castle go up in flames, satisfactorily staged. Eva Bartok brought a whiff of European sex to the proceedings but the movie, like Douglas himself, was too stolid and curiously dated in appearance. A-rated in Britain, it wasn't a great success at the cash registers when released in January 1956.

1955 was the year British science fiction at last obtained a footing on the global stage. First broadcast in July/August 1953, BBC-TV's six-part serial *The Quatermass Experiment*, the brainchild of writer Nigel Kneale, had shocked television audiences into submission, a harrowing antithesis to all the euphoric festivities and general air of optimism taking place in the Queen's Coronation Year. Two days after the final episode on August 22, which drew an audience of five million (huge for the time), Hammer Films successfully bid for the film rights and shooting commenced in October 1954.

Unbeknown to Kneale, Hammer and director Val Guest had other ideas for the BBC's groundbreaker, initiating a number of drastic revisions to the teleplay. They reasoned, quite correctly, that what was classed as suitable for a TV audience wouldn't necessarily pass muster in a cinema. It needed to be more filmic in outlook. Consequently, Guest and Richard Landau's translation of Kneale's telescript became a condensation of the BBC serial: scenes were trimmed, subplots jettisoned, dialogue modified, certain characters' roles shortened and the climax restructured, much to Kneale's dissatisfaction. To cap it all, the company hired American Brian Donlevy, veteran of countless Hollywood Westerns and gangster thrillers, to play the Professor, a wise decision as it turned out; Donlevy, fueled by coffee laced with brandy, brought a tough, arrogant energy to the part that perhaps an Englishman was unable to accomplish (it's interesting to compare Donlevy's rude Americanized scientist against Jack Warner's textbook, very polite, English police inspector). Hammer had to defend these decisions to an appalled Kneale, arguing that if they were to stand any chance of breaking into the lucrative overseas market, it was imperative that an actor of Donlevy's standing would have to be employed. The company also made darned sure that their exciting new product would receive an "X" rating, disregarding the censor's demands for minor cuts, the reason why, on first release, *Experiment* became *Xperiment*.

The film was premiered in London in August 1955, going out on general release as *The Quatermass Xperiment* in November of that year, paired with Jules Dassin's definitive crime caper, *Rififi*. The release date was purposely set by Hammer to coincide with Kneale's second *Quatermass* teleserial, *Quatermass 2*, whose third episode was aired to a record-breaking audience of eight million on November 5. Thus was created the *Quatermass* legend; Kneale's Professor appeared on the small screen and big screen simultaneously, becoming a household name in England, a name synonymous with other-worldly terror. *The Quatermass Xperiment* c/w *Rififi* became the U.K.'s highest-grossing double bill of 1955 and the rest, as they say, is history.

The Quatermass Xperiment was a giant leap forward for Hammer, displaying a remarkable self-assurance in all things connected with space never experienced before in a British science fiction picture. After years of churning out passable thrillers, the company had finally blossomed into a force to be reckoned with, much like the Professor himself. It was the international breakthrough that they had hoped for, making critics and fans sit up and take notice and cementing, in Britain at least, their fast-growing reputation. Shot in newsreel–style to add urgent realism and a sense of "it's really happening" to the narrative, Kneale's ambitious concept of an astronaut returning to Earth, infected by an alien organism, proved to be a nationwide sensation, vindicating the alterations in script and personnel

Quatermass (Brian Donlevy) stares on at astronaut Carroon (Richard Wordsworth) in *The Quatermass Xperiment*.

that Hammer had felt necessary. Gaunt Richard Wordsworth, brilliantly portraying the agonized spaceman mutating into something very nasty indeed, was responsible for a spate of faintings among female punters, one of the many factors that contributed to record till receipts. In retrospect, one can't help but wonder how Terence Fisher's more controlled pace would have fared with this material, but he was destined for fame and fortune in other arenas of the Hammer sphere—*his* breakthrough would occur two years later with *The Curse of Frankenstein*, the first British horror movie in color.

Timeslip (aka *The Atomic Man*) was the second of Ken Hughes' low-budget sci-fi/horror movies of the '50s, produced by Merton Park Studios for Allied Artists. British science fiction author Charles Eric Maine wrote the script—Maine's novels and plays in the '50s and '60s (Hammer's *Spaceways* was based on one of his radio plays) gravitated toward new science technology rather than men versus aliens. *Timeslip* began promisingly: A man (Peter Arne) is fished out of the River Thames with a bullet in his back. Taken to hospital, he clinically dies for seven and a half seconds. When he revives from the operation, he is seven and a half seconds ahead of time. Photos of him exhibit a strange halo, X-ray scans of his head turn out blank and his body has traces of radioactivity. Who is he? Journalist Gene Nelson and photographer Faith Domergue (brought over from America to add international interest) discover that Arne is a famous atomic physicist known as "The Isotope Man" and that his double (a crook surgically altered to look like him) has been substituted in his place. The clone plans to sabotage the Brant

Nuclear Research Institute by blowing it up. Why? The labs are producing synthetic tungsten and the boss of a South American tungsten mining company (Vic Perry) wants Arne dead and the facility destroyed, seeing the work the scientist is undertaking as a threat to his business empire.

For about 50 minutes, *Timeslip* intrigues as we wonder who Arne is, how can he be in two places at one time and how can he possibly answer questions before they are asked. Once the cat is out of the bag, however, Hughes opts for a fragmented cops/investigative reporters versus spies chase thriller, ruining the cohesion set in the first part—the final 28 minutes is formulaic roughhouse stuff, abandoning the scientific possibilities brought on by Arne's radiation-induced condition. The police remove the plutonium bomb from the facility before it is activated, Perry and his gang are shot dead, Arne the scientist acts normally and Domergue falls into the arms of Nelson. Despite going off the rails, *Timeslip* is a weighty piece of British sci-fi action, bolstered by a noisy stock score by George Melachrino and winning performances from the two American leads. Arne is also excellent in his twin roles of physicist and saboteur.

1956

The Quatermass Xperiment may have been a classic in the making but elsewhere, the small independents were still intent on inflicting garbage of the first order onto a very patient English cinema-going public. Eros' *Fire Maidens from Outer Space* (or *Fire Maidens of Outer Space*) has entered the pages of cinema history as the worst British sci-fi picture released in this decade; perhaps the worst produced of all time. A team of astronauts blasts off for Jupiter's 13th moon to determine the source of a mysterious signal. When they arrive, they find the remnants of the lost civilization of Atlantis, comprising 16 women dressed in skimpy tops and short skirts ruled by aged priest Owen Berry; this motley bunch are continually harassed by science fiction's ropiest monster, a man in body-hugging tights wearing a fanged mask who skulks in the shadows. "Men at last!" the Maidens gasp in delight when they set their sex-starved eyes on the masculine desirability of Anthony Dexter, Paul Carpenter and crew, viewing them as possible mating partners.

Classical composer Alexander Borodin must have been turning in his grave at the misuse of his *Polovtsian Suite* (better known as "Stranger in Paradise"); attired in diaphanous gowns, the women prance around to his music, hoping that Dexter and company will take notice and ferry them back to Earth. When the monster kills Berry, the astronauts make sure the thing follows the dead leader into a fiery pit; they then take a senior Fire Maiden back to Earth, promising to pick up the remaining 15 later.

No attempt was made by Eros and director Cy Roth to imbue their product with at least a modicum of visual style. The control deck of the space rocket resembles the interior of an old wartime airplane, while Surrey's green and pleasant countryside incongruously stands in for the 13th moon of Jupiter. As for that alien; it should have been consigned to the waste bin, along with the rest of the film. A cack-handed addition to the school of "lonely females on a planet awaiting Earthmen with which to copulate" filmmaking popularized by *Queen of Outer Space* and *Missile to the Moon, Fire Maidens from Outer Space* is a turkey of mammoth proportions, and something of an embarrassment to British sci-fi fans.

Underdeveloped in many areas, Michael Anderson's *1984* was a depressingly dark first stab at George Orwell's notorious novel about a dystopian future ruled by the omnipresent Big Brother. Defiant Edmond O'Brien played a worker in the records office of the Ministry of Truth, challenging the totalitarian state's doctrine and finding solace in the arms of Jan Sterling in a society where sex was outlawed. Imaginative set pieces made full use of Orwell's autocratic vision of what might lay ahead for all of us: telescreens, like blinking eyes, overseeing every move a person made; monitors piping mindless Muzak nonstop to the masses, informing them that "Even in your sleep, Big Brother is watching you"; loudspeakers blasting out propaganda; Hate Weeks directed at the enemy; anti-sex leagues; the zombie-like Thought Police and torture in Room 101 by tapping into one's elemental fears. Oceania, the London of the future, looked impressive, blending detailed model shots into the scenario, and the constant threat of atomic war with neighboring Eurasia was well handled, Malcolm Arnold contributing a stirring score. But O'Brien and Sterling's doomed romance didn't tug at the heart strings as it should have done; Michael Redgrave, the boss of the Ministry, emerged tops in the acting stakes, an arrogant figurehead for the new movement who betrays O'Brien without batting an eyelid. Two endings were filmed: In U.S. prints, O'Brien and Sterling have been brainwashed, embracing Big Brother and all that it stands for; in the United Kingdom, O'Brien, after torture, continues to flout the state's ideology and is killed. Despite its failure in some areas, *1984* showed that British science fiction was at last getting serious and growing up; it was the second sci-fi picture to be classified "X" and it wouldn't be the last.

Filmed in Warnercolor and CinemaScope, the Danziger Brothers' *Satellite in the Sky* was a giant step upward from the duo's *Devil Girl from Mars* and boasted imaginative space effects by Wally Veevers, almost bordering on those paraded in Paramount's more expensive *Conquest of Space*. But the subject matter was flat as handled by director Paul Dickson; the entire 85 minutes was composed of long shots, resulting in a marked absence of dramatic impetus needed to drive the storyline forward. Another in the "first man into space" series of '50s space operas, *Satellite in the Sky* had jet pilot Kieron Moore and a crew of four taking off from a launch ramp (copied from *When Worlds Collide*) in the Stardust rocket with a tritonium bomb on board; scientist Donald Wolfit's mission is to detonate the device above Earth's atmosphere, the blast intending to act as a deterrent to nuclear war. When the bomb becomes attached to the rocket through magnetic attraction, Wolfit and Barry Keegan sacrifice their lives by leaving the ship and pushing the bomb away, the pair steering it into space where it explodes without harming the Stardust.

It's all very stiff-upper-lipped, earnest and talkative; James Bond's Miss Moneypenny, deliciously sexy Lois Maxwell, plays a stowaway pacifist reporter who falls for Moore's dark good looks, and the cast, including Jimmy Hanley and Bryan Forbes, have to contend with an outrageous piece of overacting by Wolfit as the exuberant inventor. Veever's detailed model work, especially the vast underground installation housing the rocket, is the chief reason for catching this rather lifeless space melodrama that seems to go on a lot longer than it actually does.

To capitalize on the British "X" certificate, Hammer's unofficial follow-up to *The Quatermass Xperiment* left no doubts as to where their filmic ambitions lay—*X: The Unknown*, the big "X" emblazoned in red on the posters, one in the eye for the British censor. The company had asked Nigel Kneale for permission to use Professor Bernard Quatermass in the story but the request was flatly refused (Jimmy Sangster wrote the screenplay); Kneale was still smarting over their treatment of his character in *The Quatermass Xperiment*, even though he grudgingly admitted that the film had been a critical and commercial success, the public obviously unconcerned that Brian Donlevy had played the principal role instead of an English actor. Therefore, dour American Dean Jagger took on the Quatermass mantle, a nuclear scientist sent to Scotland to investigate a mysterious radioactive blob that emerges from 2,000-foot-deep fissures every 50 years, causing havoc. Leslie Norman's opening scenes are terrific—a tracking shot of a soldier crossing a gravel pit, his Geiger counter registering an immense source of radioactivity, the ground suddenly opening at his feet as a minor quake occurs. A subplot focuses on the tensions between Jagger's scatterbrained man of science (a direct opposite to Donlevy's forthrightness) and Edward Chapman's stubborn authoritativeness as boss of the Atomic Research complex. Chapman reckons that Jagger is a crackpot; Jagger thinks Chapman has no scientific vision. As they expostulate over the origins of the creature, the glowing blob oozes its way through dark woods and down country lanes, homing in on high tension cables and the power station to feed off electrical/nuclear energy and stripping the flesh from those who venture too close (Les Bowie's effects work was minimal but potent, as it had been on *The Quatermass Xperiment* and would be on *Quatermass 2* and *The Trollenberg Terror*). Jagger finally destroys the protoplasmic terror by enticing it out of the abyss with a cobalt isotope and bombarding it with electronic waves.

X: The Unknown is austere, sober science fiction for grown-ups, featuring, as did *Quatermass*, a spare but menacing score by James Bernard. Hammer Films was now forging ahead, the likes of *Spaceways* and *Four Sided Triangle* all but a distant memory. The adult market was theirs for the taking and this is where they would aim all their future material, whether or not the censor objected to what was submitted for classification (and Hammer's ongoing spats with the censor during the 1950s are almost as legendary as their films).

1957

The Electronic Monster was based on Charles Eric Maine's novel *Escapement*, the picture's alternative title. Maine's script again explored new technology; the movie was a predecessor of more sophisticated efforts such as *Videodrome* (1982), *Brainstorm* (1983) and others of their ilk. In Merton Park's rather stodgy thriller, a machine has been invented by scientists at the Amercon clinic near Cannes that can brainwash patients' disturbed minds by feeding them erotic images which later surface as pleasurable, or murderous, dreams—a self-dependant "drug" produced under unethical electronic hypnosis. Unfortunately, the rich and famous who are using this course of action to relieve them of psychiatric disorders are dying in fatal accidents, their brain tissues fried. American insurance investigator Rod Cameron steps in to uncover the truth behind the death of a film star who died *before* his car crashed. Cameron meets up with old flame Mary Murphy, engaged to the clinic's unscrupulous owner, Peter Illing, and with the help of caring scientist Meredith Edwards discovers what goes on behind those closed doors.

Director Montgomery Tully does his best with this (for the time) fanciful material, but the movie appears labored, hampered by leading man Cameron's unsympathetic, wooden performance. Skulduggery, brutal murder, lascivious dancing scenes, torture (one of the scientists is an ex-Nazi) and a happy ending (Cameron and Murphy back together after he's rescued her from becoming another victim and the lab going up in flames) highlight the production. It's quite a brew, but fails to connect, one of the reasons why the film didn't receive a wide showing in U.K. cinemas and passed most fans by.

Still stuck in some kind of artistic wasteland, Eros' *The Man Without a Body* was a cheapjack mad doctor-type offering jointly directed by W. Lee Wilder and Charles Saunders (Saunders' input was apparently minimal). George Couloris played a highly strung financier affected by a brain tumor who hits upon the crackpot idea of stealing the head of the prophet Nostradamus (buried in France), rigging it up to apparatus in Robert Hutton's laboratory and then cajoling the thing into predicting how his business interests will benefit from the undoubted words of wisdom that will spill from those age-old lips. Couloris secretly plans to have Hutton transplant the head onto his own body, so that he can more readily control his empire.

Twelve long minutes into this risible British shocker, we are informed of the results of Couloris' brain scan. Thirty even longer minutes after that, Nostradamus'  head gets to speak. While Couloris communicates with the 16th-century prophet, his mistress (Nadja Regin) is carrying on behind his back with Doctor Sheldon Lawrence, so sexual betrayal is tossed into the mix for good measure. Nostradamus, understandably annoyed at having been disturbed after 500 years of rest, feeds the businessman erroneous information, leading to the downfall of his empire. Out of his mind Couloris strangles Regin and shoots Lawrence, but only wounds him. Back in the lab, the plastic-looking head is grafted onto Lawrence's body; the resulting creature, a square papier maché box surrounding its head in an absurd parody of the Frankenstein Monster, stalks the dark London streets, falling to its death from a bell tower after Coulouris has fallen to *his* death in identical fashion.

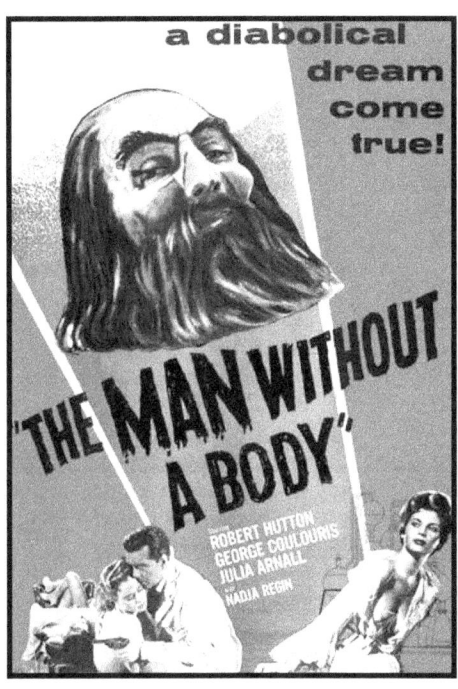

Drab and plodding are two words that best sums up *The Man Without a Body*. Coulouris never did cut it as a mad businessman/doctor (he was equally miscast in *The Woman Eater*, released the same year) and his eye-rolling turn here is laughable rather than laudable. Most of the action takes place in Hutton's sparsely equipped laboratory, the monster in the closing 10 minutes will invite titters from the audience (as it did when I caught it in 1965, on a double bill with *Fiend Without a Face*) and Wilder's direction lacks pace. The movie becomes a tired addition to '50s British sci-fi/horror that does little or nothing to add to the genre's standing or, indeed, supposed progression, as the decade wore on.

Hammer's second *Quatermass* outing, *Quatermass 2*, consolidated the company's position as purveyors of top-quality fare and is now rightly regarded as the highpoint of British science fiction in the 1950s. Val Guest and Nigel Kneale's complex screenplay took in alien invasion, dormitory town paranoia and covert government conspiracy, coming across like a mix of *Invasion of the Body Snatchers* and *1984*. Guest's treatment of Kneale's multitude of ideas is tough and involving: Professor Quatermass (Brian Donlevy reprising his role from *The Quatermass Xperiment*) is up against one frustrating problem after another in trying to persuade an obstinate British government to finance his moonbase project. Meanwhile, colleague William Franklyn is monitoring showers of meteorites falling over Southern England, originating from an asteroid orbiting the Earth. When Donlevy finds to his consternation that his pet project has been replicated at a secret military site near Winnerden Flats, and those gleaming domes, supposedly producing synthetic food, are harboring deadly organisms from outer space, the scene is set for an apocalyptic thriller that rivets from start to finish.

Despite Kneale's continued objections to the actor's involvement, Donlevy, surly and bull-headed, carries *Quatermass 2* with conviction and verve, rattling off his lines with machine-gun ferocity. Whether steamrolling his raincoat-suited bulk through Whitehall and Scotland Yard's corridors of power in order to get at the truth, or organizing a mass revolt at the center of alien operations, Donlevy is a one-man force of nature, not to be treated lightly or easily dismissed; this has to go down as one of the actor's greatest-ever performances, brandy or no brandy. From disquieting beginnings, the film quickly escalates into a nightmare of alarming events as the domineering Profes-

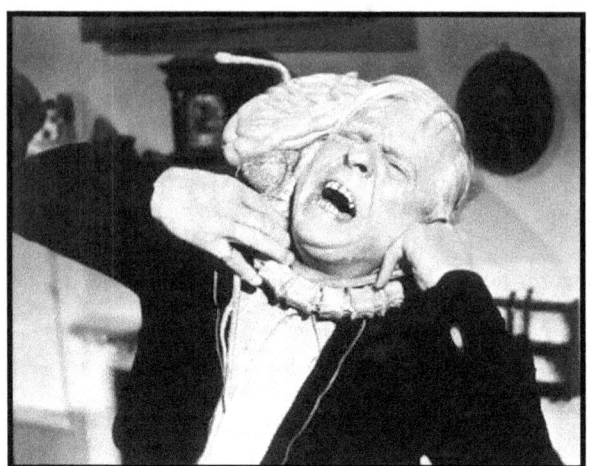

The animated flying brain monsters, suddenly becoming visible, created a sensation in *Fiend Without a Face*.

sor single-handedly attempts to foil an alien takeover, one that members of the upper reaches of the cabinet and police are aware of. Shot in and around the Shell Haven Refinery in Essex, *Q2* benefits from Gerald Gibbs' vivid cinematography, a sterling cast and Guest's energetic direction. It perpetuates, even today, an undeniable power that places it firmly in the very top echelons of science fiction film history. And, as stated, Donlevy is outstanding.

1958

Fiend Without a Face continued the run of lean but effective British X-rated sci-fi horror, and the American star taking center stage this time was the ubiquitous Marshall Thompson, once again playing an officer in uniform and flying jacket. Marshall's stolid presence ensured that this story of brain-like monsters materialized out of the thought processes of scientist Kynaston Reeves didn't plummet into silliness. A murky, gray England stood in for Canada; Reeves is a miserable professor venting his dislike for his fellow folk by tapping his deranged thoughts via an experimental machine into an airbase's atomic reactor. Inadvertently, he releases invisible creatures from his unbalanced mind that scuttle, rustle and slurp through the undergrowth, leaping on people and sucking their brains out through the back of the neck. A mad GI is blamed for the deaths, but all-round regular guy Thompson reckons it's something far more sinister.

Director Arthur Crabtree conjures up several nerve-racking interludes, assisted by Lionel Banes' artful back-lighting. It all leads up to the extraordinary climax when Thompson, Kim Parker and a few locals, holed up in a house, come under attack from the animated flying brains. This lengthy sequence alone ensured the film's everlasting status among fans, making one forget the final schmaltzy seconds when hero Thompson, after blowing up the base's power plant which, as a result, destroys the miniature "Ids," appears in a doorway; Parker rushes up to him and plants a big, wet smacker on his soppy face. Yes, in the 1950s, these movies always had to end with a kiss!

Proving that anything Bert I. Gordon could do, the British could do as well, although even more ineptly, *The Strange World of Planet X* (aka *Cosmic Monsters/The Cosmic Monster*) receives the dubious honor of being the country's one and only '50s giant insect film, and an extremely poor one at that. Based on an unremembered television serial (it looks like a TV sitcom in parts) and shot in three locations—a public house, a laboratory and a wood—Gilbert Gunn's tepid sci-fi drama told of glum-looking Forrest Tucker and Alec Mango's experiments in playing around with Earth's magnetic field. By doing so, a hole is created in the ionosphere; cosmic rays bombard the English countryside, causing insects to grow to huge dimensions. Friendly alien Martin

Benson warns the scientists about the possible disastrous effects of their experimentation. The hole is then sealed by an alien race; Benson solemnly informs one and all that Earth is not fit to join the Federation of Planets and departs in a flying saucer (which resembles a silver spinning top.)

B.I. Gordon was the king of the back-projected magnified beastie but even his efforts look champion compared to what was on offer here; millipedes, caterpillars, crickets, cockroaches and a spider, all blown up to create an illusion of gigantism, the army blasting away at these images, having no real contact with the creatures. A tramp, turned into a homicidal strangler by the rays, patently fails to liven things up. Yes, Britain still had a long way to go before it could hope to catch up with our American cousins, judging by Eros' effort. Hadn't Hammer and their two *Quatermass* classics taught other filmmakers anything?

An Italian movie poster for *The Trollenberg Terror*

Well, judging by Tempean's *The Trollenberg Terror* (aka *The Crawling Eye*), they had. Yet another adaptation of a British TV serial (broadcast December 1956/January 1957), Hammer scriptwriter Jimmy Sangster was hired to give added bite to this sub-*Quatermass* excursion into extraterrestrial activity on a Swiss mountain. Cyclopean octopus-type beings reside on the slopes of the Trollenberg Mountain, concealed by a radioactive cloud. U.N. science investigator Forrest Tucker (the imported actor was up to his eyes in British fantasy pictures in 1957/1958) has seen this before, in the Andes, but the authorities chose to ridicule his claims of alien creatures. Mind-reading sisters Janet Munro and Jennifer Jane arrive in the town and soon, Munro is communicating with the monsters by telepathy; they need thin air to survive on Earth, hence the mountains are an ideal environment. Climbers are decapitated, another taken over mentally by the things and the exciting showdown takes place on a mountain observatory busy monitoring cosmic rays. The giant octopi/jellyfish aliens attack the building, their writhing tentacles seeking human prey, before they're finished off with a combination of Molotov cocktails and firebombs dropped by the air force.

Twin British lovelies Munro and Jayne offset Tucker's dour presence, but the rest of the cast, especially Professor Warren Mitchell and Laurence Payne, are just as sullen. Still, the performances, plus Stanley Black's fine score, match the movie's downbeat mood, and Les Bowie's monstrous alien effects work well despite the low budget. This remains one of the more atmospheric of the British X-rated sci-fi thrillers to emerge from this period. It was also, for a change, a satisfactory release from Eros.

1959

Behemoth the Sea Monster lays claim to being the only British dinosaur-on-the-loose picture released in the 1950s, the stop-motion effects created by veteran Willis O' Brien and Pete Peterson. In contrast to the more flamboyant American monster movies, it has a spartan, European air to it, the imported actor on this occasion being Gene Evans. Eugene Lourie directed (American prints list Douglas Hickox as co-director); he was responsible for *The Beast from 20,000 Fathoms* (which *Behemoth* resembles in parts) and would unleash *Gorgo* onto London's population in 1961. *Behemoth* had a somewhat checkered history; soon after general release in England, the censor ordered severe cuts to the "X" certificate print in order to satisfy Allied Artists' demands that the film be made accessible to a wider and younger audience. With several scenes omitted (victims charred and blistered from radiation burns; the radioactive monster stomping through London's streets; the smashing-down-the pylons sequence), *Behemoth* was reissued as an "A" and renamed *The Giant Behemoth*. Ironically, *both* versions went the rounds in England during the mid-1960s; usually, seasoned buffs made a beeline for the X-rated *Behemoth*, curious to discover what exact footage the censor had judged unsuitable for the under-16s when those under-16s were later quizzed about what *they* had witnessed in the A-rated flick.

As monster movies go, *Behemoth the Sea Monster* in its unedited form is a pretty good '50s dinosaur-at-large romp. Granted, audiences have to wait 45 minutes for the main action to take place, but when it does, the stop-motion animation is superb (not so convincing is Jack Rabin's fake-looking model upending the Woolwich ferryboat). Not really gifted with star charisma, Evans is gruff but adequate, André Morell lends articulate support as a professor and the black-and-white photography is needle-sharp. This was to be O'Brien's final work on a monster flick, and how Lourie must have detested the British film censor's office—he came up against an identical set of circumstances regarding censorship problems when *Gorgo* was released in 1961 as an "X," not the "A" the distributors would have wished for.

First Man into Space took its cue from *The Quatermass Experiment*, the plot modeled on similar lines. Bill Edwards played a cocky space pilot who defies his superiors' orders (and that includes brother Marshall Thompson) and guides his rocket, the Y13, 250 miles into space, a lot further than scheduled. Losing control of the craft, he flies through a shower of meteorite dust and disappears off radar screens. The Y13 crashes to Earth, Edwards coated in a glistening rock-like substance (a form of "cosmic protection"), needing the oxygen content from blood to survive. Director Robert Day obviously had minimal funds at his disposal, so a wintry-looking England inappropriately stood in for sunny New Mexico, with stock footage of American airbases inserted at intervals. Nevertheless, this efficient shocker, filmed in stark black-and-white, managed to produce some effective scenes: The tortured Edwards in his bulky spacesuit blundering into a blood bank and savagely ripping open a nurse's throat; the deranged astronaut murdering two police officers and a prolonged climax in which Thompson, positive that Edwards can be saved ("If he can drive a car, he's still retained some intelligence. He's not all monster."), lures his brother into a high-pressure chamber in the hope that the alien organism covering his body will be destroyed by increasing the altitude. Edwards, managing at last to communicate with the authorities and tell them what happened in space, expires through oxygen starvation, leaving Commander Thompson to take up with not-so-grieving Marla Landi, Edwards' girlfriend.

Thompson was never out of uniform at this stage of his career, playing a commander not only in this picture but also in *Fiend Without a Face* and *It! The Terror from Beyond Space*. Solid and dependable, he does everything asked of him with a script that doesn't plummet into silliness. Landi is darkly attractive but spends most of her screen time screaming, and Edwards' make-up job, one eye staring out of a ravaged, pockmarked face, was considered too frightening for a younger audience, hence the "X" classification. Buxton Orr's music is a little strident at times but never over-prominent, incorporating a weird electronic whistling sound to announce the monster's approach. All in all, *First Man into Space*, given a major release in England in 1959, is an austere piece of sci-fi that races through its 77 minutes, a reminder of the sleeves-rolled-up ethic prevalent in British filmmaking that hallmarked this period, prior to the brassy '60s taking over.

Yes, progress *had* been made since the days of *Dick Barton at Bay* and *Mister Drake's Duck,* as *First Man into Space* showed, but British sci-fi of the '50s was very much a down-to-earth, black-and-white affair. It lacked both the color and expense that highlighted the movies flooding in from the States but did throw up a few classics along the way. However, compared to the gaudiness and tackiness that was to blight many a production in the 1960s, British '50s sci-fi can, in hindsight, be viewed in a much more approving light; adult-orientated pictures that embodied solid craftsmanship allied to a "let's get on with it" mindset, everything created on tight budgets, the end product successful at the box-office. It was this "hard graft on low finances" principle that summed up the decade perfectly.

Chapter 20
Two Schlock Classics!

Schlock: n. N. Amer. colloq. Inferior goods; trash; of low quality.

Paul Blaisdell's cucumber-shaped Venusian from *It Conquered the World* has entered the annals of '50s low-rent sci-fi movies as the screen's corniest monster. But it has a serious rival in this category—the perambulating tree-monster in *From Hell It Came*, also designed by Blaisdell. Released in 1957 by Allied Artists, this tale of a radioactive tree stump causing havoc on a Pacific atoll is schlock personified, a glorious helping of nonsense lasting 71 fairly insane minutes; monster action, South Sea action and romantic action all rolled into one, containing a script crammed full of amusing exchanges, a truly bizarre, over-the-top performance from Linda Watkins and that scowling rubbery tree waddling after its enemies. Grade Z trash? A monumental turkey? Well, perhaps, but any 50-year-old horror film that brings a smile to the face, isn't a bore and keeps audiences watching throughout its running time, with the one thought of "They don't make 'em like this anymore" predominant, has a lot going for it. Many '50s cheapies (*Robot Monster*, *The Killer Shrews*, *Teenage Monster*, *Killers from Space*) are so mind-numbingly dreadful, they can only really be viewed once and that's it. Once is enough. Dan Milner's infamous tree-monster movie may indeed, in many eyes, be taken for laughable nonsense but it's certainly not mind numbing. The picture has genuine moments of cunningly hidden brilliance that can be winkled out after several run-throughs. Let's find out what these hidden gems are.

First, the credits. The "It" in the title graphics is composed of, not the letters as such, but two elaborate sketches of the tree-monster. Nice touch of detail this, representative of most '50s monster lettering. Darrell Calker's drum-laden, Xavier Cugat-type orchestral title score is straight out of a 1930s/1940s jungle feature—we half expect Dorothy Lamour to shimmy on set as the music starts up—and then it's straight into the South Sea action. Native Gregg Palmer lies spread-eagled and tethered on the ground, awaiting death by sacrificial dagger. He's been betrayed by his wife, falsely accused of dallying with other women; as a result, Palmer's shameful infidelities have caused the premature death of his father. It's a put-up job, of course, the woman carrying on with the tribe's chief behind Palmer's back. Moreover, his father's death, in truth, is attributed to radioactive fallout drifting onto the atoll from A-bomb testing 1,500 miles away. Another factor in this scenario is that the natives (most wearing patterned Bermuda shorts) wish to get back at the Americans who have set up base on the atoll to monitor radiation levels; they blame the "Devil Dust" for causing sickness among their people, mistrust the Yanks and want them off the island. "I promise you all, I shall come back from hell and make you pay for your crime," curses Palmer, just before the dagger is hammered into his heart. A native dance is performed (Yes—the women *do* wear grass skirts!) and then his body is placed in an ornate wooden cask, to be buried upright in the ground.

So, we witness a busy first 12 minutes. Professor John McNamara and Doctor Tod Andrews are introduced, the incessant throb of drums getting on Andrews' nerves. McNamara states, "Drums don't bother me, Doc. In fact, they have a nice anthropological beat." Andrews smiles. "Well, maybe we ought to record it. Get it on the hit parade." But Richard Bernstein's tongue-in-cheek screenplay rises magnificently to the occasion with the arrival of Linda Watkins, a twice-widowed, man-hungry blonde speaking in a "cor blimey" cockney accent so excruciatingly awful that it makes Dick Van Dyke's much-derided London dialect in *Mary Poppins* sound positively Shakespearean by comparison! Was the actress enlisted to provide comic relief in a movie that didn't need it? Watkins chanced upon Palmer's murder and wants McNamara and Andrews to know all about it, sparing no

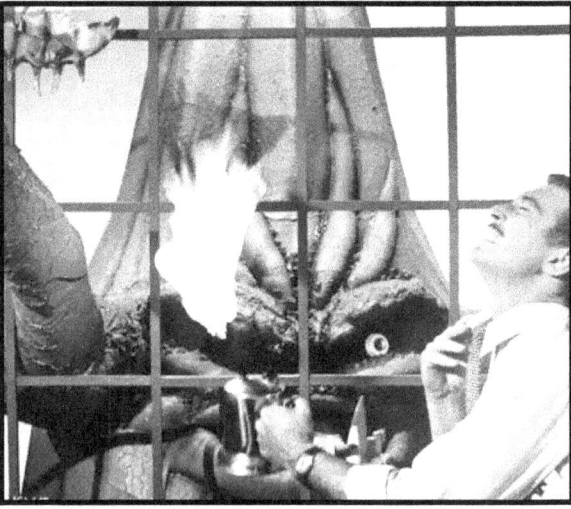

Lee Van Cleef tries to defeat the Venusian monster in *It Conquered the Earth.*

lurid details. "The bloomin' cannibals. They stuck a knife right through 'is 'eart," she squawks, mangling her vowels and lapsing from cockney accent to pseudo-Australian (the actress was actually born in Boston!). "It was 'orrible. Simply 'orrible." Andrews tries to soothe her nerves but to no avail. "I'll have nightmares the rest of me natural life," she continues, downing one drink after another. "The 'eathens. They ought to drop a bloomin' hydrogen bomb on 'em all and blow 'em to pieces."

Andrews, however, has more pressing matters on his mind other than native rituals. Another blonde, Tina Carver, arrives via helicopter to boost the scientific team and he's got the hots for her, big time. Unfortunately, the haughty Carver doesn't want to play house or discuss marriage, leaving lovesick Andrews looking as wooden as the monster he will shortly have to combat. "Why, that's right nice of you, ducky," chortles the garrulous Watkins when Carver gives her a spare bottle of perfume, sounding suspiciously like Britain's much-loved actress Dora Bryan. Meanwhile, at the burial site, the ground begins to move ominously over the spot where Palmer was interred and the chief and witch doctor devise a plan to get rid of the Americans, tipping their arrows with poison, the dialogue strictly of the "Me Tarzan, You Jane" variety, spoken in broad New York accents.

At last, a weird woody growth in the cemetery draws the attention of the three scientists. "Could a tree trunk grow out of a coffin?" asks Carver incredulously, but according to native superstition, it can and it's called a Tabanga. One has turned up before when a chief was buried with seeds—his evil spirit returned as a tree-monster, stalked the island, killed many people and disappeared without trace. Now a native issues a further dire warning: "The Tabanga will soon remove itself from the ground." McNamara scoffs at the notion. "You mean this wooden zombie's gonna uproot itself from the earth? Your grandfather must have been quite a storyteller," he sneers. But Palmer's coffin has absorbed radiation, giving life to the glowering stump; it has a heartbeat and oozes green blood, the handle of the dagger lodged in its chest. "You know what. I have

an eerie feeling that this thing knows what we're saying," says Carver, eying it nervously. On orders from Washington, the trio digs the object up and takes it to the laboratory for further scientific investigation.

Back in the lab, the tree-man chained to a bench, Carver has ideas on reviving it, but the only thing Andrews wants to revive is Carver's flagging libido. "Maybe we ought to ship it back to the States. It'd make a good scarecrow," and "Why keep this freak of nature alive," are his offhand responses to Carver's morbid curiosity over the creature. Eventually giving in to her demands (no doubt in the hope of getting back into her good books *and* underwear!), they attach an intravenous drip containing blood and experimental chemicals with the aim of stimulating the monster's heart, and then retire for the night.

In the morning, the lab has been smashed to bits—Blaisdell's legendary tree-monster *has* been revived and is on the loose! The plot and those wonderfully droll asides are jettisoned post-haste; what now follows is standard '50s "the monster is coming" shenanigans, Milner raising the pace to a more urgent tempo ("You know, I know it sounds crazy, but maybe Tabanga is for real and if it is, we're gonna need help," says a worried-looking Andrews). The shuffling menace throws his disloyal wife into a bog and somehow manages to dispatch both the crooked chief and witch doctor, even though it only moves at a steady one mile per hour. Stumbling into a pit dug by the natives who toss in burning torches, the tree-monster emerges slightly scorched and homes in on Carver, all to the sounds of Calker's strident score, blaring away merrily in the background. Grabbing hold of Carver, who shrieks, faints and then gives in to a prolonged (and irritating) bout of caterwauling ("Do you think that bloomin' monster got hold of her?" blurts Watkins in full overdrive, stating the obvious), the woody menace is cornered on a ledge overlooking the swamp. Carver breaks free and Andrews fires his rifle, the bullet hitting the sacred dagger, which re-enters the heart; the monster topples backward into the quagmire and sinks, defeated, leaving the natives to grudgingly admit after their foe has met its end that "American magic is the best." Hero-of-the-hour Andrews finally gets to kiss the reluctant love of his life and, quite wisely, the producers leave the last word to the flighty Watkins. Andrews now spoken for, the sex-starved hussy sets her rampant sights on McNamara. "By the way, Professor, I never asked you. Are you married?" she simpers, fluffing up her hair and making a beeline for the retreating scientist who looks more alarmed at the sight of her than he ever did with the Tabanga.

An undisputed cult classic and a hoot of the first order, *From Hell It Came* (yes, even *this* was X-rated in England!) wholeheartedly deserves the accolade of being the campiest, hammiest, dopiest yet in many ways the most endearing 70-plus minutes of schlock ever to emerge from a decade notorious for rolling out scores of cheapskate efforts, all of which could be included under this particular banner of moviemaking (Ed Wood's *Plan 9 from Outer Space* runs it a close second). Like a vintage wine, it actually improves with age! Let's extol the cheesy virtues inherent in the Milner Brothers' best-ever effort. Long live Tabanga!

There is no walking tree in *Mesa of Lost Women*, only the '50s worst-looking fake spider, a large puppet on strings wisely kept out of sight behind screens in Jackie Coogan's sketchy laboratory. Conceived in 1951 by Hungarian writer Herbert Tevos (aka Herbert von Schoellenbach) under the working title of *Tarantula*, Howco International deemed the results so bad that exploitation producer Ron Ormond, an affiliate of Ed Wood, was hired in 1952 for a re-shoot, the movie completed in 1953. Ormond and Tevos shared directorial credits; Tevos wrote the script and composer Hoyt Stoddard Curtin was enlisted to come up with a suitably bizarre soundtrack to match the similarly bizarre storyboard—and boy, did he succeed, in spades! Their joint endeavors resulted in one of the decade's most vilified mad doctor movies, 69 minutes of "100% dreck" as one critic succinctly wrote.

The sultry Tarantella (Tandra Quinn) may be the best thing about *Mesa of Lost Women*.

But step back a little and view it in the cold light of day. *Mesa of Lost Women* belongs to an entirely different age of filmmaking to that experienced by audiences of today, a cinematic universe where amateurs, by hook or by crook, managed on peanuts to get their skew-whiff ideas onto celluloid, everyone oblivious to the critical damnation that was sure to follow. No, filmmakers couldn't get away with it nowadays: 21st-century punters demand mega-bucks big screen excitement with top Hollywood stars to match and anything less won't do, thank you very much. In a way, films like *Mesa of Lost Women*, *Robot Monster* and *The Gargon Terror*, as well as Ed Wood and Jerry Warren's efforts, are cinema's equivalent of fossils. You unearth them, dust them off and treasure every lame minute of them; after all, pictures like these will never be made again, so make the most of what's available, warts and all.

As the camera pans over Mexico's arid Meurto Desert (actually California's Red Rock Canyon), we hear, for the first time but unfortunately not the last, the stentorian tones of another member of Ed Wood's entourage, Lyle Talbot, who acts as the voice-over narrator: "Strange, the monstrous assurance of this race of puny bipeds with overblown egos. The creature who calls himself man. He believes he owns the Earth and every living thing on it exists only for his benefit. Yet how foolish he is. Consider, only the lowly insect that man treads underfoot outweighs humanity several times, and outnumbers him by countless billions. In the continuing war of survival between man and the hexapods, only an utter fool would bet against the insect…" and so on, and so forth, for a full four minutes. And if Talbot's droning utterances aren't enough to contend with, Cur-

tin's flamenco guitar/piano-based accompaniment jangles away incessantly in the background, rising and falling in volume; the dual effect of Talbot's narration and Curtin's discordant notation will have audiences desperately searching for earplugs, and we're not even into the main story yet! (Ed Wood used part of Curtin's soundtrack from this movie in 1954's *Jail Bait*.)

Oilman Richard Travis picks up Robert Knapp and Mary Hill, found wandering in the desert ("He cannot believe his eyes. Images produced by roasting the optic nerves."). Taken to a field hospital, Knapp in his delirium mumbles "Blow them up" and "Super-bugs as big as we are. They can kill you with one bite." Knapp recovers and then, as the shadow of a camera creeps over his shirt, begins to tell his tale (the voice of Talbot cuts in: "Quite a story he's telling, isn't it Pepe?" referring to Mexican peasant Chris-Pin Martin. "You heard through your people out at Zarpa Mesa ... the mysterious Doctor Aranya."). However, Knapp's recollections are rudely interrupted: Tevos and Ormond (for artistic purposes? A flash of inspiration?) opt for a shift in gear by diving into a second flashback and return to the events of a year ago, the action working its tortuous way back to the point where Knapp and Hill were spotted in the desert.

Doctor Harmon Stevens is flown to Zarpa Mesa to meet Doctor Jackie Coogan ("Oh, we've arrived," he says unblinkingly under his panama hat) whose laboratory is situated deep inside the mesa. Coogan, sporting a big black mole under a ruined left eye, is injecting tarantula serum into human pituitary glands, creating, in females, predatory super-women who can regenerate damaged flesh; in males, pug-ugly dwarfs are the by-product. Mercifully, at this stage of the proceedings, Talbot gives us all a break by putting a sock in it; he stops blabbering on for about 10 minutes. Coogan's lab is home to grimacing dwarf John George, sexy, deadly Tarantella (played with dark allure by Tandra Quinn) and several women assistants wearing black mop-head hairpieces. Seventeen minutes into the picture, a giant spider's appendage appears over a screen just as Coogan is intoning, "If we are successful, I shall have a super female spider with a thinking and reasoning brain. A creature that someday may control the world—subject to my will." But that's not a hexapod, my dear doctor. Hexapods only have six legs!

At the sight of the spider and a girl strapped onto an operating table, Stevens gets an attack of medical ethics and decides he's had enough of Coogan and his crackpot crew. "You can't do these things. Ghastly experiments! This place must be destroyed." Quinn stabs a syringe in his neck, Curtin's cacophonous music breaks the pain barrier and the next we see of Stevens, he's an imbecilic patient in the Meurto State Asylum.

A minute later, the loony escapes by climbing out of a window.

The next scene takes place in Perkin's Frontera Cantina and, from this point on, we plunge into absurdity (as if we hadn't done so already!). Allison Hayes look-alike Quinn performs an erotic three-minute dance, flashing her underwear in front of newlyweds Mary Hill and Niko Lek, with Samuel Wu, their shifty looking Chinese servant, in attendance. In walks Stevens holding a gun, followed by his orderly, George Burrows. Grinning like a simpleton and talking in an eight-year-old's voice, Stevens (a dreadful bit of acting, it has to be said) shoots Quinn and forces the others by gunpoint to board Knapp's plane ("I command. And thou shalt obey!"). He wants a showdown with Coogan and nothing will stop him ("We fly. Now!"). Even though burly Knapp or hefty Burrows could disarm the idiot in the blink of an eye. Back in the bar, Quinn, negating her fatal bullet wound through the use of her super spider powers, rises from the floor ("Sheriff. The body just got up and walked outta here!") at the precise moment Knapp and company take off for Zarpa Mesa.

These superwomen, made inhuman by tartantula serum, are not ready to allow their human captives to escape, from *Mesa of Lost Women*.

As the mesa comes into view, one of the engines malfunctions, giving rise to another ridiculous quote from Stevens: "Birds fly without motors. And so will we." Crash-landing on the 600-foot-high plateau at night, they make camp, and Wu chips in with his own Chinese proverb: "The curtain of darkness veils the sharpest eyes." Burrows goes off to explore and is killed by a huge hairy spider, while the others, all hand-in-hand, are herded into Coogan's domain by a crowd of circus midgets and women with black nine-inch fingernails ("Who is he?" asks Knapp of Coogan. "He's a brilliant madman," replies Stevens). Faced with his nemesis, mad-as-a-hatter Stevens rejects Coogan's offer to restore his sanity on condition he helps with the experiments. He grabs a bubbling flask full of explosive and throws it at the scientist whose "greatest achievement of science" goes up in flames; the spider, Quinn, the women, the dwarfs and himself, all dead. Knapp and Hill are the only two to make it out alive and we are back where we started.

Mexican Martin believes Knapp's version of events, even if skeptical Travis doesn't ("Anybody thinks I'm gonna load one of my trucks with oil and send it up on top of a mountain to burn a bunch of imaginary spiders?"). The last word, as if we haven't already guessed, is left to Talbot: "Yes, you're right, Dan (Travis). Commonsense tells you there isn't anything to his story, doesn't it? Giant spiders on a desert mesa! Fantastic! Pepe's just a superstitious native. True, no one has ever been on top of the mesa, but it's just like any other bit of tableland. Not a thing different about it." Then we get a shot of a blonde super-woman on a cliff in a revealing dress (cue for *Mesa of Lost Women 2*? Surely not!), and to the racket of Curtin's aural backdrop, Talbot ends with "Or, er, is there?" Yes, folks—you can now remove the cotton ball from your ears!

There's no getting away from the fact that *Mesa of Lost Women* is a seriously weird motion picture; it's either the zenith of lousy moviemaking or a mad, bad masterpiece, or both, according to one's tastes. It virtually defies description, but just simply rubbishing it won't do; Tevos and Ormond's almost anti-film is as much a part of the '50s scene as *The Thing from Another World*, a schlock howler to beat all schlock howlers, rubbing shoulders with thoroughbred classics, contributing to the rich diversity that was the hallmark of this decade. *From Hell It Came* and *Mesa of Lost Women*—the world of fantasy cinema would be a much poorer (and far less interesting) place without them!

[Note: Tandra Quinn played a deaf-mute housekeeper in United Artists' *The Neanderthal Man* and Tevos was never involved in feature film production after he had left his one and only legendary mark on the industry. Ormond produced a string of exploitation movies, including *Outlaw Women* (1956) and *Untamed Mistress* (1956), and Hoyt S. Curtin's musical output throughout the 1960s, 1970s and 1980s was truly prodigious, especially in the world of TV cartoons, composing, among other things, the title theme to *The Flintstones*.]

Chapter 21
Let's Take Another Look: Part Three

4,000-year-old Mummy in Pajamas Sucks the Blood of the Living

Bel-Air/United Artists' 1957 quickie, *Pharaoh's Curse*, may not have figured very highly in the company's horror repertoire of the 1950s and was rarely seen in England, but this Mummy movie was 66 minutes of tomb-raiding action that didn't shatter any illusions one bit. Lee Sholem shot the story at breakneck speed: The British, in the middle of a revolt in Cairo circa 1903, send a team to locate the whereabouts of an expedition that has failed to return from the Valley of the Kings. Midway into their journey, Egyptian temptress Ziva Rodann (Ziva Shapir) appears like a mirage out of the desert and, by using her wiles, leads the four members to the expedition's camp. There, headstrong archaeologist George Neise has excavated a sarcophagus containing the bandaged remains of Pharaoh Ra-Ha-Tet's royal priest. Rodann, in fact, is the reincarnation of the Egyptian Cat God Bast and the mummy is that of her original brother. Ignoring Rodann's warnings of a curse, Neise makes an incision in the mummy's facial wrappings; the priest's spirit enters the body of Rodann's modern-day brother, Alvaro Guillot, who faints, revives

The Pharaoh's Curse features the reincarnated spirit of an Egyptian royal priest who goes on a murderous rampage in modern times.

and embarks on a murderous rampage, draining the blood from his victims and rapidly aging into a shriveled old man sporting a set of rotten teeth.

Moving swiftly through its paces, Sholem finds time to chuck in a burgeoning romance between nice-but-wooden Mark Dana and Neise's dissatisfied wife, Diane Brewster, while Guillot stumbles through the stone passages dressed in what appears to be striped pajamas, his crumbling features containing more lines than a railway yard. Not even losing an arm can halt him on his bloodsucking quest. Obnoxious Neise meets his end when the ceiling of the pharaoh's tomb collapses over his head, and the mummy returns to its coffin. Guy Prescott removes a golden mask from its face (how did that get in there?) to reveal ancient, wizened features.

Okay, this isn't Lon Chaney, Jr. and classic Universal or Christopher Lee and glossy Hammer, but *Pharaoh's Curse* contains enough shocking incidents to satisfy most B movie horror buffs; Rodann is a sexy delight and Les Baxter's Egyptian-themed score is another admirable example of the composer's importance in getting these minor program fillers off the ground.

"Lamentable."

I Was a 19th-Century Irish Housemaid

The subject of regression to a previous state by hypnosis, scientific experimentation or chemicals took many forms in the 1950s: Bobby-soxer into vampire (*Blood is My Heritage*); juvenile into wolf man (*I Was a Teenage Werewolf*); scientist into ape man (*The Neanderthal Man*) and woman into feline (*Cat Girl*). But none have treated the topic quite so seriously as Paramount's *The Search for Bridey Murphy* (1956). Amateur hypnotist Morey Bernstein wrote a bestseller in 1956 about the real life case of Ruth Simmons who, under hypnosis, recounted her former existence as a housemaid in 19th-century Ireland. The book was a sensation at a time when America was in the grip of theoretical debates on hypnosis, reincarnation, age regression and whether one could go back in time, find an ancient remedy for modern-day illnesses and return with a cure. Paramount rushed out a film adaptation in VistaVision, director Noel Langley co-writing the script with Bernstein, Louis Hayward playing the role of the author. Comparisons will be made with *The Three Faces of Eve*, released the following year, which dealt with multiple personality disorder, but *The Search for Bridey Murphy*, made on a more modest budget, wins the contest hands down; it has moments of genuine unease, strengthened by a bravura, underrated performance from Teresa Wright as the woman caught up in a century-old nightmare not of her doing.

Addressing the audience at the start, Hayward (as Bernstein) tells us how he became involved in hypnotism, practicing his new-found dexterity on Richard Anderson's fiancée, sick children and wife Nancy Gates before, 22 minutes in, he chooses Wright as his next volunteer—or should that be victim? Over the course of a number of taped sessions observed by Gates, Anderson and her increasingly concerned husband (Kenneth Tobey), Wright is regressed back to the age of seven, then two, and then a one year old. But Hayward isn't content to stop there—under deep hypnosis, Wright, in a lilting Irish brogue, begins to recount her life in Cork, Ireland, from the date of her birth in 1798, through her childhood, schooldays and marriage, to her death in 1864. Played out in misty flashbacks, like a series of faded photographic prints, and backed by Roy Webb's haunting score, we witness key episodes in Bridey Murphy's life as they unfold. But when Wright begins to sneeze, eerily aping Murphy's cold, and, on awakening, performs an Irish jig, Tobey and Anderson call a halt to the proceedings, worried about where all this leads. Hayward, obsessed with finding out every little detail about Murphy, calls in four experts, forces Tobey to change his mind and hypnotizes Wright up to the point of Murphy's death ("Tell me. How did you die?") and beyond, her confused spirit roaming the afterlife, trying to communicate with the living.

Tobey puts his foot down, stating, "That's enough," afraid of what effect this is having on his pregnant wife, but Hayward, shutting his eyes to warnings from everybody, persists in continuing: He takes Wright back even further, *before* she was Bridey

Murphy; she's a young child in Iowa, dying from plague-like symptoms. As Wright begins to sneeze constantly from a long-forgotten complaint, appears agitated, sings an Irish tune and asks for "linen," Hayward tries desperately to bring her back to the present but is unable to do so, the woman trapped in events enacted a century ago. This unsettling moment is one of sheer terror, chillingly conveyed by Wright who spends most of her screen time laying on a couch with her eyes closed. After several attempts, she wakes, perfectly normal, much to the relief of Tobey (and the audience!). Hayward, exhausted, decides to end the sessions.

It's talkative and stagy but *The Search for Bridey Murphy* is totally engrossing because it will beg the viewer to consider, "Can this past life be present in *all* of us?" That daunting question, together with Wright's acting nous, changing from chic suburban housewife to Irish scullery maid in the blink of an eye, is one reason for catching this psychological drama that has gone unnoticed for far too long.

"Suspends belief … slow and aimless."

A Nautical Dorian Gray

Ealing Studios are a renowned name in British film production. During the war years, they specialized in making a string of stirring motion pictures designed to keep up the morale of the troops (*Went the Day Well?* and *The Foreman Went to France*). After the war, comedies were the mainstay of their output, classics in the shape of *Whisky Galore*, *Hue and Cry*, *The Ladykillers* and *The Lavender Hill Mob*, built around the Studios' main strengths: larger-than-life characters, faultless film-craft, top-notch acting and inventive plots. *The Ship that Died of Shame* (1955) is inclined to be overlooked among the Ealing jewels in the crown as it's neither comedy nor social drama. Adapted from Nicholas Monsarrat's largely forgotten novel, this unsung thriller with a suggestion of the fantastic concerns Gunboat 1087, bought from a scrapyard by the trio who ran it during the war. When Messrs. Richard Attenborough, George Baker and Bill Owen decide to use her for smuggling contraband, to supply the starved-of-indulgencies postwar public with a few much-needed luxuries, the vessel rebels against these illegal activities, seemingly with a mind of its own.

"Ships don't have souls," intones Baker at the beginning, but this one apparently has. Following the tragic death of his wife near the end of the war (Virginia McKenna is killed when a bomb hits their holiday cottage), Baker, a bitter man, teams up with his former buddies, sallying to and fro across the English Channel with illicit goods, customs officer Bernard Lee on their tail. But when the contraband turns to counterfeit banknotes, guns and lastly, a creepy child killer the French police are after, Gunboat 1087 starts to play up. Instead of the sleek, reliable craft that saw them through thick and thin in many a battle, she seems to be deteriorating, mirroring the moral decline in her crew; the engines continually stall, the steering goes haywire and the deck, from being scrubbed and spotless, appears dirty and neglected. Baker, who, since his wife's death, treats the boat as his mistress, is aware that something is wrong. "She's losing heart," he says to a skeptical Attenborough. "She's got her pride like all of us." "I reckon she just don't want to know," adds Owen, gravely. Baker and Owen want to quit, but Attenborough doesn't, greed taking precedence over ethics. Lee is eventually shot dead by Roland Culver, an accomplice in the racket, but Gunboat 1087 gets her revenge. During a storm at sea, Baker shoots Culver, the ship lurches (on purpose?) to one side and Attenborough falls overboard, sucked into the propellers. In the final moving moments, Baker and Owen swim ashore and watch with feelings of horror and sadness as their old nautical friend, the one they adored so much during the war and which served them so well, self-destructs in shame; now a grimy shadow of her former glorious self, she slides off the rocks into the boiling waters to *her* death.

This wasn't the first time that Ealing had dipped its toes into the world of the mysterious; 1945's *Dead of Night* is a classic tale of the supernatural, much revered by enthusiasts. *The Ship that Died of Shame* isn't of the same caliber but has plenty to commend it to fans: producing/directing team Michael Relph and Basil Dearden's fast-paced handling of the material; the stereotypical English seaside resort locations; Gordon Dines' crisp photography; William Alwyn's rousing score, conducted by the Royal Philharmonic Orchestra and it goes without saying that the respected all-British cast is beyond reproach. Any feature film that can elicit sympathy for the plight of an inanimate object such as a ship must have something going for it, and *The Ship that Died of Shame* does just that, with a great deal of the company's rich expertise on show. An unusual morality play masquerades as a beguiling fantasy and becomes a superb addition to the Ealing stable.

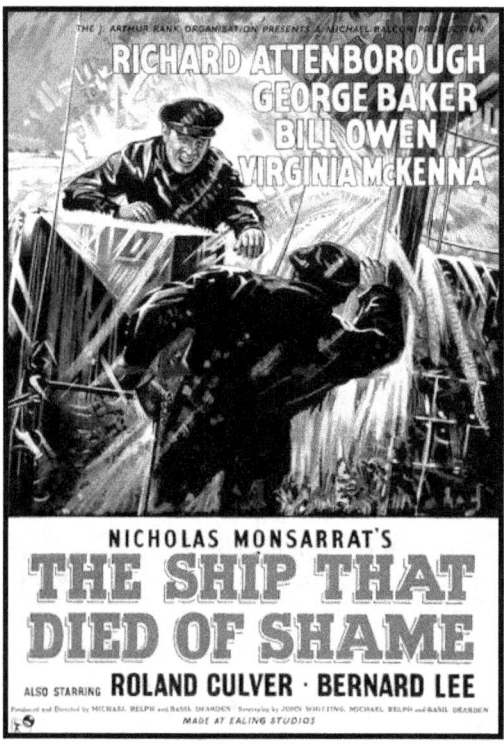

"Thin and obvious."

Venusian Robots Conquer Chicago

A half-open window, a ticking clock, a woman asleep on a rumpled bed, a bottle of sleeping tablets and deserted city streets become vivid images from the opening few minutes of Sherman A. Rose's *Target Earth* (1954). The film has such an atmosphere of impending doom that we can almost forgive the harbingers of that doom—seven-foot-tall robots from Venus—looking for all the world as though they have been constructed out of empty cereal boxes. Before they appear, however, we are treated to a tense, end-of-civilization background built mainly around four characters: Richard Denning, Kathleen Crowley, Richard Reeves and Virginia Grey. This disparate bunch winds up in a silent Chicago that lacks people, electricity and radio contact, with the odd corpse splayed on the sidewalk. What is the cause of this seemingly mass evacuation? Director Rose intercuts between survivors, army headquarters and Whit Bissell's laboratory; scientist Bissell and colleagues have captured a disabled robot and reckon that if they can discover a way to penetrate its faceplate, which masks a transmitter, our army can wipe out their army.

Back in Chicago, a psychotic gunman (Robert Roark) bursts in upon Denning and company in their hotel refuge, making a play for Crowley; his hostile presence triggers a tragic series of events, culminating in Grey getting shot and boyfriend Reeves strangling Roark. One of the robots crashes in on the fight, killing Reeves with a death ray beamed from its helmet (just like Gort in *The Day the Earth Stood Still*). Cornered by the robot on the hotel roof, Denning and Crowley are saved by the intervention of the army who fires an ultrasonic beam at the metallic alien; the vibrations shatter the faceplate, rendering it harmless.

To be frank, *Target Earth* isn't up there among the greats. Allied Artists didn't have the mega-bucks to pull off something bigger and better. But the movie's entertaining nonetheless *because* of this lack of funds. Rose put everything he had at his disposal into creating an air of disbelief and tension without the backup of elaborate special effects, aided by Paul Dunlap's impressive score, and the director came up with something special. A literate script is delivered without resorting to over-dramatics by the cast, and Denning was always a trusted lead in these modest sci-fi flicks anyway. Filmed in downtown Los Angeles on traffic-free Sunday mornings, Rose's depiction of deserted city blocks and the catastrophe such scenes conjure up in the mind is as good as it gets, even in big-budget features. Unassuming, yes, but also respectable: Those tacky robots typified the 1950s; they add to, rather than detract from, the downbeat look. Look upon them with a fondness for times past!

"Cheap and unconvincing."

Nice Body—Shame about the Face!

Jobbing actor Whit Bissell appeared in over 300 films and television programs throughout his long career, an instantly recognizable face in many '50s horror features, but only once did he receive top billing—in American International's *Teenage Frankenstein*. Bissell also starred in *I Was a Teenage Werewolf* the same year (1957), but Michael Landon pushed him to third billing on the posters behind himself and Yvonne Lime. These two movies were prime exponents of the mid-to-late '50s teenage horror cycle, and, in retrospect, the two leading examples. *Teenage Frankenstein*, on first viewing, can appear somewhat mundane; even Richard Cunha's schlock classic, *Frankenstein's Daughter*, is far livelier! Herbert L. Strock dispenses with anything resembling flamboyancy and sets out his stall, getting straight down to horror basics: Bissell plays an American descendant of Baron Frankenstein, creating a teenager (Gary Conway) from body parts with the help of unwilling assistant Robert Burton. Fiancée Phyllis Coates pays for her constant moaning and snooping, murdered by Bissell's creation and fed to a crocodile. After being given a new face (and boy, does he need one!), Conway learns that Bissell plans to disassemble his body and reconstruct it in London; understandably not too keen on the idea, he strangles his creator and feeds *him* to the croc. Two cops burst into the lab with Burton, guns blazing, forcing Conway to back into a bank of power cables; he's electrocuted to death at the same time the action switches to Technicolor for its final two minutes.

So far, so good. The laboratory scenes, showing Bissell severing a bloody hand and shattered leg, were gruesome for the day, and Conway's ruined features would surely have been a prime nominee for the most grotesque Halloween mask of the century. Strock drums up a few shocks (Bissell and Conway lying in wait in the bushes,

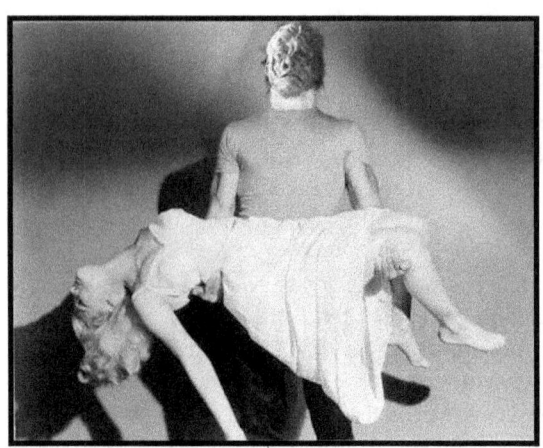

Gary Conway as the teenage monster, in a publicity shot from *Teenage Frankenstein*

observing a young couple necking, waiting to pounce because of the need for a new head) and Bissell's bad-tempered, obsessive scientist is totally devoid of sentiment and warmth for anybody, including Conway. However, what makes *Teenage Frankenstein* a cut above the average is Kenneth Langtry's wonderful script, overflowing with sardonic one-liners and demonstrating a neat line in self-parody.

Bissell's colleagues, at a lecture, state that, "Dead tissue cannot be reactivated." He sets out to prove his critics wrong ("They all said 'Don't dare' to my ancestor"), planning to use the "ingredients of youth" in his creation, as the elderly are too worn-out for his purposes. "This is a morgue. My own private morgue," he proudly states to a worried-looking Burton as they push the victim of a car crash into the deep freeze. Like every other Frankenstein committed to celluloid, Bissell is a control freak, announcing loftily, "What I create I must control." After cutting off the damaged limbs, he procures substitutes from a plane crash in which a number of young athletes die ("All those fine athletic bodies gone to waste."), stitching them onto Conway's pumped-up body ("Strong hands of a champion wrestler ... the leg of a football star."). The film's most risible line, and one of the most infamous snippets of '50s horror dialogue, is when Conway, head swathed in bandages, awakes from an operation. "Good morning, my boy," says Bissell, but receives no answer. "Come come, my boy, say good morning to your creator. Speak, you've got a civil tongue in your head, I know you have because I sewed it back myself." To compound the sense of absurdity, Bissell then adds, "You do have vision, you know, at least in one eye." And when Conway starts to cry, Bissell looks a tad smug: "It seems we have a very sensitive teenager on our hands."

Bissell teaches Conway manners, as in the following exchange:

Conway: "Yes."

Bissell: "Yes, Sir would be preferable. In England, you know, we have a little more respect for the older generation."

Conway, who wants to "walk among people," breaks out of the lab and strangles a blonde. "Women interfere with our plans," is Bissell's cold reaction, deciding to stir things up between Conway and interfering Coates, inferring that Coates is going to report the experiment to the authorities ("I know you are hiding something. I saw your monster."). And, far from happy with his hideous looks, Bissell makes his creation a promise: "Pick the face that pleases you. Then it will be yours."

It's undoubtedly the dialogue that makes *Teenage Frankenstein* such a pleasure to sit through. This teen horror offering has a hard-boiled edge to it due to Strock's whittled-down direction, Bissell's terse, tactless performance, Lothrop Worth's barebones photography and Paul Dunlap's brassy score. The accent is on matter-of-factness, not stylish Gothic thrills. Teamed up with Strock's *Blood Is My Heritage*, the movie was box-office gold in England for a great number of years and, ironically, one of only a handful of films that the dependable Whit Bissell is remembered for.

"Lame and tame."

Futuristic Mutant Comes A-Knocking at the Door

Scientists work on a prototype time machine that can penetrate the future, a love/lust triangle surfaces, a peeping Tom appears and a radioactive disfigured female from the future all decorate American International's *Terror from The Year 5,000* (1958) and incorporates all these tasty elements within its framework, plus a rumbustious score from Jack Shaindlin. But what it also urgently needed was a decent budget. Frederic Downs' lab was unadorned to say the least, not too far removed from what you might find in your local school, while Salome Jens as the female mutant from 5,200 AD, covered from head to toe in a glittery, sequin anti-radiation suit, was only around for the final 10 minutes. Without doubt, the germ of a good idea needed the big-budget treatment, but that budget failed to fully materialize. This cheeseparing production, however, manages to rise above its limitations and has one or two worthwhile moments, and one or two that are not so worthwhile!

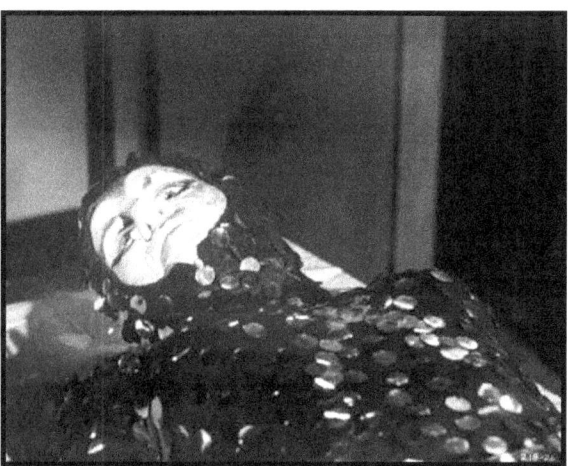

Salome Jens plays the female mutant from the future who wears the sequin anti-radiation suit in *Terror from the Year 5,000*.

Museum curator Ward Costello is sent a statuette of a headless woman by old friend Downs. Carbon-dating it to the future, and noting with alarm that there's enough radiation in the object to kill a human being if they were exposed to it for two weeks, Costello sets out for Downs' island retreat to learn more and immediately clicks with the scientist's sassy daughter, Joyce Holden. Unfortunately, her fiancé, John Stratton, flares up in a jealous rage over the mutual attraction and, in the shadows, handyman-cum-Peeping-Tom Fred Herrick also lusts after Holden. Back in that ramshackle lab, Downs and Stratton are exchanging objects with whoever lives beyond the time barrier ("Do you mean you actually think that you've contacted human beings of the future?" queries Costello), a metal disc returned with "Save Us" inscribed on it in Greek. A four-eyed cat also emerges from the chamber, swiftly buried in the lake by Stratton. When Stratton reaches the bursting point over Costello and Holden's blossoming relationship, he pushes the time-apparatus to its limits and Jens appears with a face like an uncooked pizza, her deadly touch producing radiation burns, intent on hauling Stratton into the nuclear-devastated future so that he can mate and revitalize the human race. After a climatic struggle in the laboratory, Jens and Stratton are electrocuted, the film finishing on a typical '50s downbeat note emphasizing the dangers of meddling with the atom and the cause it might have on future generations: "The future is what we make it," intones Downs solemnly over the closing credits.

There are shades of *The Fly* in this seldom-seen sci-fi feature, with objects materializing via an experimental matter machine, including the grotesque Jens who kills a nurse and conceals her malformed features behind a mask made from the dead woman's facial skin. Acting-wise, the cast goes through the motions adequately enough, apart from Stratton who wears a pained expression throughout. And look out for Beatrice Furdeaux playing Costello's secretary, a cameo of comically inept proportions. Robert J. Gurney, Jr.'s direction is perfunctory, content to allow the actors to get on with things without the aid of fussy camerawork. If all this sounds like a recipe for disaster, it isn't. A curiosity of sorts, *Terror from The Year 5,000* may be small-time fodder, but at 74 minutes, it doesn't outstay its welcome and entertains on an uncomplicated level. This is one of AIP's forgotten B treasures.

"Intriguing but clumsy."

Panther-Man at Loose on Philippine Island

A variation on H.G. Wells' *The Island of Dr. Moreau*, *Terror Is a Man* (1959) hardly saw the light of day in the United Kingdom and the same goes for director Gerardo de Leon and producer Eddie Romero's series of Filipino *Blood Island* movies which followed: *The Blood Drinkers* (1966), *The Mad Doctor of Blood Island* (1968) and *The Blood Devils* (1971), among others. A conventional mad scientist plot is given a bleakly intelligent perspective in this joint U.S./Philippines tale of surgeon Francis Lederer's attempts to remold a panther into a manlike being, thereby speeding up the evolutionary process by producing a new species. Fifty-six major operations and dozens of minor ones over a two-year period have resulted in a heavily bandaged creature drugged and stored in Lederer's underground laboratory, screeching like the tortured animal it is, shackled in its cell and able to croak only a single word, "Man." This is one mistreated creation we feel really sorry for; so does the surgeon's wife, Greta Thyssen, who vents her pent-up sexual frustrations on Richard Derr, shipwrecked on the island and promising the girl that he will help her get away from the accursed place and her fixated husband. The moment when Thyssen surrenders to her lust is shot like a scene from an art-house sex movie by de Leon. Halting by her room, Thyssen turns and stares at Derr sitting in his room, waiting, back to camera. Then slowly, her mind made up, she sidles toward him seductively, just one thing on her mind. Hinting at smoldering emotions, this raunchy scene is brilliantly handled, just one of the picture's many strengths.

Harry Paul Harber's script is succinct and intelligent, matching scene for scene de Leon's taut direction and believable acting from Lederer, Thyssen, Derr and Oscar Keesee as the surgeon's slime-ball assistant. The unusual Philippine locations convey an atmosphere of gloomy hostility in the opening section, the monster, on the loose, sneaking through the dense foliage to terrorize the local natives who flee the island en masse after a couple are savaged to death. Recaptured and experimented on further, the creature again becomes the victim. Keesee becomes the focus of the creature's blind hate; after beaten with a club by the heartless slob, it ferociously breaks free, kills his tormentor and carries Thyssen off to a cliff. Derr shoots the beast when it throws Lederer over the cliff edge, but a sympathetic native boy hides the wounded man-beast in a boat, pushing it out to sea. Derr and Thyssen walk off in the surf to an uncertain future.

Originally, the William Castle-like gimmick of an alarm bell rang prior to moments of fright (Lederer's scalpel slicing flesh) and this still exists in some prints. An offbeat variation on the Frankenstein theme, *Terror Is a Man* contains a lot of sobriety in its "tampering with nature" message, a sobriety that many American counterparts do not possess. The movie's firmly on the side of Lederer's hapless creation, a pain-racked victim of one man's single-minded quest to achieve the scientifically impossible, never mind who, or what, gets hurt in the process.

"Obscure ... not frightening."

16th-Century Head Runs Riot on Ranch

Universal-International's *The Thing that Couldn't Die* (1958) is an unpretentious little B-effort that was produced in the wake of their unbroken run of classics stretching from *It Came from Outer Space* to *Monster on the Campus*. Overlooked by many mainstream horror writers (quite a few film guides omit this movie from their lists), Will Cowan's 69-minute disembodied-head thriller has its creepy moments after a methodical buildup, despite being hampered by a wildly exaggerated central performance from Carolyn Kearney, playing a reluctant psychic water diviner who uncovers an ornate 16th-century chest under an oak tree on her aunt's ranch. ("Don't dig here. There's something evil down there.") The heavily inscribed object contains not, as hoped for, a fortune in treasure but the head of one Gideon Drew. In 1579, when Sir Francis Drake set foot on Californian soil, sailor Drew (Robin Hughes), on orders from Drake, was beheaded for dabbling in the black arts, his head and body buried separately to damn his soul to eternity. Ranch hand Charles Horvath unwisely forces the lid off the chest, disclosing Hughes' scarred head, eyes glaring hypnotically; knifing accomplice James Anderson, dimwitted Horvath, under the head's spell, lumbers off into the night, grasping his unexpected booty and lugging Anderson's corpse behind him. Now it has been uncovered, the head exerts a baleful influence over both Kearney and Andra Martin, mentally commanding the women to locate its body so that the two can be joined, thus enabling the devil-worshiper to repeat his practices. In the closing scene, the cast gathers in the lounge, the coffin (unearthed by a black-dressed Kearney) on the floor; the lid is opened and the headless corpse clambers out. Kearney places the head on the trunk and Hughes is reactivated. "At last, I breathe again!" he cries. "Satan still lives. Four centuries have not reduced his power. After so long at fast, I thirst for human blood" His reign, however, is short-lived. William Reynolds forces him back into the coffin by waving a magic amulet in his face that can ward off evil (found by Kearney in the opening few minutes); the charm is thrown in the coffin and Hughes decomposes into a skeleton.

The head of Gideon Drew (Robin Hughes) searches for his body, in *The Thing that Couldn't Die.*

To save on costs, musical director Joseph Gershenson utilized snippets from previous Universal horror/sci-fi movies to form a composite soundtrack (see chapter four); soundtrack nuts will easily pick out the refrains from *This Island Earth, Tarantula, Creature from the Black Lagoon* and *The Monolith Monsters* buried in the mix (Gershenson resorted to the same trick in *Monster on the Campus*). This works mainly because the arranger's cobbled-together score isn't intrusive, adding to the darkly atmospheric tone. Compared to other Universal productions of the day, *The Thing that Couldn't Die* is usually viewed as a two-bit second feature, but it was still a popular attraction on the English horror circuit for a number of years despite its sniffed-at status; fans would usually find it sharing the bill with another of Universal's lower-level outings, the vampire Western *Curse of the Undead*. Cowan (this was his only full-length picture) ups the pace after a talkative, slow-moving 26 minutes, delivering some spooky shocks; the climax, when that headless corpse emerges from its coffin, is oddly unsettling, one more remarkable Universal final sequence to add to their many others. If we try to ignore Kearney's bad case of overacting, *The Thing that Couldn't Die* is an unusual supernatural-cum-horror outing, miles ahead of all those "disembodied-head" movies churned out during the 1950s.

"Low-grade horror."

There's a Lobster on My Back

Columbia's *The Tingler* (1959) was probably director William Castle's most successful movie playing in England during the early '60s, more popular with the fans than his magnum opus, *House on Haunted Hill*. Time and time again, it showed up with *The Werewolf, Night of the Demon* and *20 Million Miles to Earth*. To label this film "ridiculous" is ridiculous in itself. Granted, Castle's camerawork didn't really flow as it should have done, parts of the action resemble an inexpensive TV production, but the production had horror maestro Vincent Price at the top of his game, Robb White's coherent script, two creepy, drug-induced hallucinatory scenes, Castle's most infamous gimmick "Percepto" and an engaging creature unlike any other found in '50s horror. What more could Castle devotees wish for?

Price stars as a doctor convinced that at the precise moment of fright, a force in the form of a living organism, fed by fear, materializes on the spine and shatters the vertebral column, disappearing when the person screams and releases tension. To test his theory, he shoots his wife with blanks, causing her to faint, immediately X-raying her for signs of the force that shows up on X-ray plates, presented to young assistant Darryl Hickman. Price then injects himself with lysergic acid (LSD), needing to feel the pain of terror, but he hallucinates and screams ruining the experiment. Befriending Philip Coolidge who runs a cinema with his deaf-mute wife (brilliantly played by Judith Evelyn), Price hits upon a way to obtain a specimen of the Tingler; frighten Evelyn to death, after first injecting her with lysergic acid. After all, the woman's incapable of uttering a single sound, let alone scream. Castle orchestrates Evelyn's "scared to death" sequences by the use of distorted angle shots, underlined by Von Dexter's eerie music. Windows close, doors shut, an apparition wields a knife, a hairy arm holds an axe, blood runs from taps and a blood-filled bath (tinted red in U.S. prints) provides the final nightmarish image. Price quickly performs an autopsy on Evelyn's corpse, removing a parasitic crustacean from her back, proof that the Tingler actually exists. In an about-turn of events, Price's two-timing wife (Patricia Cutts) laces his drink with drugs and releases the rubbery lobster from its cage to finish him off; sister-in-law Pamela Lincoln enters the room, screams (there's an awful lot of screaming in this movie) and the creature falls from Price's neck.

In America, various theaters had seats wired to administer a mild vibration during *The Tingler*'s most notorious scene: The oversized creepy-crawly breaks loose during a screening of the (pointedly) silent classic *Tol'able David*; as it scuttles among the audience, Castle opts for a total blackout which in those days, with a lack of peripheral lighting in auditoriums, was the equivalent to watching a film in a coal cellar. A voice shouts, "Scream! Scream for your lives!" (audience participation gone berserk!) and, when the lights come back on, the scaly monster is chomping away on the projectionist's throat. These shock tactics were effective at the time, Castle replacing suspense with promotional gimmickry, and it worked, although this would never be allowed to happen today! Insurance companies would have kittens!

Coolidge, not Price, is the man who scared his wife to death, wanting to lay his hands on her cash. Price restores the Tingler to Evelyn's body to kill it and leaves to call the police; Coolidge, stricken by guilt, backs off in alarm as his wife's body rises from her bed, the windows shut, the door closes and it's now *his* turn to die of fright! This is an X-rated gem from Castle, among his best work ever.

"Ridiculous shocker … dull handling … corny."

A Subterranean Sanctuary from the Atomic Bomb

Fifty-two years before John Amiel's multimillion-dollar boring machine headed into the Earth's interior in *The Core*, in *Unknown World* (1951) low-budget producer Robert Lippert had his Cyclotram undergoing the same exercise, at a fraction of the cost. An early warning of what might happen to the human race following a nuclear war, Terrell O. Morse's enterprising fantasy actioner begins with a stark message delivered at a lecture by scientist Victor Kilian: The atom poses a threat to mankind—it can cause the death of every living thing. Man, he states, needs a refuge to hide from fallout, and where else to look but deep within the bowels of the Earth. Kilian is a leading

member of the Society to Save Civilization. Unfortunately, his plans to construct a giant tunneling machine that will enable scientists to seek out a suitable "geological shelter" are thwarted through lack of money and public interest. Rich, bored benefactor Bruce Kellogg, with money to burn, is willing to finance the building of the Cyclotram on one condition—he's to be included in the expedition with Kilian and five others.

Thirteen minutes into the picture, the machine ("Imagine the submarine with the ability of a tractor," states Otto Waldis) trundles up the side of Mount Neleh in Alaska, an extinct volcano. Descending into the crater's depths, the crew pauses at the site of a 1938 expedition that got no further in their explorations, and they blast a passage in the rock wall and begin their journey. Jules Verne's *Journey to the Center of the Earth* seems to have been the main source of inspiration for the producers. Like Verne's explorers, Kilian and crew descend a volcano, travel through miles of volcanic vents, encounter an underground ocean 1,640 miles below the Earth's surface, experience an electrical storm and are returned to the surface via an eruption. Filmed in the Carlsbad Caverns, the special effects and production design by Irving Block and Jack Rabin are simple but effective, the vast cavern the team breaks into a subterranean delight. However, this isn't the paradise they have been seeking. The atmosphere renders life sterile; when Marilyn Nash's rabbits give birth to dead babies, the team realize that human beings cannot possibly live, or reproduce, in such a place, a "haven for the dead." And this is after depression, feelings of isolation and in-fighting has set in because of their claustrophobic abode ("Crops can survive without sunlight." "Perhaps. But can we?"). Only three out of the seven return, Kilian electing to stay behind in the marvel he has discovered (his "promised land"), only to drown in a raging sea.

Ernest Gold's quirky score perfectly matches the picturesque underground settings and the script is hilariously self-deprecating at times, the picture not taking itself too seriously. The acting is above average as well. In a period of fantasy cinema where millions are expected to be spent on CGI state-of-the-art effects, *Unknown World* may seem extremely primitive by comparison, but there's no denying the bumbling charm it radiates, a kind of innocence lost on modern-day audiences. Like an artifact from a distant age, it has worn amazingly well over the years, a laudable reminder of what sci-fi fantasy used to be like when resources were limited and those involved worked overtime to bring their imaginative ideas to the big screen.

"Cheap … lacks purpose."

Diamonds are a Zombie's Best Friend

Prolific director of B pictures Edward L. Cahn had, in the eyes of many a film writer, a slight misfire with 1957's *Zombies of Mora Tau*, also released as *The Dead that Walked*. Over a decade before George A. Romero's blood-spattered living corpses stalked the countryside in *Night of the Living Dead*, we had 10 zombified sailors guarding a 60-year-old stolen chest of diamonds located in the hull of a sunken ship off the African coast. Their leader is the husband of tottering grandmother Marjorie Eaton who, with granddaughter Autumn Russell, lives in a mansion overlooking the wreck and is quite used to seeing dead-eyed sailors draped in seaweed roaming across her land. What's more, these amphibious zombies can survive underwater! Crosses dated 1906, 1914, 1923, 1928 and 1938 mark the graves of previous treasure seekers who have perished at the hands of these nautical necromancers. Will Gregg Palmer, Morris Ankrum, Joel Ashley and Allison Hayes have better luck in grabbing the goodies, even though fresh graves have been dug in preparation for their early demise.

Five of the 10 zombified sailors who guard the undersea treasure in *Zombies of Mora Tau*

That oft-used word "wooden" sums up *Zombies of Mora Tau* to a tee. The acting is as lifeless as the zombie sailors, but with Bernard Gordon's leaden script to work from, what more can we expect. Cahn's camerawork stays rooted to the spot, surprisingly so when we consider his expert use of the lens in *The Four Skulls of Jonathan Drake* and *It! The Terror from Beyond Space*. Elsewhere, Mischa Bakaleinikoff reprised his title score from *The Werewolf* and attempted to boost the action by adding a noisy stock soundtrack, including incidental music from *20 Million Miles to Earth*. His valiant efforts were only partially successful.

So, the movie becomes a debacle all round, particularly in comparison to other Columbia classics of the day. But is it *that* much of a debacle?

The answer has to be "no" because *Zombies of Mora Tau*, like so many badly made films from the 1950s, becomes inherently enjoyable *because* of its badness, as is the case with Weissmuller's *Jungle Jim* features, the subject of chapter 31. Audiences can sit back with the popcorn and take pleasure in the absurdities and not feel ashamed in doing so, further evidence that B movies from this period, and this period alone, retain the uncanny power to exert this effect on a viewer, however lame they can be at times. Cahn's humdrum zombie flick has the following to tickle the palates of those in a less-discriminating frame of mind.

Allison Hayes: Her sultry, sex-charged looks make Autumn Russell appear virginal, even though Russell herself is a blonde stunner.

Marjorie Eaton: Maria Ouspenskaya, the wise Gypsy soothsayer in Universal's *Wolf Man* series, revisited. Her withered old crone make-up and croaking words of wisdom add some vitality to the proceedings.

The screaming scene: When a zombie lurches into Hayes and Russell's bedroom, the girls take it in turn to scream; first Hayes, then Russell, then Hayes, then Russell—a full minute's worth!

The underwater sequences: Purportedly filmed through the side of an aquarium tank, these make the similar scenes in Paramount's *Road to Bali* seem like the work of Sergei Eisenstein!

Candles: Yes, lighted candles are the devices that keep the zombies at bay and drive them back into the mausoleum they inhabit.

Hayes zombified: What a waste! Trollop Hayes gets turned into a zombie, somehow managing to keep a straight face in the part.

The acting: Hayes, Ankrum and Eaton, passable. Ashley and Palmer, so-so. Russell and the boat's crew, rotten.

Script: Russell to chauffeur: "Sam! You hit a man!" Chauffeur: "It wasn't a man. It was one of them!" Hayes falls into an unmarked grave: "That grave. It's for me. I know it!" Palmer to Eaton, asking what could the zombies possibly do if the diamonds were sold in America: "What they would do? Look in all the jewelry stores on 5th Avenue."

In the end, Palmer reluctantly hands the diamonds to Eaton (only because he's asked granddaughter Russell to marry him and wants to turn over a new leaf); she ditches the rocks back into the sea, lifting the curse, the zombies finding eternal rest at last. Her long-dead husband, resplendent in naval uniform and observing all from the bushes, promptly vanishes, his empty suit falling to the ground.

Seventy-one minutes of disarming voodoo baloney sums up *Zombies of Mora Tau*. Perhaps all concerned, who had a lot of experience in making these kind of programmers, could have put a tad more effort into what they were achieving, to make their movie a more uplifting exercise in zombie-horror and eliminate the overall flatness. But was that possible with producer Sam Katzman pulling the strings? Britain's less-severe "A" classification said it all. Nevertheless, it still remains an interesting artifact, one of the few zombie pictures to emerge from the '50s, albeit not a very frightening or bloody example of the genre, that's for certain.

"Silly … abysmal acting and effects."

Chapter 22
The Abominable Snowman in the 1950s

When Sir Edmund Hillary and Sherpa Tenzing Norgay conquered Mount Everest in 1953, their expedition had reported to the world's press not only news of the victorious ascent but also descriptions of huge footprints seen in the snow-covered wastes made by an unidentified animal. Mountaineer/explorer Eric Shipton, trekking through the Himalayas in 1951, had also come across similar prints; this lead to the *Daily Mail* "Snowman Expedition" of 1954 which set out for Nepal to either confirm or debunk the Yeti legend, returning empty-handed. Tales of a quasi-human beast roaming the Himalayan wilds have circulated since the middle of the 19th-century, but up to the date of Shipton's discovery, no concrete evidence had ever been produced to suggest that such a creature existed, although in 1921, a member of the first Everest Reconnaissance Expedition claimed to have spotted one at a distance. Much speculation and theorizing about the possibility of a missing link inhabiting the Nepalese heights followed as a result of these expeditions. Given the nature of the beast, it's therefore surprising to note that during the whole of the 1950s, only four movies were produced that centered on the Yeti myth: *The Snow Creature* (1954), *Man Beast* (1955), *Half Human* (1955) and *The Abominable Snowman* (1957). In the United Kingdom, apart from the Yeti, all four films had one thing in common: Each was A-rated, the monster felt to be not sufficiently horrific to warrant an "X" classification. The productions each had their merits and faults and, although there isn't a great deal to choose from between them, Toho's *Half Human* (the original, uncut Japanese version) comes out tops as being the more thoroughgoing of the quartet. Even the first of the four, W. Lee Wilder's *The Snow Creature*, isn't the limp effort one might imagine, despite this director's deserved reputation as a supplier of below-standard horror fare knocked out on shoestring budgets.

Wilder (brother of ace director Billy Wilder) had botanist Paul Langton, photographer Leslie Denison, Sherpa guide Tbru (Teru) Shimada and 10 porters trekking through the desolate Himalayan wastes (actually California's Bronson Canyon, combined with footage of Nepal) in search of rare plants. When the wife of one of the Sherpas is abducted by a Yeti, Shimada forces Langton to abandon the quest for unrecorded flora and focus his mind on a higher priority—apprehending the creature with the intention of taking it alive to America. Full marks to Wilder for introducing the monster after only seven minutes instead of the normal 20 minutes and for showing some flair in the long opening passage leading up to the capture of the snowman in his lair. Stark black-and-white photography, hostile rocky terrain, an incessant moaning wind and Manuel Compinsky's raucous soundtrack all add to the

suspense, compensating for the play-it-by-numbers acting from Messrs. Langton and Denison.

Forty-two minutes into the 69-minute running time, we are in Los Angeles where the immigration department discusses whether or not the creature is human in origin (if it is, should it have applied for a visa?). Midway through the debate, the Yeti breaks free from a refrigeration unit, kills a woman and hides out in the sewers (how '50s monsters loved those Los Angeles sewers!). The police and Langton eventually corner the beast, throw a net over it and rather callously shoot it dead. The L.A. scenes are darkly lit to provide a semi-documentary style, but unfortunately this also applies to the snowman itself, whose face remains firmly rooted in dimness; all we see is a tall furry humanoid without any discernible features, a major disappointment.

In many ways, *The Snow Creature* was a fairly inauspicious beginning to the short-lived *Abominable Snowman* cycle of movies but that can hardly be blamed on Wilder or his production company, Planet Filmways. After all, the major studios appeared not to be the slightest bit interested in the Yeti, snubbing it as a viable screen monster despite the press publicity it was receiving. Therefore, it was left to the independents to pull something out of the hat, on meager resources. And next on the list, Jerry Warren, working for Favorite Films, did just that.

Warren's *Man Beast* might just well qualify as the director's finest hour, especially when you compare it to *Teenage Zombies* and *The Incredible Petrified World*, two infamous Warren '50s dead ducks. It has pacing, reasonable acting (apart from Virginia Maynor), a decent score (Josef Zimanich), picturesque Himalayan scenery proficiently blended with Californian location work and a none-too-risible Yeti. First off, let's put to bed the Rock Madison issue: There is no such person as Rock Madison. Warren

made the name up from Rock Hudson and Guy Madison (according to the IMDb) and was originally going to offer it to Tom Maruzzi. He then changed his mind and kept the name to boost the cast list! So it's Maruzzi who leads an expedition to discover the whereabouts of Maynor's missing brother; the brother set out to find a Yeti and disappeared without a trace. Also tagging along is Maynor's reluctant and rather cowardly boyfriend, Lloyd Nelson. Climbing higher into the Himalayan foothills, they meet with anthropologist George Wells Lewis and two guides. He's on the lookout for George Skaff, who was expedition leader when the brother went missing; it transpires that on each expedition Skaff has lead, one person from the team vanishes. Skaff turns out to be half man, half Yeti, and he communicates with the shaggy-haired snowmen by telepathy, luring humans into the Yetis' domain in order that they can mate and preserve their race.

Maruzzi and Maynor are the only two who make it back to civilization: The snowman kills Nelson and Lewis and the evil Skaff falls to his death from a cliff face.

An awful lot of footage of the actors trooping over endless snowfields in *Man Beast* occurs but at least these outdoor scenes (background projection is virtually absent) lend a certain degree of atmosphere, as do the impressive rock climbing passages, expertly (yes, expertly!) directed by Warren. A tall, white-haired Yeti makes its first appearance after 26 minutes (not bad for a 67-minute movie) and the action doesn't nosedive into farce toward the end, as was often the case in so many cheapskate '50s productions. What lets audiences down is Maynor's attempts at meaningful acting. Gazing off-camera for most of her screen time, as though she's reading an autocue (perhaps she was!), the actress resembles a blonde hooker on the hunt for clients, not somebody who is overly concerned about a missing brother. Her delivery is hilariously stilted, a real shame as B. Arthur Cassidy's script sizzles with lively exchanges and warrants better treatment. Wells: "There it is. Yeti country." Maruzzi: "As far as I'm concerned, you can have it!" and Maynor, looking at a drawing of a Yeti: "More beast than man." Wells: "It may be to your eyes. But I believe it's human." Guide to Maruzzi: "See Yeti—die!" All in all, Favorite Films' *Man Beast* is an agreeable *Abominable Snowman* romp that is put together with a moderate amount of dash by Warren, a feat he seemed unable to replicate in his subsequent cinematic efforts.

Hammer's *The Abominable Snowman*, the third of the '50s Yeti pictures, is a little *too* restrained and should really have been let off the leash. It has distinct advantages over the other three films: Nigel Kneale's rapid-fire, articulate script; classy acting from the entire cast; taut direction from Val Guest and striking black-and-white photography by Arthur Grant, in RegalScope to boot. But it also has drawbacks: The action is 90% studio-bound; although location filming took place in the French Pyrenees, very few exterior shots found their way into the finished production. And the Yeti isn't fully shown until a shameful 81 minutes have passed, leaving just 10 minutes to tie up all the loose ends. Hammer had to drop Kneale's title, *The Snow Creature*, as it would have clashed with W. Lee Wilder's earlier effort (*The Creature* had originally been a BBC-TV play, broadcast in January 1955, before Hammer acquired the movie rights), and Peter Cushing, who starred in the play, reprised his role in the feature film. He's a botanist who embarks on an expedition with hard-nosed opportunist Forrest Tucker; humanist Cushing wishes to study the creature (if they can locate one), while Tucker wants to take it back to America for exploitation and profit. Veering backward and forward between the monastery (presided over by gnome-like lama Arnold Marle) and the snowy backdrops (Humphrey Searle provides an excellent gong-laden score), the movie takes time to get into gear, a fleeting glimpse of a Yeti's gnarled hand introduced after a lengthy 50 minutes. Tucker's expedition turns out to be jinxed from the outset: Timid cameraman Michael Brill goes mad, mentally destroyed by the snowmen's

The noble and family-oriented Yeti of Japan's *Half Human*.

distant wailing, and wanders from the camp, only to fall off a cliff; hunter Robert Brown, after shooting a Yeti ("Man the destroyer," declares Cushing acidly), dies from shock and Tucker is buried under an avalanche. Cushing, alone, finally meets the snowmen, benign 11-foot beings that erase all thoughts about themselves from the botanist's mind. Back at the monastery, in the arms of worried wife Maureen Connell, Cushing professes to have no memory of the Yetis, which pleases Marle no end as the wily old bird was in cahoots with them all along, by telepathy.

Kneale's intelligent scripts were always multi-layered and here, he and director Guest expound the hypothesis that the creatures Cushing, Tucker and company are up against represent, in a way, reflections of man's own fears, and that those fears will cause unforeseen reactions and conflict, leading to the undoing of the expedition. This message was probably lost on a '50s audience who were more dismayed by the fact that the company had issued a black-and-white A-rated picture, not a Technicolor "X" as in *The Curse of Frankenstein*, still raking in a fortune at the ticket office at the time *The Abominable Snowman* was released. Guest's thoughtful addition to the Yeti cycle is too talkative for its own good and, although drumming up a sense of unease, paranoia and isolation, is unable to shake off those artificial studio settings that work against it. Cushing revealed once again what a formidable English actor he was, effortlessly undergoing the transition from television to cinema; Tucker was suitably bullish as the American huckster and Connell was simply lovely, angst-ridden or not. Worthy can sometimes equate with dullness: *The Abominable Snowman* certainly isn't uneventful, but it could have been improved by introducing some fire into its belly. This might have promoted the film to a higher status, along with other Hammer productions of the day. As it stands, it's ever so slightly dreary.

But before Hammer's foray into the Yeti legend came Toho's *Half Human* (*Ju jin Yuki Otoko*), translated as *Beast Man, Snow Man* or *Monster Snowman*. An American version of the film turned up in selected English theaters in 1964, running at 72 minutes, and in 1986, a 63-minute print appeared on Britain's Channel 4 station; this is the edit found on current DVDs. Neither bear much resemblance to

A Japanese poster of *Half Human*

Toho's 94-minute original. The Americanized hatchet job equals the butchery performed on *Varan the Unbelievable*, omitting 50 minutes of Japanese footage and making up the difference by splicing in 19 minutes of newly filmed material featuring John Carradine (in six separate segments), pontificating at great length to his colleagues on all things Yeti-based. To give some idea of the sheer scale of trimming, the creature

doesn't appear in the original until 39 minutes elapse after an almost funereal but careful buildup. In the revamp, it's a short 20 minutes—and that includes seven minutes of American footage! The beatings that the Yeti, mountain girl Akemi Negishi and Akira Takarada are subjected to are also missing (the central section is quite cruel in its depiction of prolonged violence toward both man and beast), numerous sequences have been drastically reshaped while the 12-minute climax in the cave has been reduced to five minutes. Parts of Akira Ifukube's scores from *Godzilla* and *Rodan* can be detected in the soundtrack medley. Ironically, Kenneth G. Crane is listed as director on the Carradine print, Inoshiro Honda not even getting a mention; there *is* a postscript stating that "segments of this picture were written and filmed in Japan," hardly what you would term gracious in view of the fact that all Japanese dialogue has been wiped clean (Carradine narrates) and Crane only directed the American footage, which lasts a paltry 19 minutes. Honda was responsible for the remaining 44!

The 94-minute, unedited *Half Human* is told in flashback to a reporter. Five skiers take to the mountains of Northern Japan; two vanish, one later found by the mountain police mauled to death, every bone in his body broken. Near the body are tufts of fur and large footprints. An expedition is sent into the mountains to see if the Yeti exists. There, a native tribe worships the ape-like creature and his infant, who inhabit a nearby cave. Also arriving at the same time is a group of gangsters who want to exhibit the creatures in a circus. The thugs capture the creatures, cage them and head back to civilization (the only sequence to make it more or less intact into the Carradine film). However, the infant manages to free the adult but is shot dead; blind with fury, the enraged snowman wipes out the gang, razes the native village to the ground and captures a member of the expedition (Momoko Kochi). The finale sees mountain woman Negishi tussling with the Yeti before they both topple into a volcanic vent filled with sulfurous waters. Kochi is rescued and we are back at the start, in the railway station, the group having related their adventures to the reporter.

Honda's splendidly pictorial exercise into the Yeti myth was withdrawn by Toho in the 1960s for vague reasons: The company, it has been whispered, was disturbed and more than a bit sensitive by the implications tacitly hinted at that some of the imbecilic, malformed villagers were the product of interbreeding between natives and Yeti. When the monster carries off Kochi, is it to procreate and preserve his species? Even by Japanese standards, that streak of sadism apparent in the middle section doesn't sit well with the material; animal activists would have had a field day in this day and age, whether or not the snowman was fictional or real. Sedately paced at first, packed with atmosphere (the keening wind, the remote snowscapes, distant howling) and full of incident, *Ju jin Yuki Otoko* boasts scenic mountain backdrops and a Yeti with which we can empathize, a reclusive, shy figure prowling the wastes, minding its own business, at the mercy of man and his barbaric traits (the picture is notable for its lack of incidental music at key moments, imbuing the general mood with a sense of foreboding and isolation, happy to allow the action to speak for itself). And Honda's homage to *King Kong* is only too evident in the wonderfully composed scene where the kindly creature hauls Takarada up from a precipice where he has been left dangling on a rope, a few minutes of unadulterated fantasy at its peak.

Toho's original, uncut *Half Human* is long overdue for a deserved release on digital disc. Lovingly crafted and truly memorable, it beats all the other suitors to the Yeti throne hands down. Like most other product from Toho during this fruitful chapter in their history, the movie doesn't pander to the kids and has that traditional Japanese fantasy ambience that elevates it to near-classic status. Inoshiro Honda and his team served the Yeti legend proud; hopefully, one day, fans will be given the opportunity to see just how great this picture is.

Chapter 23
Let's Get Serious

The Cloud of Death, starring John Agar, Robert Clarke and Allison Hayes, directed by Lee Sholem. *The Last Three on Earth*, starring William Marshall, Richard Carlson and Beverly Garland, directed by Roger Corman. Sound familiar? Well, they shouldn't because these titles have been fabricated. *The Cloud of Death* becomes *On the Beach*; *The Last Three on Earth* becomes *The World, the Flesh and the Devil*. The two fictitious movies, if made, would have been classed as Bs and included in many a book on guilty pleasures, revered by fans of the cheap and dreadful. But in the sphere of film criticism, the two *true* movies hardly ever get a look. Why so? There is a case to argue that because they're expensively produced, classed as highbrow fodder for a mainstream audience, contain A-list stars, are a bit like a soap opera now and again, contain no radioactive mutants and put their end-of-the-world message across with subtlety and lack of tacky effects, it's customary to give such productions the cold shoulder. Never in a million years would Gregory Peck, Ava Gardner or Harry Belafonte subscribe their illustrious names to a low-budget sci-fi outing, while a director of Stanley Kramer's reputation would never have been involved in such fare in the first place. There's a hint of snootiness in this blanket denial of two of fantasy cinema's more potent, heavyweight '50s undertakings, as if to say "Huh! They're for the grown-ups or the serious cinema set. We've got no place for them here." Well, like it or not, both films fall into the same post-nuclear category that formed the basis for a host of '50s sci-fi product focused on the after-effects of an atomic bomb blast, so it's high time they received a fair hearing, enabling them in the eyes of the disbelievers to be slotted side-by-side with the likes of *Day the World Ended* and *Five*. In this chapter, we are going to get serious!

Adapted from Nevil Shute's bestseller, United Artists' *On the Beach* (1959) ran for a lengthy 134 minutes, boasted a stellar lineup which included four major stars to ramp box-office takings and had Stanley Kramer, one of Hollywood's foremost directors, at the helm. "Banal" and "clichéd" are hardly the right terms to use in describing this picture, nominated for two Oscars, but they *have* been applied in some blinkered circles. The setting is Melbourne, 1964. The Northern Hemisphere has been destroyed by atomic warfare; a vast cloud of radioactive fallout is drifting south toward Australia where the inhabitants have only a few months to live. With this post-apocalyptic premise to work on, Kramer splits his work into two critical phases: How a bunch of disparate people react to their impending death and Gregory Peck's mission to determine the source of a mysterious radio signal emanating from San Diego.

Peck, who spent most of his fine acting career perfecting the strong silent type, plays the stoical naval officer with consummate ease as befits an actor of his standing, commanding the nuclear submarine Swordfish that docks into Melbourne, bringing updated news of the disaster to the authorities. Burying haunting images of his dead wife and two children (left behind in America) at the back of his mind, he's pounced upon by alcoholic socialite Ava Gardner, desperate to find true love before they all perish. A young, pre-*Psycho* Anthony Perkins (being groomed as an up-and-coming romantic lead; Hitchcock soon shot that notion down in flames!) is a naval lieutenant, having to cope with nervy wife Donna Anderson. She refuses to acknowledge the fact that the world

219

Ava Gardner and Fred Astaire appearing in a lobby card from *On The Beach*

is doomed, skating around the distressing subject of radiation sickness and not wanting to hear any morbid discussions about it, horrified at the thought of taking a suicide pill and giving one to her baby ("And this cures it?" she asks Perkins, hopefully. "No," he bluntly replies. "This ends it."). Last but not least, Fred Astaire crops up as a hard-drinking playboy, intent on living life to the full before going out in a blaze of glory.

The hopes, fears and bitter disillusionment felt by the leading characters is presented as a series of personal vignettes that, due to John Paxton's wordy script, tends occasionally to inhibit the narrative flow, as in the lengthy interlude where blowsy, intoxicated Gardner tries her hardest to seduce Peck at a party thrown by Perkins (her come-ons are unsuccessful). To impart an air of intimacy, Kramer, throughout the film, frames his cast in repeated close-ups, pushing the background and foreground shots out-of-focus, leading to some critics denigrating the film to the status of a slushy romantic drama along the lines of *Peyton Place*, with the issue of atomic war and its cataclysmic aftermath brushed to one side in favor of the Peck/Gardner "will they, won't they" scenario.

With this in mind, Kramer changes track in the 64th minute: Peck, Perkins and Astaire board the submarine and head north on a reconnaissance mission, to check radiation levels, to see if any life exists and to discover the source of that persistent signal. This 30-minute segment is powerful stuff, bringing home the full impact of a world where nobody draws breath anymore. Composer Ernest Gold, who won the 1960 Golden Globe for his score, ditches the overused *Waltzing Matilda* leitmotif, initiating a menacing sci-fi undercurrent that lowers the mood, while Giuseppe Rotunno's needle-sharp monochrome gives way to a murky gray wash—this is used to great effect when the *Swordfish* passes under the Golden Gate Bridge and noses into an eerily deserted San Francisco, Peck scanning the empty streets through his periscope. The puzzling signal that had raised so many people's hopes turns out to be a window blind pull-cord wrapped around a coke bottle, hitting a Morse key, a crushing denouement. "Who would ever believe that human beings would be stupid enough to blow themselves off the face of the earth." For once, a profound statement from the garrulous Astaire, reflecting the crew's innermost thoughts as they make hasty preparations to leave America's lifeless West Coast for good.

Back in Melbourne after that heart-stopping interlude, Peck and Gardner start an affair, people line up for suicide pills and Astaire wins a Grand Prix in his Ferrari. As the radiation begins to take effect ("The background level of radiation in this very room is nine times what it was a year ago. Don'cha know that? Nine times! We're all doomed, y'know," states Astaire, dampening the spirits of those around him), Peck decides to depart with his men and return to the States; they want to die on home ground, not in Australia. Gardner, having found genuine love for the first time in her worthless existence, is left alone, movingly watching Peck sail off in his submarine to certain death. And Perkins, after a difficult period, persuades his traumatic wife to take a pill ("Peter, I think I'll have that cup of tea now."), their final moments together truly heartbreaking, an extremely touching piece of cinema. Astaire, true to his word, locks himself in his garage, sits in his Ferrari and starts her up, gassed to oblivion, a broad smile on his face; a poignant final few words are uttered by Admiral John Tate to assistant Lola Brooks, raising their glasses to a "blind, blind world." The closing shots of Melbourne's streets, denuded of traffic and people, mirror those of San Francisco, a Salvation Army banner fluttering in the breeze proclaiming "There is still time Brother."

Fred Astaire and Gregory Peck appearing in a lobby card from *On The Beach*

On the Beach is a solid, prestigious sci-fi motion picture bereft of the grandiose posturing that heralds much of today's juvenile "Act of God" offerings. Peck, Gardner and Perkins act with total conviction, while Astaire proved that he was more than capable of rising above his song-and-dance routine to elicit a fine performance of some considerable authority. Yes, the picture does drift periodically and overplays its hand in dealing with Gardner's simmering passion for reticent Peck, but Kramer is professional enough to overcome such narrative dips. An emotionally charged warning of the catastrophic dangers to be had in messing with the A-bomb given the adult treatment, Kramer's excursion into '50s post-nuclear paranoia is pretty serious stuff; surely that's not a good enough reason to turn your nose up and ignore it, is it?

Film writers often quote that MGM's *The World, the Flesh and the Devil* (completed in 1958 but not released until 1959) owes its conception to M.P. Shiel's Victorian novel *The Purple Cloud*. In fact, it bears very little resemblance. Shiel's remarkable end-of-mankind saga, first published in 1901, tells the story of a young doctor who embarks on an historic expedition to the North Pole to prove his worth to his pernicious fiancée. After several fateful confrontations with hostile team members, he finds himself utterly alone; working his way south, he discovers a world decimated by an immense cloud of cyanide gas, millions of decaying corpses littering the streets. Gradually losing his faculties, the doctor travels the length and breadth of the globe, destroying city after city by fire until he chances upon a single female survivor, the Eve to his Adam. Perhaps the time has long since passed when an enterprising filmmaker would have seized upon this spellbinding novel, lovingly written in classic English prose, and conveyed Shiel's startling images to the big screen. No, if anything, *The World, the Flesh and the Devil*

is comparable to Arch Oboler's *Five*, placing the spotlight on a small group of post-holocaust survivors rather than the masses, changing its theme midway through from survival of the fittest to racial discord.

Trapped underground in a mine collapse for five days, Harry Belafonte emerges to a world devastated by atomic poison, newspapers in the manager's office proclaiming the End of the World. Puzzled, he heads to New York to seek survivors, eventually meeting blonde Inger Stevens. The initial sequences showing Belafonte surveying a silent, deserted New York pack an almighty punch, still managing to be, after 50 years, the equal of anything that modern-day cinema can throw at an audience. Harold J. Marzorati's widescreen black-and-white photography brilliantly evokes a sense of soulless desolation, framing Belafonte in one well-placed shot after another as he wanders aimlessly through the city's canyon-like avenues, his shouts echoing back to him among the towering skyscrapers. Thousands of vehicles clog up bridges, the dockyards are devoid of life and radios don't function. Despite being surrounded by all this calamity, Belafonte still feels disposed to place his rubbish in a trash container, a nice humanitarian touch by director/writer Ranald MacDougall, demonstrating that, although he may be alone, the man still abides by conventional rules. As for the lack of bodies, well, it's a case of what you don't see that makes this part of the film all the more unsettling. There wasn't the need to have everything ladled out on a trowel to audiences in the 1950s. Less was more.

With the arrival of Stevens, the movie's racial tone begins to emerge; she wants to live with him ("We haven't said anything about love, have we."), but he won't consider it because he's black and therefore looks upon himself as inferior to her, questioning the morality of the situation. "No!" he says with finality, to which Stevens sarcastically replies, "I'll never get married." His inbuilt prejudices will not allow him to get close to Stevens, despite the desire to do so, not even when he cuts her hair, presents her with a diamond pendant and arranges a birthday party, spurning her advances and obvious need for a deep, meaningful relationship.

Sixty-three minutes in, bearded Mel Ferrer turns up in a boat, the worse for wear. Shaved, rested and recovered, he quickly makes his intentions known to Stevens—he wants her as a mate; Belafonte, a "Negro," can go to hell ("I have nothing against Negroes," he mocks to Belafonte, unable to fathom out why the woman should be attracted to a man who is not white). Jealousy and racial intolerance rear their ugly heads (Belafonte buys a painting of a black slave adrift on a boat: "Poor slob. All alone in the world," he says with resentment, bemoaning his own fate); although Stevens craves male physical contact, she has set her sights on Belafonte, not the bigoted Ferrer, whose caveman approach to getting her into bed is to announce "Me man, you woman. How about it?"

Some might say that the action slows down a pace at this point in the picture, the director immersing himself in the mounting tensions between the trio, but give MacDougall his due, he manages to keep the momentum going because of the highly unusual circumstances the threesome find themselves involved in. After all, if the human race is to carry on, which of the two men, at loggerheads with one another, will the girl choose ("Why don't you toss a coin," Stevens suggests acidly to her pugnacious suitors). Both of them, in the end, appear to be the solution to keeping the peace. After a gunfight in Manhattan's thoroughfares between Ferrer and Belafonte, which ends in stalemate (Belafonte throws down his weapon after reading the inscription on the peace memorial fronting the United Nations building), the three walk off hand-in-hand to face an uncertain future, their grievances put to one side—for the moment. The movie finishes with "The Beginning" rolling up on the closing credits.

A plea for racial harmony … the disappearance of racial purity? This seems to be the message, loud and clear; tagged onto a stunningly mounted depiction of an unpopulated New York, *The World, the Flesh and the Devil* lacks the pomposity and self-importance prevalent in 21st-century blockbuster moviemaking and sticks in the memory as a great example of "what if…?" The film could have been at least 10 minutes longer (the 95-minute running time ends rather abruptly) and Miklos Rozsa's biblical-type score is so reminiscent of his work on *Quo Vadis* and *Ben-Hur* that we wouldn't be all that surprised to see Charlton Heston trundling down the street in a chariot at any time, but it's a rewarding experience all the same, the anti-nuclear stance resonating over the decades. Like *On the Beach*, *The World, the Flesh and the Devil* becomes a true grade-A post-apocalyptic drama not given its due because of (strange as it may seem) its classy credentials.

Chapter 24
Under the Knife:
Franju's Surgical Masterpiece

In June 1960 at the Edinburgh Film Festival, seven members of the viewing audience fainted during a screening of *Eyes Without a Face* (1959), which the British censor had passed uncut with an "X" classification after months of deliberation. Vilified by the critics and hesitantly given a limited showing at art-house and independent theaters, the film caused further outrage when more faintings, and even vomitings, were reported in the press. On the Continent, Georges Franju's audacious (and misunderstood) movie that kick-started the revisionist surgical horror sub-genre suffered minor cuts. However, the biggest insult of all made to what is now regarded as the pinnacle of European New-Wave medical/mad surgeon cinema was reserved for its American release. Cut by six minutes, re-edited, dubbed and lumbered with the crass title of *The Horror Chamber of Dr. Faustus*, Franju's masterwork was finally issued by producer William Shelton and Lopert Pictures in 1962, double billed with *The Manster* (aka *The Split*). In doing this, Shelton was pandering to the drive-in, sensation-seeking brigade rather than a discerning clientele who would appreciate the movie for what it really was. It is only in recent years that the uncut print of *Eyes Without a Face* has become available on the market, while its bastardized American cousin has quite rightly vanished without trace. But what are the major deviations, if any, between the two versions, apart from that inappropriate title change? [Note: Although listed in some quarters as a 1960 production, *Eyes Without a Face* was completed and copyrighted in 1959, hence the inclusion of Franju's landmark horror picture in this book.]

The mask is one of horror cinema's most potent images, dating right back to the early years of cinema; in *Eyes Without a Face*, it has never been more effectively used as an object of beauty and innocence hiding something truly terrible underneath. And that something terrible are Edith Scob's features. Destroyed in a car crash in which her father, surgeon Pierre Brasseur, was the driver, Scob (the actress possessed a fragile, gamine allure) wears a porcelain mask to veil her horrific facial injuries, wandering restlessly through her father's rambling mansion, an ethereal figure whose luminous eyes reveal her inner turmoil. It is said that the eyes mirror the soul, and that is most certainly the case here; Scob's expressive eyes are a key factor in the production, as significant as her iconic mask ("My face frightens me. And my mask terrifies me even more.")

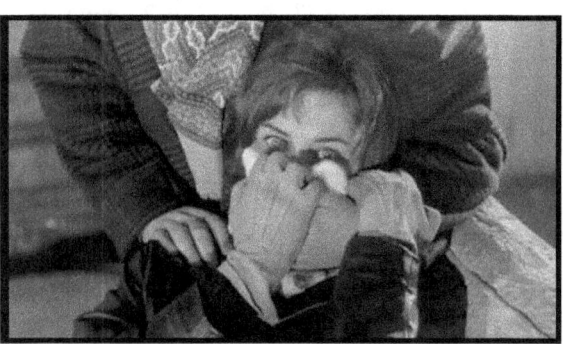

Young female victims are rendered unconscious and used for skin grafts to restore a damaged face.

Clad in black, one-time French glamour queen Alida Valli loiters in the shadows, stalking homeless young girls and taking them back to Brasseur's house in her Citroen. Once there, they are rendered unconscious and used for skin grafts in an attempt to remodel Scob's ravaged face. Brasseur had also operated on Valli in the past, giving *her* a new face, so she owes him a debt of gratitude as well as being in love with him.

The moment when Scob, without mask, approaches her strapped-down tissue donor demonstrates horror cinema at its most bone-chillingly brilliant. Scob

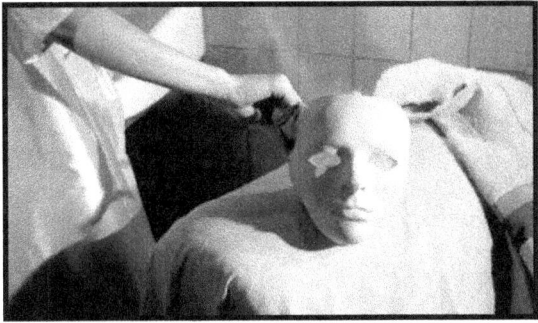

Edith Scob is about to confront her strapped down tissue donor, but first she takes off her mask and leaves it on a cushion.

warily circles the laboratory (you can almost smell the ether and feel the cold), studies the equipment and the comatose victim, walks to a mirror and removes her mask. The mask is left on a cushion, but we, the audience, are not allowed a glimpse of Scob's disfigurement. Franju shoots the actress from behind, only the back of her head in camera as she makes her steady way to the operating table. She stares down at the girl, her long, delicate fingers cautiously stroking the unblemished skin, soon to be *her* skin. The girl comes to, looks up at Scob and emits a single piercing scream. Scob slowly backs away like a wounded animal, out of focus, her ulcerated face vaguely visible, the guard dogs barking furiously, adding to the sweaty tension—we are finally permitted to see what the unfortunate girl has seen. With Maurice Jarre's eerie musical tones a muted, malevolent undercurrent, this one galvanizing scene alone promotes Franju's bold enterprise to everlasting status.

Franju's authoritative control of his subject matter is masterful in directorial pizzazz: his expert use of light, shade and pace; the reverential, lingering close-ups of Scob's haunting, doll-like mask and her radiant face after the operation; the five-minute tissue graft performed in one unflinching take (*not* for the faint-hearted!); the sterile laboratory and the three central characters—Brasseur, stern, clinical, totally focused; Valli keeping her emotions in check, a relentless procurer of young women, eager to please her icy lover and the wonderful Scob, childlike, a lost soul caught up in a wretched chain of events where no solution exists. Ably assisting Franju was respected cameraman Eugen Shufftan, bathing the picture in glacial monochrome imagery, while noted composer Maurice Jarre's Gallic score must surely rank as one of cinema's top-10 horror soundtracks, a lyrical, nursery rhyme leitmotif that jangles insidiously throughout and embeds itself in the mind.

It cannot be stressed how vital Jarre's musical arrangements are to *Eyes Without a Face*, particularly in the scenes involving Scob. As her slim figure, clothed in high-necked dress, drifts from one room to another, the unblinking eyes behind the mask taking in all that is happening, Jarre's score perfectly complements her every move, adding poignancy here, a menacing note there. Scob seems to inhabit a Grimm's fairy-tale world, divorced from the grisly business of restoring her good looks, curling herself up in a fetal position during bouts of depression. Great movie composers can flesh out a character as well as a director can, and *Eyes Without a Face* is a case in point. Both

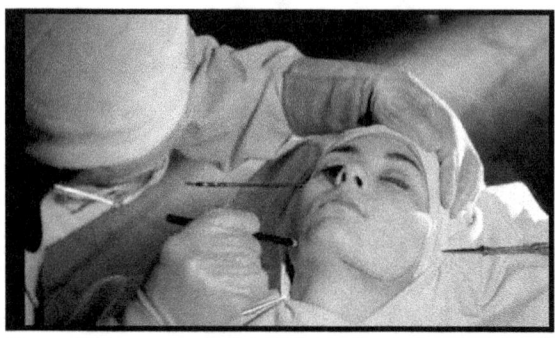

Pierre Brasseur as the mad surgeon prepares to surgically remove the face of another victim.

Jarre and Franju created a tragic female persona that audiences could identify with, and the composer's part in this must never be underestimated.

In a picture of so much depth, the three standout scenes are the aforementioned girl-in-lab segment; the skin graft operation, as cool and matter-of-fact as the man performing it and the unforgettable climax. Stabbing Valli in the throat with a scalpel, Scob turns the ferocious dogs loose on her father in an act of perverse rebellion, of release, of failure, of pity for the victims (the audience is left to draw its own conclusions). As the dogs rip their master to shreds, she almost floats into the night like a specter, white doves wheeling in the air, one perched on her shoulder as Jarre's musical cadences reach a crescendo. A powerfully poetic and moving last act with no real resolution—but there wasn't supposed to be one.

Eyes Without a Face may indeed, along with Hitchcock's *Psycho*, be the precursor to the slasher genre that was to come. It spawned a rash of surgical-horror dramas of some renown, *The Awful Doctor Orlof* and *Seddok, Son of Satan* being two important examples. But its violence isn't gratuitous, although it does carry an air of morbidity. The movie owes a great deal to the old Universal Karloff and Lugosi flicks of the '30s and '40s, with a nod in the direction of the great Jean Cocteau, while remaining individual and influential in its own right. It was a film way ahead of its time and could so easily have been made today. It is a film which horror lovers will repeatedly savor, to acknowledge Franju's sheer virtuosity and technique and to marvel at Scob's never-to-be-forgotten performance as the piteous girl trapped in a medical nightmare.

Where, then, and why does *The Horror Chamber of Dr. Faustus* go so drastically wrong? How did it manage to comprehensively tarnish a work of such repute? Many foreign films, before and after, have been inexpertly altered to suit English and American audiences so, preposterous title notwithstanding, *Faustus* in that respect follows a well-trodden path: Poor dubbing replacing subtitles, characters' names Anglicized/Americanized and drastic editing leading to jumps in continuity. But Shelton and Lopert were tinkering with a textbook classic here, not any old run-of-the-mill production. Their one major *faux pas* was in the misuse (or abuse) of Maurice Jarre's soundtrack, as we shall discover. That, more than anything else, is the main reason for *Faustus*' undoing.

First, let's cover the cuts. *Faustus* is 84 minutes long compared to *Eyes*' 90 minutes. Those missing six minutes occur principally in the opening credits, shorn by 70 seconds (the original's credits run just over two minutes), the skin graft operating scene, heavily edited from five-and-a-half minutes to a little over two (the original take was considered too strong) and the sequence showing Brasseur torn apart by the dogs. The sight of the surgeon's mangled face has been edited out, a fatal omission as Franju, in incorporating this crucial shot, was reflecting upon Scob's own ruined features, subtly ramming home the point of the daughter's redress. A few minor trims en route contribute to the remainder of the cuts, although the disturbing montage of four photographs capturing the gradual deterioration in Scob's unsuccessful facial graft survives the American cut.

The dubbing is blighted with the usual translation problems of lips not matching words, but give *Faustus* its due, it sticks pretty closely to the original and concise French script, with one or two silly digressions chucked in to pander to the non-European customer.

But in rearranging and unnecessarily cranking up the volume of Jarre's hypnotic score to suit their own objectives, the American distributors calamitously messed up the picture's natural flow, solid proof that the fine artistic meld between director and composer, if interfered with, can upset a film's equilibrium and damage the narrative drive. Because of the truncated credits, Jarre's title theme, a macabre fairground-type melody, comes straight in at the middle section and is therefore incomplete. This middle section is then applied rather harshly into the opening minutes that show Valli disposing of a corpse, and the score has a tendency to be overused in areas that, in the original, remain silent. Silence works wonders in building atmosphere, as Franju was fully aware. Too much music, however exceptional that music may be, can spoil the mood, which it does constantly in *Faustus*, to the movie's detriment. What's more, additional, dissonant sounds can be heard, notably when Brasseur and Valli leave the funeral and arrive at the surgeon's house. Who was responsible for this? Not Jarre, that's for certain. The careful pacing seems to fall apart with this unwarranted meddling, diminishing the original's standing and giving it a ragged appearance; *Eyes*, in its *Faustus* guise, has been relegated to just one more badly dubbed foreign exercise in sleaze and sadism. Yes, Franju's startling images remain more or less intact, but they don't marry with Jarre's music as they do so magnificently in the original cut. And remember, Jarre won an Oscar for his work on *Lawrence of Arabia*—he, above all others, didn't deserve Shelton crucifying his score to such a disastrous effect.

So steer clear of *The Horror Chamber of Dr. Faustus*. It is not worthy of your consideration. Mingling Gothic values, medical science fiction, unethical surgery and the contrast between beauty and ugliness into a complex whole, Franju's uncut *Eyes Without a Face* is an out-and-out classic, the director's big statement that rewards time and time again on so many levels. And when Scob, after her operation, gazes at the camera with those huge eyes and says wistfully, "When I look into a mirror, I feel I'm seeing someone who looks like me, returning from far away," your heart will melt. How many horror films can induce that feeling in a viewer?

Chapter 25
Tales of Mystery, Imagination, Noir, Horror And Suspense—British Style

From 1950 onward, American horror cinema gained momentum and began producing a string of big-budget shockers featuring radical new directors and fresh, exciting stars. The Europeans were not that far behind, and neither were the Mexicans and Japanese. But in Britain, things were markedly different. The Second World War had severely depleted the country's finances; Britain was dragging itself out of the mire of the conflict and unlimited funds were not at hand to splash out on the cinema industry as a whole, let alone the horror genre. Truth be told, British horror drama, in its narrowest form, had never made any sort of impact on the international market anyway. Somebody had to grasp the bull by the horns and come up with a revolutionary style of horror filmmaking that would shake the staid British film industry to its very core *and* successfully conquer those lucrative overseas markets. Hammer's garishly gruesome *The Curse of Frankenstein* achieved precisely that in 1957, redefining the horror films of yore and raising attendance figures to unheard of heights. It was an unqualified critical and commercial success in the United Kingdom and America and remains a foremost contender (along with *Dracula*) for the title of the most influential English picture to be made in the 1950s. This one film also verified the fact that the "X" certificate feature was big business, quelling reservations felt by distributors nervous at the thought of banning under-16s from their theaters.

But until Terence Fisher's groundbreaking masterpiece appeared, scaring audiences in a blaze of Eastmancolor glory and eclipsing all others that had gone before, British horror as such still fell into the stuffy old 1930s/1940s category of "Mystery and Suspense," with a smattering of the macabre hinted at here and there to spice up matters. The product reeked of dusty prewar theaters, eccentric character actors, traditional British reserve and stage-bound direction; it also lacked color photography, weighed up as being too expensive. Compared to what was coming out of the States in the 1950s, British pictures seemed like whimsical black-and-white artifacts belonging to the Dark Ages, low-key and sparely financed, produced by independent studios, somewhat dour in approach and usually A-rated (the U.K.'s first homegrown "X" films were the 1953 crime thrillers *Cosh Boy* and *The Yellow Balloon*). It was a world in which well-groomed chaps politely referred to sophisticated women as "my dear" or "darling" and smoked like chimneys. Everyone spoke the Queen's English in precise, clipped tones. It was where you would catch the bobby on his bicycle, doing his best to control the working class population, who were invariably shown to be cloth-capped, beer-swilling "cor blimey" ruffians carousing in public houses. British films of that hard period reflected the austerity of a country still recovering from repeated wartime bombing raids, a million miles away from Hollywood's professional gloss and wealth. "Unglamorous" would best sum up British cinema in the early 1950s.

So, as Warner Bros. prepared to unleash their expensive, spanking-new *House of Wax* on an unsuspecting public in 3-D, with Vincent Price the new star on the block, and Universal-International nurtured similar plans to let loose their gill-man in identical format, U.K. audiences had to be content with Old Mother Riley scuttling around a gray, wet London after an aging Bela Lugosi in the antique-looking *Mother Riley Meets the Vampire*. What better way to illustrate the yawning gulf in cinematic values, culture, ideas and ready cash. This "softly-softly" trend continued on and off throughout the decade, despite the fabulous box-office smashes bequeathed upon the fans by Hammer Films. But some minor gems were thrown up along the way, including pre-*Curse of Frankenstein* Hammer features. Most are now long forgotten, relegated to a level of obscurity and quite unknown outside of the United Kingdom (as are many of the sci-fi flicks described in chapter 19). Let's sample a few of these morsels and see just what was out there to entertain England's post-war cinemagoers other than the big-budget output from the major players across the Atlantic.

1950

John Gilling's screenplay for *Dark Interval* (Present Day Films, directed by Charles Saunders) foreshadowed the House of Hammer psycho thrillers of the 1960s and at precisely one-hour long didn't hang about too long. Zena Marshall plays a radiant young bride who returns from her honeymoon to her handsome husband's spooky house. Once there, Andrew Osborn drops his mask of goodwill and exhibits signs of intense jealousy, imagining Marshall has fallen in love with family doctor John Barry. John Le Mesurier plays a sinister butler, aware that his master is insane, as is Barry; both have kept this secret to themselves, Marshall unaware that she has married a madman. After going out of his mind, Osborn is shot dead by his butler who then poisons himself, leaving Marshall to take up with the doctor. Osborn switches from charmer to wide-eyed psycho with ease and Marshall possesses that mature poise prevalent among English actresses in the '50s. Unseen for many years, *Dark Interval*, a standard quickie rushed out to meet Britain's required film quota, needs to be exhumed from the vaults and included in a retrospective of Gilling, regarded as one of England's most underrated screenwriters and directors.

Zena Marshall in a publcity pose for *Dark Interval*

In 1904, 16 years after the infamous Jack the Ripper murders, which took place in London's Whitechapel district, a doctor (Valentine Dyall) takes up lodgings in Christine Silver's Victorian house. Tall, bearded and dressed in black, the sinister medic begins to exert a baleful influence, treating the place as if he owns it—guests are barred from seeing Silver and daughter Constance Smith, lights are kept dimmed, blinds are drawn, loud noise is forbidden and Smith discovers a map of the Whitechapel area in his room, together with a drawer full of surgical instruments. Smith's would-be boyfriend, reporter Jimmy Hanley, becomes worried for the women's safety, starts to rummage around and reaches the conclusion that the mysterious doctor is none other than England's first and most notorious serial killer, Jack the Ripper. But the police refuse to

Reporter Jimmy Hanley points an accusing finger in *Room to Let*.

believe it, thinking the man could be a mental patient who escaped from an asylum on the night of a fire that Hanley was covering for his paper. Which of these is he? Hanley determines to find out, putting the lives of mother and daughter at risk; does the creepy lodger plan to satisfy some deeply hidden urge by killing the women, especially when he says to Silver, "In four days' time, I shall begin again where I left off."

Based on Margery Allingham's radio play, Hammer's *Room to Let*, an excursion into the Ripper legend, seems like a trial run for the psychodramas the company began to specialize in 10 years later. At the end of the day, the film falls short of expectations by an unsatisfactory winding-up narrated by Hanley as an old man (Dyall is shot dead by Silver, so we never know who he was), but director Godfrey Grayson manages to imbue Dyall with an aura of ill-omen, shooting from floor level to give the actor added height and threat and repeatedly closing in on his severe features. Even as far back as 1950, Hammer's black-and-white photography was moody and carefully wrought, as in the scenes of Dyall slowly descending the stairs to intimidate Silver and Smith, and in the gloomy interior shots. For students of early British horror thrillers, *Room to Let*, running at 68 minutes, is a must, *if* you can lay your hands on a copy, now as rare as hen's teeth. And what a hoot to see a young Charles Hawtrey cast completely against type as Smith's second boyfriend. Hawtrey's camp frolics in Britain's *Carry On* series betrayed his gay leanings; a romantic lead he was not!

Not screened on British television since 1964, never released on VHS and, as I write, unavailable on DVD, *Shadow of the Past* is the rarest of the rare, like so many other early '50s U.K. films, a shadow of *its* past. Directed by Mario Zampi for his own production company, this 83-minute police/ghost thriller tells of a woman (Joyce Howard) whose sister has been brutally murdered. Howard is perfectly aware that her wicked brother-in-law (Andrew Osborn) is the killer, so she takes on the persona of the "Lady in Black," in effect becoming her sister's vengeful ghost. Teaming up with Terence Morgan, she plans to scare Osborn into confessing that he committed the deed as the police are getting nowhere with the case. It is believed that the British Film Institute holds a 35mm print of this picture in their archives (as they do with *Dark Interval*). If so, plenty of aficionados exist out there that would love to see Zampi's 62-year-old melodrama released on digital disc.

Viewing Hammer's *Someone at the Door* today, it's almost impossible to believe that this was the selfsame outfit that would produce all those blood-curdling Gothic thrillers from 1957 onward. But that was seven years away. In 1950, Francis Searle's antique horror-comedy came over like a watered-down *Old Dark House,* smelling of mothballs, more suited to the stage than celluloid. In fact, it owed its origins to a London West End play dating from the 1930s. Hard-up journalist Michael Medwin, owner of a creepy old mansion replete with priest holes, sliding panels, underground passages and a resident ghost, has the crazy idea of faking his sister's murder in order to scoop the headlines, and then discover her "body" later, cashing in on the resultant publicity. The previous caretaker mysteriously vanished; when his corpse is fished out of a lake, suspicion falls on Medwin, who now has two stories on his hands.

The play-it-by-numbers plot has new caretaker Danny Green in cahoots with smarmy neighbor Garry Marsh. Both are trying to scare Medwin, Yvonne Owen and boyfriend Hugh Latimer out of the mansion in order to locate a fortune in jewels hidden in a suit of armor. Inspector Campbell Singer turns out to be a killer and there's a great deal of scurrying from one part of the set to the other, while Searle's camera remains stationary. Medwin overacts to the point of lunacy, as Frank Spencer's twee score sums up the comedy elements perfectly. There are two scenes where, suddenly (and out of context), the film gets serious: Marsh threatens to burn out Owen's eyes with a lighted cigar if she doesn't let on about the jewels, and Singer is shot dead in a struggle with Medwin. Putting these violent episodes to one side, *Someone at the Door*, as English as roast beef and Yorkshire pudding but nowhere near as tasty, resembles, at best, a creaky British musichall farce and seems to go on forever, even at 61 minutes.

1951

Cloudburst is a gratifying Hammer/Exclusive *noir* thriller that many buffs have never heard about. It epitomized the company's output prior to Professor Quatermass and Baron Frankenstein, two characters that put them on the map in 1955/1957. *Cloudburst*, directed with professional discipline, short (83 minutes), expertly constructed, contains psychotic overtones and a serpentine plot. For the first 17 minutes of Francis Searle's tragic revenge drama, the director is obviously in love with Elizabeth Sellars' refined bone structure, his lens caressing her lovely features in a succession of close-ups, but for a purpose—she won't be around that long. Sellars, pregnant, is married to Canadian ex-espionage agent Robert Preston. In a country lane, viewing a field they might purchase for their unborn child, Sellars is brutally mown down by a speeding car, the driver and his female companion already wanted by the police in connection with the murder of a night watchman. In contrast to that serene, lovey-dovey opening, *Cloudburst* suddenly turns venomous.

Preston, grief-stricken, enraged and embittered by his wife's wasteful, premature death, vows vengeance, using his skills accrued in wartime sabotage to track down the pair responsible and make them suffer in copycat fashion. Whether he breaks the law in doing so is of no consequence to him because Preston is now a cold, calculating killer on the loose, always remaining several steps ahead of the police inspector (Colin Tapley), who is watching his every move.

How Preston, a menacing figure in hat and trench coat, sets about achieving his goal by covering his tracks makes for compulsive viewing. "You made me the perfect murderer," he snarls at the captured driver, Harold Lang. "Our instructors used to hammer home one thing. When you're being tortured, remember the first lie's the most important. You may never get the chance to tell another." Beating him senseless after inserting a bare electrified wire into his flesh to gain information about his passenger, Preston drives Lang to a remote country lane and repeatedly runs him over. Tapley deduces what Preston is up to but can't prove anything, not even when the code-breaker cunningly positions himself in a side road to await the arrival of his second victim (Shelia Burrell) in a police escort. A small blast in the road, triggered by Preston, forces the vehicle to stop. Burrell steps out and Preston, driving a white sports car, hits her at full speed. Finally, the war veteran, a spent force, turns himself in to the authorities after almost swallowing a cyanide tablet.

Bleak and violent, with Preston a dynamic leading man, *Cloudburst* possesses a workman–like confidence belying its budget, a feeling of technicians rolling up their sleeves and getting on with it. This confidence took root in early Hammer productions such as this, coming into full bloom in their future classics. A fast-paced gem, this is worth seeking out.

Alongside *Shadow of the Past*, British horror movies don't come much more obscure than *Death is a Number*. Running at 51 minutes, this Delman/Adelphi Films production, directed by Robert Henryson, is a complex supernatural tale centered around numerology and the three mystical connotations attributed to the number nine: passion, violence and destruction by fire. Writer Terence Alexander narrates the story to wife Lesley Osmond, and what a tangled series of events it turns out to be, involving his old college friend Denis Webb. Webb, a car designer and reckless racing driver, died in a fatal crash at the Brooklands circuit 10 years back. Alexander reckons his death wasn't by chance; the man was the victim of a family curse somehow linked to the one number that had figured so prominently in his life, and he wants to get all the facts down in print.

Webb was born on September 9, 1890 (a double nine if you add the one and the eight). He was badly burned in an accident in 1917 (another double nine when you add the seven and two ones together) and he inherited a castle with a turbulent past in Sussex (if you correspond words with numbers, Sussex is a nine). Where is all this leading to, audiences might well ask? Webb is the ninth generation son to have lived in this castle; a witch (Ingeborg Wells) haunts the battlements, as does a Lady Beatrice, both women figuring in the life of Webb's descendent who died 300 years ago. Webb is led astray by the witch's seductive powers and has a habit of venturing into the forbidden East Wing, where ghostly phantoms and misty vapors, drawn to the room by an arcane window, torture his mind, enacting scenes of violence and fire. Not long after, Webb perishes at Brooklands; his car was number nine. When Alexander visits the castle, the East Wing is in ruins and the mysterious window no longer there.

Death is a Number crams more into its brief running time than many films manage in twice the length (predictions, superstition, fate, occult influences and creepy apparitions). Horace Shepherd wrote the fanciful score (credited to Ecaro Pastore), while Phil Grindrod and Harry Long conjured up some atmospheric, brooding photography, especially in the scenes of translucent ghosts floating through the castle's malignant stone-lined passageways. Not screened commercially since 1959 (it was A-rated) and hard to come by today, this densely plotted spooky oddity, omitted from the majority of movie compendiums, is a vital cog in the works that made up the British horror industry of 60 years ago. Regrettably, the picture is so rare that it will probably never officially see the light of day.

Also scoring high marks in the rarity factor is Christopher Lee's 13th movie, Independent Sovereign Films' *Valley of Eagles*, distributed by Lippert Films in America. Lee's role, is, however, minor; he plays a policeman, on screen for a couple of minutes only. A mystifying amalgam of Cold War *noir*, cop thriller and outdoor adventure, this tells of a Norwegian scientist (John McCallum) who has invented a "barium record," a metal disc that converts sound waves into electrical energy. As proof of the machine's power, he melts an iron bar after playing the disc like a gramophone record. Jealous, treacherous colleague Anthony Dawson steals McCallum's notes plus a box of vital parts and, together with McCallum's bored wife (played with icy detachment by Mary Laura Wood), drives off into Lapland's snowy wilderness, headed for the border, planning to hand the formula to the Russians. McCallum and Inspector Jack Warner follow the pair and are soon up to their necks in stampeding reindeer, man-eating wolves and Laplanders who inhabit a lost valley, training flocks of demonic eagles to attack anything on sight.

Director Terence Young sets out the opening 15 minutes as a semi sci-fi offering shot in *noir*-style, addressing the twin issues of McCallum's revolutionary machine and his unhappy marriage. Once Dawson and Wood have done a bunk, we switch to darkly plotted crime drama for a further 15 minutes. The remaining 55 minutes takes place in the tundra; McCallum and Warner team up with Laplanders, hoping to catch up with the criminal duo that are having to trek across country following a collision with a snow plow. After several incidents en route to a village overlooked by a huge mountain, Dawson and Wood are buried in an avalanche. Laplander Nadia Gray invites McCallum to investigate what lies beneath her furs—this, at long last, brings a smile to his somewhat doleful features.

Nino Rota's rich score is a real treat, considering the picture's lowly ambitions, while Harry Waxman's vivid cinematography expertly blends live action and Scandinavian location footage to bring those wintry wastes to life. *Valley of Eagles* is so different from the norm, and equally so invigorating, that lovers of obscure British cinema will want to hunt it out, regardless of the high cost of obtaining a decent copy on DVD.

1952

A deftly made, unpretentious haunted boat yarn, Vernon Sewell's *Ghost Ship* (Merton Park) was actually filmed on the director's own steam yacht. American Dermot Walsh and his English wife (26-year-old Hazel Court, the very picture of English rose loveliness) buy the *Cyclops*, standing in a state of disrepair in a boatyard on the South Coast, despite the harbormaster warning them that the vessel is haunted. Proceeding with the purchase, Walsh spruces up the yacht and the original bosun is maintained. When a number of unexplained incidents occur (the smell of cigar smoke; a man seen in the engine room), the couple call in psychic investigator Hugh Burden and medium Joan Carol. Carol, in a trance, gives an account of the *Cyclops*' previous dark history, shown in flashback. On a trip to France, the captain discovered his wife was carrying on with his chief engineer. Shooting them dead, he hid the bodies in a disused water tank and jumped overboard. The twist is that the present-day bosun is, in fact, the murderous captain; when the bodies are discovered, he shoots himself and the curse is lifted.

Low-key, wordy, with some clammy moments, *Ghost Ship* rewards the viewer with strong performances, a concise script, pleasing English seaside locations, efficient direction and luscious Hazel Court in full bloom. Sewell virtually remade this movie in 1961's excellent *House of Mystery*—both pictures are worthy of any buff's undivided attention.

Stolen Face was Hammer's 35th feature, made at a period when the company was just one of several independent studios supplying the British public with thrillers, social dramas, comedies and semi-fantasy fodder. It was also fledgling director Terence Fisher's first foray into the world of surgical pre-Hammer horror. Georges Franju's *Eyes Without a Face* and Anton Giulio Majano's *Seddok, Son of Satan* owe a debt of gratitude to Fisher's early exercise in sexual obsession and split personality, themes that would occur time and time again in Hammer's later output and the flourishing continental horror movie. Hollywood stars Paul Henreid and smoky-voiced Lizabeth Scott were flown in to England to give the movie an international flavor. Henreid is a noted surgeon who falls in love with sultry concert pianist Scott while on vacation in the country. Learning that Scott is to be married to kindly André Morell, he performs complicated plastic surgery on a facially scarred woman serving

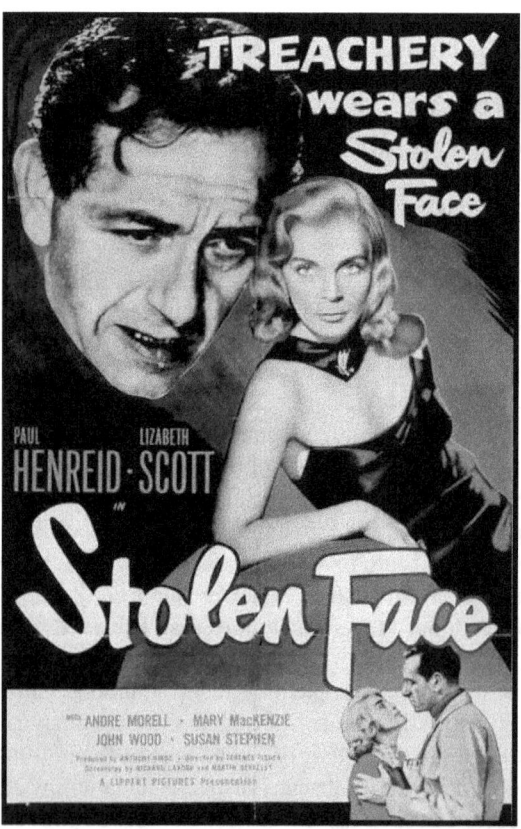

time for theft in London's Holloway Prison. The result? He delivers a spitting image of his already-spoken-for lover. But his creation (whom he marries) reverts to her scheming, thieving, drunken ways, preferring jazz clubs to concerts and making life hell for the doctor. The frantic climax sees the surgically enhanced wife falling from a moving train after confronting her double; Henreid is now free to take up with Scott, as she has ditched Morell.

Fisher's assured direction and talent for composition was a taste of much greater things to come, while Scott, in her dual role as the cool blonde and crazy harridan, lit up the production. Henreid, his ardor kept fully under control, turned in a polished performance. Malcolm Arnold's rich score was on hand when required. A grim warning that beauty is only skin deep and can mask a dangerous inner-self, *Stolen Face*, part romance, part horror, is a medium-budgeted hors-d'oeuvre, whetting the appetite for the fare that would feature on Hammer's main menu five years hence. *Stolen Face* remains an important addition to the company's extensive back catalogue.

1953

John Gilling was the man behind Mid Century/Kenilworth's *Deadly Nightshade*, a minor effort showcasing his talent for turning out briskly paced and intriguing thrillers, with an edge to them. The old theme of mistaken identity was given a razor-sharp twist here; sometimes, taking on another person's identity can land a person in much deeper water than he/she would wish. Filmed around the Cornish fishing port of Looe, the film showcases Emrys Jones as a saboteur (Matthews) in league with foreign atomic scientists and agents that blow up British ships as they sail past. An escaped convict (Barlow), behind bars for murder (he claims it was manslaughter), is the spitting image of Matthews (Jones played both roles). One night, he bursts into Matthews' cottage, accidentally kills him during a fight, hides the body in an outhouse and takes on his identity to evade police capture. But can he keep the ruse going long enough to hoodwink those who knew Matthews only as the reclusive cottager, those confederates in cahoots with Matthews' treasonable operations *and* those acquainted with Barlow, the escaped convict? Juggling his twin personas (himself and Matthews) and afraid to let the pretence slip, the situation is further complicated by the arrival of Barlow's on/off girlfriend, elegant Zena Marshall, who is convinced that the man isn't who he says he is.

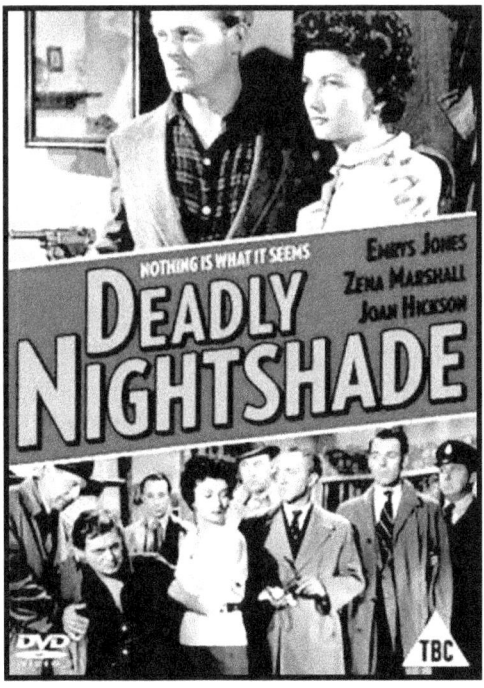

At just 60 minutes long, Gilling's snapshot tale taking in recognition, betrayal, insecurity, espionage, accusation and wrongful murder races along without a pause for breath, capturing the uncertainty of those Cold War times. Jones, Marshall, John Horsley (the inspector on Jones' tail) and the remainder of the British cast act with purpose; look out for a fleeting appearance from George *The Mummy* Pastell as a sinister foreign scientist. Obviously shot on a shoestring budget, *Deadly Nightshade* presents '50s communist high anxiety from an English viewpoint in a low-key but effective manner.

1953/1954 saw several examples of the portmanteau film, made popular in the 1960s in horror anthologies such as *Dr. Terror's House of Horrors* and *Torture Garden*. The Danziger Brothers' *Gilbert Harding Speaking of Murder* was a collection of three short mystery tales narrated by curmudgeonly, bespectacled BBC television personality Gilbert Harding, all of which formed part of a teleseries entitled *Calling Scotland Yard*: "Falstaff's Fur Coat," "The Missing Passenger" and "Thirty Days to Die." The first told of an actor (Robert Adair) who dons a luxurious fur coat and is hounded by crooks that mistake him for a dealer in stolen jewels. The latter concerned a playwright (Hubert Gregg) who plots to murder critic Lawrence Naismith for continually panning his works. "The Missing Passenger" had two sisters (Kay Walsh and Betty Ann Davis) locking their mutual ex-boyfriend (Patrick Barr) in an attic for 20 years, a plot device that recurred in numerous '60s thrillers, *The Collector* and *Fanatic* being two examples. Directed by Paul Dickson, the picture was released in 1954 and hasn't been seen for years.

Neither has *Three's Company*, whose trio of stories was edited from the television series *Douglas Fairbanks, Jr. Presents* (1953-1957) and theatrically issued under Fairbanks' own production company. Fairbanks acted as the narrator of the following: "The Surgeon," "Take a Number" and "The Scream." Terence Fisher directed the first two while Charles Saunders was responsible for "The Scream," the best of the three. Fairbanks and treacherous wife Constance Cummings buy a house that is haunted by a piercing scream occurring at 11 o'clock each night that is the prelude to a murderous event; Fairbanks then decides to kill his evil wife, resulting in her scream of death.

The Triangle also consisted of three anecdotes from the Fairbanks' TV show and again has never been released on tape or disc: "A Lodging for the Night," "American Duel" and "Priceless Pocket." In the first (directed by Bernard Knowles), a thief in 15th-century Paris escapes from the police and takes refuge in a house owned by an ex-military man; the second (directed by Lance Comfort) deals with two men who decide on a Russian roulette-type duel involving choosing a poison and the third (directed by Leslie Arliss) involves an ordinary man whose trouser pockets supply him with an endless quantity of pound notes.

Eight more omnibus movies made up of episodes from *Douglas Fairbanks, Jr. Presents* were given a limited commercial release in England as support features: *The Accused, The Death of Michael Turbin, Destination Milan, Forever My Heart, The Genie, The Last Moment, The Red Dress* and *Thought to Kill*. These appear to have vanished off the British cinema map many years ago, although the BFI may hold prints in their vaults.

Three Cases of Murder (London Films/Wessex) is yet another early illustration of the film omnibus, the narrator here played by future TV personality Eamonn Andrews. Not up to the standards set by Ealing's similar *Dead of Night* (1945), the movie is a little-seen treasure of expertly crafted British cinema (not released until 1955), Georges

Perinal's gleaming photography and Doreen Carwithen's lovely English score complementing each tale to perfection. First off we have "In the Picture," directed by Wendy Toye. Alan Badel (he starred in all three) plays a deceased, anonymous artist who periodically materializes out of his own landscape canvas, retrieving items from the museum to display in his house as objects of desire. In his quest for artistic perfection, Badel transports curator Hugh Pryse into the painting's mysterious house where resident taxidermist Eddie Byrne kills him. Illusion and reality become blurred in this somewhat twee opener, only the final shot (Badel leading an unsuspecting young girl into the picture's frame toward the baroque door of the house) guaranteed to raise the hackles.

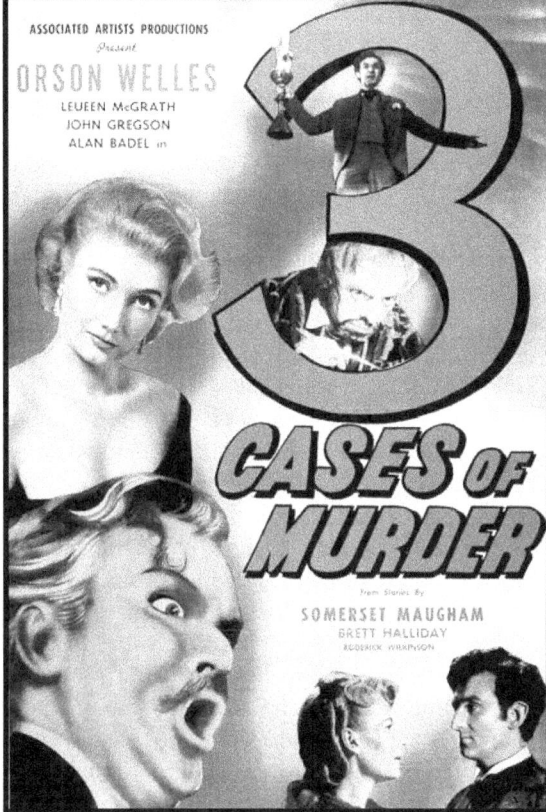

The second tale, "You Killed Elizabeth," is the most interesting of the three, tighter in plot and forcibly directed by David Eady, like a mini *film noir*. John Gregson and Emrys Jones are business partners who have remained friends since childhood. When Gregson, a notorious womanizer given to blackouts caused by heavy drinking, goes off to court a potential client, the reserved Jones meets and falls in love with Elizabeth Sellars, planning to marry her. Gregson returns, fancies the girl himself, dates her behind his friend's back and then blithely announces that they are going to marry. The next morning Sellars is found beaten to death in her flat. Is Gregson the guilty party, committing the murder in one of his blackout phases? It turns out to be mild-mannered Jones—when Gregson uncovers the truth, his one-time pal pushes him to his death through an open window. In the end, Jones inadvertently leaves incriminating evidence with a barman (Badel again), ensuring that he won't get away with the double murder after all.

Larger-than-life Hollywood actor Orson Welles was the star of the third episode, "Lord Mountdrago," directed by George More O'Ferrall. A bullying foreign secretary, he ridicules his Welsh opponent (Badel) in Parliamentary meetings to such an extent that the man's career is ruined. But retribution follows in a series of nightmares; Welles, in various bizarre situations, finds himself humiliated in front of friends and family, Badel an ominous presence, the man gloating at his adversary's discomfort. Doctor André Morell is unable to offer a solution to the politician's disturbed mind and, in a final dream, Welles pushes Badel in front of a train; Welles later falls down steps and dies, stating to his wife and Morell that Badel has reaped his revenge from beyond the grave.

Welles, as expected, hammed it up to the point of parody, wonderfully verbose in his role as the flamboyant Lord Mountdrago and topping off this satisfying triplet of vignettes in grand style. The omnibus format as presented here would be revived in the 1960s, chiefly by Amicus Productions; rarely seen, *Three Cases of Murder* is a fascinating period piece, combining supernatural elements and murder effortlessly, a reminder of sound British cinema in its most rewarding era.

Summit Films' *The White Huntress* (aka *Golden Ivory*) wasn't released until 1957, part of a distribution deal with American International Pictures, and has hardly been glimpsed by addicts of the obscure over the intervening years. Like a version of *King Solomon's Mines* without the mines, director George Breakston's jungle safari trek was actually filmed in Kenya's unspoiled wilderness and therefore benefits greatly from authentic location work. But the promising storyline—the search for a lost elephant graveyard gleaned from information scrawled on a scrap of paper by a dying explorer—never amounts to anything and Susan Stephan, the female lead, is certainly no white huntress. She wrestles with a python, wears low-cut outfits and projects a sexy attitude, but that's about all. Brothers Robert Urquhart and John Bentley, both hunters, act as guides to a party of settlers seeking a new African home in 1890. There's talk of a fortune in ivory hidden in a remote valley; a prospector, on the run after killing three of his colleagues, joins up, hinting at gold in the region and hostile Masai warriors stage an attack midway through (and quite bloody it is as well). Urquhart and Stephan start making eyes at each other, and Bentley (an alcoholic waster) dies in a second native assault, a dozen spears sticking out of his body, as the movie ends, the wagons trundle onward to Philip Green's meandering soundtrack.

The White Huntress has a refreshingly raw look about it (not a stage set in sight) and cuts down on the cutesy animal footage; it's also reasonably well acted and directed, moving quickly enough over 70-odd minutes. If only the "hidden elephant valley" element had been expanded upon to add a tantalizing speculative angle to the chronicle of events, the picture might have been a minor action/adventure winner. As it stands, it's mainly of interest because of its sheer rarity value.

1955

Mister Tall, Dark and Gruesome himself, Christopher Lee, played a schizophrenic killer in the Danziger Brothers' *Alias John Preston*, a 66-minute psychiatric romp of importance to fans because of the actor's involvement. Here we had a pre-*Frankenstein* and *Dracula* Lee, and looking at the movie now (it's very hard to acquire an acceptable copy), it seems impossible to believe that two years down the road, everlasting fame and fortune in the horror field would be his for the taking. Lee, speaking in a peculiar Anglo-American accent, arrives from nowhere at the village of Deanbridge, loaded with cash. In a matter of months, he's bought a failing factory and farm, ordered a new hospital wing, become a member of the hospital board, purchased a cottage and inveigled his way into the home of banker John Longden. The attraction is Longden's daughter, Betta St. John, engaged to drippy Peter Grant, winner of a local golf tournament. A suave man of the world, in her eyes, Lee appears to be a far better prospect than Grant.

She ditches the lovelorn sap and starts dating the town's mysterious benefactor; soon, their wedding is made public.

But when the hospital announces the appointment of a psychoanalyst (Alexander Knox), Lee gets twitchy and develops worrying traits. He continually fiddles with cigarettes without smoking them, states to all and sundry his hatred of "witch doctors," as he acidly terms psychiatrists, loses his temper without provocation, doesn't give his fiancée his full attention at musical concerts, refuses to go to Paris on business and begins to have bad dreams.

In *Alias John Preston,* Christopher Lee's character has bad dreams where he strangles a blonde Frenchwoman.

The nightmares, which he relates to Knox, revolve around a blonde Frenchwoman visiting him at his cottage. Is she an old flame? Is she a blackmailer? In the dream, Lee strangles her and her ex-husband finds out. Together, the two men bury her corpse in the garden. Then, in another dream, Knox turns up at the cottage. Lee, during a fight, kills the husband, hits Knox over the head with a poker and wakes up. After telling Knox of the final dream, we see the back of the psychiatrist's head—it sports a large surgical dressing. Lee's nightmares are fact, not fiction. His real name is David Garrity, a deserter, criminal and murderer with a split personality; the ex-husband was a French detective on Lee's trail. "It's all over now," Knox tells Lee as, sweating and shaking, he's led away by orderlies, Knox informing St. John that she has had a lucky escape—she was days away from becoming the wife of a psycho. St. John goes back to Grant, poor compensation for losing handsome Lee, whether he was nuts or not.

A typical Danziger Brothers potboiler of the day, made by the same team behind *Devil Girl from Mars* (directed by David MacDonald; musical score by Edwin Astley), *Alias John Preston* forms an integral cog in Christopher Lee's cinematic wheel of fortune. Those rich baritone tones and imposing presence carry the movie, which isn't a bad example of the true to type English co-feature that was to be found in cinemas throughout the 1950s. But, as mentioned, its availability is limited these days.

In 1950, Hammer Films cut a five-year deal with producer Robert Lippert to produce a series of low-budget crime-based thrillers, the intention being to beef up the allocation of second features which were part and parcel of U.K. screen presentations in those days (American actors were drafted in to add Hollywood glamour to the cast). Short in length (60-75 minutes), these mainly forgotten B features form a legacy of screencraft founded on good old-fashioned elbow grease that has long since vanished from the British film industry. *The Glass Cage* (aka *The Glass Tomb*) is one of the more intriguing, set in the world of carnivals, a favorite Hammer motif that cropped up in many of their '60s/'70s productions. Eric Pohlmann played "The Starving Man" whose act involved him being locked in a glass cage where he hoped to remain without food for a record-

The Glass Cage was retitled *The Glass Tomb* for its American release.

breaking 70 days. At a pre-launch party, a girl is strangled in an upstairs apartment by suave psychopath Geoffrey Keen; Pohlmann lets on to boss John Ireland that he *thinks* he spotted the killer ascending the stairs to the woman's door but can't put a name to his face. When Keen hears this, he attempts to find a way to break into Pohlmann's cage and silence him before he recollects who he saw.

Over its 59 minutes (the unedited print lasts 74 minutes), *The Glass Cage* crams in murder, blackmail, sexual desires, abduction and poisoning, plus a macabre party scene in which Ireland's freak-show performers make merry while, upstairs, Keen strangles his victim and then joins Ireland's party as though nothing unexpected has happened. Sid James, who was having an affair with the murdered girl, is blackmailed by lowlife Sydney Tafler and then shot dead; Sam Kydd guns down Keen after the killer has broken into the cage disguised as a nurse and shot the impostor who has taken the place of the poisoned Starving Man.

Director Montgomery Tully did a decent job in aping the American *noir* style, all close-ups, shadows and overlapping dialogue, helped by stark photography depicting a London still living through the after-effects of the Blitz. And young Honor Blackman was on hand as Ireland's delectable wife, nine years before she uttered those immortal words to a bemused Sean Connery in *Goldfinger*: "My name is Pussy Galore."

The second of Ealing Studio's fantasy-type thrillers of 1955 (see chapter 21 for *The Ship that Died of Shame*) was *The Night My Number Came Up*, an airline disaster movie built around the themes of premonition and coincidence. Due to fly from Hong Kong to Tokyo via Okinawa with a select group, Michael Hordern informs Michael Redgrave at a dinner party about a strange dream he had the previous night. In the dream, Redgrave took off in a Dakota that became lost in a thunderstorm, ran out of fuel and crashed in the mountains of northwest Japan. Hordern details the exact number of passengers on the flight, who they are, how they react to the sequence of events and the circumstances leading up to the crash. Thinking nothing more of it, Redgrave and seven others take off but soon alarming incidents begin to occur that were foretold in Hordern's nightmare. Are they all doomed to perish? Is the omen of disaster about to become a horrifying reality? As each passenger faces his/her own personal fears, the Dakota plunges into a lightning storm; radio contact is lost and the plane is way off course, heading toward a mountain range hundreds of miles from their chosen destination.

Robbed of a twist ending, which is a marginal letdown, Leslie Norman still manages to pump up the pressure as coincidence upon coincidence piles up, Redgrave, the passengers and the sweating pilots convinced that they are the victims of fate. Fine aerial shots, the kind of black-and-white photography many modern-day films would die for, a tip-top all-British cast and a blistering Malcolm Arnold score make this one of Ealing's top-grade outings of the decade, but one that is rarely heard of today.

1957

On the surface, Insignia Films' *Cat Girl* is a fairly straightforward tale of a woman inheriting a 700-year-old family curse whereby, in moments of passion, she turns into a feline monster, able to control her muse, a savage leopard. But dig a little deeper and you'll discover that this lesser-known horror outing broke a few sacrosanct rules. It dared to present overt carnal desires in English heroines that had been suppressed in the realms of British cinema for decades, a liberation of sexual mores unique in such a low-key production. The catalyst was young Barbara Shelley, in her first-ever role as a newly married heiress, unknowingly next in line to take over the curse. Visiting her uncle's creepy old house with husband Jack May and another married couple, Shelley is told about the curse but refuses to believe it. Shelley's former lecturer (and ex-beau) Doctor Robert Ayres turns up, thereby setting the scene for hidden emotions to rear their ugly heads. Shelley is still in love with Ayres, who is married, while the weak-willed May hungers after Patricia Webster, whose husband is permanently tipsy. When May sneaks off into the woods with Webster for some midnight canoodling, Shelley catches them in the act and transfers her soul into a prowling leopard that slaughters her cheating husband.

Director Alfred Shaughnessy quite plainly had a fondness for Shelley's figure; there are two lingering shots of the actress' bare back, racy for 1957, and the intense look of ecstasy on her face as she views the two adulterers embracing on the ground speaks volumes. Carted off to a London institution on the advice of Ayres, Shelley changes into a cat-woman at night, a superficial but effective transformation sequence used. We see her clawed hands and furry face shot in fuzzy focus. She also controls her leopard muse through barred windows. Released and given a room in a swanky hotel, Shelley spends a day in the company of Ayres' wife (Kay Callard); engulfed with jealousy, she decides to kill her, chasing the terrified woman through London's dank back alleys. Ayres and the police drive to the Denmark Street area to prevent another murder; the doctor's car hits the leopard and it morphs into Shelley, lying dead on the wet street.

Transposing Jacques Tourneur's *Cat People* to wintry England worked wonders in this minor picture that went the rounds in England and the States with *The Amazing Colossal Man*. The British censor's office was unusually lenient in passing the film with an "A" certificate—or did its veiled air of eroticism pass them by? *Cat Girl* is a miracle of dark, psychological suspense, and deep-voiced Shelley, at the start of her horror career, will set any hot-blooded male's pulse racing.

Michael Anderson's string of '50s hits—*The Dam Busters*, *1984* and *Around the World in Eighty Days*—culminated in a taut thriller, ABP's *Chase a Crooked Shadow*. After languishing in the cinematic vaults for half a century, the film has finally seen the light of day on DVD. Hitchcock would have loved David Osborn and Charles Sinclair's incisive screenplay: Anderson, from the very beginning, lets the audience in on the secret. Richard Todd and Faith Brook are up to no good, targeting heiress Anne Baxter in her swanky Spanish villa, Todd taking on the persona of her brother who died in an automobile accident. The woman has inherited the family villa following the collapse of her father's business and his subsequent suicide over the loss of a fortune in company diamonds. Does Baxter know the whereabouts of those missing diamonds? Todd has a hard time convincing Baxter that he is her brother, and her belief that the man is an impostor is shaken to the core when her uncle, Alexander Knox, welcomes him into the household with open arms. Puzzled detective Herbert Lom has his doubts about Todd, but he has nothing to go on, even when Baxter claims that he and Brook are planning to kill her for her inheritance.

Anderson, with economic use of the camera, lays on the suspense with a trowel; we are fully aware that the sinister Todd is not who he says he is, so why can't anyone else realize it apart from the increasingly nervy Baxter? Here comes the spoiler alert! In a totally unexpected twist that will fool even staunch addicts of this kind of fare, Todd and Brook turn out to be police officers, working closely with Lom and Knox. All four have played a part in breaking Baxter into giving a confession, which she does; collapsing in tears and on the verge of madness, she admits to killing her brother by tampering with the brakes on his car, blaming him for their father's suicide. But this premeditated murder wasn't enough to prevent the deranged Baxter from stealing the diamonds to satisfy her own greed.

A legendary Hollywood good-looker (she was breathtakingly gorgeous as Nefretiri in Paramount's *The Ten Commandments*), Baxter, as the conniving heiress under duress, demonstrates her acting chops laudably, her role fortified by Todd and company. An underrated British drama that, once the surprise is out of the bag, will force audiences into catching it all over again in order to spot the clues and red herrings cunningly littered throughout the 87-minute running time.

The Danziger Brothers produced their own budget version of *Double Indemnity* and *The Postman Always Rings Twice* with *The Depraved*, a 70-minute helping of British *noir* boosted by the sultry screen presence of Anne Heywood, a true English beauty. Danziger Brothers' regular director Paul Dickson didn't hang about, getting straight down to the nitty-gritty without any preamble. Heywood is married to Basil Dignam, a drunken bully whose idea of marital bliss is to bark at Heywood, when she wants to go out, "You stay, little bird." No wonder she falls for Captain Robert Arden from the nearby American army camp at Deningley, when he turns up on her doorstep asking to use the phone as his Jeep has run out of fuel. What follows is classic *noir*—as Dignam refuses to divorce Heywood (she only married him for his money), the duplicitous duo hatch a plot to have the vile wife abuser die in a car crash and make it appear like an accident, so that they can be together. After the deed is successfully carried out, Inspector Denis Shaw, investigating the incident, begins to suspect that Arden is behind it all;

the American officer has failed to cover his tracks in one or two vital areas, leaving possible incriminating clues. When Arden, full of remorse, realizes that the game is up and that wily Heywood has already cashed in one of her husband's insurance policies, he guns her down and surrenders to the police.

Bracingly shot, grimly atmospheric and played out to a jazzy score (Albert Elms), *The Depraved* has long since vanished into that cinematic black hole which is the graveyard of so many British A-rated co-features dating from this heady period. This is a shame as femme fatale Heywood sizzles, especially in a highly suggestive nude scene (not shown,

The sultry Anne Heywood, a true English beauty, as she appeared in *The Depraved*.

but left to the imagination), while Dignam excels as the kind of chauvinistic male pig women would wish to avoid at all costs. This remains one of the Danziger Brothers' more accomplished efforts, but it is very hard to lay hands on today.

Undoubtedly one of Michael Gough's more unrecognizable feature films, Archway's *The House in the Woods,* had the actor, for a change, toning down his customary theatrical method of role-playing. A neurotic reporter who requires peace and quiet to write his new book, Gough and wife Patricia Roc leave their noisy London apartment block and rent a cottage in the country, miles from anywhere. But the sinister owner (Ronald Howard) is not the affable landlord he appears to be. Grieving over the death of his wife, he takes an unhealthy liking to Roc and decides to paint her portrait, submerging his tortured soul in a mournful tune, "Fantasy of Lost Love," which he listens to continuously. Gough grows suspicious over Howard's lies and irrational behavior. Why does he warn the couple about the supposed dangers of walking in the nearby woods when he ventures there? What exactly is buried under a large rock in those woods? Why does the artist insist his wife died several years ago, yet Gough finds a book with an inscription made by Howard's wife only three months ago? Why does he angrily destroy his wife's portrait after Roc's has been completed? Unknown director Maxwell Munden piles on the eerie tension over a space of 62 minutes, discarding the need for an intrusive score. The disclosure surfaces that Howard murdered his wife too soon for her to gain her aunt's inheritance, so now he must kill Roc *and* Gough and pretend to the legislators of the will that Roc was *his* wife, thus maneuvering himself in a position whereby he can lay his hands on the cash. This reveal is adroitly tied up in the hectic climax. It's hard to believe that this long-forgotten B picture came out a year before Hammer's masterful *Dracula*, and that Gough starred in both films. Munden makes excellent use of the cottage's claustrophobic interiors and threatening, isolated setting, and the trio of Gough, Roc and Howard play off each other admirably. This one comes recommended for those with a taste for the unfamiliar.

So inept that it was hardly ever given an airing after its initial release date, Fortress Films' *The Woman Eater*, produced and directed by the same team behind the equally bad *The Man Without a Body*, was a tawdry piece of rubbish, whose one saving grace was Edwin Astley's rowdy score. George Couloris gives a third-rate impersonation of a mad scientist who transports a sacred tree back from the Amazon jungle. When the monster feeds off sacrificial women, it produces a serum that can revive the dead. Stuck in a corner of Couloris' basement laboratory, the carnivorous, multi-armed tree embraces females that the doctor abducts, his native assistant (Jimmy Vaughan) drags them into the tentacle-like branches. Petite blonde Vera Day turns up as an assistant to housekeeper Joyce Gregg; Gregg is the doctor's ex-love, but the doctor lusts after Day. Sick of Gregg's jealousy, he strangles her and then attempts to bring her back to life by injecting her corpse with the serum. She's reactivated as a brain-dead zombie, expiring after a few minutes. In a blind rage that the experiment has failed, Couloris sets fire to the tree and gets a knife in the back for his troubles, thrown by Vaughan. Day flees the house, seeking solace in the arms of local garage owner Peter Wayn.

Seventy-one minutes of pure tedium sums up this insipid picture. Day is playful but dim, the cops live up to their British nickname of "woodentops," as does would-be hero Wayn. Couloris rolls his eyes and leers but is unable to reach the heights set by Lugosi in his mad doctor poverty row epics, and that hairy tree makes Tabanga (*From Hell It Came*) look downright artistic. From the opening scenes of Couloris wading through a fake jungle set to the quickie ending, *The Woman Eater* is one big dud of a horror movie. No wonder U.K. cinemas refused to include it in their "What's on next week" schedules.

1958

A Hammer film in all but name only, Henry Cass' *Blood of the Vampire* is the only color picture in this chapter and, while not as obscure as others mentioned, it warrants inclusion because it is often overlooked in favor of the Hammer productions of the day. Scripted by Jimmy Sangster and produced by Robert S. Baker and Monty Berman for Tempean/Eros (the duo made *The Trollenberg Terror* the previous year), this hefty chunk of British horror, photographed in lurid Eastmancolor, was distributed by Universal-International in America (*Monster on the Campus* was the co-feature), marketed as competition to the Hammer horrors making inroads abroad. The film features a mad

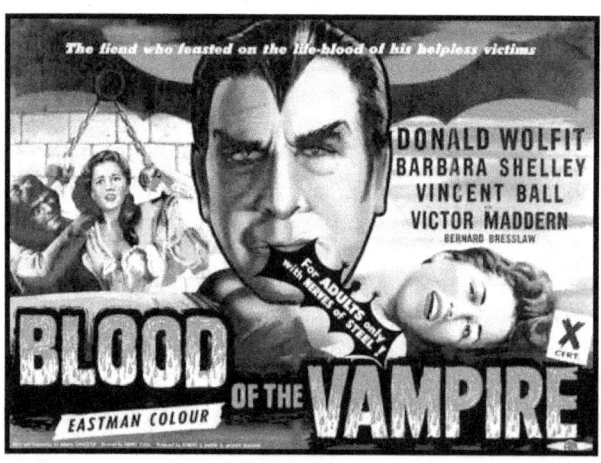

doctor requiring constant blood transfusions (Donald Wolfit in full flow); a hunchback servant (Victor Maddern's career-best role); a luminous Barbara Shelley; torture; gruesome surgical procedures; a bawdy, cleavages-on-display tavern scene; bodies in suspended animation and an asylum for the criminally insane that resembles Castle Dracula. It's little wonder that this popular movie was in circulation for

12 years in England, doubled-billed with either *Behemoth the Sea Monster* or *The Brides of Dracula*. The fans loved every minute of it.

And why was it so popular? Victor Maddern is the answer. The actor's portrayal of Carl, Wolfit's mute assistant, is miraculous. His right eye akin to a fried egg that has slid down his deformed cheek, a bushy mop of hair overhanging maniacal features, left hand a hairy claw, a small hump on his back and shuffling on a twisted right leg, Maddern's English Quasimodo commands the attention and deserves a higher standing in the '50s order of outstanding horror performance. Crafty (like a naughty child), servile and, in the end, disobedient (he falls for Shelley, just as Quasimodo fell for Esmeralda, and refuses to harm her), ever quick to flash his knife to prove a point, Maddern created one of horror's most endearing characters, but one that is made light of today.

Wolfit was just as memorable, resembling a well-fed Bela Lugosi; as expected of a thespian of his stage reputation, he played the part of the unscrupulous Doctor Callistratus with unrestrained gusto. Against the formidable pairing of Maddern and Wolfit, Vincent Ball, on paper, stood little chance to shine as the earnest young medic who exposes the asylum's dark secrets (the actor was fresh from children's TV), but he was respectable enough, and Shelley simply had to walk on set to get the pulses racing. Despite that gory stake-in-the-heart beginning, there are no vampires (a bat is seen briefly when Maddern murders a blackmailing doctor who has given Wolfit a heart transplant); Wolfit suffers from a degeneration of the blood cells and needs constant supplies of the red stuff from the asylum's inmates to keep him alive. He's torn to pieces by the ferocious prison dogs in the closing minutes after Maddern, dying from bullet wounds, unleashes the canines on him.

Blood of the Vampire, sourcing its gallows material from *The Curse of Frankenstein* and *The Black Sleep* among others, is gilt-edged British X-rated Gothic horror. Supposedly a racier version concocted for the Continent and Japan, with additional sequences of female violation, was edited but seldom screened. *Blood of the Vampire*, in retrospect, gives Hammer's better-known fodder a run for its money, both critically and commercially.

Hammer's 64th production, *The Camp on Blood Island*, rang box-office tills at the time despite universal condemnation from the critics. With its accent on sadism and brutality, a heady combination that the public was getting a taste for, the film was a guaranteed success—an "X" certificate Japanese prison camp drama remolded as Hammer horror. Why, then, include it in this chapter? Not screened on British television for 34 years and last appearing in cinemas in the 1960s with *The Revenge of Frankenstein*, this is one Hammer film that resides in a kind of Hammer backwater, regardless of its winning credentials: Val Guest's incisive direction; Jack Asher's sharp black-and-white MegaScope photography; a sterling repertory cast led by André Morell; Gerard Schurmann's military-type score and a grimly realistic air of suffering and degradation. Morell plays a stoical British officer, determined that thuggish Japanese Commander Ronald Radd shouldn't get to hear that the war has ended because, if he does, Morell's compatriots and the inmates of a nearby women's camp will be executed en masse, both camps razed to the ground. Dutchman Carl Mohner is assigned the hazardous task of sabotaging the Jap's radio while the unexpected appearance of motor-mouth American pilot Phil Brown, crash-landing his plane and eager to tell everyone that hostilities have ceased, poses a serious threat to the lives of both men and women held prisoner.

Filmed with pace and a commendable lack of sentimentality, the opening scene of a soldier machine-gunned into a grave he has dug sets the cheerless tone, one that ruffled the censor's feathers at the time; even the original poster was banned as being too "crude and offensive" (ironically, ex-POWs unanimously gave Guest's picture the thumbs-up). Marne Maitland was in his element as a sneering, psychotic martinet and Barbara Shelley (looking far from glamorous) made her first major appearance for the company (she previously had a tiny part in 1953's *Mantrap*). Like a low-budget, X-rated cousin to David Lean's *The Bridge on the River Kwai*, *The Camp on Blood Island* offers enough blood, guts, beheadings, mass executions, atrocities, explosive action and authenticity (all the actors look half-starved; and no subtitles appear for the Japanese dialogue) to appease horror and war fans alike. Why it continues to be ignored, even by a lot of Hammer appreciators, remains a mystery.

By mid-1958, Hammer was well into its stride, beginning to garner an international reputation as producers of top-quality, handsomely mounted horror fare, and in color no less. But there was another side to the company's output: psychological black-and-white drama. Many of Hammer's psychodramas get left behind in the wake of *Dracula*, *The Curse of Frankenstein*, *The Revenge of Frankenstein* and others, but in continuing to produce them, Hammer remained true to its lower-ranked origins. A few caused as much furor among the critics as their colorful cousins had done; in 1960, the X-rated *Never Take Sweets From a Stranger*, dealing with the taboo subject of child molestation, had the British press and censor's office baying in shock horror—how could *any* film company worth their salt stoop so low as to make a motion picture on the public-sensitive issue of pedophilia.

But we digress, necessarily so, to show that Hammer films were never afraid to go where others feared to tread, and that their monochrome suspense thrillers were just as well made, and could be just as controversial, as their Gothic horror counterparts. The company often chose to walk a fine line between seriousness and pure sensation, *The Snorkel* an excellent example of their *modus operandi* from this period, a capital little movie of which many Hammer fans are perhaps unacquainted. It's based on the age-old question: Can man commit the perfect murder? Well, Peter Van Eyck reckons *he* has. Drugging his wife, he places her on a couch, seals windows and doors with tape, turns on the gas lamps, dons a diving mask with twin snorkel outlets, clambers through a trapdoor under the floor, connects a hose from outside air pipes to both outlets and lays in wait. His wife expires, the police are baffled by the crime and a verdict of suicide is entered. But stepdaughter Mandy Miller isn't fooled. She thinks Van Eyck murdered her father on a fishing trip and has done the same thing to her mother. But how was it executed? Spotting a poster in the street showing a diver wearing breathing apparatus, she has a hunch and sets about proving that her wicked stepfather is the man responsible. Van Eyck twigs that the youngster is doggedly on his case and puts into motion plans to kill her in identical circumstances.

Wisely, director Guy Green opted for an analytical approach; the lengthy opening scene showing Van Eyck's meticulous preparations was presented without musical accompaniment, all the more tension-fueled because of it. In fact, Green eschewed an orthodox soundtrack, content to let the actions speak for themselves as Miller, trying vainly to convince the police and guardian Betta St. John of Van Eyck's guilt, goes it alone and, in doing so, nearly loses her life, twice (Van Eyck cold-heartedly poisons

Miller's dog). The payoff sees Miller undergoing the same treatment as her mother; however, the tables are turned on cocky Van Eyck. William Franklyn and St. John burst into the room and save the girl, thinking *she* was committing suicide. On her protestations to the contrary, they search the room for the culprit; a heavy cabinet is yanked away from the wall, trapping Van Eyck below the floorboards. Miller returns for a last look, hears Van Eyck screaming for help and walks off ("Just my silly imagination," she muses). Driving to the airport, Miller's conscience pricks her and she asks Franklyn to stop. Entering the police station, the girl advises

Susan Beaumont and Lee Patterson in *The Spaniard's Curse*

the inspector to visit the villa and look under the carpet in her mother's room. That will prove her theory about Van Eyck.

Attractive Italian Riviera location work (the French and Italian Rivieras were a favorite mainstay for later Hammer thrillers) coupled with a "will he get away with it" plot add up as a suspenseful, stripped-down 90 minutes. Eyck is smoothly sinister while St. John glows with that elusive English blend of femininity and sensuality. As for 15-year-old child star Miller, the critics' opinions were divided; stilted and awkward, or wide-eyed and innocent. In my estimation, her performance is a bit of one, a bit of the other.

Another long-lost '50s British rarity is Wentworth Films' *The Spaniard's Curse*, which turned up occasionally on the U.K. horror circuits in the early 1960s, rated "X" or "A" depending on which area of England it was being presented. Director Ralph Kemplen commenced with a touch of the mystical: A man (Basil Dignam), wrongly convicted of murdering a woman during a burglary, invokes a 15th-century Spanish curse (The Assize of the Dying) on the judge, court officials and jury, condemning them to death. Before Dignam is hung, he dies from a heart attack. When the foreman of the jury is run over and killed, Susan Beaumont (the judge, Michael Hordern, is her guardian) thinks the curse has come home to roost because the accused criminal was innocent all along. Hordern's son, preening reporter Tony Wright, thinks so too, as does the dead woman's half-brother, Lee Patterson. All three set out to discover who the real culprit was; in changing tack, Kemplen's tantalizing premise of supernatural reprisal re-tailors itself as a psychological whodunit centered around missing jewelry, a shady pickpocket and Hordern's friend Ralph Truman, who was having a fling with the pianist up to the time she was murdered. The real killer turns out to be the narcissistic Wright. He married the pianist during the war, left her over her incessant demands for a family title and then strangled her after she refused to finance his lifestyle. To cover his tracks, Wright callously shoots Truman and Hordern dead to prevent them talking to the police. The movie ends with the psycho having a change of heart and confessing the crimes to his editor, another scoop for the newspaper.

A 72-minute program filler it might well be, but *The Spaniard's Curse*, blessed with fine cinematography by Arthur Grant (he worked with Terence Fisher on a few early Hammer classics) and good all-round performances, is no better or worse than many other British dramas of the day. It's a hard-to-find curiosity that collectors of the unusual will appreciate.

1959

The Danziger Brothers (Harry Lee Danziger and Edward J. Danziger) continued turning out brisk little assembly-line B thrillers up to the end of the '50s, the 65-minute A-rated *The Child and the Killer* being one of the least known. Directed by Max Varnel and scripted by Brian Clemens, who cut his teeth on stuff like this before going on to write a slew of classic television crime actioners over the next two decades including *The Avengers*. *The Child and the Killer* presented a gray England where children as young as seven were allowed to run free and were punished with a sharp slap if they misbehaved. Patricia Driscoll is a young widow being romanced by American army captain Robert Arden (reprising his role from *The Depraved*). Her cowboy-mad son Richard Williams befriends an escaped psychopathic soldier (Rod Steiger look-alike Ryck Rydon) who has gunned down an officer at the nearby military base, the killer hiding out in a dilapidated house. Obsessed with the Wild West, the kid is under the impression that the handcuffed Rydon is a real life outlaw who can introduce him to Jesse James if he does what's asked of him. The moronic deserter bullies Williams into helping him evade the police, ordering the youngster to ferry food, clothing and a file to the house without letting his mother know what is up. On his own initiative, Williams also steals Arden's gun. Eventually breaking free of his cuffs, Rydon drags the protesting boy over to Driscoll's house where she's brutalized and sexually assaulted before Arden bursts in and shoots the schizoid dead.

The relationship between innocent child and violent criminal has been explored in many films, very few possessing the gritty edge that Varnel gives it here. Rydon's hulking savagery plays off wonderfully against Williams' blonde gullibility, Albert Elms' score switching from jazzy to cutesy to strident at the drop of a hat to match the mood. Directed at a furious pace, *The Child and the Killer*, at present almost impossible to come by, should form part of a package devoted to the digital restoration of all of Danziger Brothers' '50s *noir* thrillers. At the time, these formed an essential component of the British film industry; they must not be allowed to fade from sight.

Butcher's Film Distributors was an independent producer of small-budget films formed in the 1930s, grinding out (much like Danziger) one hour-plus potboilers at the rate of four to five titles a year to fulfill the need for second features on the Odeon and ABC circuits. Terry Bishop, who made a name in television by directing the *William Tell* and *The Adventures of Robin Hood* serials, was responsible for two of Butcher's best efforts, *Cover Girl Killer* and *Life in Danger*. Both dealt with psychopathic killers, coming in at 62 minutes, and each showed that Bishop's talent was undoubtedly wasted on the small screen. *Life in Danger* was classed as a B release, but *Cover Girl Killer*, Butcher's finest '50s hour, was promoted to A status and given an "X" rating by the censors.

Several years before he found immortality as Harold Steptoe in TV's *Steptoe and Son*, Harry H. Corbett donned pebble-lens glasses, wore a slicked-down toupee and joined the dirty raincoat brigade, leering at provocative photographs of indecently dressed showgirls in Soho's seedy backstreet district. The sexually frustrated weirdo targets young women who have appeared half-naked on the front cover of *Wow!* glamour rag; he arranges appointments with them on the bogus pretext that he's a noted film producer and pumps their bodies full of morphine, leaving the bikini-clad corpses in poses similar to those displayed on the lurid magazine covers. Spencer Teakle, owner of *Wow!*, joins forces with the police (led by Victor Brooks) and, after four murders, reluctantly agrees to use girlfriend Felicity Young as bait. She models for cover number five but wily Corbett, using smoke and mirrors tactics, latches on to the fact that the cops are close to catching him. He sends an out-of-work actor to meet Young and the man is arrested, but in steps Corbett to finish off the girl just as Teakle

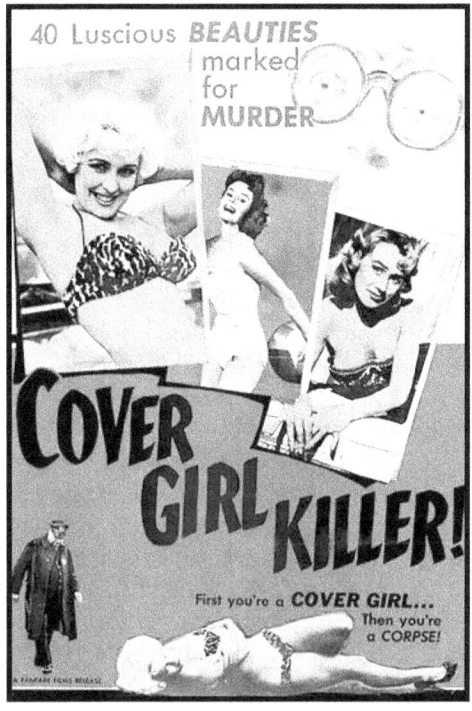

and the police arrive at the Kasbah Club in the nick-of-time and, after a struggle, the maniac falls to his death from a stage gantry.

Don't expect glossy Hitchcockian suspense or any kind of psychoanalytical babble in *Cover Girl Killer*; Butcher's didn't have the budget for such luxuries. What they did have was an awareness of tempo and determination, Bishop capturing the seamy side of London's notorious striptease joints with unerring accuracy. Corbett is a revelation; not really known for his serious roles, he is creepiness personified as the sweating, goggle-eyed lunatic. The moment when he approaches the camera resolutely, about to strangle screaming Christina Gregg, makes the flesh crawl. A variation on Michael Powell's *Peeping Tom*, Butcher's neat little psycho chiller is a far cry from today's graphic serial killer flicks but all the more grittily realistic for it.

Life in Danger, shot in rural locations, starred Derren Nesbitt as a suspected child murderer on the run after escaping from Parkway Asylum. He hides in a barn, befriended by a flighty teenager (Julie Hopkins) who takes a lustful shine to him. As the villagers arm themselves with farm implements and surround the hideout, paranoia, prejudices and lynch-mob mentality rise to the surface, revealing darkly unpleasant sides to their natures. The revelatory climax, whereby Nesbitt, shot and wounded, turns out to be an unemployed laborer (the real killer has surrendered), is handled with aplomb by director Bishop in a cut-price take on Hitchcock's *The Wrong Man*, where the innocent is thought guilty through the vagaries of fate.

American producer Herman Cohen came to England in 1959 to oversee two projects: *Horrors of the Black Museum* and *The Headless Ghost*. Both movies were released as a double-bill in America: The first is deservedly stuck with the status of being a forerunner to the cycle of sadistic slasher movies that emerged from the 1970s onward; the second has sunk without trace. Independent outfit Merton Park Studios was responsible for *The Headless Ghost*, an innocuous haunted castle comedy scotched by woeful miscasting: The three main characters, Americans David Rose and Richard Lyon, plus Scandinavian Liliane Sottane, patently lack screen presence and acting know-how, dragging the production down into stupidity. Filmed at Allington Castle in Kent, the threesome play tourists who decide to spend the night in Jack Allen's Gothic pile as a dare. Ghost Clive Revill appears, charging them with the task of locating a secret chamber containing a mystical pouch. When the pouch is thrown at the portrait of an ancestor beheaded 600 years ago, the head will join with the body and the Castle's disturbed spirits, all in a state of limbo, will be able to rest in peace.

A clutch of popular '50s British comedians would have been in their element with this kind of scaredy-cat material—Frankie Howard, Charlie Drake, Norman Wisdom and Bob Monkhouse each possessed the requisite comedic forte to turn Peter Graham Scott's 61-minute co-feature into a rollicking farce, but Rose, Lyon and Sottane didn't, looking completely out of their depth and thereby contributing to the film's poor standing. Despite the "U" certificate, the picture included a suggestive belly dancer scene and Scott threw in a couple of jumpy incidents (the floating head connecting to its body) that probably induced the odd shudder in younger children. One question remains. Just *how* did the trio manage to waltz into the castle after the coach party had departed and the doors were securely locked? Shot in DyaliScope, containing a blaring Gerard Schurmann score that was totally inappropriate and completely at odds with the juvenile pranks taking place (his similar piece on *Horrors of the Black Museum* was, however, befitting), *The Headless Ghost* would have been a real crowd-pleaser as an Ealing situation comedy taken on by a company of seasoned eccentrics. In casting the central roles with three non-English actors to aim for the overseas teen market, Cohen and his team torpedoed the English ambience required to pull off the slight, very British, story. Allington Castle was undoubtedly the star of this show. A clear-cut case here of "what might have been…"

The producing/directing team of Robert S. Baker and Monty Berman, fresh from their success with *Blood of the Vampire* and intent on usurping Hammer's supremacy abroad, turned their attentions to England's greatest unsolved murder case in *Jack the Ripper*. Low-budget or not, this version of the notorious serial killer's grisly exploits pressed all the right buttons: murky but effective photography, highlighting the foggy, cobbled Whitechapel alleyways; salacious murders; sharply directed with an eye for detail and a strong cast. With a raucous soundtrack and "X certificate-Adults Only" emblazoned across the lurid posters, the public responded in droves, and this Mid Century picture, distributed by Paramount, was an unexpected box-office success.

Two Americans, Eddie Byrne and Lee Patterson, were brought in to play detectives hunting the killer. Patterson looked as though he had just stepped out of a jive joint (this *was* supposed to be London in 1888), but the producers were banking on his sex appeal to boost their product on the overseas market. In a familiar storyline, John Le Mesurier was a haughty surgeon working in the Mercy Hospital for Women, as was excitable Ewen Solon. Which of the two was responsible for the stabbings and mutilations of down-and-out women, preceded by the words asked of them by the killer, "Are you Mary Clarke?" It turns out to be Solon; his mind affected by venereal disease, he blames prostitutes for his complaint and has decided to rid the streets of them. More or less found out at the end, he's crushed to death in an elevator shaft, the screen igniting into color for all of five seconds.

Baker and Berman had Victor Maddern playing a memorable hunchback in *Blood of the Vampire*; here, the duo saw fit to include another hunchback, Endre Muller, Le Mesurier's disfigured assistant, mistaken for the Ripper midway through. Muller's one-dimensional hunchback lacked finesse and is hardly thought of today, but the part suited a production that, although rough around the edges, stands up with the best of all the cinematic variations on this macabre chapter in English criminal history. This grim little shocker held on to its popularity well into the late 1960s, going the rounds on a double bill with Lugosi's *The Return of the Vampire*.

Endre Muller played the disfigured red-herring in *Jack the Ripper*.

Two Hammer films released in 1959, *The Stranglers of Bombay* and *The Ugly Duckling*, couldn't be more far apart in content, yet they have one thing in common—like *The Camp on Blood Island*, they remain overshadowed by the Technicolor pomp of *The Revenge of Frankenstein*, *The Hound of the Baskervilles*, *The Man Who Could Cheat Death* and *The Mummy*, released around this period. Terence Fisher, in the period of his greatest success, directed *The Stranglers of Bombay,* which caused quite a bit of fuss and bother (reported in the press) when it first appeared. Originally earmarked for an "X" certificate, the censor demanded cuts, notably in the scenes involving busty Marie Devereaux gloating orgasmically at the sight of two men having their eyes and tongues ripped out and leering over spread-eagled Guy Rolfe, at the mercy of a cobra (from Mondo Exploito.com). Even trimmed of these lascivious moments, the papers bayed in disgust when the film went on general release as an "A," Fisher milking the inherent violence and sadism in Indian culture for all it was worth. "Vicious and nasty," wrote one snooty reviewer, voicing the opinions of many critics who were not in the mood to be kindly disposed toward the director's overripe colonial horror show

Taking place in the 1820s, Rolfe played an officer determined to bring to ground the Thuggee cult, worshipers of Kali who waylaid caravans, strangled their victims and buried the bodies in mass graves. Class snobbery within the armed forces was represented by Allan Cuthbertson and Andrew Cruickshank, both stubbornly stonewalling Rolfe's desire to end the cult's reign because of their own selfish ambitions. George Pastell chewed the scenery as the cult's fanatical religious leader, Jan Holden was the token wife and slimy Marne Maitland was just as evil as he was in *The Camp on Blood*

Island. Hammer horror dressed up as period drama, capitalizing on the subject's intrinsic shock value—with a list of atrocities as long as your arm. It's very hard to believe, even today, how this one Hammer production, out of all the others released around this time, escaped the "X" classification. Because of the controversy surrounding the film and its subject material, *The Stranglers of Bombay* is dissimilar in many ways to what the public was getting used to from this fertile period in the studio's history, due in part to the non-appearance of Cushing and Lee and the fact that it wasn't in color. Fisher piles on the grit and gristle (a severed hand, decomposing corpses, mutilations, a hanging, stomachs slit open, strangulations, hot irons gouging out eyes and tongues) to the sound of James Bernard's walloping bang/crash music, and the MegaScope photography by Arthur Grant is black-and-white clarity itself. Having seen the original movie at the cinema in November 1960 and January 1965, I can confidently state that current DVD releases contain the edited version. One day, perhaps, the uncut print will be available to all Hammer fans.

Hammer's comic take on the Jekyll/Hyde fable, *The Ugly Duckling* (1959), starred TV-regular Bernard Bresslaw as the buffoonish Henry Jekyll. A social misfit working as a pharmacist in a chemist's shop, Bresslaw concocts a potion that turns him into urbane Teddy Hyde, the master criminal behind a gang of crooks. Directed by Lance Comfort and boasting a splendid British cast (Jon Pertwee, Richard Wattis, David Lodge and Michael Ripper), this must count as one of Hammer's hardest-to-find features, unavailable, as I write, on tape or disc. Hammer allied to comedy didn't really work in the eyes of their fans, perhaps one of the reasons why *The Ugly Duckling* remains so elusive and has never been up for consideration as a picture worthy of a digital makeover. The same can be said for the majority of the films mentioned in this chapter.

Chapter 26
From Around the World

America and Britain were not the sole provenance for horror, science fiction and fantasy movies during the 1950s. Other countries in various parts of the globe were coming up with the goodies, albeit in markedly different guises to their U.S. and U.K. source references. Granted, the pictures in question, by and large, were more inscrutable than your average feature, interpreted as custom-made for a highbrow clientele by mainstream buffs. Moreover, they were not the result of conveyor belt production, being one-offs, crafted (in most cases) with artistic care and attention, reflecting a particular country's ethnic cinematic tastes and not conforming to the norm. Rarely, if ever, presented to Western audiences (unless it was a film convention or art-house venue), the likes of *Valkoinen Peura* (Finland), *El Crimen de Oribe* (Argentina) and *La Corona Negra* (Spain) are first-class examples of non-American, non-British horror and fantasy, another little-known component added to the '50s rich fantasy fabric. In choosing a selection of pictures from such far-flung places as Russia, Italy, Czechoslovakia, Norway and Austria (including a couple of joint collaborations), I hope to illustrate just how unconventional foreign moviemakers could be in their methods of bringing the fantasy genre to the silver screen in their native homelands. Japan is included because there was another side to the Japanese horror industry other than Toho's output. Let's see what the foreign film industry contributed to the '50s fantasy scene, however small that contribution was.

***Arzt Ohne Gewissen: Privatklinik Prof. Lund* (*Physician Without Conscience*)**
Divina/Gloria Films 1959; West Germany; 94 minutes; Director: Falk Harnack

The Italians, the French and the Spanish were not alone in spearheading the new wave of medical horror movies throughout Europe—the Germans were pushing back the boundaries of unethical surgery in a few critical productions of their own. The '50s highpoint of West German cinema in this field is probably *Die Nackte und der Satan* (*The Head*), Joseph Green's *The Brain that Wouldn't Die* being its less effective (but more enjoyable) U.S. counterpart. Both were made in 1959, the same year that Harnack's seminal chiller touching on the "off limits" subject of illegal heart transplants caused a scandal in its home country when first shown. As is the general norm in Latin cinema, *Arzt Ohne Gewissen* was blessed with stark black-and-white photography and a cold, clinical precision not usually found in American movies of the same nature. Baroque vaulted sets, acting from the school of neo-realism and a magisterial, Handel-type title score from Siegfried Franz rounded off a deeply satisfying, seldom-seen European surgical horror opus overshadowed (as so many were) by Franju's *Eyes without a Face*, the classic film of its type to emerge from the Continent.

Ewald Balser stars as a modern-day Frankenstein (Professor Lund), abducting prostitutes and removing their hearts, which are kept in his castle laboratory, beating merrily away in fluid-filled tanks attached to innovative equipment, to be given to those deserving (in his eyes) of a transplant. The women's corpses are dumped in a nearby swamp. The film opens with Balser's sumptuous funeral, the story told in flashback by Wolfgang Preiss, Balser's conscience (mirroring the fractious Robert Urquhart/

Peter Cushing relationship in *The Curse of Frankenstein*); he's a noted doctor escorted to the professor's rambling old castle to help out with transplant operations. Alarmed at Balser's twisted ideals, he vehemently argues over the ethics involved in obtaining organs from unsuspecting donors. A third viciously callous practitioner is also in on the act, crippled ex-Nazi torturer Wolfgang Kieling (playing a Doctor Stein!), wanted by the police for questioning in connection with several missing prostitutes. A famous singer (Cornell Borchers), desperately ill from a failing heart, is due for a transplant, Balser's criminal assistant having procured a young prostitute for that purpose. The mad doctor is also in love with the woman. The whole corrupt enterprise falls apart when one of the professor's heart recipients escapes from his room. Making his way to town, the poor man staggers into a marketplace and promptly drops dead in a police station from a heart attack. The investigating officers soon arrive at the castle; unable to cope with the infamy that will be heaped upon him should his activities be exposed, Balser swallows a cyanide tablet. Kieling hobbles off into the surrounding marshes with his pet dog (the only thing he loves) and sinks in a quagmire.

For connoisseurs of little-known European Gothic cinema, *Arzt Ohne Gewissen*, overlooked in favor of *I Vampiri*, *Eyes Without a Face* and, later, *The Awful Doctor Orlof*, makes for essential viewing. It's far more worthy of our attention than the more familiar but somewhat overblown *Die Nackte und der Satan*. Echoes of the German expressionistic movement that manifested itself in bygone classics (1919's *The Cabinet of Dr. Caligari* is the template) can be spotted in Harnack's artful approach to his subject: the play of light and shade in the interior shots; the air of frigid bleakness and the claustrophobic castle vaults. Unembellished with extraneous trappings, the movie is a brave (for the time) fusion of practical science, sadism and voyeurism (the film includes one semi-nude shot), the cinematic equivalent of a cold shower after feasting on one-too-many glossy color pictures from Britain and the States. The current (2012) DVD release doesn't have English subtitles, so here's a great opportunity to brush up on your German while reveling in a classy piece of Euro medical horror.

***Ch'ien-nu Yu-Hin** (Enchanting Shadow)*
Shaw Brothers 1959; China; 85 minutes; Director: Li Han-hsiang

If ever the word "beautiful" can be used to describe a horror film, then that word perfectly sums up Shaw Brothers' bewitching account of a haunted temple, shot in divine, saturated colors by Ho Lu-ying that are a feast for the eye. Based on a tale taken from Song-Ling Pu's 17th-century anthology of 400 short ghost stories, *Strange Stories from a Chinese Studio*, the Shaw Hong Kong studios constructed an architectural set worthy of any early

Hammer film, a Byzantine pagoda fallen into ruins where travelers are able to spend the night if they choose to disregard its reputation of being haunted. A young scholar (Chao Lei) stops in the temple's South Lodge for two nights, his only companion a hermit (Yang Chih-ching) who has lived there for years. Venturing out into the overgrown courtyard during the misty early hours, he hears strange music; stepping through the ornate portals of an ancient doorway, Lei is greeted by the sight of a gloriously lit East Lodge. There, young Betty Loh Ti is seated, painting on scrolls, three older women playing cards nearby. Lei introduces himself to the ravishing girl but in doing so triggers off a series of alarming events. This lodge (as he later discovers) is also in ruins, reeking of death and decay. Loh Ti died of a sickness 10 years ago and her evil grandmother's phantom (Tong Jo-ching) encourages the girl's spirit to lure passing visitors into having sex so that she can murder them and drink their blood ("Granny intends to take your life," says Loh Ti to a bemused Lei. "I seduce people so that she can suck up the blood."). Lei is Loh Ti's next target but she falls in love with him, leaving Jo-ching in a blind fury, determined that the scholar will not be the one person to escape her spectral clutches.

Set to Yao Min's chilling soundtrack, ranging from traditional Mandarin to idiosyncratic continental and including a doom-laden *Pit and the Pendulum*–type undercurrent, *Ch'ien-nu Yu-Hin* is classical Chinese horror, slow-moving, carefully thought out, every scene bathed in deep, inky colors and constructed for maximum impact. Sound effects play an important part in creating the right mood, bells tinkling and birds screeching, heralding the arrival of the ghosts. Loh Ti's radiant presence lights up the screen, given added poignancy by the fact that her lost spirit yearns to be freed from her grandmother's curse, imploring Lei to help her find eternal peace. The climax in the forest is straight out of a Grimm's fairy tale. Having dug up Loh Ti's remains for reburial, Lei and the girl are chased by Jo-ching, but the witch is vanquished when the hermit hurls a magical sword into her back. She crumbles into a skeleton just as the cock crows, a sound that, since time immemorial, signifies the death of an evil spirit. Lei, having unknowingly been killed by the witch, is reunited with Loh Ti in the spirit world.

Mixing romance, horror and the supernatural with a degree of artistry very rarely encountered in fantasy cinema from the West, Shaw Brothers' Far Eastern opera–like ghost story is a reminder that this kind of fare *could* be found outside of America, England and the Continent; Li Han-hsiang's movie proves it. As enchanting as its title suggests, this is an outright Oriental winner that lingers long in the mind.

***Cisaruv pekar—Pekaruv cisar** (The Emperor's Baker; The Baker's Emperor; Return of the Golem)*
Czechoslovensky Film 1951; Czechoslovakia; 150 minutes; Director: Martin Fric

The Golem first appeared on the silver screen in 1914, scriptwriter Paul Wegener remaking the film in 1920 in what many critics regard as the definitive telling of the Eastern European legend. A huge automaton made of clay is brought to life by a 16th-century Jewish alchemist in Prague to save the people from repression. Wegener's masterful Germanic picture influenced the *Frankenstein* movies of the next decade and remains an essential piece of silent cinema to this day.

Martin Fric's Czech version came in two parts: The first, *Cisaruv pekar*, ran for 84 minutes; the second, *Pekaruv cisar*, for 66 minutes. Photographed in bright-as-a-button colors by Jan Stallich, Fric's semi-comic fantasy (it even includes a musical interlude) took in astrology, alchemy, politics, sexual dalliance, court subterfuges and the mighty Golem itself, entwining its intricate plot threads into a sometimes perplexing whole. Producer/cowriter Jan Werich played the principal role of Rudolf the Second, a cantankerous emperor obsessed with eternal youth, women and seeking the whereabouts of the Golem. As the buffoon conducts a series of calamitous meetings with his cronies in Prague Castle, a baker (Werich again) gets thrown into a dungeon for daring to give bread to the needy. The baker also resembles Rudolf, so a case of swapped identities rears its head in the film's second half as the baker, through a series of bizarre occurrences, takes on the mantle of the emperor, falling in love with an "artificial woman" (Natasa Gollova) created by the devious alchemist Jiri Plachy, a conspirator who, with others, plans to overthrow the court of Rudolf.

What about the Golem? It's discovered in an underground crypt and only really comes into its own in the end scenes when the baker places the shem (or force) into the head in order to give life to that massive body. Designer Jan Zazvorka's 12-foot mechanical/robotic model has eyes like glowing red coals, smoke billowing from the eye-sockets as the hulk crashes through walls and lumbers after the emperor's fleeing subjects and enemies ("Don't mess with the Golem or you'll pay for it," Werich warns the crowds). It's a fabulous, almost overpowering creation, all the more so when you consider how long ago the movie was made; what a pity Fric didn't feature it in more sequences.

As in Wegener's 1920 esoteric classic, the Golem becomes a champion of the poor who wish to live in peace, even though its unbounded natural energy can be harnessed for evil intent. In a joyous climax, it supplies the bakery with enough heat to produce hundreds of bread rolls for the impoverished, starving locals. In this respect, Fric's film can be viewed as a thinly disguised political allegory about the potential dangers of tampering with nuclear power at the moral expense of the less fortunate among us. Or it can simply be enjoyed as a very colorful period romp (the production values are absolutely superb) with a phenomenal mechanical monster thrown into the bargain. Either way, the director's flamboyant adaptation of the Golem fable, which belies its age on repeated viewings, is a richly rewarding, multi-layered experience for lovers of exotic, and very different, foreign cinema.

La Corona Negra (The Black Crown)
Suevia Films 1950; Spain; 105 minutes; Director: Luis Saslavsky

Adapted from a story by Jean Cocteau, Argentinian director Luis Saslavsky's tortuous drama concerns an adulteress descending into madness and will appeal to those movie lovers who are not afraid of challenging, thought-provoking cinema requiring 100% concentration. Filled to the brim with ambiguities, where one begins to doubt his or her own eyes, the movie begins in surreal fashion, reminiscent of an Ingmar Bergman masterwork—a woman on horseback, dressed in black, rides over a harsh, windswept desert landscape, groping arms appearing out of the sand, a skeletal corpse riding toward her. Then when she wakes as if from a dream, the woman (Maria Félix) is seated in a bar, recently widowed. Befriended by handsome engineer Rosanno Brazzi, Félix suffers from sporadic loss of memory, acute anxiety and hallucinatory flashbacks. Did she stab her bullying husband to death with scissors following a row over her affair with hot-headed Vittorio Gassman? Or did Gassman commit the deed when the three of them had a confrontation? Gassman arrives on the scene with a dwarf helper (Piéral), the duo seeking the dead man's jewels. Félix claims they were buried with her husband inside his coffin. The police suspect Gassman of the killing; he, in turn, is insanely jealous of Félix's relationship with Brazzi. In a showdown at a mine, the two men fight it out and Brazzi is shot dead, his corpse draped across a horse that trots toward the villa where Félix is staying. On seeing the battered, bloodied body of her new lover, she screams and goes mad, flocks of screeching birds hovering overhead.

It all sounds straightforward, but it isn't. The narrative is repeatedly punctuated with symbolic images: squawking ravens wheeling in the sky, their circular formation the black crown of the title; vultures feeding off a corpse; scissors the dominant motif; blood dripping from a lifeless hand; tarot cards foretelling death and the black-clad widow pursued by the evil dwarf through a gleaming white

cemetery. Has Félix been crazy all along (she's constantly shadowed by two nuns who have to subdue her on occasions)? As if things weren't complicated enough, the film, midway through, jumps from one location to another with little in the way of continuity, the same characters appearing in these different settings without rhyme or reason.

Viewed logically, what *La Corona Negra* appears to be all about is guilt and how this corrosive emotion can warp one's personality. It's a complex interweaving of *noir*, horror and the semi-supernatural, held together by a great cast. Brazzi and Gassman were giants in European cinema but the plaudits must go to titan-haired Mexican diva Félix. Looking like Rita Hayworth in her prime, this voluptuous screen goddess has enough lust appeal to inflame the passions of most men (apparently, her private life was as lurid as her role in this picture). Shot in the neo-realist manner that highlighted Spanish/Italian cinema from 1950 onward (the stark photography by Antonio Lopez Ballesteros and Valentin Javier is superb), *La Corona Negra* (as at 2012) is far from easy to pick up on DVD, even from specialists (and it won't be subtitled either). It should form an essential part in any fan's collection of hard-to-come-by European horror; hopefully, one day, the film may surface as an official release.

El Crimen de Oribe (*The Crime of Oribe*)
Estudios Mapol 1950; Argentina; 84 minutes; Directors: Leopoldo Torres Rios/Leopoldo Torre Nilsson

A mysterious house stands alone in a dark wood, occupied by a widower and his three vivacious daughters. Each night, the family re-enact Christmas Eve, lighting candles, going through the same motions, singing "Silent Night" and arranging figurines in set positions. By doing so, Raul De Lange can halt the passage of time; his fourth daughter (Maria Concepcion César) was cruelly afflicted with an incurable disease and tragically died from a heart attack one Christmas Day. Only by performing this daily ritual can the grieving father prevent his daughter from dying, thus keeping her presence in the house, as though she still lives.

El Crimen de Oribe is a superbly constructed obscurity dating back to the early years of Argentine horror cinema, combining fantasy, romance, the supernatural and sinful deeds into an entrancing whole. Oribe is an arrogant, narcissistic poet, played with haughty indifference by Carlos

Thompson. He meets journalist Roberto Escalada one night in an hotel where the reporter relates that following the breakdown of his car on a lonely road, he was taken to a strange house by a passerby and through high gates watched an elderly man and three girls place lighted candles on a Christmas tree. Intrigued, the poet accompanies the journalist to the house but they cannot gain entrance through the gates or draw anyone's attention. Escalada later discovers that the widower cannot abide visitors and will go to great lengths to deter them, so he returns on his own and tells the poet of a peculiar series of events. He managed to sneak in through the gates, entered the house, went upstairs and saw the family ritual taking place around the tree; as the clock struck midnight, a fourth daughter appeared, looking wan and distressed. Her sisters fussed over her, she played the piano and a crucifix was placed around her neck. Suddenly, she spotted him looking at her in the semi-darkness. Alarmed, the girl flew upstairs and laid down on her bed. In that brief instant, he fell in love with her and that love was returned. Escalada then states that he remembers nothing more and woke up in his own hotel bedroom.

The following morning, the police go to the house as César has been found dead. However, the perplexed doctor claims he issued the girl's death certificate over a year ago and it should have been signed on that Christmas Day. This mystery without a logical solution fascinates Thompson so much that he decides to write a poem about it, embellishing the details to make it appear that it was he who broke into the house, knew César and fell in love with her, boastfully presenting the experience as his own, not Escalada's. But in his quest for fame, he pays the ultimate price for his deceitful "crime." De Lange blames the intruder for breaking the cycle of the spell he carried out to preserve his daughter's presence, precipitating her death. Thompson's published poem points the finger at *him* being the intruder, not the journalist. In sweaty fear of his life, the poet finds himself hunted by a man in black carrying a parcel; running from a train, he calls Escalada from a subway station but is shot in the back by the hunter who turns out to be De Lange. The final moving moments show the old widower lighting candles in memory of his lost daughter before being led away by the police.

Unfortunately, decent prints of this poetically dark fantasy haven't survived the years; a faded, ragged version in Spanish is all that's available today and fails to do the film justice. Direction, cinematography, editing, script and music are faultless, as are the performances, especially César who brings pathos to every scene she's in as the girl trapped in a twilight existence. And the moral? Do *not* interfere with unknown forces and capitalize on others to feather your own nest. What *El Crimen de Oribe* needs, to erase the decades of neglect, is a digital restoration job (to include subtitles), enabling fans of the hard-to-trace to view this hauntingly beautiful masterpiece in all its former glory. Perhaps one day…

De dodes tjern (*Lake of the Dead*)
Norsk Film 1958; Norway; 76 minutes; Director: Kare Bergstrom

Never have dense woodlands containing a lake appeared so menacing than in Kare Bergstrom's chilling ghost/murder tale, shot in widescreen (AgaScope) and crisp black-and-white. Not given a wide showing outside its native country, this Norwegian spookfest benefits from eerie location work and Gunnar Sonstevold's ominous score. Writer Henki Kolstad tells the events of the story in flashback. Kolstad and five friends travel to an isolated 100-year-old cabin standing in woods, near which is the reputedly haunted Blue Lake. The director gives us a lot to think about in the opening minutes: Henny Moan's brother (Per Lillo-Stenberg) isn't at the cabin to greet them when they arrive; the pair are twins and share a telepathic bond (and an incestuous one, as it turns out) and the sister claims that something has happened to her brother, something connected with the cabin's past history.

Years back, a man killed his sister and her lover with an axe, threw their bodies into the lake and jumped in after them. People who visit the cabin are haunted by the killer's evil spirit and drowned in the lake, the ghost luring them to a watery grave. When Moan starts having dreams about her missing brother and is seen sleepwalking by the lake's edge, psychiatrist-cum-hypnotist Erling Lindahl gets in on the act, stating that "Science doesn't believe in goblins," and that there is a rational explanation to all of this. But Georg Richter, who was having a fling with Moan, falls into the lake and is fished out, dead from fright. Lindahl's beliefs are shaken to the core and he decides, with Kolstad, to uncover the truth behind the supposed visitations from the one-legged specter by staging a trap; Kolstad's wife, Bjorg Engh, standing in for the neurotic Moan, floats down to the lake at night in a white gown in order to flush out the real perpetrator of these inexplicable acts.

Bjorg Engh floats down to the lake at night in a white gown to attract the killer, from *De dodes tjern*.

Like *Psycho* and other psychological thrillers that felt the need to put forward a clarification of events in their final wrapping up, *De dodes tjern* offers the same deal, but in guarded tones. A sub-Freudian text spouted by Lindahl purports that Moan was in love with Lillo-Stenberg *and* Richter; when the jealous brother found out about Richter, he faked his disappearance, pretended to be the peg-legged ghost, murdered his rival and drowned himself in the lake, therefore subconsciously mimicking the previous tragedy. However, the final shot of Kolstad holding the feather of a one-legged crow, the specter's familiar, indicates that, despite the psychiatrist's biased reasoning, a vengeful ghost might be inhabiting these woods after all! And on that tempting note ends a very satisfactory supernatural outing that shows how a gripping ghost film should be made—with care, attention and an eye for muted, but effective, shocks.

El Hombre y el Monstruo (*The Man and the Monster*)
Cinematografica ABSA 1958; Mexico; 78 minutes; Director: Rafael Baledon

Borrowing judiciously from *Dr. Jekyll and Mr. Hyde*, *The Phantom of the Opera*, *Beauty and the Beast* and *The Wolf Man*, this handsomely photographed film is up there among the best of the Mexican horror movies dating from the 1950s. It's more straightforward in approach, less in the way of camp histrionics. Art replaces science as the catalyst that causes pianist Enrique Rambal to transform into a cross between Mr.

Hyde and a werewolf. The reason for this transformation unravels over the opening 25 minutes and requires a viewer's undivided attention, even with subtitles.

A woman crashes her car into a tree; she knocks on the door of a nearby house and is savaged to death by something or someone. Concert organizer Abel Salazar appears on the scene and we are now inside the old house, where a strange story unfolds. At a piano recital he attended some time ago, Rambal, whose mother (Ofelia Guilmain) was a famous pianist, heard a stunning piece performed by Martha Roth from an ancient transcript. Envious of Roth's talents on the keyboards, he invoked the dark powers, slashed her across the neck with scissors and interred her mummified body in a niche inside his house. But by committing murder, Rambal entered into an unholy pact and has to pay a terrible price; when he plays the enchanting opus, he changes into a hairy beast-man ("You sold your soul to the Devil," screams his mother on seeing her son morph into a monster). Only the comforting touch of his mother's hand can contain the beast and return him to normality. To atone for the heinous crime, Rambal trains a beautiful young pianist (again played by Roth) to be a top soloist, although he soon becomes jealous of her prowess. He wants to be "the best piano player in the world," and his protégé isn't going to stand in his way.

Salazer becomes involved in Rambal's terrible secret when he steals into the house and takes the musical parchment from the mummified corpse's hand. Rambal, as the wolf man lusting for blood, goes berserk and embarks on a rampage, tracking Salazer down to his lodgings; the monster slays a young girl, fights the concert promoter and terrorizes Roth in her bedroom before his doting mother restores him to normality. The final 10 minutes takes place at a concert. Roth is playing Tchaikovsky's *Piano Concerto No. 2*, with Rambal conducting the orchestra. Five minutes into the concerto, Roth forgets Tchaikovsky, drifts into a semi-trance and starts to play the forbidden composition. In front of the horrified audience, Rambal becomes the wolf man, hurling himself at the bewildered pianist and attacking Salazar before the police shoot him dead. Guilmain cradles her son's body in her arms and, through her touch, his human features return; the parchment containing the musical notations disintegrates in flames.

It's easy to imagine that *El Hombre y el Monstruo* originated from the Continent, such is its flamboyant use of light and shade. Raul Martinez Solares' brilliant black-and-white cinematography is diamond-hard, while Rafael Baledon directs with touches of Gothic horror sourced from the classics of yesteryear: vaulted, gloomy interiors; grand set pieces; a vase of flowers withering at the touch of a clawed hand; the monster infatuated with a young, desirable girl; a mummified corpse; admirable transformation scenes and a melodramatic soundtrack by Gustavo Carrion. Guilmain carries off the acting honors, playing a possessive mother, clasping a black cat to her bosom, with whom no one dare mess. Psychological

man-into-monster thrills don't come more expertly made than this rare Mexican masterpiece. It's an absolute cracker of a horror movie.

El Hombre Sin Rostro (*The Man Without a Face*)
Orofilms 1950; Mexico; 91 minutes; Director: Juan Bustillo Oro

Oro's highly charged psychological thriller is a film years ahead of its time; this could so easily have been a product of the 1960s. A precursor to *Psycho* and even '70s and '80s slasher fodder, containing elements of Hitchcock's *Spellbound* (1945) and the symbolism of Jean Cocteau, the director's journey into the darker regions of a tortured mind is a veritable *tour de force* and a visual feast for lovers of bizarre set design. And unlike much of the Mexican horror genre, there isn't a trace of any light-heartedness— it's played deadly straight throughout.

The pre-credits sequence sets the right mood: A funeral procession filing down an avenue of twisted trees in a swirling mist, a man sitting on a bench, watching. He arises, spotting a figure in coat and hat walking down another avenue of streetlights. Taking a gun from his pocket, he fires. The figure falters. The man approaches. The mysterious figure turns to reveal a face devoid of features, a blank mask.

This is one of four crucial dream/flashback sequences in the picture, and avenues play an important part in Oro's game plan, not only in these dreams but in the night exterior shots as well. Psychiatrist Miguel Angel Ferriz narrates the story. Arturo de Cordova is a police doctor, obsessed by a number of Jack the Ripper–style murders talking place in the city; prostitutes are being slain by a madman, and could it be him? Why does the sight of couples canoodling in a nightclub provoke him into such a rage? Disturbed by his irrational behavior, he consents to Ferriz analyzing his hidden thoughts, and three more atmospheric dream sequences unfold, forming the bulk of the film's central section. In the first, the doctor is back on that expressionistic set, wandering among tall, sexless statues of women and descending a spiral staircase. A chained monster is unleashed from below, smashing the statues and changing into the faceless man. The second sees Cordova at odds with his smothering mother (Matilde Palou) over his relationship with Carmen Molina; she wants her son all to herself and tries her best to sabotage the romance by lies and deceit. The third episode has Cordova following Palou through the mist. They reach a pool, his hands covered in blood. He sees the faceless man down the avenue of lights. The figure turns to reveal his mother's face.

The mysterous figure with a face devoid of features, a blank mask, appears in dream/flashback sequences throughout *El Hombre Sin Rostro*.

What Oro appears to be telling us is that Cordova, having a negative identification with his mother through her despicable treatment of Molina, murders prostitutes *as* his mother, the women of the streets guilty of provoking male sexual desire, much like Molina has done in her beloved son.

Following another slaying, Cordova, his fevered mind tipping over into insanity, almost stabs Molina (now his wife) to death with a scalpel but is shot in the back by Ferriz. But the closing reel hints that perhaps Cordova wasn't the insane killer—it *may* have been the psychiatrist all along.

This early Mexican Gothic barnstormer is topped off by Raul Lavista's full-bodied horror soundtrack (overused at times) and Jorge Stahl, Jr.'s dazzling camerawork (the two men collaborated on 1956's *The Beast of Hollow Mountain*). As a psychoanalytical case study in split identity, Oro's masterwork has few equals in '50s horror cinema for sheer brio and panache—an official release with subtitles is long overdue.

Mannekang i Rott (*Mannequin in Red*)
Sandrew/Baumanfilm 1958; Sweden; 108 minutes; Director: Arne Mattsson

Who murdered the beautiful model dubbed The Red Mannequin? Her corpse displayed sprawled in the window of fashion house La Femme, a 17th-century dagger protruding from her back. The woman was also an infamous escort who blackmailed her married clients, so it could be one of any number of people, including other models jealous of her looks and notoriety. Arne Mattsson's plush psychological melodrama (he was termed the Swedish Hitchcock) had the appearance of a 1960s continental movie without the nudity and bloodshed; it's been said that Mario Bava based his groundbreaking slasher opus *Blood and Black Lace* (1964) on this one film. Photographed in gorgeous Eastmancolor by Hilding Bladh, Mattsson assembled a larger-than-usual cast of characters, all retaining grievances and hidden agendas: La Femme's domineering boss, wheelchair-bound Lillebil Ibsen; Anita Bjork, her conniving second-in-command; Lissi Alandh, show organizer and three family members—niece Gio Petré, foster son Bengt Brunskog and nephew Lennart Lindberg.

Annalisa Ericson goes undercover as a model to discover the killer of the Red Mannequin in *Mannekang i Rott*.

Private investigator Karl-Arne Holmsten arranges for his wife (Annalisa Ericson) to go undercover at the fashion house, posing as a model, to find out all about the dead girl. But when Ibsen, trapped in her mansion by persons unknown, perishes in an inferno, the vultures circle around her business empire in a labyrinthine plot of Hitchcockian proportions.

Mattsson makes full use of Bladh's inky color photography, drenched in reds, greens and blues in several scenes, and settles for little or no music to heighten the tension, notably the end sequence set in a musty theater and the murders that follow Ibsen's demise. Petré is strangled, her corpse hung from a gibbet, and Brunskog is shot in the head. He also tosses in red herrings left, right and center (what has the shadowy Alandh got to do with any of this?) and uses Ibsen's cat as a portent to forthcoming unpleasant occurrences. The surprise ending reveals that Ibsen didn't die in the fire; she survived, scarred, and can now walk unaided. Bjork is the loopy killer, desperate to prevent Ibsen's family from getting their hands on the business empire, which she secretly covets. Confronting her old boss, she's strangled by Ibsen who doesn't want her to marry Lindberg, heir to the family fortune. Bjork's lifeless body falls from a balcony and Ibsen then calls the police.

The addition of a pair of incompetent private eyes, stuttering Nils Hallberg and girlfriend Lena Granhagen, spoils the film's mood in places and makes one wonder why the director chose to include this not-so-funny double act. At 108 minutes, *Mannekang i Rott* loses pace at times and the plot machinations become a tad confusing, Mattsson lingering on those heavily made-up faces, almost forcing the viewer to discover for themselves what subterfuges and lies are hidden beneath the masks. Like the shallow world it portrays, this Swedish psycho thriller is all style and very little substance, like a glitzy fashion magazine tainted by death—the color, though, really is the bee's knees.

Moln over Hellesta (*Moon over Hellesta*)
Sandrew/Baumanfilm 1956; Sweden; 106 minutes; Director: Rolf Husberg

Is this a Swedish variation on Hitchcock's *Rebecca*? Or is it an elegant forerunner to all those Hammer '60s psychological thrillers? Perhaps it's a touch of both. Like an upscale coffee-table book transferred to celluloid, Rolf Husberg's family drama, melding Swedish *chic* with supernatural undercurrents, leisurely unfolds in rich monochrome imagery produced by photographer Rune Ericson, the acting spot-on and the framework backed by a lush score from Torbjorn Lundquist. Swedish stunner Anita Bjork stars as the fiancée of Count Birger Malmsten. Driven to the family estate of Hellesta, Bjork gradually becomes aware, through gossip, innuendo and small-talk, that Malmsten's former fiancée died in mysterious circumstances seven years ago, falling

off a rock, breaking her neck and drowning in a lake. Strange happenings then begin to occur that mirror the events leading up to the first fiancée's death: Bjork's bedroom window flies open in the middle of the night, a ghostly face appears in a mirror, roses wilt in the greenhouse, she almost has a fatal car crash, there's talk of a curse and hauntings and she's locked in a creepy old church for a whole day. In an empty bedroom, she deciphers scribble on a pad that reads, "Dear Papa, I'm afraid," obviously written by a person terrified of something or someone. Determined to get to the bottom of the mystery, especially as everybody, including Malmsten, is tight-lipped on the subject, Bjork decides to carry out her own investigation into Hellesta's dark secret.

That dark secret turns out to be Malmsten's schizophrenic sister, Doris Svedlund. Suffering from a severe case of arrested development, she murdered her brother's first fiancée through insane jealousy and attempts to do away with Bjork in an identical fashion, but she fails. The family covered up the crime and tried to help the demented girl to the best of their abilities, but to no avail; screaming about life's injustices and that no one in the family has ever loved her, Svedlund drives off like a maniac, piling into Malmsten's car on the road and dying from a broken neck, like her victim. Ironically, *her* fiancé, seated next to the Count, emerges unscathed from the accident. Needless to say, Malmsten and Bjork are now free to kiss and get on with life; a rose blooms in the greenhouse which he gives to the girl of his dreams, a romantic touch which brings to a close an opulent, carefully wrought chiller, a splendid example of Scandinavian '50s cinema not often seen outside its native country.

La Morte Viene Dalla Spazio (*The Day the Sky Exploded*)
Royal Film/Lux 1958; France/Italy; 80 minutes; Director: Paolo Heusch

A film of two halves: The first 34 minutes are gritty and tense, the remainder less so. A joint U.S., U.S.S.R. and U.K. space mission has American astronaut Paul Hubschmid blasting off to the moon in atomic-powered rocket *XC*. Hubschmid may be remembered under his American pseudonym of Paul Christian, the name he used in *The Beast from 20,000 Fathoms*. Here, he brings a whole new meaning to the term "wooden," his features frozen solid when relayed over monitors to space control. The acting doesn't get much better when he returns to Earth in a capsule after aborting the *XC*, the rocket having developed a life-threatening fault; hospitalized, his wife (Fiorella Mari) fusses and frets over him and then goes into the "you're not spending enough time with me and your son" routine when an unforeseen problem occurs that needs the pilot's undivided attention ("We've launched a missile into outer space and it's loaded with potential death."). She drives off in a huff while he's called upon to deal with a possible threat to Earth. The *XC* carried on into space, hit a meteorite, exploded and fused together a massive cluster of asteroids. This cluster is now set on a course for Earth, attracted by its magnetic field; once above the planet, intercontinental cataclysms will occur, meaning the end of mankind. And all this 40 years before *Deep Impact*!

After that suspenseful opening round, *La Morte Viene Dalla Spazio* becomes unstuck and disjointed. There are umpteen scenes of mass panic and rioting, news footage of fires and floods and a glowing ball of light fills the sky, heralding the approach of the asteroids. Italy's

Mario Bava works wonders with the cinematography, imbuing the panic sequences in nightmarish tones of shadowy darkness, while director Heusch keeps things moving up to the splendid finale when hundreds of atomic missiles streak through the sky, pulverizing the gargantuan lump of rock back into space. The script, though, is clichéd (made worse by poor dubbing), Hubschmid is unable to raise the level of his performance above that of a B-movie extra and we have the obligatory scientist going off his head, gunning down his colleagues whom he blames for the catastrophe. But the picture is a lively enough reminder that disaster movies *did* exist way back in the 1950s, but not made on the kind of mega-budgets that became commonplace in film production from 1970 onward.

Nebo Zovyot (*The Sky Calls*)
Dovzhenko Studio 1959; Russia; 77 minutes; Directors: Aleksander Kozyr/Mikhail Karyukov

Let it be said that the special effects and hardware offered in Russia's first '50s space opera present a level of realism not seen in similar American movies, including George Pal's efforts. The look of the film is the late '60s brought forward several years; not quite *2001*, but getting there. No wonder Roger Corman plundered footage from this film, combined it with his own newly shot material and issued it in 1963 as *Battle Beyond the Sun*. But forget Corman's cheeky rip-off—*Nebo Zovyot* gleams with pin-sharp color photography and authentic sets, an outer space extravaganza unfortunately betrayed by that Waterloo of many a science fiction feature: poor characterization and lack of narrative drive.

A reporter (S. Filimonov) accompanies a scientist (Ivan Pereverzev) to a giant artificial satellite above the Earth where the Russians are making preparations to send a manned rocket, the *Rodina*, to Mars. Americans Konstantin Bartashevich and G. Tonunts make a stopover, docking their spaceship the *Typhoon*, which is heading for the moon. When they discover plans for the Russian Mars voyage, NASA orders them to take off for the Red Planet instead, to beat the Russians at their own game. But the *Typhoon* gets caught in a meteor shower and, damaged, drifts toward the sun. The Russians come to the rescue, the two Americans boarding their ship. The *Rodina*, running short on fuel, has to land on the Icarus asteroid and await an unmanned fueling vessel sent from Earth before they can return home.

The Russian *Nebo Zovyot* offered realistic hardware and special effects in 1959; Roger Corman plundered footage for his *Battle Beyond the Sun*.

Nebo Zovyot went all-out for stunning visuals and succeeded admirably: rockets docking at the satellite; Earth surrounded by a blue halo; several life-like space walks; Icarus bathed in a red glow as Mars rises above its rocky horizon and the interior of the satellite, equipped with gardens and laboratories. Yuli Meitus' eccentric organ-based music complemented these sequences perfectly. However, this very matter-of-fact approach worked against the movie, with an emphasis on repeated shots of astronauts strolling about outside the satellite and close-ups of a space-suited male and female posing for the camera, as if on the front cover of a glossy magazine. The flip side to all those lavish space sequences also lies in the acting; it's a little on the dour side, leading to a dissociation with the people involved, much in the same way Kubrick's *2001* managed nine years later, the characters become inessential to the hardware on display, becoming mere human props. And the ending, with the astronauts safely back on Earth and feted as heroes, is given over to several minutes of flag-waving Russian patriotism, a rebuff perhaps to the scenes of gaudy New York transmitted to the satellite's TV monitors midway through the action.

Many years ahead of its time, *Nebo Zovyot*'s production values, for the year it was made, are second-to-none, but the fact remains that, again like *2001*, it remains as cold as the icy vacuum of space it so accurately brings to the screen.

Onna Kyuketsuki (*The Lady Vampire; The Woman Vampire*)
Shintoho 1959; Japan; 82 minutes; Director: Nobuo Nakagawa

Japan's first vampire movie taking place in contemporary times would come as something of a surprise to those brought up on a diet of Christopher Lee and Bela Lugosi. Shigeru Amachi's vampire walks around in daylight in suit and sunglasses, his image is reflected in mirrors and he turns into a bloodsucker only when the moon is full and shining its rays on him. But combined with the modern-day setting are facets of traditional Japanese cinema: The bald karate wrestler, one of Amachi's three aids (a witch and a dwarf are the other two); inserted scenes of 17th-century feudal battles and a fencing duel near the end. Filmed in widescreen and sharp black-and-white, Nakagawa's caricature of accepted vampire movie virtues is unusual to a degree, a weird mix of the Western and the Oriental, spoiled by a protracted, rather silly climax.

Twenty years after vanishing on a visit to her ancestor's grave, Yoko Mihara turns up at the family home having not aged a single day, although her scientist husband now looks old enough to be her father. Moreover, she bears an uncanny resemblance to a half-nude portrait of a woman that has just won a nearby art competition. Dazed and listless, Mihara tells her strange story to her family. On visiting the grave, she was abducted by Amachi and taken to his underground castle in the hills. The man was a vampire, feeding off the blood of virgins; any woman who denied his lust was turned into a statue. It was Amachi who painted her portrait so that he could gaze longingly at her buxom figure, a clear-cut case of "look but don't touch" as the woman was certainly no virgin and, in his eyes, tainted. Mihara managed to escape from her imprisonment and the vampire has followed her to Nagasaki, intent on taking back his prize.

Amachi's transformation into vampire is triggered by the moon's light: doubling up in agony, he emerges with fangs, talons and black-rimmed eyes. In one scene, he slaughters six women in a bar before disappearing into the crowds with his malicious dwarf assistant. The vampire kidnaps Mihara a second time, whisking her off to his castle. As stated, the climax descends into farce, with the police, reporter Keinosuke Wada and Mihara's daughter Junko Ikeuchi charging around the castle vaults, trying to dispatch Amachi and his attendants while hoping to rescue Mihara at the same time. Mihara is changed into a waxen statue ("Mother!" screams Ikeuchi three times); Amachi

Onna Kyuketsuki was Japan's first vampire film and starred Shigeru Amachi as an undead whose transformation is triggered by the moon's light.

(in Dracula cape), caught in the moonlight, morphs from satanic good-looker to wizened old man sporting a shock of white hair. He walks into a poisoned pool to his death and the witch ignites the castle's powder room, blowing the place to pieces.

There are one or two scenes at the start which bode well: Mihara drifts through the dark night in a diaphanous gown, black lank hair hiding her features (yes, decades before the Asians started doing it!), and her elderly husband and butler creep up the stairs with a candle to find out who, or what, is in the bedroom. But the remainder of the picture struggles to prolong the eerie atmosphere of the first half. If treated more seriously, *Onna Kyuketsuki* might have become a classic Japanese vampire shocker, but as it is, hardcore foreign movie buffs will enjoy it, even if mainstream fans might well give it the thumbs down.

Return to Glennascaul
T.R. Royle 1952; Ireland; 23 minutes; Director: Hilton Edwards/Orson Welles

On a break from filming *Othello* in Ireland, Orson Welles got together with the Dublin Gate Theater Company and rattled off this M.R. James–type ghost story that was nominated for an Oscar as Best Short Subject in 1953. Although Edwards was given a director's credit, *Return to Glennascaul* has the celebrated Wellesian signature stamped all over it: vivid black-and-white photography; deep-focus shots; odd camera angles; clipped, echoing dialogue and a *Citizen Kane*–type dissolve near the end when the haunted house resolves into the fogged-up windscreen of Welles' car. Welles probably acted as co-director but, for reasons of his own, declined the credit. Forming part of the *Three Cases of Murder* DVD set, this riveting supernatural short is a thumbnail sketch of Welles' adroitness both behind and in front of the camera.

Welles acts as narrator. One windswept night, he picks up a stranger (Michael Laurence) by a crossroads. The man's car has broken down and the driver would appreciate a lift to Dublin. Laurence then relates *his* eerie anecdote. One similarly foul night, two women by the crossroads (Shelah Richards and Helena Hughes) flag him down, asking for a lift to their house, Glennascaul (meaning "The Glen of the Shadows"). Once there, Laurence is invited in for a drink, notices a Chinese tapestry on the wall and produces a cigarette case given to him by his uncle who, coincidentally, once lived, and eventually died, in China. The case is engraved "For PJM from Lucy 1895" and the younger of the women (Hughes) shows great interest in it. Leaving the house and driving a short distance, he has to return because he left the case behind. What he finds is a weed-choked drive leading to a locked derelict house displaying a "For Sale" sign. Next day, on further investigation with the estate agent, he discovers that Richards died 10 years ago aged 80, while Hughes (her daughter) expired two years later, aged 60—yet both women looked years younger when Laurence met them. Going back to the house with a key, he enters the building to a scene of cobwebby neglect. Everywhere is coated with dust and patches on the walls show where pictures *used* to hang. Upstairs, to his consternation, damp footprints from the previous night still mark the bare floorboards, as a non-existent clock chimes and a voice cries, "Don't go." He flees the house in terror.

Orson Welles as he appears in the ghostly short *Return to Glennascaul*.

He then tells Welles that the daughter's name was Lucy! Thoroughly spooked, Welles drops the man off and, spotting another two women asking him for a lift, one of cinema's most gifted exponents in the art of acting and directing puts his foot down and heads for the hills! This wonderful two-reeler may well be a curiosity piece; nevertheless, it's a perfect reminder of Welles' formidable talents, one of the many reasons why he is still looked upon, to this day, as a giant of 20th-century cinema.

Sadko

Mosfilm 1952; Russia; 85 minutes; Director: Aleksandr Ptushko

Watching *Sadko* is akin to opening a treasure chest and gazing in awe at the glittering, precious stones within. This little-seen Russian fantasy, charting the voyages of a minstrel (Sergei Stolyarov) who searches for the fabled Bird of Happiness, has the same overpowering aroma of wonder that permeated Alexander Korda's *The Thief of Bagdad* (1940). The color, set design, costumes and artistic vision are nothing short of fabulous, as is the Rimsky-Korsakov score. *Sadko* is straight from the Arabian Night's storytelling of Scheherazade; all it needed to round things off was a Harryhausen–type exotic monster to appear on set, but we can't have everything.

For lovers of Eastern fantasy and cinematic virtuosity, *Sadko* is a long-lost marvel.

The inhabitants of ancient Novgorod live under the yoke of rich, greedy merchants who regard the poor as riffraff. Stolyarov, dismayed at the poverty and sea of miserable faces, decides to set sail to locate the Bird of Happiness, hoping that its appearance in the city will change attitudes and bring peace and harmony to the downtrodden populace. First, the new people's champion requires three ships—betting with the merchants that he can produce the gold to build them on forfeit of his head, he charms the Princess of the Lake (Ninel Myshkova) into letting him catch three golden fish (like many a mythical being, she has to return to her kingdom when the cock crows). This he does by singing to her; the fish are netted, converted to gold and Stolyarov, with his specially chosen crew, sails off to find the legendary Phoenix, leaving behind his grieving sweetheart, Alla Larionova.

Director Ptushko shifts pace and scenery effortlessly. From a quasi-Russian backdrop of domes and minarets set in a shimmering blue sky, the voyagers come face-to-face with a warring Viking tribe inhabiting a bleak, rainswept rocky region, then a dazzling temple in India, an Egyptian sojourn, a storm at sea, an underwater domain and, lastly, the return to Novgorod. The lengthy Indian segment sees Stolyarov and his men winning the sweet-voiced Phoenix in a game of chess played with the local prince. As they leave the palace, hundreds of armed warriors close in for the kill, but the Bird of Happiness (looking like an eagle with a female head) puts the whole lot to sleep, including their elephant steeds ("Sleep, sleep … bliss … calm bliss," the entity hypnotically chants). Escaping, Stolyarov then has to jump into the raging ocean to pay penance to the undersea god by marrying one of his daughters (which he doesn't) and finally squelches ashore at Novgorod, into the arms of the lovely Larionova. Back in the city square, he proclaims to the multitudes that happiness shouldn't be sought; it's right here, in their native land. In other words, there's no place like home.

The allegory of the poor versus the rich was given the fairy tale treatment in this lush extravaganza, winner of the Silver Prize at the 1953 Venice Film Festival. But *Sadko* can only be fully appreciated in its original Russian form. In 1962, Roger Corman's Filmgroup acquired the rights to the picture; Corman and Francis Ford Coppola trimmed seven minutes of footage, dubbed the speech (badly) and released it under the title of *The Magic Voyage of Sinbad*. Sadko became Sinbad, Novgorod was altered to Kobasan and the original's splendid color wound up a fuzzy travesty of the real article. Avoid this version—*Sadko* has recently been restored by the Russian Film Council and must be seen to be believed. Yes, there are no fanciful monsters on display, but nevertheless, for lovers of Eastern fantasy and cinematic virtuosity, *Sadko* is a long-lost marvel to luxuriate in.

Sampo (*The Day the Earth Froze*)
Mosfilm/Suomi Filmi 1959; Russia/Finland; 91 minutes; Director: Aleksandr Ptushko

Based on Scandinavian legends and folklore, plus the works of Hans Christian Anderson and the Brothers Grimm, Ptushko's wondrous adaptation of Elias Lonnrot's dark fairy tale is not (as I write) available in its original release format. Produced in vibrant colors and DyaliScope, a truncated, clumsily dubbed 68-minute edition was licensed by Roger Corman's Filmgroup and marketed in 1964 as, of all things, a sci-fi feature under the title of *The Day the Earth Froze*. Only recently has Filmgroup's drastically cut print become obtainable on DVD, but even in its shortened incarnation, Ptushko's sublime masterpiece is a cornucopia of fantastical delights that will sweep fans of the arcane off their feet.

The Sampo of the title is the "Mill of Everything," a crystalline edifice that spews forth grain, salt, flour, gold and silver at the wishes of its masters. Anna Orochko, a witch residing in the mountainous, barren land of Procura, kidnaps maiden Eve Kivi, forcing her blacksmith brother (Ivan Voronov) and suitor (Andris Oshin) to come looking for her.

The witch hungers for a Sampo of her own and the blacksmith is one of the few people who can forge one. After Oshin has cultivated a field of snakes as a test of his courage, Voronov constructs a Sampo for Orochko and her minions, using as the final ingredient her treasured "Heavenly Flame," a glowing animal skull. Leaving the witch's domain with the girl in a metal boat that Voronov has forged, Oshin decides to go back to Procura, stealing the crystal dome from the Sampo and returning with it to Kalevala. Enraged, the witch follows in vengeance and, during Oshin and Kivi's joyful wedding feast, snatches the sun from the sky, imprisoning the orb on Procura (she has also trapped the four winds in giant sacs). Freezing to death in a world plunged into darkness and beset by blizzards ("There can be no happiness without the sun."), the community fashions magic harps out of sacred trees, sails to Procura and, by playing the instruments, forces Orochko's tribe of gnomes to fall into a trance. The evil witch, her power destroyed, changes into a pillar of salt and the sun is retrieved, bringing warmth and life back to the villagers.

Backed by Igor Morozov's superlative music, Ptushko and photographers Gennadi Tsekavyj and Viktor Yakushev created, out of both miniature models and huge sets, a phantasmagorical, mythical universe bathed in vivid hues. Many of the exquisite backdrops, in particular the Witch's Hades–like rocky kingdom, resemble the paintings of Gustave Doré, exhibiting a richness in detail almost unheard of in modern-day cinema; certainly, a computer would be unable to conjure up the depth of composition seen on display here. Ptushko, who early in his career experimented in cinematic effects, is a forgotten master of the truly pictorial fantasy movie, as *Sadko* proved so conclusively in 1952. Marred by abrupt breaks in continuity (several musical interludes are missing, as well as the extended sequence showing Oshin's distraught mother searching for him before he returns to Kalevala), *Sampo*, even in its edited version, still serves up a marvelous, evocative spectacle. Hopefully, one day this unique gem will be restored to its full-length glory.

Tempi Duri per i Vampiri (*Uncle Was a Vampire*)
Maxima Film 1959; Italy; 90 minutes; Director: Stefano Vanzina

It's rather ironic that Christopher Lee, refusing to be typecast as a vampire after achieving worldwide fame in Hammer's *Dracula*, should appear as precisely that in this jokey Italian tale of the undead. What's more, this is a rare chance to see Lee as a black-and-white bloodsucker, given that the original Technicolor/widescreen prints appear to no longer exist. Filmed on the Italian Riviera, Lee is the scornful uncle of comedian Renato Rascel, who has just sold the ancestral castle to a group of hoteliers to stave off a debt crisis. Vampire Lee turns up at the castle-cum-hotel in a huge trunk, demanding a resting place in the family crypt that, unfortunately for him, now forms part of the hotel bar. Annoyed at having to sleep in a nearby graveyard, he vampirizes Rascel who turns into a pint-sized version of Bela Lugosi, scampering around the hotel after dark and feasting on a bevy of blonde female guests. But the love of gardener Sylva Koscina rids Rascel of his curse; she smothers him in kisses and he returns to normal. Lee is last seen waltzing off with two young girls for a spot of necking.

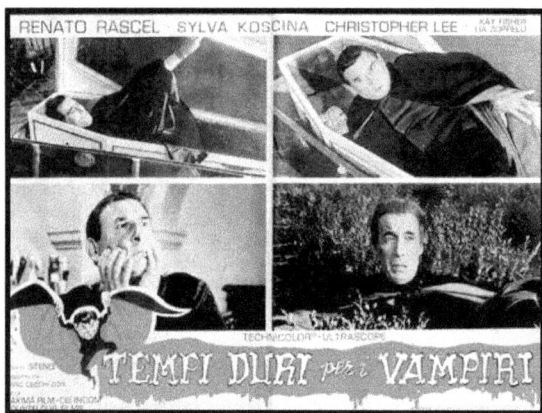

For audiences who enjoy horror comedies, *Tempi Duri per i Vampiri* might just tickle your funny bone, with its inaccurate references on vampire lore and Lee's poker-faced intonation (his lines are dubbed by an actor with a phony Italian accent and given an echo) serving as a direct contrast to Rascel's clownish, Lou Costello–type antics ("Cross, garlic, stake, cock," he mutters incessantly). One fairly amusing sequence has Rascel trying to force a cock to crow to rid him of his troublesome uncle. As for any vampire chills, thrills and bloodletting, forget it. The sunny locations and flirtatious swinging set dispel all sense of the macabre, and the stately English actor, who fades from the action after his nephew becomes a vampire, looks ill at ease, probably wishing he was back on the Hammer backlot. This one's for diehard Lee fans only.

Le Testament du Docteur Cordelier (*The Doctor's Horrible Experiment*; *Experiment in Evil*)
RTF/Consortium Pathé 1959; France; 95 minutes; Director: Jean Renoir

Famed director Jean Renoir's free and easy adaptation of Robert Louis Stevenson's classic, *The Strange Case of Dr. Jekyll and Mr. Hyde,* originally started life as a television broadcast, shot quickly over 10 days; it was given a theatrical release in 1961, rated

"X" in England. In fact, the opening few minutes see Renoir enter a TV studio, sit at a desk and narrate the story as *Jean Renoir Presents*. Updating the scenario to modern-day Paris to suit the times, Renoir hired Jean Louis-Barrault to play both distinguished, silver-haired Doctor Cordelier and his bestial alter ego, Monsieur Opale. Barrault, an expert in mime, put his talents to good use in his scenes as Opale, creating a nihilistic tramp-like figure (beetle brow, untidy shock of hair, bristly hands) running amok among pedestrians on the Parisian streets. Sadistically kicking a crippled man to death, molesting innocent women, viciously attacking those who pass by with his twirling cane, spying on courting couples and prancing down the sidewalks like a dervish, face twitching in mischievous glee, Barrault's Mr. Hyde is nothing short of astonishing, easily on an equal footing with (and outdoing, in some cases) most other cinematic variations on this fabled character. There are no transformation scenes to speak of—they would be completely out of place in a Jean Renoir film. The doctor simply drinks a potion in his laboratory, writhes on the floor and, with minimal make-up, staggers to his feet as his debauched other half.

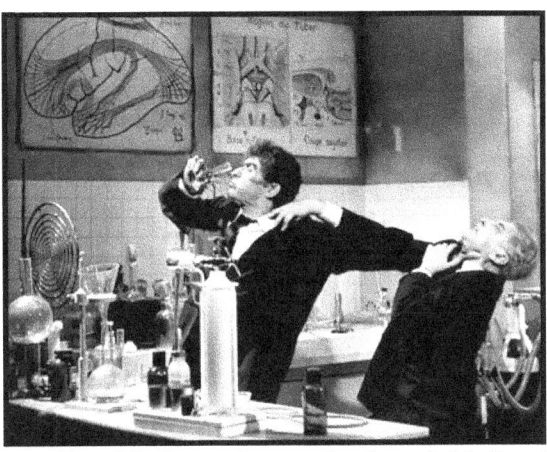

Jean Renoir's free and easy adaption of *Jekyll and Hyde* stars Jean Louis-Barrault in the dual role.

Renoir, through his leading man's lips, gave us his thoughts on what would happen if the bonds of morality were no longer existent by splitting the personality into good and evil. Opale represents Cordelier's hidden cruelty, lust and sexual deviations, these ungodly desires dormant in all men. Only by separating the soul can they be unleashed. It's because the doctor is aroused by his female patients' undisguised passion for him that he goes down this route. As Opale, he can indulge; as the doctor, he is strictly forbidden to (in one erotically charged sequence, Cordelier puts a patient to sleep, gives in to his urges and rapes her). And Cordelier's androgynous manservant, Jean Toppert, isn't called Désiré for nothing!

Teddy Bilis is the doctor's lawyer and, in the final reel when the secret is out—while psychoanalyst Michel Vitold lives to regret the day he chose to scoff at Cordelier's experiments in dual personality—he is murdered by Opale who finally takes his own life by drinking poison. If there is one jarring note in this highly polished picture (we would expect nothing less from a director of Renoir's repute), it is Joseph Kosma's noisy score; the xylophone leitmotif used to emphasize Opale's malicious antics works well, but the blaring cacophony in other areas sounds like a thunderstorm inside a Chinese temple, all bangs, crashes and gongs, ruining the mood. But this is a minor distraction—Renoir's movie isn't Hammer or a big-budget outfit dealing with Stevenson's subject in flashy color; it's model European cinema, vaguely French *nouvelle vague* in feel, blessed with earthy monochrome photography, Renoir's artistic camerawork welding it all together. A more sophisticated than usual horror film from the Continent that generally goes unnoticed by buffs and critics who are more used to the better-known American versions of this story.

Ein Toter hing im Netz (*Horrors of Spider Island*; *It's Hot in Paradise*)
Rapid Film 1959; West Germany/Austria; 82 minutes; Director: Fritz Boettger

The late 1950s/early 1960s boom in nudist films meant that English schoolboys who had surreptitiously peeked at half-naked women in under-the-counter naturist magazines now had an opportunity to see these female delights on the big screen, if they lived in or around London, that is. The U.K.'s capital city was about the only place allowed by the censor to show movies like *Nudist Paradise* (1959) and *Naked as Nature Intended* (1961); most, unusually, were granted lenient "A" ratings, not the prohibitive "X." The sexploitation movie was born during this period, eventually spilling over into the horror medium; on the Continent, *Ein Toter hing im Netz* appeared in 1960 and was promptly refused a British certificate. Like a trashy Russ Meyer '60s soft-porn flick, Fritz Boettger's abomination was nothing more than what all those young lads had ogled at in those forbidden magazines, with an added trace of horror. For lovers of genuine European cinema, read no further; *Ein Toter hing im Netz* lets the side down, badly.

On their way to a gig in Singapore, seven dancers, their manager and his secretary are marooned on a desolate Pacific island when their plane crashes. They discover a professor's body snared in a huge spider's web inside a cabin and, guess what, the island has those all-important uranium deposits (as they all do!). Manager Alexander D'Arcy wanders off in a storm, is bitten on the neck by a radioactive spider and turns into a furry-faced, fanged maniac with a predilection for strangulation. Two men (Harald Maresch and Rainer Brandt) turn up in a boat, accordingly setting the scene as to who can escape D'Arcy's murderous claws, who can't and who will make out with who.

Tottering around in high heels, stockings and suspenders, skirts up to their armpits, breasts spilling out from flimsy tops and more worried about the state of their hair and cosmetic foundation than the threat posed by D'Arcy's clownish monster, buxom Barbara Valentin and her troupe are a sight to behold, even more so when they make themselves bikini-style "island costumes." And how on earth can these sexy wenches disport themselves over the deeply unattractive Brandt? German heartthrob Hardy

Kruger—yes. Brandt—no! Combined with an out-of-place jazzy score is the atrocious dubbing; the crass translation from German to pigeon-English states the obvious to the nth-degree:

The girls see the cabin: "Look. A cabin."

The girls see the professor in the web: "A dead man—in a spider's web!"

The girls hear gunfire: "Those were shots. I heard them clearly."

The girls hear screaming: "I heard a scream. I heard it plainly."

The girls see a ship: "A ship. There—a ship."

The girls shout to the ship (about two miles away): "Hello, we're over here. Don't forget us."

Fifty minutes into this farce, that jazz score shifts into good old rock 'n' roll; the bikini-clad bimbos writhe all over the two men ("We'll dance and raise the roof."), fondle each other's breasts, get tipsy, engage in a catfight and generally act like a bunch of hookers in heat. Fifteen very long and tedious minutes later, the director suddenly remembers that he is supposed to be making a horror movie and goes for a quick wrap up: D'Arcy reappears, kills one of the girls and also cocksure Brandt and finally sinks in a quicksand.

Like an Ed Wood production, Boettger's preposterous feature entered the domain of the "It's so bad it's good" category of ineptness years ago. Even peroxide blonde, Diana Dors look-alike Valentin, exuding sluttish, sensual wantonness, can't prevent the movie from being classified D, as in D for Dud. *Ein Toter hing im Netz* could well qualify as the worst-ever foreign horror picture.

Valkoinen Peura (*The White Reindeer*)
Suomi Filmi 1952; Finland; 73 minutes; Director: Erik Blomberg

Winner of the prize for Best Fantasy Film at the 1953 Cannes Film Festival, *Valkoinen Peura* is one of only three horror/fantasy films to have been made in Finland during the 1950s, the others being *Noita Palaa Elamaan* (*The Witch Comes to Life*), directed by Roland af Hallstrom in 1952, and 1959's *Sampo*. Blomberg's feature, drawing on Finnish folklore, is a vampire film with a difference. In the inhospitable, snowbound wastes of Lapland, sexually frustrated Mirjami Kuosmanen yearns for male company when her husband (Kalervo Nissila) goes off for a week herding reindeer. Visiting the local shaman, she is given a love potion that will work if she kills the first living thing to be met after leaving his abode; only then will men find her alluring.

Sexually frustrated Mirjami Kuosmanen, at the height of passion, turns into a vampire.

Sadly, her pet baby white reindeer is the sacrificial lamb, knifed to death in a reindeer graveyard. This has an extraordinary effect on Kuosmanen; she transforms into an adult white reindeer, is chased by a hunter into the Demon's Valley, morphs back into human form and is overwhelmed by lasciviousness. At the height of passion, she turns into a vampire and kills the man, reverting to her reindeer guise and leaving the herders to puzzle over the bloody corpse. Is witchcraft to blame? Several more murders follow, Kuosmanen visiting the antler graveyard and begging to be released from the evil spell cast upon her. It falls to Nissila to finish her off with a steel-tipped lance. Cornering the reindeer in the Demon's Valley, he hurls his missile, which enters the heart; the beast falls and Kuosmanen materializes in front of her horrified husband, dead.

Although 73 minutes long, Blomberg's poetic take on the vampire myth unwinds slowly but surely, in keeping with the pace of life in this bleak, strangely melancholy wilderness. Blomberg's harsh photography (the director was a noted cinematographer) parallels the pitiless lives the people have to endure and he coaxes an emotional performance from dark-haired Kuosmanen as the cursed woman paying the price for giving in to her carnal desires. Foreign vampire movies don't come more eclectic than this; *Valkoinen Peura* is strictly for those with a penchant for the rare and unusual, a potent fantasy that enchants and fascinates on many different levels.

Chapter 27
A Classic Short

Never in the history of fantastic cinema has 34 minutes passed so enchantingly as in Albert Lamorisse's *The Red Balloon* (*Le Ballon Rouge*, Films Montsouris 1956). Winner of eight awards, including the Cannes Palme D'Or and an Oscar for best screenplay (even though the picture is virtually dialogue-free), this French children's classic was an extremely popular co-feature in British cinemas throughout the 1950s. A whole generation of families grew up watching *The Red Balloon* and it left a lasting impression, but with the advent of the '60s, the film faded from sight. Recently restored in pristine condition on DVD, this is one motion picture short that might even captivate today's gadget-mad children, to remind them that long before the age of technology, fun and magical games could be had from something as elementary as a balloon on a white piece of cord.

Taken at face value, that is exactly what *The Red Balloon* appears to be about—a simple fable of a boy and a balloon, which he discovers one morning tethered to a lamppost. But delve a little further and we will find that this urban fairy tale operates on a much deeper, more rewarding level—it didn't win all those awards for being a shallow exercise concerning a kid with a novel toy. The balloon represents both an escape and an outlet from the cruel, hostile world that young Pascal Lamorisse (the director's son) inhabits. From the opening shot of the boy stroking a cat as dawn breaks over a hazy city backdrop to the climax showing Lamorisse floating over rooftops supported by dozens of different colored balloons, not a single frame of this captivating little film is wasted. Lamorisse and photographer Edmond Sechan present the Belleville area of Paris (demolished for redevelopment in the late 1960s) as though painted by a master artist on canvas; shot in autumn, the wet cobbled streets reflect the cracked, crumbling facades of the rundown buildings, the misty horizons bathed in a watery light, every scene rendered in shades of blue, brown and gray to provide maximum visual impact, the color as sharp as a knife. In direct contrast to the drabness given out by the city's thoroughfares and edifices, the balloon is a vibrant, brightly polished red object, almost standing out in mock 3-D, and purposely so; it is, after all, the star of the show.

Played with adorable naturalism by Lamorisse, we follow the child as he scampers along the pavements, past the bakeries, cafés, patisseries and bookshops with his new companion in tow, involving disinterested pedestrians in his high-spirited antics. The mischievous balloon appears to possess a mind of its own, reacting to Lamorisse's commands—"Balloon! You must obey

Pascal Lamorisse is about to be lifted from the cruel, hostile world by the army of balloons.

The lad lives in a decaying tenement block and the balloon symbolizes his means of creative and imaginative escape.

me and be good!," nudging a blue balloon held by a little girl, looking at itself in a mirror propped up in an antiques market and sheltering under an umbrella when it starts to rain. However, the world as a whole seems to be against the youngster; love doesn't figure all that strongly in *his* day-to-day life. His grumpy grandmother won't allow the balloon indoors, so it hovers outside his bedroom window, waiting patiently for its new playmate to come out. He's refused entry onto a tram, the church closes its doors to the balloon and his teachers bar the balloon from school, keeping the lad in after hours as punishment for being late—the teacher involved in the discipline is harassed by the boy's glossy red friend who takes umbrage at the penance.

The lad lives in a huge decaying tenement block and seems utterly alone, so when a gang of ruffians pursues him through alleyways and sidestreets, intent on grabbing the balloon through malicious envy, our hearts ache for the little boy, the film taking on a darker tone. The law of the jungle decrees that what this gang cannot possess, they'll destroy; cornered ("Fly away, balloon!" the mob yell with hatred), a stone from a catapult punctures the balloon and it slowly deflates, the director focusing on its death throes for a full minute. Then it is callously stamped on and we feel witness to the violent end of a loved one, not just a balloon being burst. Certainly, this is how Lamorisse reacts, slumped in sorrow at his tragic loss. This is the signal for dozens of balloons of all shapes, sizes and colors to congregate above the forlorn boy, coming to his rescue in acknowledgment of the loyalty he has shown to his (and their) stricken comrade; grasping the tangle of cords, he's lifted high into the air, sadness giving way to elation as he drifts over the city's rooftops, away from the isolation and repression that taints his small universe, the picture fading as he is taken to ... where? Hopefully it's a better place than that from which he has come.

Maurice Le Roux's memorable score is just one more highlight in Lamorisse's poetic essay into a small child's unhappy existence. "Acutely observed," "perfectly timed," "bravura technique," "timeless quality," "sheer artistic flair," "expertly composed" and "exhilarating visual style" are phrases often bandied about by many critics to describe many films, but in the case of *The Red Balloon*, they all ring true. This is a movie that still has the ability to touch the heart and soul in all of us. Think about it—how many of today's directors could make a feature about the innocent relationship between a boy and a balloon and manage, within its brief framework, to stir an audience to the point of tears and bring a lump to the throat in its joyous but poignant closing minutes. Not that many, I'll warrant.

Chapter 28
A Monster Double Bill: Mexican Dinosaur Meets Outer Space Turkey

One double bill that didn't go the rounds in the early 1960s was *The Beast of Hollow Mountain* paired with *The Giant Claw*, the first reason being that two different companies were involved (in the United Kingdom, if nowhere else, legislation demanded that film couplings had to be composed of movies from the same company). The second reason would have to be the pictures themselves: *The Beast of Hollow Mountain*, more suited to a younger audience, takes an interminable amount of time to get to the point where the monster makes its entrance, which would have lead to restless bums on seats; as for *The Giant Claw*, this would have lead to said bums on seats getting up and walking out in derision. 1956 and 1957 were peak years for monster movies and these two faced stiff competition. Let's see why both failed to rise to the occasion by hoisting a metaphorical white flag in surrender.

Under its joint Mexican/U.S. title of *El Monstruo de la Montana Hueca*, United Artists' dinosaur-on-the-loose adventure from 1956 sounds promising, on paper at least. Scripted from an idea by Willis O'Brien, the film features Jorge Stahl, Jr.'s lush CinemaScope and DeLuxe Color photography; presents a rousing Raul Lavista score and debuts a new process termed by producer/director Edward Nassour as Regiscope. Nassour, aided by Louis DeWitt, Jack Rabin and Henry Lyon, constructed a fully armatured two-foot Tyrannosaurus Rex, which was blended into the live action by conventional stop-motion animation. Several other models were plaster-built, each in a different pose. When these varying models were shot two frames at a time, it gave the appearance of movement, termed "Replacement Animation" or "In Depth Animation." Big rubber feet were used in close-ups. Did this imperfect combination of traditional stop-motion animation and electronically controlled (Nassour's description) animation work, though?

Although at 45 minutes there's the briefest-of-brief glimpse of the giant lizard, attacking Pascual Garcia Pena near a swamp, it's 62 minutes before we are treated to a full-on view. Before then, we are rooted in Western soap opera territory. Gringo rancher Guy Madison is herding cattle over the Mexican border, some of which are ending up dead in the swamp at the foot of Hollow Mountain. Madison blames greedy land baron Eduardo Noriega, who's jealous of fiancée

The jerkily animated T-Rex (Allosaurus?) becomes the star of *Beast of Hollow Mountain* for the final 18 minutes.

Patricia Medina making eyes at the American. He wants Madison to vamoose back over the border for good. Carlos Rivas plays Madison's sidekick, while Pena and urchin son Mario Navarro are roped in to supply comic relief (all three Mexicans starred in *The Black Scorpion* a year later). The movie's eye-catching and attractive to look at, with fistfights, wedding preparations, fiestas, fireworks and striking scenery, but hell, this is supposed to be a monster movie, so when's that darned monster going to appear? When it does, the beast chasing Navarro out of the swamp into the arms of Medina, the two seeking refuge in a dilapidated building, audiences can't help feel moderately disappointed. Looking large one minute, small the next (particularly in long shots) and sporting a ludicrously long tongue, the jerkily animated T-Rex is novel if nothing else, becoming the star of the show for the remaining 18 minutes (depending on which text books read at school, it *could* be an Allosaurus). The composite shots are admittedly rendered with skill, especially when the monster drags Noriega out of a cave and mauls him to death. The same can be said of the lively finale, the cowboys riding in to help Madison, who lures the dinosaur into the quagmire by swinging Tarzan-style on a rope, recalling Harryhausen's *The Valley of Gwangi,* made 12 years later. In this sense, Nassour's newfangled process was years ahead of its time. Budget restraints meant that the beast didn't show up until later, but if it had been allowed more screen space, the picture could have been a minor classic. It's that hour-long stretch of filler that almost kills *The Beast* stone dead. But give the film its due—it *was* the first to introduce an animated dinosaur in widescreen as well as color. That alone makes Nassour's effort a tiny bit special.

Those of a certain age born in England will remember comedian Rod Hull and his pet puppet Emu (the author caught his act at a convention in 1994). Well, if you're English, the mighty buzzard from outer space in Columbia's *The Giant Claw* (1957), flying millions of miles simply to lay an egg on Planet Earth, will unfortunately remind Brits of Hull's threadbare ornithological prop. Director Fred F. Sears and producer Sam Katzman hit the heights with *The Werewolf,* but here, the duo laid a curate's egg of titanic proportions, coming up with a monster that suffers the ignomiy of being labeled the '50s worst. Only Denmark's *Reptilicus,* released by American International in 1962, can equal this creature in sheer cinematic shabbiness. It's in a class of its own—lower class, that is!

Alternatively christened "A flying battleship," "A big bird," "An overgrown buzzard," and "The feathered nightmare on wings" by a bemused cast featuring Jeff Morrow (who later felt embarrassed by the results), Mara Corday (a criminal waste of the lovely actress' talents) and Morris Ankrum (the doyen of countless B movies was used to spouting lines of gibberish with a straight face, so no change here), this colossal bundle of squawking feathers arrives on Earth, gobbling up model trains, planes and automobiles and refusing to reveal itself on radar screens because of its antimatter composition. Electronics engineer Morrow, romancing mathematician Corday, puzzles over how to defeat the creature which causes global havoc, his brow furrowing in thought as Ankrum reels off samples of Sam Newman and Paul Gangelin's let's-play-it-for-  laughs dialogue: "It's some kinda bird alright." "Hundreds of planes are searching for this overgrown buzzard." "This should be the end of the big bird that was there but wasn't." "People having fun" states the narrator near the beginning, showing the cast at work. It doesn't seem to apply here, judging by Morrow and Corday's dismayed expressions! At first reckoned to be a UFO (farmer Louis Merrill babbles on about it being a legendary flying witch!), then "An extraterrestrial. Comes from outer space," the monster lays an egg that is blasted to fragments by Morrow and Corday. It then flies off to New York, perching atop the Empire State Building (the film's one half-effective scene) and demolishes the United Nations (note the footage of crowd panic borrowed from *The Beast from 20,000 Fathoms*). Morrow eventually hits upon the solution to defeat the winged menace, a machine that can pierce the bird's force field, installing the device in a plane. As they are attacked, the monster is enveloped in gas and bombarded with rockets—dead, it falls into the ocean, one huge claw showing above the waves as a lasting reminder of just how tatty this thing was. Morrow takes solace in Corday's womanly embrace. Oh boy, after this picture, he needed an embrace!

Completed in two weeks (the effects were drummed up in a Mexican laboratory), *The Giant Claw* sucks audiences hook, line and sinker into its cack-handed 75-minute narrative, making us feel sorry for Morrow and Corday in their thankless roles and wondering what the whole crew felt when all and sundry viewed the rushes. Even composer Mischa Bakaleinikoff's score was plundered from his other Columbia fantasy arrangements, sounding stale and unoriginal. That scrawny neck, those glassy eyes, that plastic

Jeff Morrow was Guest of Honor at FANEX 3 classic horror film convention held in 1986 in Baltimore, MD, USA. He good-naturedly accepts this giant claw autographed by the convention staff.

beak full of plastic teeth and the visible strings working the model were hard to ignore. This (in the eyes of English fans) is Rod Hull's Emu magnified a thousand-fold. To those non-English buffs, it is the quintessence of the word "turkey." *Not* one of Columbia's better features, it has to be said.

So goes *The Beast of Hollow Mountain* and *The Giant Claw*. Two of the '50s least-favored monster movies, and two that rarely dared to announce their presence on England's horror circuits (both A-rated, *The Beast* showed up occasionally with family-based features while *The Giant Claw* was usually paired with *Zombies of Mora Tau*). They let the side down and couldn't meet the challenge set by *The Deadly Mantis, Rodan, The Monster that Challenged the World* and *20 Million Miles to Earth*, all grade A creature-features from the same period. Viewed decades later, *The Beast of Hollow Mountain* can be appreciated as an early attempt to produce a monster feature in 'scope and color which didn't quite come off; *The Giant Claw*, on the other hand, is so hilariously corny that one cannot help but laugh every time the camera zooms in on that beady-eyed face. For diehard addicts of jerry-rigged monster outings only!

Chapter 29
Fifty Fabulous '50s Scenes

From *The Thing from Another World* to *Journey to the Center of the Earth*, '50s fantasy movies were crammed with noteworthy incidents, incidents that firmly lodged themselves into the public psyche, to be recalled years later with fond remembrance. A great many top-class features didn't only contain one great sequence; they contained as many as half a dozen. Even the grade Z quickies had at least one moment of pure brilliance that rose above the dross. The following 50 sequences can be classed as either pivotal sequences, memorable scenes or typical '50s scenes—or a mix of all three! They don't all automatically appear in big-budget efforts either; a few from much-humbler origins sum up the tacky spirit of the times exquisitely. I make no apologies for mentioning a handful of scenes that were included in *You're Not Old Enough Son*. In the realm of horror cinema, some sequences in a particular movie simply cannot be bettered!

The Amazing Colossal Man
Sixty-foot giant Glenn Langan pulls a mighty big syringe out of his leg. Bert I. Gordon's inept process work sums up the decade's cheapskate ethos perfectly—but back then, audiences weren't all that bothered anyway!

The Beast from 20,000 Fathoms
Ray Harryhausen's Rhedosaurus scrambles onto the Manhattan dockyards, raises its head and roars, causing widespread panic, heralding the arrival of the atomic bomb-activated monster movie. And let's applaud David Buttolph's overlooked, full-blooded score, boosting the dynamics involved to perfection.

The Black Scorpion
Richard Denning and the military versus Willis O'Brien's gargantuan animated arachnid in a Mexican stadium. This becomes an explosive climax to a very dark '50s monster fest.

Blood Is My Heritage
Sandra Harrison turning into an X-rated co-ed vampire among the bushes, guaranteed to put the wind up all those underage British kids who sneaked in to see the movie in the early 1960s.

Blood of the Vampire
Victor Maddern as Carl, Donald Wolfit's one-eyed, hunchback assistant, captivates in every scene that he's in. This is a much-undervalued '50s horror character that deserves recognition; Maddern never turned in a better career performance.

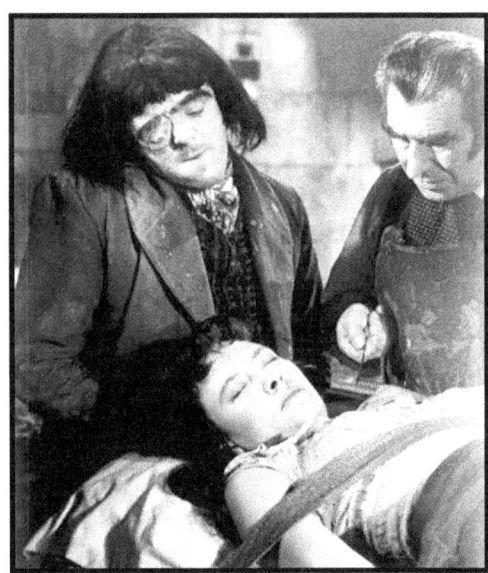
Blood of the Vampire: Victor Maddern as Carl (left) with Donald Wolfit

Creature from the Black Lagoon
The gill-man's scaly forearm and claw rakes the riverbank to the sound of Hans J. Salter's bombastic music, giving birth to the '50s creature-feature.

The Creature Walks Among Us
The genetically altered gill-man seeks retribution, pursuing his hated enemy, Jeff Morrow, and trashing his house in the process. This movie contains one of Universal's most riveting, underrated climaxes.

The Curse of Frankenstein
Christopher Lee rips the bandages from his face, Terence Fisher zooms in to capture those ghastly features in Eastmancolor and scores of females faint in British cinemas. The modern-day horror film starts right here.

Seconds before Christopher Lee rips the bandages from his face, in *Curse of Frankenstein*.

The Day the Earth Stood Still
Iconic, seven-foot minimalist robot Gort materializes silently from the flying saucer following the shooting of his master, Michael Rennie, unleashing his awesome alien power and reducing military hardware to ashes.

Devil Girl from Mars
Haughty Martian female Patricia Laffan, arched eyebrows and flawless complexion, steps into a Scottish inn, dressed from head to foot in black, shiny PVC, an S&M dream come true.

Dracula
Cushing and Lee's final showdown in Castle Dracula is horror cinema at its finest. Director Terence Fisher, composer James Bernard and the two actors fashioned, over the course of a few minutes, one of horror cinema's greatest climaxes, a head-to-head to beat them all!

The Emperor's Baker
The 12-foot Golem, a full-sized mechanical model, smoke billowing from red glowing eyes, stomps after a terrified crowd in Prague Castle. An amazing creation for the year (1951) it was made.

Eyes Without a Face
Minus her doll-like mask, Edith Scob's ruined features are seen in blurred focus as she backs away from her screaming skin donor. Georges Franju's masterpiece hikes up the tension, reaching new heights in surgical horror.

Fiend Without a Face
The animated flying brains climax, unique in late '50s British sci-fi and probably eating up 90% of the film's budget, becomes unforgettable.

The Fly
David Hedison reveals his fly-features to startled audiences, in CinemaScope and color to boot, leading to yet another welter of fainting fits in the United Kingdom.

Forbidden Planet
The roaring Id monster (created by Disney studios) sheds its cloak of invisibility in a canyon on Altair 1V as Leslie Nielsen and crew bombard it with ray guns.
Frankenstein 1970
Boris Karloff's blundering, bandaged, blind creation loiters in the castle vaults, waiting to pounce on unsuspecting body-part donors. England's hordes of underage horror addicts lapped up this CinemaScope movie, and this particular Frankenstein Monster, for years, ignoring its more obvious shortcomings.
From Hell It Came
The first sight of the lumbering tree-monster as it waddles after its enemies still sticks in the memory. Only the '50s could come up with something as risible as this and still entertain the public!
Godzilla
Godzilla's 14-minute trashing of Tokyo counts as one of monsterdom's greatest scenes of mass destruction, filmed in nightmarish, X-rated tones that are quite unknown in today's family-friendly fantasy climate.

The lumbering tree-monster waddles away with another victim in *From Hell It Came*.

Grip of the Strangler
With virtually no make-up, King Karloff's features hideously twist into the insane strangler from whose grave he has plucked an incriminating knife. Not bad going for a 70-year-old!
The Hideous Sun Demon
Robert Clarke as the lizard-man bursts in upon startled girlfriend and doctors, proving that even B movies could come up with the goods on occasions and cause a stir among audiences.
House of Wax
Mad, disfigured Vincent Price, in cloak and hat, scuttling through foggy, gaslit streets after intended victim Phyllis Kirk. American Gothic *par excellence*!
I Was a Teenage Werewolf
Salivating werewolf Michael Landon approaches his co-ed victim, viewed upside down by the horrified girl in the gym. The '50s teenage horror cycle kicks off here.
The Incredible Shrinking Man
Miniature Grant Williams fights to the death with a tarantula on a bench top over who gets a bite of the stale cake, superbly orchestrated by Jack Arnold and effects ace Clifford Stine.
Indestructible Man
Lon Chaney scrambles out of the sewers and onto a gantry, exposing his flayed, scarred features, Albert Glasser's vibrant score upping the excitement level.

Invasion of the Body Snatchers
The classic greenhouse sequence: Kevin McCarthy, Dana Wynter and friends face their worst nightmares as the pods from outer space spew forth blank human replicas.

It Conquered the World
Paul Blaisdell's Venusian being trundles out of its cave to confront Lee Van Cleef, the fool who unwisely brought the thing to Earth in the first place. Hilariously conceived but the film produces archetypal '50s monster thrills.

It! The Terror from Beyond Space
Ray Corrigan's Martian monster bursts out of the grilled hatch in a cloud of grenade-smoke, blindly crashing into cabinets as Marshall Thompson and his crew listen nervously on the ship's intercom.

Journey to a Primeval Age
Four boys on their raft, drifting slowly toward the dense, silent Carboniferous forests, becomes an evocative sequence capturing a lost world that vanished over 300 million years ago.

Journey to the Center of the Earth
James Mason and fellow explorers gaze in awe at the glittering crystal grotto miles beneath the Earth's surface, a scene of pure wonder underlined by Bernard Herrmann's vivid score.

Kronos
The 100-foot-tall robot poised above a power station, flashing, beeping and whirring as it prepares to drain the plant of electrical energy. This becomes an amazing scene born out of the decade's Atomic Age.

The Land Unknown
As the mists clear, Jock Mahoney and colleagues catch their first glimpse of the primeval landscape inside the crater. Imaginative set design created on relatively low finances by monster specialists Universal International impresses, and it's photographed in CinemaScope.

A studio publicity photo of an artist's rendering of the massive Kronos draining the planet of electrical energy. Too bad the actual execution of Kronos as seen in the actual movie does not equal the artist's imagination.

The Monolith Monsters
The wall of towering black crystals, toppling then rising up, approaches the small desert community as Grant Williams tries desperately to halt them in their tracks. The film features tremendous effects from Clifford Stine and his technicians.

The Monster that Challenged the World
The prolonged, edge-of-the-seat climax occurs as Audrey Dalton and her young daughter are cornered in a laboratory by the room-sized mollusk.

The Mummy (1959)
George Pastell, reading the Scroll of Life and watching with a mixture of reverence and fear, watches as mud-encrusted Christopher Lee rises shakily from Hammer's Technicolor swamp. A crowning moment from Terence Fisher, photographer Jack Asher and composer Frank Reizenstein is realized.

Night of the Demon
As Maurice Denham attempts to escape, a giant medieval demon materializes out of the night sky to slay him, summoned by devil cult leader Niall MacGinnis. Jacques Tourneur's long opening sequence sets the tone of things to come, mirroring the film's climax in which MacGinnis meets *his* end.

The Quatermass Experiment
Richard Wordsworth exposes his fungoid arm to the horrified chemist. Dozens of female patrons fainted in British cinemas circa 1955/1956 at this one sequence alone.

Quatermass 2
The too-inquisitive minister, plastered in steaming, corrosive slime, slides down the dome's stairway to his death as Brian Donlevy looks on in revulsion.

The Red Balloon
Albert Lamorisse's lyrical journey into a child's repressed existence climaxes with the boy (Pascal Lamorisse) hoisted over the Parisian rooftops by dozens of different colored balloons, his only companions in an unfriendly, uncaring world. Unforgettable.

The Revenge of Frankenstein
Savagely beaten to within an inch of his life by a brutal janitor, handsome Michael Gwynn reverts to his previous deformed state, his dribbling face contorting with rage as he strangles his tormentor.

Rodan
Kenji Sahara stares in disbelief and terror as a colossal egg, nestling among boulders, splits open, revealing a monstrous prehistoric chick that fills the underground cavern with ear-shattering squawks. Toho's superb art direction ensured that, in Japanese monsterdom, this scene, along with Godzilla's wrecking of Tokyo, was the one that fans remembered for a long time.

The 7th Voyage of Sinbad
Ray Harryhausen's fabulous cloven-hoofed Cyclops strides from a cave entrance in full view of a flabbergasted Kerwin Mathews, introducing audiences to a new type of fantastic visual never before experienced.

Tarantula
Leo G. Carroll's colossal spider crushes to splinters the house from which it was created. X-certified monster

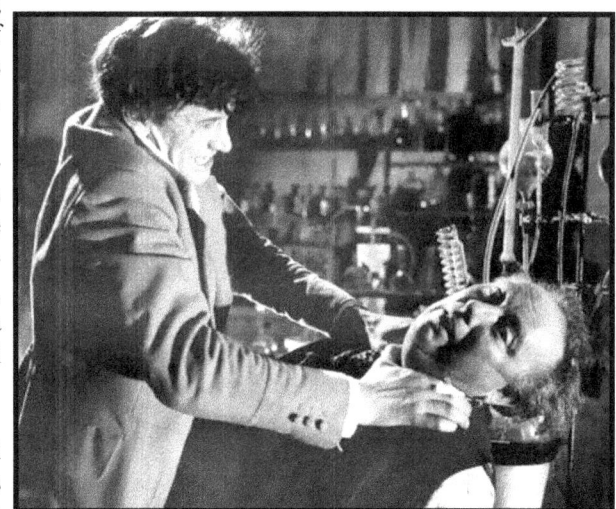

Michael Gwynn reverts to his previous deformed state, from *Revenge of Frankenstein*.

pandemonium from Universal's second golden age when horror movies laid it on the line.

Target Earth
In front of a startled Richard Denning and friends, a Venusian robot crashes through the hotel window in all of its cardboard glory.

Them!
The final blazing confrontation in the Los Angeles storm drains between military and giant mutant ants never fails to impress.

The Thing from Another World
Kenneth Tobey and colleagues trudge through snowdrifts in a howling gale to view the flying saucer embedded under the Arctic ice, Dimitri Tiomkin's soundtrack an ominous aural backdrop. The aliens have arrived in '50s sci-fi cinema.

The headless body of Robin Hughes scrambles out of its coffin, from *The Thing That Couldn't Die*.

The Thing That Couldn't Die
The headless body of Robin Hughes scrambles out of its coffin, a startling "let's jolt them out of their seats" moment livens up one of Universal's lesser efforts.

20 Million Miles to Earth
The baby Ymir hatches on the tabletop, proving that long before computers came along, Ray Harryhausen invested his fantastic models with depth, character and, in the eyes of his legion of devoted fans, longevity. His Venusian creature, an alien victim trapped in Earth's hostile environment, is arguably the special effect magician's greatest stop-motion achievement.

20,000 Leagues Under the Sea
The giant squid's attack on Captain Nemo's Nautilus becomes an immortal action sequence from the Disney studios that held a generation of schoolchildren in its thrall.

The War of the Worlds
The first confrontation between U.S. military and Martian war machines, a spectacular shoot-'em-up that had never been experienced before at the time of the film's release. Sixty years later, this all-guns-blazing sequence can still galvanize the senses and hold its head above water, despite the progress made by computers in the field of special effects.

Almost made it...

The Alligator People
Richard Crane runs through the Louisiana swamps sporting the head of an alligator. Filmmakers could never get away with it nowadays!

Chapter 30
Spawn of Dr. Jekyll

Between 1908 and 2008, there have been a total of 134 film adaptations of Robert Louis Stevenson's classic Victorian novel of split personality, *The Strange Case of Dr. Jekyll and Mr. Hyde*, first published in 1886. The 1950s came up with a few variations on the "good versus evil" theme expounded by Stevenson, including two oddities: *The Son of Dr. Jekyll* (1951) and *Daughter of Dr. Jekyll* (1957). Why oddities? The first is rarely mentioned in movie compendiums despite its above-average sheen and expert handling, an unwarranted omission on behalf of film writers; the second because Mr. Hyde turns out to be a werewolf! And did the infamous Doctor Jekyll ever produce a son and daughter? Let's have a look at both pictures and put forward the rock-solid case that film compilers who continually ignore them in their lists are totally unjustified in doing so.

The Son of Dr. Jekyll is the least-seen, and least remembered, of any Columbia horror movie made in the 1950s. During the halcyon days of the U.K. Sunday one-day programs and late-night shows that catered to English horror fans from the late '50s through 1969 (dealt with at length in *You're Not Old Enough Son*), *The Son of Dr. Jekyll* was notable by its absence (the writer recalls it being screened at a provincial cinema on the outskirts of London sometime in 1961); the picture has never been given an official DVD release, either. Why this is so is a puzzle. The production is well-mounted, with a good eye for period detail, the predominately British cast act with conviction, Seymour Friedman directs with purpose, Henry Freulich's rich black-and-white photography brings London's 19th-century streets to shadowy life, Paul Sawtell provides a lush score and Mortimer Braus and Jack Pollexfen's script steers clear of the usual banalities. The suggestion lingers that the main reason for its lack of fame in fans' estimations is a dearth of mad doctor–type horror. *The Son of Dr. Jekyll* is more of a murder mystery than an out-and-out horror feature, with

Jekyll's barbarous alter ego, Hyde, only putting in a fleeting appearance; if more had been made of the Hyde character, this would have been, without doubt, a classic Jekyll and Hyde movie of some repute.

1860: In a fiery opening sequence worthy of a bodice-ripping Victorian melodrama, Mr. Hyde is pursued through the gaslit London streets by an angry, torch-bearing mob. Entering his house, he's cornered in his burning laboratory and dies falling from a top window. Flash forward to 1890: Louis Hayward stars as Dr. Henry Jekyll's son, unaware of his notorious birthright as Lester Matthews and Alexander Knox have reared him from the time he was an infant (Knox points to a baby in a crib: "Utterson. Come and see young Jekyll—or young Hyde.")—Jekyll/Hyde, in a blind rage, having murdered the mother. Dismissed from the Royal Academy of Science for dabbling in radical experiments verging on what his tutors term witchcraft, Hayward is told about his father by Matthews and estate executor-cum-guardian Knox, both of who are concerned that their protégé might have inherited Dr. Jekyll's warped traits. Hayward's regal-looking fiancée, Jody Lawrance, reluctantly agrees to delay their marriage by three months, enabling the doctor to refurbish the family home, now reduced to a blackened ruin, hire an assistant (Rhys Williams), assemble a laboratory and commence his own experiments in "abnormalities and changed personalities" in order to clear his father's tarnished reputation ("Legends don't die. They have to be killed.")

Alexander Knox becomes the villain of *Son of Dr. Jekyll*, not Louis Hayward.

As news of Hayward taking up residence in his father's old house spreads, the mob camp out on his doorstep, newspaper headlines scream, "Mad Doctor's Son at Jekyll House" and Knox tries to force Hayward to drop his intention of discovering his father's magic formula without success; he's not even interested in a plum job offered to him in Leipzig, such is his obsession. And what sinister motive is behind shifty Knox tampering with Hayward's potion one night? By this stage of the proceedings, audiences will be patiently waiting for a man-into-monster scene to perk things up and it occurs after 36 minutes. Hayward mixes the powdered potion in the liquid and quaffs the foaming mixture, taking notes as the effects of the drug slowly kick in, staring at his face in a mirror for any signs of alteration. Suddenly, his hand morphs into a gnarled, hairy claw, dark lines etch his features, a row of fangs sprout over his bottom lip and shaggy hair flops across a creased brow. It's a terrific transformation job, as good as any other executed in this decade, but annoyingly it's only seen once; Hayward falls to the floor in agony and faints, and that's it. Make the most of this effective sequence—it won't happen again!

What does happen is that, with headlines still reporting his every move ("New Jekyll Incident!") and the mob refusing to back off, Hayward is arrested on a trumped-up assault charge after a young boy has been found near his house, badly beaten. He appears in court and is released on condition that Knox cares for him in a clinic for lunatics ("Wonderful service," Hayward dryly tells Knox. "How would you like your drink. With or without a straitjacket."). Then the woman who looked after Hayward as a newborn attempts blackmail (she wants the young doctor to suffer as his mother did) and the movie steers a somewhat unsatisfactory course away from the original Jekyll and Hyde tale to that of "Who exactly is it that's running around in a cloak and hat, looking vaguely like Mr. Hyde, and acting in a sadistic manner if it's not Jekyll's son" series of developments. Knox is the villain of the piece—insanely jealous of the first Dr. Jekyll's success. He's been committing a number of violent crimes in the hope that Hayward will be blamed and put away, leaving himself free to lay his hands on Jekyll's estate. The end mirrors the beginning—Knox, after setting fire to Dr. Jekyll's journal and notes detailing his experiments, is trapped in his old mentor's burning house and falls to his death from an open window; Hayward is finally exonerated of the criminal acts committed by Knox and walks off with Lawrance.

X-rated in the United Kingdom, *The Son of Dr. Jekyll* isn't a failure by any stretch of the imagination. Seventy-five minutes of solid cinematic craftsmanship equates to an enjoyable dish of Victorian derring-do that may not be the be the most blood-curdling Jekyll and Hyde flick ever made, but it remains a credible addition to the many films based on Stevenson's most fabled twisted persona.

Allied Artists' *Daughter of Dr. Jekyll*, although containing a degree more "X"-certificate monster thrills than *The Son of Dr. Jekyll*, is inferior in a lot of ways to the Columbia flick and patently lacks any kind of Victorian atmosphere, having the feel of a '40s Universal B-horror picture. Fifties scream-queen Gloria Talbott, dressed as though she's just stepped out of the Folies Bergere chorus line, turns up at her guardian's mansion with fiancé John Agar to claim her 21st-birthday inheritance, unmindful of the fact (just as Louis Hayward was) that her father was Dr. Jekyll and that he, not Arthur Shields, left the estate to her. But Shields wants the estate for himself and plans to have the heiress locked away for crimes she hasn't perpetrated. To begin with, he lets Talbott in on the big secret, revealing who her father actually was; horrified, she, in turn, refuses to get married to nice Agar, fearing she may be cursed with Jekyll's depraved genius. There's talk of vampires and werewolves among the superstitious household, all stating that when the full moon rises, "That's when the monster Jekyll rises from his tomb."

Shields puts the second part of his plan into motion; he hypnotizes Talbott into thinking that she has a split personality just like her father, and that she's responsible for a spate of murders

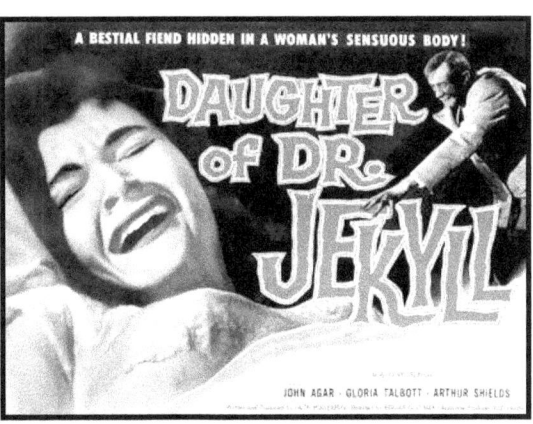

Arthur Shields becomes the villain of *Daughter of Dr. Jekyll*, not Gloria Talbott.

in the area, even going to the extent of smearing blood over her hands, bed sheets and nightdress. He, of course, is the real killer; drinking Jekyll's potion, he changes into not, as you would expect, Mr. Hyde but a werewolf on the night of the full moon, savaging to death the household maid and a blonde bimbo before being staked through the heart in the family crypt by a mob of angry villagers, led by John Dierkes. "He will never prowl the night again," intones a voice over the closing credits, to which Shields, in pretty poor wolf man getup, turns to the camera and growls, "Are you sure?"

Although Jack Pollexfen produced and, like *Son*, wrote the script (the reason for the many similarities between the two films, including almost the same length, 74 minutes), the result, allied with Edgar G. Ulmer's uninspired direction and a mediocre stock score, is rather stodgy, hampered by muddy photography that over-relies on a profusion of misty effects to a point where, in outside shots, it's difficult to see what's taking place through the murk. The normally reliable John Agar appears lethargic, particularly if we compare his performance in this film to his authoritative, energetic turns which were a highlight of his two outstanding Universal features, *Tarantula* and *Revenge of the Creature*. The only gem of a line the actor gets to utter is when Talbott, in the family mausoleum, sees her father's tomb; Agar stares at the engraving on the slab and, with a start, exclaims, "Not *the* Dr. Jekyll!" And as for his striped jacket—it compliments Talbott's Victorian corset. There are one or two imaginative touches, such as Talbott's dream sequences in which she imagines herself to be a female Hyde, her snarling vision distorted in a mirror; and although Shields' wolf man make-up is rudimentary to say the least (he looks more like an unkempt Mr. Hyde than a lycanthrope), at least we have a monster of sorts roaming the countryside. Not one of Allied Artists' choicer morsels from this highly productive period in their fantasy/horror history, that's for sure, and it does stray into territory far removed from Stevenson's book. But the film has Agar and Talbott, two horror stalwarts whose like we will never see again and who gave fans so much pleasure in the movies in which they appeared. If nothing else, that alone ensures *Daughter of Dr. Jekyll*'s immortality in the eyes of true aficionados of the genre.

Chapter 31
The Adventures of Jungle Jim in the Atomic Fifties

In 1948, Johnny Weissmuller, after starring in 12 *Tarzan* movies, swapped his loincloth for the safari boots and slouch hat of Jungle Jim. The character originated from Alex Raymond's 1934 comic strip; in 1937, Universal filmed a 12-part serial with Grant Withers in the title role. Weissmuller, after completing his final *Tarzan* film in 1948 (*Tarzan and the Mermaids*), stepped straight into the Jungle Jim Bradley persona, an all-action part that fitted comfortably with his limited talents. Columbia knocked out 16 movies from 1948 to 1955, all classed as Bs and each containing a fantasy element in their blueprint. The first two in the series, *Jungle Jim* (1948) and *The Lost Tribe* (1949), fall outside the scope of this book; we will concentrate on the 14 that followed in their well-trodden boot-prints. Produced by cheapie specialist Sam Katzman (he didn't earn the sobriquet "Jungle Sam" for nothing!), the *Jungle Jim* features never exceeded the 73-minute mark, each drummed up in double-quick time. They're about as low-brow as one can possibly get on celluloid, but they remain perfect vehicles for a nostalgic giggle—rollicking, knockabout fun, with *Killer Ape* the nearest to being classified as a horror outing (A-rated in England). Tarzan's Cheetah becomes Tamba (later, Kimba), Jane is replaced by a selection of relatively unknown Hollywood starlets and Weissmuller, the Arnold Schwarzenegger of his day, romps through the jungle backlot with athleticism, if not a great deal of acting ability. But then, it wasn't needed in flicks of this caliber.

So ignore those snooty critics who have pilloried the *Jungle Jim* movies. What do they know? Park your brain on the doorstep, grab the popcorn and cokes, get comfy and enter a numbskull world of thrills and spills where dastardly Nazis dress up in gorilla costumes; where Mischa Bakaleinikoff's musical arrangements blast out nonstop; where Weissmuller's features remain, for the most part, an expressionless mask; where the villain nearly always topples to his/her death from a cliff top; where JJ tangles with every savage form of animal life imaginable (many not from Africa!), emerging without a scratch; where indigenous tribes are stocked with American B actors and where audiences wonder whether or not there's a woman in Jungle Jim's life (or are we getting too deep here?). A good time is guaranteed by all—audiences won't be bored for a second! And let's give these movies ratings, as follows:

☒☒☒	A big bunch of bananas for Jungle Jim, Tamba and Kimba
☒☒	Jungle Jim and his pet pals must try a little bit harder to catch the baddies
☒	Drama lessons for Jungle Jim; animal behavioral lessons for Tamba and Kimba

To round off each synopsis, some priceless lines of dumb dialogue will be quoted, and there's an awful lot to choose from!

1950

Jungle Jim and *The Lost Tribe* sets the precedent for the 14 Jungle Jim adventures that were to be foisted onto a disbelieving public: dialogue that could have been written by an English schoolboy sitting his 11-plus exams; skittish female leads; pugnacious villains; missing persons; lost cities; hidden treasure; stock wildlife footage; and the man himself, bravely striding from A to B without pausing for breath. But before we plunge into the jungle, we must, for the sake of posterity, mention snippets of prose taken from the above films, to get into the swing of things, as it were:

Jungle Jim
Virginia Grey: "Well, I suppose you and Kolu and Zia will be off on another adventure, huh?"
Weissmuller: "I suppose so. Would you like to come along?"
Grey: "Could I, Jim? Could I?"
Weissmuller: "Anytime, Hilary. Anytime."

The Lost Tribe
Myrna Dell: "My name's Norina."
Weissmuller: "Jim. Just Jim."
Dell: "Just Jim, eh, from the jungle."

You have been warned! On with the action!

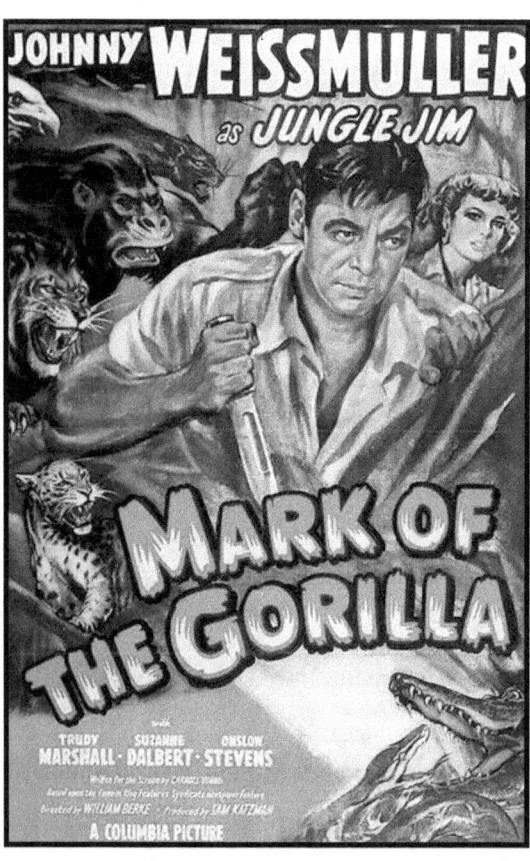

The first of the new decade's *Jungle Jim* movies and third in the series was the shoddy (by *Jungle Jim* standards) *Mark of the Gorilla*, a jungle-Nazi flick of ludicrous and hilarious proportions directed by William A. Berke, the man behind the first two entrants. A group of Nazis led by spy Onslow Stevens has infiltrated a game reserve, searching for hidden treasure worth a million bucks, left there during the war. To deter the inquisitive, a few of the men periodically roam the jungle and cliffs kitted out in 1940s gorilla costumes, killing rangers. Weissmuller, after wounding one of the gorilla-men with a knife, smells a rat ("We don't get gorillas around here."). When the warden is murdered, Jim decides to track the Nazis down to their cave hideout, aided and abetted by Skipper the dog, Caw-Caw the crow and two juicy dames, Trudy Marshall and Suzanne Dalbert. Tamba the cheeky chimp, after performing his party tricks in the first reel by stealing his owner's catch of fish, disappears, only to reappear in the final couple of minutes.

What can you say about this 68-minute chunk of tosh without ripping it to pieces? Five minutes of wildlife footage (whose theme is the prevention of hunters slaughtering animals for trophies) follow the credits. After this, the ex-Tarzan star steps into the action, fighting a leopard, tiger and giant eel, clambering up cliffs, tussling with the enemy, donning a gorilla suit himself, engaging in gun battles and manipulating Stevens into falling off a rock face to his death. Weissmuller looks slightly stupefied by it all, his flat tonal range not boding well for the remaining 13 outings in the series, but the kids will lap it up while adults will sit and ponder this all-important question—with one bout of heroism after another to his name, how is it that Jungle Jim doesn't get to kiss either of his leading ladies? ☒ ☒

Weissmuller to Dalbert after throwing a knife into a man in an ape suit: "It looked like a gorilla. But that yell sounded almost human."

Berke retained the director's chair for *Captive Girl*, which starred three ex-swimming champions: Weissmuller, Buster Crabbe and Anita Lhoest. A spirited edition to the long-running saga, *Captive Girl* cut down on the wildlife footage and included some inventive action, not only from Weissmuller and company but from Tamba, Skipper and Caw-Caw. Lhoest (this was her one and only film role) played a bleached blonde babe in a leopard-skin bikini whose parents were killed by native chief John Dehner (unrecognizable under a thick layer of black greasepaint and an outlandish feather headdress) and his witch-men. Left alone in the jungle to fend for herself, she surveys her domain from on high above a waterfall, a savage tiger her sole guardian. Crabbe and his gang are engaged in searching for treasure in the Lagoon of the Dead, the exact spot where Lhoest's parents were dumped. Affable native boss Rick Vallin needs Weissmuller's assistance in locating Lhoest, otherwise known as "The White Witch," "The She-Devil" and "The Wild Girl of Lake Bokonji" because she's in danger of joining her parents at the bottom of the lagoon. Dehner wants the girl dead so that he can take over leadership of the tribe and cause trouble. Jungle Jim, Vallin, Tamba, Skipper and Caw-Caw set off to find the buxom wench before Dehner sacrifices the orphan and disposes of her body in the forbidden waters.

Captive Girl moves like an express train over 73 minutes, with more close calls and scene jumping than we can shake a stick at. By the final reel, audiences will be yelling, "Stop the action!" Crabbe, in cahoots with Dehner, is strangled by a rope while diving in the lagoon, the bottom littered with skeletons; Dehner chokes to death on a golden chain after falling from a temple into the lagoon; Dehner's witch-men are driven out of the village by hundreds of tree-monkeys (how on earth did they manage to shoot this scene?) and Lhoest, after stuttering through about three words in broken English, is fluent enough by the end of the film to offer her undying gratitude to Weissmuller and Vallin. As is the case with most of the *Jungle Jim* features, there are repeated shots of characters wandering aimlessly along the same old trails to pad out the running time but, notwithstanding this, *Captive Girl* is lively enough to keep the interest going; it doesn't lack incident, that's for sure. ☒☒☒

An example of Jungle Jim's powers of deduction, addressed to his dog: "You notice how quiet it is in the jungle, Skipper? I think I get it. She's telling the birds and the animals to keep quiet. So as long as we don't hear any noises, we're on the right track. Right, Skipper?"

Berke carried on with *Pygmy Island*, whose themes were staple ingredients of most *Jungle Jim* films. An expert searching for a precious tropical plant has disappeared, the baddies are after her and natives have enlisted the aid of Jungle Jim to trace the woman. In this opus, Captain Ann Savage has vanished while hunting for the rare Nogambo swamp plant that possesses the unique property of producing indestructible rope. Her dog tags plus a lasso made from the rope have been found in a Pygmy charm bag, and the Pentagon are anxious to locate her whereabouts. It turns out that Billy Curtis and his Pygmy tribe have not abducted Savage; she wants to locate the plants without crooked Steven Geray, boss of the Bugandi Trading Post, laying his hands on them. Geray and his mob plan to utilize the plants for warlike purposes, terrorizing the Pygmies into submission by wearing grotesque masks and calling themselves the Bush-Devil cult. Weissmuller intervenes to upset Geray's plans, coming to the rescue of damsel-in-distress Savage, defeating Geray, sniffing out the plants and bringing peace to the Pygmies. David Bruce and his squad of marines accompany Weissmuller on his mission, as does Tamba. Caw-Caw and Skipper no longer figure in the series.

Carroll Young's comic book script states the blindingly obvious at every twist and turn of this 69-minute jungle farce, Weissmuller uttering his two much-favored phrases "I'll take a look up ahead" and "I'll scout around" with the resigned air of a man trying to learn his lines. In fact, twice during this movie, he trips over his words, but all credit to the actor, he swiftly recovers. And how on earth can the jungle savior in the well-laundered safari suit march through the wilderness like an automaton without ever stopping to eat or drink? At every bend of the trail, men with guns are waiting to mow him down, but our intrepid hero emerges unscathed. Highlights of *Pygmy Island* (where, by the way, is the island) include Weissmuller and Tamba tangling with a guy in a gorilla costume on a rickety rope bridge over a ravine; a barnstorming elephant stampede; Bruce looking ever-so-slightly dazed, as though he's about to turn into his most famous screen identity, *The Mad Ghoul*; Weissmuller wrestling with a rubber crocodile and Curtis swinging through the trees like a Mickey Rooney/Lou Costello hybrid in a loincloth. The roughhouse fistfights are also surprisingly violent for a picture of this nature. Needless to say, Geray and his criminals are eventually eliminated, the plants are returned to the pygmies and Tamba performs one of his renowned back flips in celebration. This is highly enjoyable nonsense. ☒ ☒ ☒

Weissmuller to Tamba, picking up a spent cartridge and smelling it: "Somebody just fired this, Tamba. Maybe at the elephants. Funny we didn't hear the shot, though."

1951

Number six in the series, *Fury of the Congo*, was a weak offering compared to the previous five. Berke once more directed what amounted to a 69-minute chase movie in which Weissmuller, native girl Sherry Moreland, plane crash survivor William Henry and Tamba pursue a gang who are holding Professor Joel Friedkin prisoner. Friedkin is being bullied into abstracting a narcotic from a rare species of animal, the Okongo. The drug is worth millions and Lyle Talbot wants a slice of the action. The male members of Moreland's tribe have also been rounded up to assist in the capture of these animals. Henry turns out to be a baddie, an agent in cahoots with Talbot and his crew, but Moreland and her Amazonian warriors defeat them in the final reel; the striped Okongo are left to freely roam undisturbed.

Two tolerable sequences—Weissmuller ensnared by a giant desert spider, and Tamba, swinging on a vine, hysterically knocking his master off a log into quicksand—do not a good *Jungle Jim* adventure make. The bad guys chase after Jungle Jim; Jungle Jim runs after Moreland and in one drawn out five-minute interlude, two of Talbot's thugs stalk Moreland through the jungle, the scrub and over precipitous cliffs. All vestiges of a plot become swallowed up (as does Weissmuller, thanks to Tamba) in a mire of tediousness, cinematic padding at its worst. And the intrusive score doesn't help either, not letting up for a second. Weissmuller actually gets to swing across a chasm in true Tarzan style and has a scrap with a leopard, but, apart from Moreland's attractive allure and Tamba's chuckleheaded pranks, that's just about it. And it's very hard to dispute the oft-quoted jibe that Weissmuller couldn't act his way out of a wet paper bag on the evidence shown in this picture. This is a *Jungle Jim* film to forget. ☒

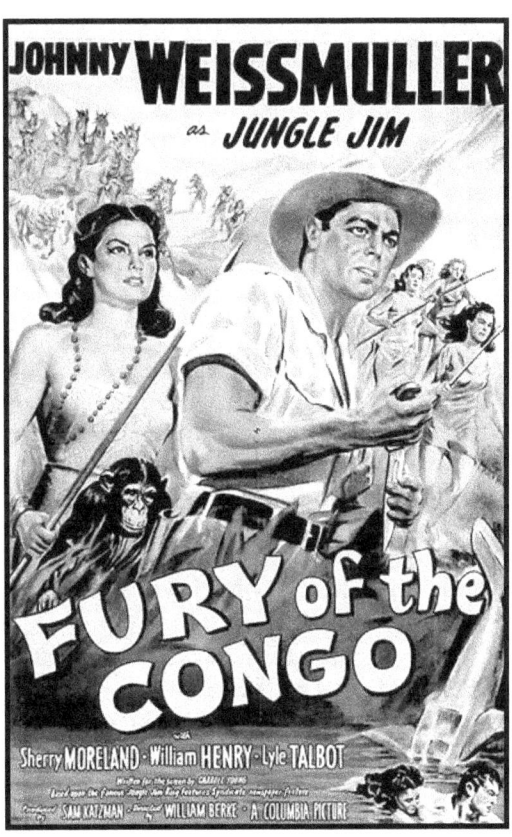

Moreland to Weissmuller: "You make sign of obedience to Okongo god. How you learn that?"

Weissmuller: "I belong to the jungle."

Jungle Manhunt saw a change in personnel: Lew Landers took over the director's role while Samuel Newman was brought in to replace Carroll Young as scriptwriter, maybe hoping to inject some life into Weissmuller's monosyllabic delivery. The result was a marked improvement on *Fury of the Congo*: Weissmuller got to smile more; there was less music and wildlife footage and the 66-minute plot was cohesive rather than shambolic. But it still dealt with a missing person, this time played by real life American football star Bob Waterfield. He's a war hero-cum-soccer star who has gone AWOL in the jungle for nine years, and feisty photographer Sheila Ryan, rescued from raging rapids by Jungle Jim when her canoe capsizes, wants the beefy one to help her find him. In the meantime, a tribe of savages led by Lyle Talbot is attacking villages, capturing the males for some unknown purpose. The raids are announced by the arrival of the skeleton-men, three guys attired in skeleton costumes that leap up and down, scaring the natives half to death. Ryan thinks that Waterfield is somehow mixed up in all of this, so hiring Weissmuller as a guide, they set off with Tamba and native chief Rick Vallin to find out what's going on.

Talbot, an industrial chemist, is engaged in manufacturing synthetic diamonds out of a mixture of igneous rock, magma, sugar, water and carbon, a recipe designed to have all budding geologists rooting around for these ingredients in order to create their own goodies. He requires a constant supply of natives to work his mines as, after a few weeks, they fall sick and die from radiation poisoning. After chancing upon two battling giant lizards (footage from *One Million B.C.* was used; a man-in-dinosaur suit sequence was dropped from the final print) and skirmishing with oily Talbot and his mob, Weissmuller infiltrates the mine tunnels, comically dressed as a native, filches a quantity of explosives and dynamites a lake bed. The tunnels are flooded, the slaves freed and Talbot, after a chase, falls off a cliff to his death. To cap it all, Ryan decides to plant a smacker on Waterfield in the closing seconds, even though Jungle Jim has saved her from drowning twice; taking her cue, Tamba does the same to Weissmuller!

Jungle Jim doesn't get to fight a single animal in *Jungle Manhunt*, content with plunging his knife into a rubber shark (the shark versus octopus scene appears in the opening five minutes of Jerry Warren's *The Incredible Petrified World*); he's more active than usual, seems to be enjoying himself *and* he remembers his lines! That new scriptwriter must have made all the difference! ☒☒☒

Talbot to Ryan: "You're a very attractive girl. If I were you, I shouldn't exchange the glow of beauty for the glow of radioactivity."

1952

There's no getting away from the fact that *Jungle Jim in the Forbidden Land* is 65 minutes of politically incorrect, outrageous camp concocted by writer Samuel Newman and director Lew Landers: Weissmuller stabs a stuffed panther to death and wrestles with a man-eating hippo; hundreds of elephants are to be slaughtered for their tusks and white-skinned natives and a couple of lycanthropes are added to the interesting mix. Add a nice blonde heroine (Angela Greene), a nasty brunette schemer (Jean Willes), three villains (William Tannen, Frank Jaquet, Frederic Berest) and plenty of screen time devoted to Tamba's shenanigans and we have the formula for a *Jungle Jim* romp that totally defies all sensible critique, whichever way audiences look at it. This would have been a great *Road* movie 10 years back— Bob Hope in the Jungle Jim role? Stranger things have happened in the world of cinema.

Anthropologist Greene is mounting an expedition to locate The Land of the Giant People, with or without a permit. Her boss (Lester Matthews) is vehemently opposed to the idea, even though he's in touch with an ancient native shaman called The Old One regarding the whereabouts of the place. The girl wishes to study these people but, unbeknown to her, George Eldredge, Jaquet, Tannen and Willes are in collusion with native chief Berest; their plan is to herd hundreds of elephants through a secret passage in the forbidden land and butcher them for ivory. Like Greene, they have no idea where this region lies. Jungle Jim does, but he's not letting on to anyone. Two of the giant people have been captured and Tannen plans to subdue them with a sedative, hoping that in a docile state, they will lead his poachers into their domain. Greene hires Weissmuller as a guide after he rescues her from a marauding panther, carrying the shaken lass to his house near Ingaba Lake, Wasabi, where she gets the chance to gaze in awe at the ex-Olympic star's swimming prowess. It's only when Jungle Jim is framed for murder that he changes his mind about taking Greene to the forbidden land, deciding to head out there and prevent the hunters from massacring the defenseless elephants.

Thirty-two rollicking minutes whizz by before we get a glimpse of the two captive giant people in a cage—they're werewolves! The female is the most attractive she-wolf you'll ever come across, while the male resembles Matt Willis in *The Return of the Vampire*, which—surprise, surprise—Landers also directed. The male breaks loose and suddenly we're plunged into 1940s horror territory as the wounded wolf man goes on the prowl, attacking Greene and Weissmuller before Tamba comes to the rescue, sending him packing with a well-aimed rock. Weissmuller is then knocked senseless by Tannen and, under the influence of a truth drug, gives the exact location of the giant peoples' country. Placed in the hands of Matthews (who has arrived to save the elephants from drowning in a flood) on a murder charge (Tannen stabs Eldredge with Jungle Jim's knife), Weissmuller is tied up but set free by Tamba. In a riotous climax, the entire cast fight it out on the edge of the forbidden land. The elephants stampede out of the valley to safety, Berest is shot dead, the natives are routed by government troops, Tannen surrenders and Willes pays for her greed, plunging over (yes, that's right!) a cliff with the dying wolf man.

A little bit more variety was injected into number eight in the series, making this one of the better, if not the best, of the *Jungle Jim* pictures (Mischa Bakaleinikoff's composite soundtrack included the works of 11 different composers to ensure the picture received the right backup). Fair enough, the leading players put Weissmuller to shame in some scenes; it's not hard to detect a distinctive pause in his interchanges, giving him that vital second of thought before speaking his lines (which never exceed 10 words; speeches are out!). The actor would have been over his head in a Howard Hawks' film, where overlapping dialogue ruled the day. But the action moves like a rocket, not giving audiences a chance to dwell on the lunacy of it all. As for disobedient Tamba, he's a hoot from start to finish, whether performing back somersaults, flouting orders or throwing a cartridge belt onto a fire, causing bedlam. Not high art, in fact nowhere near it, but not every movie can be a *Citizen Kane*, can it? Just relax and revel in its undiluted silliness. ☒☒☒

Greene: "Jungle Jim? What's his address."

Assistant in commissioner's office: "He doesn't have any. He lives in the jungle."

Spencer G. Bennet took over the director's reins in the 67-minute *Voodoo Tiger*; it kept the same title music featured in all the others but failed to continue with the velocity that enshrined *Jungle Jim in the Forbidden Land* as candidate for the topmost *Jungle Jim* feature. A voodoo sect led by Charles Horvath worships the tiger as a deity, performing murderous rituals in front of a stuffed model of the big cat. Weissmuller and his jungle troops break up a ceremony in the opening minutes just as a native is about to be beheaded, Horvath sulking and mooching off into the jungle. Thrown into the storyline is Jean (Jeanne) Dean, owner of a performing tiger; when a plane she has boarded crashes, her pet runs amok, leaving Horvath's voodoo cult to suspect that a living tiger god has come among them. Another plot thread concerns James Seay, John Cason and Michael Fox's search for art treasures hidden in the jungle after the last war.

It's not long before Weissmuller, British Museum photographer Jean Byron, Tamba, official Rick Vallin, Major Robert Bray, Seay's gangsters and Dean (plus her tiger) are converging on Crescent Valley where the voodoo headhunters live. The missing art treasure narrative goes up in a puff of smoke as Bennet concentrates on Jungle Jim's attempts to stamp out the voodoo cult (who have built a brand-new stuffed tiger) while evading the bad guys. Seay booby-traps Dundee Pass leading into the valley, but Tamba discovers the trip-cord; Dean is worshiped as a voodoo princess because her trained tiger, in the natives' eyes, is the reincarnation of a god. Weissmuller fights a caged lion to prove his worth. Dean and the female survivors of the plane crash all wear Dorothy Lamour-type sarongs. Weissmuller is seen swimming in that instantly recognizable studio tank; and the pass is dynamited in the closing stages, bringing tons of boulders crashing down on Horvath, his tribe, Seay and Cason. Fox has to stand trial for murder.

Although moderately exciting in parts, *Voodoo Tiger* showed definite signs of laziness creeping into the *Jungle Jim* franchise: sequences from the previous eight films were slotted in at regular intervals; the over-familiar plot was ragged around the edges; the same actors were showing up in the same roles; Jungle Jim seemed to lose patience with the mischievous Tamba; and those Caucasians masquerading as African natives were beginning to look ridiculous. But the movie was popular enough to warrant the making of a further seven. ☒ ☒

Weissmuller to Byron: "The jungle drums are newspapers, radio, telephone and Western Union all wrapped up in one."

1953

Sol Shor scripted *Savage Mutiny*, with Spencer G. Bennet again directing. When I say that Tamba was the star of the show, audiences have some idea of how lame the 10th *Jungle Jim* movie turned out. Scientists plan to drop an atomic bomb on Tulonga Island to determine the effects of radioactivity on plants; Weissmuller, Field Representative Angela Stevens, Doctor Nelson Leigh and Major Lester Matthews are assigned to ensure that the native population is safely evacuated and inoculated. Lurking in the background foliage, foreign agents Gregory Gay and Leonard Penn are plotting to sabotage what is known as Jungle Project X in the hope of bringing disharmony to Anglo-American bomb testing.

Having eliminated a shack full of enemies at the start, Weissmuller meets resistance on Tulonga from chief Paul Marion, who is trading with Gay and Penn. Marion doesn't

want to quit the island as it will upset his shady financial dealings with the spies. But Charles Stevens, Marion's superior, overrules him, leading to a mutiny among the warriors. The natives only agree to leave Tulonga if Weissmuller can convince them that there are no evil spirits barring their way (shrunken heads and animal carcasses have been left on the trail by Gay to instill a feeling of fear). After the crossing, the Tulongans set up camp at Dangor, Gay and Penn then arranging for uranium dust to be sprinkled over the tribe to introduce radiation sickness; Jungle Jim finds out, pursues the two agents downriver and kills the pair of them. On his return, he's tied up with Stevens by the suspicious native chiefs but set free when "The Great Fire Bird" drops its deadly cargo, the picture ending on a pessimistic note; in Leigh's misguided opinion, the bomb is a weapon of peace, and this is "only the beginning."

Our barrel-chested hero has a free-for-all with a panther (this scene was lifted wholesale from *Jungle Jim in the Forbidden Land*) and in one protracted sequence, designed to pad out the 73-minute running time, he has to trek back to retrieve Stevens' case full of vaccine from a pack of snarling hyenas. Meanwhile, Tamba upstages all those on the set by grabbing a rifle ("I told you not to play with guns, Tamba."), performing a dozen or so back flips, getting under everyone's feet and smoking a pipe. Gay and Penn make one-dimensional villains, the story drags and Weissmuller frowns a great deal. Unlike the atom bomb blast, Jungle Jim's entry into Atomic Age cinema is a bit of a damp squib all round. ☒

Weissmuller's words of wisdom to his hairy buddy: "Never trust a woman, Tamba."

Filled to the brim with stilted dialogue, tribal ceremonies, baddies stirring up trouble with the natives for their own ends and that blessed panther scene reused for a third time, *Valley of Head Hunters* carried on where *Savage Mutiny* left off, becoming a run-of-the-mill Jungle Jim opus enlivened, once again, by Tamba's naughty frolics. Hoodlum Robert Foulk and accomplice Joseph Allen are up to no good in the jungle: Allen kidnaps native girls and sells them to construction workers as wives while Foulk is after oil discovered in River Valley, formerly known as the Valley of the Headhunters. Back in Wasabi, Commissioner George Eldredge is arranging for an expedition, led by Weissmuller and Nelson Leigh, to enter the valley; copper deposits have been located there, and the government wishes to open up negotiations with the local tribes for mineral rights. When Foulk hears about Eldredge's plans, he decides to make trouble to stop the expedition in its tracks. Foulk bribes evil chief Vince Townsend, Jr. to raid villages, loot and decapitate the dead, making it seem like headhunters are back in the area. Interpreter Christine Larsen tags along with Jungle Jim, as does officer Steven Ritch; she thirsts for revenge as Foulk's men murdered her parents. Last but not least, trigger-happy Tamba brings up the rear, fiddling with weapons, sniffing ether and applying powder from Larsen's cosmetics bag to his hairy cheeks.

Like all *Jungle Jim* vehicles, plot development and assorted characters are outlined in the first 10 minutes, thus enabling the viewer to disengage the brain and take in the action. Natives fight natives; Weissmuller and company clash with headhunters; Tamba joins in the fray with a club; Ritch and Larsen fall in lust; Weissmuller, as stated, rolls

A foreign poster for *Valley of the Headhunters*

in the dirt with that black panther and two friendly chiefs can't decide whether to sign the mineral contracts or ignore the whole business. In a frenzied climax, Allen receives three arrows in his back and Tamba's club fells Foulk. On board the riverboat, the leases are signed while Ritch kisses Larsen for the umpteenth time. And Weissmuller's acting technique shows some signs of improvement in this film; he actually interrupts someone speaking, engaging in *two* pieces of overlapping dialogue!

Over 67 minutes, *Valley of Head Hunters* doesn't really slacken, William A. Berke brought back to add vigor, but it *is* redundant in approach. After all, this being number 11 in the series, just how many variations on a theme can be employed in a Jungle Jim movie? Tamba's slow motion back somersaults, a result of the chimp inhaling ether, is the one good reason to watch this mediocre entrant. ☒ ☒

Larsen: "A village was attacked last night. The huts burned. The natives killed."
Ritch: "And their heads cut off."
Leigh: "Their heads cut—that means..."
Sudden flash of insight from Weissmuller: "Headhunters!"

Killer Ape was number 12 in the series and was rustled up in a week on miniscule funds provided by producer Katzman, director Spencer G. Bennet returning to the series. Weissmuller had his hands full with not only firebrand native vixen Carol Thurston but evil scientist Nestor Paiva. Paiva has invented a drug that, when swallowed with water, takes away an animal's fighting instincts. Naturally, Paiva wants to sell his formula to the highest bidding nation bent on using it in a future conflict. Meanwhile, Weissmuller

is being blamed for a number of deaths among a local tribe who are supplying Paiva and his men with animals for experimentation. He's not responsible—a giant ape man (Max Palmer) is running riot, fed up with everybody tramping all over his territory. In a final clash, Weissmuller, with a little help from Tamba, burns Palmer to death in a cave stacked with cardboard boxes after the brutish ape creature has tossed Paiva into a cage containing a none-too-friendly panther.

A return to form *and* a guilty pleasure of the first order, *Killer Ape* is so bad that it *is* good, a vast improvement on *Savage Mutiny* and *Valley of Head Hunters*. Everything about this picture is woeful beyond words, but that's exactly why it's such a delight: Weissmuller's wooden execution of his lines, Thurston screaming incessantly when in the arms of Palmer, the natives resembling Caucasian B-movie extras (which they undoubtedly were), Thurston pulling a knife on Weissmuller at every given opportunity, Paiva heroically trying to ham it up but failing, Weissmuller and Palmer chucking boxes at each other during a showdown, an overbearing and tuneless stock score organized from five composers' works by Mischa Bakaleinikoff (including samples of his own music), wildlife footage overkill, a dumb script and Palmer absurd as the monster, with his tree-trunk legs squeezed into fur boots, a woolly jacket standing in for body hair and a bulbous prosthetic nose projecting over a set of stained false teeth. Thank goodness for Tamba the chimp's meddlesome antics, although these begin to pall after reel four. Although it may indeed be 68 minutes of schlock personified by trying its hardest to be a cheapo horror film, *Killer Ape* somehow manages to be fairly amusing, but in all the wrong places! ☒☒☒

Weissmuller to alarmed native girl after his cheeky simian buddy tries to peek up her skirt: "Tamba's only trying to be friendly."

1954

Lee Sholem took over directorial duties for the 68-minute *Jungle Man-Eaters* and, although Weissmuller's acting ability was at this stage *almost* on a par with his co-stars, this remains at the bottom of the *Jungle Jim* pile. Nothing much happens in the first 10 minutes, simply stock footage of natives rowing the river and colorful tribal ceremonies. Then Jungle Jim rescues Karin Booth and Richard Wyler (Stapley) from savage warriors and we're into a very worn-out plot: Bad guy Frenchman Gregory Gay, buddies with renegade chief Paul Thompson, kills two mining partners in France and, back in Africa, shoots the third partner, stealing maps and papers relating to a rich diamond field. Bribing Thompson and his tribe to go on the warpath, Gay, using the rampaging natives as cover, smuggles the precious stones in animal crates back to his ship. Concerned Commissioner Lester Matthews enlists Weissmuller, Booth, Wyler and chief's son Bernie Hamilton (fretting over his pregnant wife) to prevent a native uprising and bring Gay to justice.

If you're an animal lover, one particularly disturbing scene appears in this film that might upset the delicate: A lion and buffalo engage in a head-to-head, the lion breaking loose, only for Jungle Jim to stab ferociously the majestic animal to death. Okay, it's only a stuffed toy he stabs a little too eagerly, but it would never get past the censor in these sensitive times. Weissmuller also tangles with a rubber croc and there are dragged-out shots of Jungle Jim, Booth, Wyler and Tamba in a plane looking down at animal herds stampeding from a fire. By the way, where are the maneaters? What we do have are war dances, a fight on board ship, Hamilton's wife dying after giving birth, villages torched, more ritualistic ceremonies, Wyler mooning over curvy Booth, mine workings dynamited and, wait for it, Gay stumbling off a clifftop to his demise in a raging storm. *Jungle Man-Eaters* has a "seen it all before" air to it, only Tamba, proving to be more of a pest than usual, brings the odd smile to the face (the scene when he throws a rock and knocks Weissmuller unconscious is a scream). Yes, there is a panther but, thank goodness, Weissmuller doesn't get to roll about with it. The movie becomes a dull, repetitive edition that audiences certainly won't want to sit through more than once. ☒

Weissmuller, trying in vain to stop his pet chimp from clowning around: "Never mind the monkey business, Tamba!"

It was a revision of sorts for movie number 14 in the series, *Cannibal Attack*. Columbia chose not to renew their rights to the Jungle Jim character, but Weissmuller was contracted to make a further three pictures to complete the series. Therefore, "Jungle Jim" was dropped from the credits and Weissmuller became just plain Johnny—but what remained was still a *Jungle Jim* adventure. Kimba replaced Tamba and Lee Sholem directed a marginally more coherent caper than *Jungle Man-Eaters*, this time concerning sibling rivalry over a deposit of cobalt discovered in an iron mine. David Bruce runs the mine but his power-mad brother Steve Darrell is, with the help of henchmen Bruce Cowling and Joseph Allen, hijacking the shipments of rock, spiriting them away on barges and selling the ore to the highest bidder; Darrell, along with native princess Judy Walsh, will then be wealthy enough to rule the jungle, even though he's old enough to be her father. Charles Evans, the colonists' dithering commissioner, can't make up his mind who's bushwhacking who, and whose side Weissmuller supports. Twelve minutes into the 69-minute movie, the audience is informed in roundabout fashion that we are now dealing with "Johnny," not "Jungle Jim," and that adorable Tamba has morphed into hairier but still troublesome Kimba. On the Magai River (the River of Crocodiles in Cannibal Valley) natives dressed in crocodile suits are attacking the cobalt shipments on orders from Cowling, so after fighting a leopard (from *Jungle Jim*) and an eagle (from *Mark of the Gorilla*), Weissmuller joins forces with Bruce to defeat Darrell and his gang of crooks.

Voluptuous Walsh, eyeing up Weissmuller, draping herself over Darrell and siding with Cowling, looks tasty, but her acting flair is only equal to that of Kimba's, and at least the chimp is funny. And enough pith helmets are on show to stock an army surplus store. Weissmuller races around, swims, gets knocked out every few minutes and still manages to wield those ham-sized fists in the frantic final reel. Darrell confesses to his crimes and is arrested after crafty Walsh leaves him thinking that an elephant has trampled her. The concluding engagement has all parties meeting in an uproarious confrontation on the river, the crocodile-men splashing through the water to rib-tickling effect: Allen is shot dead, Walsh throws a knife into Darrell's back, Kimba smashes a club over the croc-men's heads, Evans fires two bullets into the jungle temptress and Weissmuller drowns Cowling. The last shot is of Kimba reading a newspaper through spectacles while beating a rubber crocodile outfit with his club. It even makes Jungle Jim, sorry, Johnny, laugh out loud! ☒☒

Weissmuller, spotting Walsh's sandals on the riverbank: "Luora's alive."
Bruce: "What do you mean?"
Weissmuller: "Elephants can't open shoebuckles."

1955

For the first time in the series, Weissmuller the actor now became Johnny Weissmuller the character in *Jungle Moon Men*, directed by Charles S. Gould. Six minutes in, the local commissioner rows up, steps out of his canoe and announces to Jean Byron and William Henry: "This is Johnny Weissmuller." Introductions over and done with, we are pitched into a far less convoluted story than usual. Byron plays a writer researching Ra the Sun God; she's also seeking a legendary moon goddess called Princess Oma, thought to live in a secret temple somewhere in Baku country. This goddess, like the fabled "She Who Must Be Obeyed," has discovered the secret of eternal life. Mixed up with all the Egyptology banter is a tribe of Pygmies in panto costumes, led by Billy Curtis, known as the "Moon Men" or "Little People," who worship the goddess (Helene Stanton). When Chief Michael Granger's son is abducted by the Pygmies on orders from Stanton (she requires a new high priest) and later found dead, Granger swears revenge. He sets out to destroy Stanton; Weissmuller, Byron, Henry and Kimba also make tracks for Stanton's lost kingdom, with Curtis and his miniature cronies harassing them at every opportunity. Tough guy Myron Healy  follows in their wake, intent on snapping up the diamonds he feels sure litter Stanton's underground palace, judging by the huge specimen set in a gold pendant found on the chief's dead son.

Jungle Moon Men contains many more imaginative set pieces than *Jungle Man-Eaters* and *Cannibal Attack*, and the black-and white-photography is invested with a surprising amount of richness, an aspect of all *Jungle Jim* features and one that for the most part gets overlooked amid all the hokum (cinematographers Lester White, Ira H. Morgan, William P. Whitley, Fayte Browne and Henry Freulich deserve a mention here). But by now, the series, not surprisingly, had lost its freshness, Weissmuller content to put on an act for his devoted fans without bringing any new depth to his character (but was there any depth in the first place?). Once inside Stanton's subterranean realm, Henry, in a trance and earmarked as the next priest by blonde Stanton, wakes up and wonders where the hell he is. Healy's eyes light up with greed at the sight of all those diamonds, and Weissmuller opts to be the new high priest if the goddess promises to set the others free and not feed them to her pet lions. Healy and his confederate are ripped to shreds by the rampaging lions in the end, let loose by the Moon Men; Johnny drags Stanton out into the sunlight where she disintegrates in clouds of smoke in front of her dwarf subjects and Granger's warriors. Curtis' Little People decide to live in peace with the natives, and Kimba sits high on a rock, a jeweled pendant draped around his shoulders, the new Sun God in this neck of the woods! At 70 minutes the penultimate *Jungle Jim* (or Johnny Weissmuller) epic is amusing twaddle for the undiscriminating punter; those whose cinematic leanings aspire to higher things, steer well clear! ☒☒☒

Commissioner to Henry: "This is Johnny Weissmuller." To JW: "Bob's a friend of mine from the States."

Henry, in awe: "Johnny Weissmuller! Why, I've heard of you many times!"

The final entry in the series, *Devil Goddess*, starred Angela Stevens as the heroine, and just as well—the entire sequence from *Savage Mutiny* in which she mislays her case, forcing Weissmuller to return and grab it from a troop of hyenas, was scooped up and inserted into the movie. The actress was hired to enable this sequence to be used, the producers taking care that her new shots matched those in the previous picture. And if this wasn't enough to bring on a sense of déjà vu, the fight with the guy in the gorilla suit on a rope bridge over a chasm appears in *Pygmy Island*; look closely and observe that Kimba becomes Tamba! Commencing with a five-minute chimp tea party, Stevens wanders into Johnny Weissmuller's camp; her professor father (Selmer Jackson) is desperate for Weissmuller to take him to the Mountain of the Explosive Fire, on forbidden Kirundi land. Jackson claims that his ex-colleague, Billy Griffiths, an initiate into occult rites and Egyptian cults who disappeared in the area four years ago, *could* be responsible for the natives worshiping a sacred fire god, to whom they offer up female sacrifices. In the blink of an eye, Weissmuller makes tracks for the Kirundi Valley, closely followed by Ed Hinton, William Tannen and their band of looters. Hinton is in possession of a jewel-encrusted scimitar which forms part of King Solomon's treasure, and that treasure chest just happens to be buried right under the volcano where self-deluded Griffiths acts as god to the natives.

Although packed with countless snippets from the previous *Jungle Jim* adventures, *Devil Goddess*, directed by Spencer G. Bennet, brings the series to a close with a bang, *not* a whimper. Griffiths, resembling a cut-price Moses, is in fact looking after the sacrificial girls because, every nine years, the volcano erupts—and this is the ninth year! The nutty professor even has a 1930s-style laboratory inside his volcanic abode, where he can concoct his explosive potions to befuddle the natives. Weissmuller, as usual, escapes bullet wounds, even though he is shot at several times. The film ends with an eruption as the natives flee in terror from the molten lava, the sacrificial maidens are rescued, Griffiths is told who he really is and Hinton gets speared. How else can you finish the show but with a villain falling off a cliff, in this case Tannen. Kimba naturally has the last laugh, helping himself to a few baubles from King Solomon's treasure chest. A 70-minute jungle caper of the type that cinema, as it presently stands, will never see the likes of again (did somebody shout "Thank God" from the back stalls?). ☒☒

Stevens to Weissmuller, referring to Kimba: "What's he gabbin' about?"

Weissmuller: "He told me never to argue with a woman."

Johnny Weissmuller didn't hang up his boots and safari jacket after the series ended in 1955; in the same year, the veteran carried on as Jungle Jim in a further 26 TV episodes for Screen Gems. In summary, the *Jungle Jim* feature films are top-drawer nonsense, but endearing nonsense, viewed with a certain amount of affection 50 years on. In so many areas, they represent the very *essence* of '50s B moviemaking. The true sign of a guilty pleasure is that, no matter how lame or bad a film may be, fans will want to go back to it time and time again, to wallow in its ineptness and absurdities and, what's more, actually enjoy the experience without (of course) letting on to friends. Never was the term "guilty pleasure" more apt than in Johnny Weissmuller's 16 Columbia *Jungle Jim* movies. They were all woodenly acted, erratically directed, featured corny scripts, contained hours of padding; repeated sequences from one production to the next, regurgitated storylines, showcased attractive but shallow actresses and third-division support casts, fabricated fake jungle sets where chaos reigned over cohesion and added wayward chimps Tamba and Kimba for comedy relief. Lastly, the indefatigable Weissmuller endured the same motions over the course of 18 hours 25 minutes without turning a hair on that well-groomed head. And he *never* kissed his leading ladies. Raise your slouch hats to the man and give him a big round of applause. He thoroughly deserves it!

Chapter 32
Science vs. Folklore

Before the advent of Atomic Age cinema, those twin icons of terror, the werewolf and vampire, were portrayed, quite correctly, as the evil manifestations of traditional folklore, talked about in hushed tones by superstitious villagers who made the sign of the cross at the very mention of those unholy beings. Garlic, running water, decapitation, stakes through the heart, the crucifix, fire, sunlight, silver bullets and wolfsbane were the things these creatures of legend feared most. However, from 1950 onward, science, for a time, replaced folklore, and although the long-established representations of these two demonic figures went on to survive in movies such as Hammer's *Dracula* and the various Mexican werewolf farragoes, a few filmmakers plumped for a more unorthodox approach, choosing the cold rationality of medical science to explain lycanthropy and vampirism rather than Gypsies sitting around fires spinning folk stories. A sub-genre was born—Gothic science. Two such movies to emerge from this decade were Columbia's *The Werewolf* (1956) and United Artists' *The Vampire* (1957); the protagonists in both were the end result of scientific research, not age-old Eastern European myth. Each production was given the *film noir* treatment and remain, to this day, criminally underrated. During the early 1960s, they tended to crop up as second features on the U.K. horror circuit, but never as the main attraction. *The Werewolf*'s main cinematic partner was *Creature with the Atom Brain*, while *The Vampire* often shared the bill with *The Monster That Challenged the World*. Made on low-budgets, *The Werewolf* and *The Vampire* typify the American-made but British X-rated '50s B horror movie: atmospheric photography, well-paced direction, fairly brief running time, good horror effects/make-up, terse script and a beginning, a middle and an end.

King of the Quickies Sam Katzman and director Fred F. Sears may well have hit all-time personal highs with *The Werewolf*, starring Steven Ritch, who was last seen in the *Jungle Jim* potboiler *Valley of Head Hunters*. (Sears died tragically at the age of 44 in 1957 while working on his next Columbia feature.) Injured in an automobile accident, Ritch is taken into care by two scientists, S. John Launer and George Lynn. The duo have concocted an experimental serum formulated from wolf's blood contaminated by radioactivity; the hope is to find a cure for radiation sickness as atomic warfare might create a new kind of world where humans revert to primitive animals. Ritch is injected with a dose to determine what effect it will have, but all that the serum succeeds in doing is unleashing the beast hidden within him. When provoked, Ritch morphs into a wolf man, killing a barbum who tries to rob him of 20 bucks and then going on the run in the snowbound woods bordering Mountain Crest. There police officer Don Megowan and the local residents pursue him. ("It came out of the alley," screams an elderly lady to a startled Megowan after stumbling across the ravaged corpse.)

"The tales that say wolf men roam the Earth" intones the director over the opening scene of a haunted Ritch wandering down a darkened street, wringing his hands in despair, a look of anguish distorting his features, instantly setting the proper mood by giving a nod in the direction of the legends of antiquity. His camera then enters Chad's Bar, switching to *noir* mode: shaded interiors, faces in full-frame, pithy dialogue and a blonde dame. Quickly ratifying that there's a werewolf on the prowl (a splendid rear shot of the monster backing out of an alley; shoe tracks changing to wolf prints in the snow; a man's throat ripped out), the agonized Ritch, 20 minutes into the action, calls on Doctor Ken Christy and niece Joyce Holden (Megowan's fiancée), admitting to the murder ("I killed him. What's happened to me?") but not comprehending why he committed the crime. "I was dreaming. I know I was dreaming," he moans to Christy, pleading loss of memory. "I want to know who I am. I want to know *what* I am." Later, Holden drily says, "What a night this is going to be. Dead man in the other room and a werewolf roaming around loose." Expert horror buffs *might* detect at this point a few bars of music from *The Return of the Vampire* (composer: Mario C. Tedesco), cunningly inserted by musical director Mischa Bakaleinikoff, and this isn't the only connection with Columbia's classic vampire yarn from 1943. Clay Campbell designed Matt Willis' werewolf make-up in that movie, and Ritch's in this one. He was also responsible for the wolf man in *Jungle Jim in the Forbidden Land*, the reason why all three lycanthropes bear a marked similarity.

Audiences have to wait 35 minutes before being treated to the full transformation job, but it's well worth sticking around for. Cornered in a mine tunnel by Launer, Ritch, by means of time-lapse photography, becomes a drooling, snarling werewolf, leaping at the terrified scientist before running off; he stays that way until caught in a bear trap. After a tearful reunion with his wife and son, the hapless family man gives himself up and is put behind bars, leading to the film's best sequence. The two doctors worm their way into Ritch's cell, intent on sedating him so that they can study his behavior, but they catch him in werewolf state. Waking up, Ritch slaughters the pair of them, Sears focusing his camera on the silhouette outline of cell bars thrown against bare walls. We hear, rather than witness, this violent act of savagery. In the final reel, the townsfolk are like the villagers of yore, hunting the unfortunate wolf man through the woods at night with torches and rifles. Come daybreak, he's chased onto a road spanning a river; clambering along a dam wall, the monster is gunned down as he reaches a huge boulder, changing back into human form after he expires.

The Werewolf combined new wave science fiction with standard horror and in its own small way provides a turning point in the meeting of the two genres. With

Hammer about to unveil *The Curse of Frankenstein*, horror, from 1956/1957 onward, took precedence over sci-fi and we were back where we had started, albeit in a more graphic form, before the bomb had changed filmmakers' conceptions on how to shock an audience with a difference. Sears, in commendable Expressionistic style, made excellent use of the wintry Big Bear Lake locations in and around California's San Bernardino National Forest, bringing a sense of immediacy to the scenario. He also elicited strong performances from his cast, especially Ritch as the ordinary guy, minding his own business, tortured by an affliction not of his own making. He's as believable in this performance as Chaney and Oliver Reed were in their parts, conveying an emotional depth rarely seen in films of this nature. Spare moviemaking at its finest, *The Werewolf* ranks as one of the '50s most neglected low-key horror flicks. Science, in this instance, triumphed over folklore and successfully revamped the old fables to suit a new audience, fabricating one of the screen's more arresting wolf men in the process.

Jobbing actor John Beal's somewhat sad countenance suited his role to perfection in *The Vampire*; suburban Gothic replaced *The Werewolf*'s scientific Gothic, the vampire more of a Jekyll and Hyde monster than a traditional bloodsucker. Beal, like Steven Ritch before him, was also the unknowing (and innocent) recipient of an agent created by science, in this case pills. Calling on a sick elderly doctor who has been experimenting with animals' primitive instincts and brain regression, local medic Beal is given a bottle of tablets by the doc who then suddenly expires. Back at the office and laid low by a migraine, Beal's ballet-mad daughter, played with oodles of charm by child actress Lydia Reed, accidentally gives her father one of the experimental pills. Beal is unaware that these regression tablets have been prepared from the blood of vampire bats; at 11 o'clock every night, he turns into a wrinkly skinned, shaggy-haired maniac, loping through the dark streets in search of victims. Those caught in Beal's clutches die from heart attacks and a rare blood disease caused by a virus that leads to cellular destruction.

Director Paul Landres succeeds in conjuring up a cozy picture of small-town Americana at the mercy of a monster within its midst: the delivery boy on his bike who discovers the dying doctor; Reed, as cute as apple pie, the blossoming young girl loving her afflicted father to bits; steel-jawed cop Kenneth Tobey, eying up all the available talent, especially Beal's receptionist, Coleen Gray; the old lady taking her dog for a walk, unaware of Beal lurking in the bushes and a patient who says to Beal, "We're awfully lucky, doctor, to have you around taking care of us," entirely ignorant of what the man has become. No flashy camerawork here, just straightforward storytelling, Landres relying on Beal's skill to carry the succession of events—suspense, dread, the lot.

This the actor does with aplomb. As his craving for the pills increases, single parent Beal becomes irritable and confused, even losing patience with his delightful daughter. He looks ragged, ill and tired. When he realizes that he might be the killer after three corpses have been found in as many days, he orders Reed to go and stay with her aunt for her own safety ("Dad, Are you mad at me or something?") and arranges to meet fellow doctor and ex-college buddy Dabbs Greer, to confess all. "I killed her. Those pills turned me into a horrible thing. A beast!" cries Beal. Greer later tries to put Beal's mind at rest: "Exactly, but Paul, that doesn't make you another Dracula." This is *The Vampire*'s most telling sequence. Up until then, we have only seen partial glimpses of the monster; as the clock ticks past the hour of 11, Greer, who has forbidden Beal to take a tablet, sees the doc's hand change into a misshapen claw. Then Beal turns to face his friend, his grotesque features in full view. Killing Greer, he shoves the corpse into a furnace to cover up the crime, but an audio tape left running reveals everything to Tobey. The final transformation scene takes place in Beal's house after he has written his last will and testament, intending to commit suicide. Attacking his terrified receptionist who tries to talk him out of the act, Tobey and his partner burst in and chase the monster out into the woods. Beal grabs Tobey but is shot dead by the other officer (not, however, with a silver bullet!), falling backward into a muddy pool and changing back to the caring physician.

Mention must be made of Gerald Fried's insidious soundtrack, similar to the music he composed for *I Bury the Living*. It's slightly unorthodox but works well enough, pushing the action along nicely. No crucifixes, angry villagers, garlic or hiding from the sun; a skeletal corpse and bite marks on the neck are the only nods in the direction of the old–styled values inherent in most cinematic tales of the undead. Like *The Werewolf*, *The Vampire* is *noir*-ish in parts and reflected, at the time it was made, new attitudes toward much used themes. It didn't last long—Landres directed *The Fantastic Disappearing Man* a year later which was far more a conventional vampire outing than this turned out to be. But in that short space of time, when science overruled folklore, American fantasy cinema came up with two understated classics of the horror genre whereby scientists created the werewolf and the vampire, not mythical legend. Steven Ritch and John Beal represent twin victims of scientific meddling in things best left alone; they did nothing better in their movie careers. Both pictures unreservedly warrant a higher place in the order of horror film merit.

Chapter 33
Closing Credits: A Hammer Favorite

As the credits finally reach an end, I'll close this journey through 1950s fantasy cinema with Hammer's 1959 production of *The Mummy*. "This English writer hasn't included a single review of a Hammer horror film in his book," I hear you mutter. "Surely, this has to be an oversight!" Fair enough, there's *The Abominable Snowman*, the minor Hammers and the two *Quatermass* movies. Okay, the classics *are* mentioned, but how can the writer leave out a write-up of a major release English Gothic-horror movie made by a British film company of such great repute?

Let's put that to rest.

On Wednesday May 4, 1960, I saw my first-ever "X" film (three years under the legal age limit, but I won't tell if you won't). That film was Hammer's *The Mummy*. Fifty-two years on, it remains my favorite Hammer movie. The three pitch-perfect classics that preceded it, *The Curse of Frankenstein*, *Dracula* and *The Revenge of Frankenstein*, are precisely that—classics, which I don't dispute for a single minute. But *The Mummy* stays dear to my heart *because* it was my first adult horror picture. And, let's be frank, a bloody good horror picture as well. So no in-depth coverage as such because we all know *The Mummy*'s plot machinations by now, or *should*. I'm giving it the same treatment that Edward L. Cahn's *It! The Terror from Beyond Space* received in chapter 11: break it down piecemeal and analyze how each different component worked its magic, and continues to do so.

Christopher Lee

Let's not beat about the bush—Lee's Kharis is horror cinema's Number One mummy; Karloff, Chaney and countless others simply don't match up to his rampaging, bandaged automaton, all the more impressive because of the actor's commanding stature. Take the bog scene. The actor doesn't just simply walk out of the swamp, he staggers awkwardly on surgically damaged limbs unused for 4,000 years, a touch of sheer brilliance on the actor's part. Lee's expressive eyes mirror his inner torment (much like Edith Scob's did in *Eyes Without a Face*) as in the scene where he gazes upon Yvonne Furneaux for the first time, the reincarnated image of his long-dead love, Princess Ananka. As he holds out his arms in supplication, Lee, by expert use of mime, elicits sympathy; this is a mummy we feel sorry for. Credit must go to Roy Ashton's superb make-up, allowing Lee to bring nuances to a role other actors had been unable to achieve up to that date. And when he's on his mission of destruction, he's unstoppable, not a shambling has-been, smashing through doors, windows and grills in pursuit of those who dared to desecrate his beloved's tomb. This is a Kharis that demands respect.

Christopher Lee's expressive eyes mirror his inner torment when he gazes upon Yvonne Furneaux.

Peter Cushing

The epitome of the English Victorian archaeologist, Cushing's urbane persona, smooth vocal delivery, twitchy mannerisms and swift reactions to Lee's onslaughts brought a nervy intelligence to his role of the cursed John Banning, fast establishing him as the outstanding horror actor of his generation. The Cushing/Lee partnership was in fine fettle, each playing off the other's skills with uncanny finesse. They were as good in this as they were in *The Curse of Frankenstein* and *Dracula*.

Terence Fisher

Terence Fisher's poetic approach to the horror film was by now beginning to gather rave critical reviews and pay dividends: Fisher plus Cushing and Lee meant long lines outside British cinemas on a Saturday night, reaping box-office gold. A leisurely opening 20 minutes, taking in plot dynamics, characters and immaculate period design, bathed in Jack Asher's gorgeous, Technicolor-saturated photography; then, wham!, in with the action as Lee emerges from the swamp (a key Hammer sequence), homing in on Felix Aylmer, treated as a lunatic in the Engerfield Nursing Home and the first of the mummy's victims. Fisher's masterful use of angled shots, close-ups and swift cutting, particularly when Cushing painfully paces his drawing room, Lee approaching the French windows to wreak havoc, conveyed a macabre style unique in British horror. Fisher also had Lee marching straight toward camera (to startle the audience) and filmed him from the floor level upward in his sarcophagus, lit from below to throw those centuries-old, mud-caked bandaged features with the glaring eyes into sharp relief. Without a shadow of a doubt, *The Mummy* ranks as one of the director's most telling achievements.

Jimmy Sangster

Sangster's script is lucid and succinct, especially in the 13-minute historical flashback dealing with Kharis' attempts to bring Princess Ananka back to life. Elsewhere, juicy snippets abound, as they should in all great horror films:

Peter Cushing, the outstanding horror actor of his generation, when teamed with Christopher Lee meant box-office gold.

George Pastell to Cushing and Raymond Huntley: "He who robs the graves of Egypt dies!"

Cushing to Huntley, referring to Ananka's tomb: "There's something evil in there, Uncle Joe. I felt it."

Aylmer to Cushing: "The mummy. I wanted to tell you about the mummy. It's the mummy who lives. Remember, John, someone has found the scroll. The mummy is released again."

Cushing to Inspector Eddie Byrne: "All right, Inspector. I believe the intruder was a mummy. A living mummy."

Byrne: "A mummy? One of these Egyptian things?"

Cushing: "That's right."

Byrne: "I thought they were always dead people."

Cushing: "They usually are. By rights, this one should be dead too."

Frank Reizenstein

Here's how to top off a first-rate horror film—dress it up with a first-rate soundtrack. Reizenstein's rich orchestral score equals James Bernard's legendary music to *Dracula*; I personally rate this as one of the best Hammer musical arrangements of all time. For the movie soundtrack fanatic, he/she can quite easily sit back and listen to *The Mummy*'s score without even bothering to watch the picture, it's that impressive. Akin to a symphony written by a classical composer, Reizenstein's multitudinous notes breathe life into every vivid frame of Fisher's 88-minute barnstormer.

Bits and Pieces

This was Cushing and Lee's fourth pairing in a Hammer film, although the two had met on set before, in *Moulin Rouge* (1952); Cushing had acted in a minor role while Lee was an extra. It was also the third re-launch of a Universal monster, owing much more to the Lon Chaney *Mummy* flicks of the 1940s than Karloff's 1932 excursion into ancient Egyptian beliefs in reincarnation and the afterlife.

Out of an eccentric ensemble of Hammer supporting players, Michael Ripper again shines as a poacher who, under the influence of too much alcohol, has spotted Lee marching through the dark woods like "a great bear." Spare a thought for poor Yvonne Furneaux—the girl occasionally looked out of her depth against heavyweights Cushing, Lee, Aylmer, Pastell and Huntley, but as Victorian eye-candy went, she served a purpose. The censor demanded minor cuts to meet British "X" certificate requirements (Lee's tongue-slicing scene was retained in Japanese prints). And, in the name of art, Lee nearly broke an ankle tottering out of the misty quagmire; his shoulder almost suffered the same fate when he burst through a door to strangle Huntley.

The Mummy becomes a horror film that, although conceived during the final stages of Atomic Age cinema, owed its very existence to those shadowy classics of times gone by, before the atom bomb had been invented. As the old saying says, what goes around, comes around.

If you enjoyed this book,
please visit our website
http://www.midmar.com
or call or write for a free catalog

Midnight Marquee Press, Inc.
9721 Britinay Lane
Parkville, MD 21234
USA
410-665-1198

www.ingramcontent.com/pod-product-compliance
Lightning Source LLC
Chambersburg PA
CBHW071301110526
44591CB00010B/739